MW00774311

# THE ROOTS OF
# VIOLENT CRIME
# IN AMERICA

# THE ROOTS OF VIOLENT CRIME IN AMERICA

*From the Gilded Age through the Great Depression*

## BARRY LATZER

*Louisiana State University Press*
*Baton Rouge*

Published by Louisiana State University Press
www.lsupress.org

Designer: Barbara Neely Bourgoyne
Typeface: Whitman

Library of Congress Cataloging-in-Publication Data
Names: Latzer, Barry, 1945– author.
Title: The roots of violent crime in America : from the gilded age through
   the great depression / Barry Latzer.
Description: Baton Rouge : Louisiana State University Press, 2021. |
   Includes bibliographical references and index.
Identifiers: LCCN 2020019317 (print) | LCCN 2020019318 (ebook) | ISBN 978-0-
   8071-7429-6 (cloth) | ISBN 978-0-8071-7483-8 (pdf) | ISBN 978-0-8071-7484-5 (epub)
Subjects: LCSH: Violent crimes—United States—History. | Crime—United States.
Classification: LCC HV6789 .L386 2021 (print) | LCC HV6789 (ebook) | DDC
   364.150973/09034—dc23
LC record available at https://lccn.loc.gov/2020019317
LC ebook record available at https://lccn.loc.gov/2020019318

For Eli Faber, of blessed memory, dear friend,
excellent scholar, wonderful colleague

# CONTENTS

# PREFACE

For much of my adult life, during the late twentieth century, the United States was besieged by extraordinary levels of violent crime. From 1960 to 1990, violent crime rates per 100,000 people (the standard measure) rose a shocking 353 percent.[1] Partly as a result of the nation's preoccupation with the threat to personal security, the study of crime came into its own as an academic discipline, and I became a professor at John Jay College of Criminal Justice in New York City.

Most of my colleagues were convinced that the crime wave (more tsunami than wave) was a product of adverse social conditions—meaning poverty, residential segregation in socially isolated large-scale communities, female-headed households, and high unemployment rates—a theory sometimes called "structural analysis." Since socioeconomic conditions were improving when the crime rise began in the late 1960s, this explanation seemed questionable. When I learned that at earlier points in history, such as the early 1890s and the late 1930s, crime rates were fairly low or were declining despite sharp economic downturns, I became even more skeptical. My skepticism was reinforced by the crime drop during the great recession of 2007–8. How could it be that worse conditions produce *less* crime?

This motivated me to mount a major study of violent crime over the course of American history, from the nineteenth century to the early twenty-first. I sought to explore the correlation between social and economic conditions in the United States and violent crime levels. What, I asked, was the relationship, if any, between these phenomena? My work on the post–World War II period, *The Rise and Fall of Violent Crime in America,* was published in 2016.[2] The volume now in your hands asks the same question for the period prior to 1940.

This book focuses on violent crime in roughly chronological order, from about 1880 to 1940. However, in chapter 1, which discusses white southern violence, I look back to the immigration patterns of the seventeenth and eighteenth centuries, which have, surprisingly, influenced crime in this country ever since. In addition, I sometimes broke with strict chronology so that I could group some chapters together thematically. An example is the discussion of crime in the nineteenth-century West, chapter 5, which comes after four chapters on southern crime extending into the early twentieth century.

Once I realized that violent crime did not correlate perfectly with socioeconomic disadvantage, I sought explanations for this unexpected finding. What I found, unsurpringly, is that multiple factors were significant in the rise and fall of violent crime, including the size of the young male population, from which the bulk of violent offenders are drawn; the role of gangs made up of these young males; the immigration and migration of certain groups to or within the United States; the effectiveness of the criminal justice system in apprehending and punishing offenders; the availability of firearms; the use of narcotic drugs, and so on. These factors were pretty much as expected, although the way they play out in American history is in itself interesting.

More surprising and contentious is my finding that the cultural support for violence among social groups (ethnic, religious, racial, and regional groups, the latter exemplified by white southerners), played a major role in the history of crime. According to this "cultural theory" of crime, some disadvantaged groups commit much more violent crime than other groups, despite comparable, or even lesser, deprivation.

Not only does this cultural factor explain the variance in violent crime rates among similarly disadvantaged groups, it also partly explains why economic conditions—in a particular city, a region, or an entire nation—do not accurately predict violent crime rates. Rather, the level of violent crime depends on the cultural support for violence among the inhabitants. There is a second reason as well for the lack of correlation between violence and the economy: violent crime is usually motivated by anger due to insults, quarrels, grudges, and the like, not by money. Consequently, violent crime does not align with economic conditions, which is why economic depressions do not invariably cause violent crime upturns.

The 1890s—discussed in detail in Part III of this book—offers a notable example of this phenomenon. During that decade, when the biggest cities in the United States were reeling with massive numbers of impoverished people, many of them recent immigrants, violent crime rates were much lower than they would be one hundred years later when the proportion of the population living in poverty was much smaller. Crime historian Roger Lane once reported that "robbery at gunpoint was so rare in the urban East" that a Bronx saloon holdup in 1895 made headlines in Philadelphia and the story ran for a week![3] In 1990, by contrast, an armed robbery in the Bronx wouldn't even have produced an article, much less a headline, in New York City newspapers. If there were greater levels of urban poverty in the nineteenth century why was stranger violence—the bane of the late twentieth century—so uncommon? Why didn't big-city residents of the 1890s rob their neighbors or kill total strangers at anywhere near the levels for these crimes one century later?

Moreover, prior to the last decades of the nineteenth century and the development of a sizable middle class, elites engaged in violent crime, duels among "gentlemen" providing an especially vivid example. Starting in the twentieth century, however, elite violence diminished radically as the middle class came to realize that its benefits were far outweighed by numerous risks, including personal injury, loss of status, and criminal justice sanctions. Plus, the civil legal system provided effective alternatives for dispute resolution.[4] In other words, contrary to prevailing contemporary beliefs as well as to the structural theory of crime, history presents striking examples of violent crime without poverty and profound poverty without violent crime.

This is not to say that structural explanations are completely wrong. In the twentieth and twenty-first centuries it is clear that crime (save for fraud and other "white collar" offenses) is overwhelmingly a poor man's game. So there is, as structural analysis posits, a high correlation between poverty and crime. But is this because the poor are induced by poverty to resort to criminality, or is it that the more affluent have, for self-interested reasons, abandoned the field to the less well-off? The late nineteenth-century situation, as we shall see, and the significance of nonfinancial motivations for violent crime, such as disputes or long-standing quarrels, suggest that the latter is the better explanation. If so, then it isn't that socioeconomic adversities cause violent crime, but rather that affluence inhibits it.

There is, as I have said, a second reason to believe that poverty doesn't invariably cause crime, namely that social groups manifesting comparable or greater levels of adversity often have lower rates of violent crime than groups in less favorable positions. A notable illustration of this is provided by chapter 8, which compares the Italian and Jewish immigrations to New York. As I show, despite the similarities of circumstance—impoverishment, squalid overcrowded housing, social and economic segregation, profound divergence with the host country's culture—the crime of the Italians was much more violent than that of the Jews.

This crime/adversity mismatch is not limited to the early twentieth-century Jewish and Italian immigrants. Throughout American history, different social groups have engaged in different amounts of violent crime, and no consistent relationship between the extent of a group's socioeconomic disadvantage and its level of violence is evident. For example, impoverished Scandinavian and German immigrants had relatively low crime rates, while disadvantaged Mexican and Irish entrants committed violent crime at very high rates.

What is the explanation for this? How do we account for the crime differentials among groups with comparable disadvantages? The theory presented in this book is that some groups contain subgroups that are *culturally* disposed to violence—that is, they have what is known as a *subculture of violence;* other groups lack this subculture.

Culture is commonly defined as the set of customs, traditions, and values of a society or community, such as an ethnic group or nation. A "subculture" refers to specific practices within the subgroup of a cultural community. So a subculture of violence refers to the tendency toward violent behaviors in the subgroup. Consequently, a cultural group with a subculture of violence will engage in higher levels of violent crime than another group even though it faces fewer or no greater adversities.

As demonstrated in this book, some cultures have subcultures with a proclivity for violence, which is frequently used to establish "respect" in the community, or, to use an old-fashioned term, "honor." The honor culture of southern whites in the United States was (and still is, though to a lesser extent nowadays) such a subculture of violence.

The southern culture of violence has long been associated with high violent crime rates among white southerners. As far back as the 1870s, H. V. Redfield found that murder was four to fifteen times more frequent in the southern states than elsewhere in the United States.[5] This southern penchant for violence continued well into the twentieth century, and even seems to endure in the twenty-first.[6]

Significantly, the white southern honor culture was instrumental in the development of a black subculture of violence which in turn provides an important explanation for African American violent crime. This is one of the original, if contentious, key findings of this book. To flesh it out a bit I will conclude the Preface with a discussion of cultural explanations for high black crime rates. (See chapters 2 and 4 for a detailed analysis of African American crime during the period covered by this book.)

Being almost exclusively southern for all of the seventeenth, eighteenth, and nineteenth centuries, as well as the first two decades of the twentieth, African Americans developed their own subculture of violence in emulation of the whites around them.[7] This shouldn't be surprising. Southern blacks and whites shared many customs, beliefs, and values, including dietary preferences, religious beliefs, and even dialect. African Americans modified these customs, beliefs, and values as suited their own circumstances, but the white southern influence was powerful and omnipresent.

Among these adaptations was the testiness and sensitivity to insult that leads to violence—violence intended to preserve the aggressor's honor or, in modern parlance, command respect in the community or the neighborhood. In the late twentieth century ethnologist Elijah Anderson explained black ghetto violence in such terms. He described "an especially heightened concern about being disrespected. Many inner-city young men in particular crave respect to such a degree that they will risk their lives to attain and maintain it."[8] "The resulting craving for respect," Anderson observed, "gives people thin skins and short fuses."[9]

This violent black subculture produced high rates of black crime in the South, starting in the 1880s and 1890s. This crime typically involved assaults, sometimes deadly, commonly over sexual jealousies, gambling disputes, perceived insults, and petty quarrels. Seldom were whites the victims of these attacks, as reflects the infrequency of interaction between the races along with black fear of extreme white retaliation. When, in the early twentieth century, blacks began to move north this subculture of violence traveled with them. As I explained in an earlier work: "One can make a strong case that impoverished African Americans shared in the southern culture of violence and transported it to the North during their migrations. There, social isolation and discrimination perpetuated a version of this culture among lower-class blacks, accounting for the high rates of black-on-black violence."[10] In short, blacks developed a violent subculture in the South and brought it to northern cities along with other black cultural markers like jazz, the AME church, and soul food. The result was enormously elevated rates of violent crime among blacks in the North as well as the South.

Racist discrimination played a crucial role here, but it is not the role commonly believed. If anger and frustration over racism had fueled African American violent crime it is difficult to explain why the victims overwhelmingly were other persons of color. Yet among low-income blacks, which was the vast preponderance of the African American population, intraracial crime soared while black-on-white crime was uncommon.

For ethnic immigrants with high crime rates—the Irish of the nineteenth century and the southern Italians of the early twentieth—the rise to middle-class status eroded the cultural support for violent crime. The same class override affected blacks too—middle-class African Americans have always had relatively low violent crime rates—but blacks were thwarted in their efforts to move up the social ladder, blocked by Jim Crow and racial bias. Consequently, the lower-income black population continued to comprise a sizable portion of the black community and black violent crime remained consistently elevated for another century.

The preceding describes in a nutshell one explanation—among many explored in this book—for elevated violent crime rates among African Americans. In addition to socioeconomic class, several other factors influenced those rates. Age and gender were significant, as young males were responsible for most of the violence. Weaknesses in the criminal justice system were another important cause of high crime. Narcotic drugs played a major role, especially in the late 1980s. The widespread availability of guns was significant in raising murder rates. In short, the subculture of violence, while weighty, was not alone in accounting for high African American crime rates.

This book is a synthesis of history and criminology. Each chapter seeks to present historical conditions in the United States and relate them to the violent crime of that particular era. I have tried to avoid imposing any overarching theory of crime (or of history) on my analysis, nor have I bowed to the demands of political correctness. I can only hope that my method has produced a persuasive account of a persistent and disturbing feature of U.S. history.

# THE ROOTS OF VIOLENT CRIME IN AMERICA

# A SOUTHERN CULTURE
# OF VIOLENCE

# 1

# White Southern Crime from the Eighteenth to the Nineteenth Century

Never tell a lie, nor take what is not your own, nor sue anybody for slander or assault and battery. *Always settle them cases yourself!*
—ANDREW JACKSON'S MOTHER'S ADVICE

There was a world of violence that I grew up in. You accepted violence as a component of life. . . . You heard about violence, and you saw terrible fights . . . not violence of robbery, you see; it was another kind of violence in the air: the violence of anger.
—ROBERT PENN WARREN ON HIS KENTUCKY CHILDHOOD

## WHITE SOUTHERNERS

No other section of the country, not even the "wild" West, has been as blood-soaked as the southeastern region of the United States. Most of that violence was, of course, war-related, as the most sanguinary conflict ever to wrack America was fought by and large in the South. Much of the remaining violence was the product of social conflict—riots, lynchings, and various acts of intimidation—mainly designed to suppress blacks and keep them from assuming power in proportion to their numbers, which, in the South, have always been very high. Once one subtracts killings and maimings due to war and social discord, there remains an inordinately high number of plain old crimes of violence, mainly assaults and murders. As I will show, starting in the late 1880s, African Americans contributed more than their share to the interpersonal carnage. Indeed, throughout the twentieth century, black homicide rates have been many multiples of white rates, commonly seven to ten times higher. But while whites were apt to blame blacks for the South's elevated homicide rates, the truth is, both black *and* white southerners have disproportionately high murder rates. Or rather, they *had* higher rates. There has been a convergence in recent decades, a blurring of the regional distinctions in crime that is itself worthy of analysis—and will receive it in the chapter on southern crime in the twentieth century.

For several reasons this outsized regional crime—especially among whites—is a puzzlement. For one thing, the South, for most of its history, has largely been rural, and rurality, even combined with poverty, has since the late nineteenth century never been associated with violent crime. Violent crime, we've been told repeatedly, is an urban problem. Nevertheless, excessive southern violent crime persisted well into the twentieth century. If anything, the high crime of the South is further proof that urbanization is not a sine qua non for violence, that interpersonal violence can thrive outside of big cities.

Another anomaly of white southern crime is its tendency, in the first half of the nineteenth century especially, to cut across class boundaries. Another truism of violent crime is its monopolization by the lower classes; rarely do middle- and upper-income people engage in such activity. But in the antebellum South, as will be made clear, males from the better-off segment of society, imbued with a heightened sense of personal honor, were quick to kill one another in duels or less formalized clashes. The lower classes, to be sure, carried on their own versions of these interpersonal contests, but the high-end killings in the South seem to be unique in the history of violent crime in America.

A final curiosity is that the impact of immigrant crime—speaking here of mid-nineteenth and turn-of-the-twentieth-century immigrants—was negligible below Mason and Dixon's line. While there was *some* flow of European immigrants to the South—Italians to New Orleans, for example, midcentury Irish to coastal cities such as Charleston—this was but a trickle by comparison to the deluge washing over the cities of the northeast. In short, white crime in the South was overwhelmingly native crime. There was, however, as I will show, an immigration effect on the South seldom thought of, the effect of a much earlier eighteenth-century immigration. As historians now have demonstrated, migration to America by the so-called Scotch-Irish, a distinctive group from northern Ireland and the northern borderlands of England, brought to the South a potent heritage of honor-related violence.[1] This cultural heritage, persisting for nearly two centuries, goes far in explaining white southern crime.

## A SOUTHERN CULTURE

For over two hundred years, visitors to southern states have remarked on the levels of violence that they saw. "Even before the War for Independence," historian John Hope Franklin noted, "a British traveler in South Carolina and Georgia observed that the rural life and the constant use of arms promoted a kind of martial spirit among the people." By the early nineteenth century, the South's reputation for violence was well established. "In 1846, the Scot, Alexander Mackay, described the 'fiery blood of the South.' A decade later," Franklin added, "James Stirling was disturbed by the proneness to violence and the readiness to fight which he observed in the Southern states where 'wild justice easily degenerates into lawless violence, and a bloodthirsty ferocity is developed among the ruder members of the community.'"[2]

One of the first attempts to provide more than a merely impressionistic account of violent crime was H. V. Redfield's study published in 1880, *Homicide, North and South*.[3] Relying on reports from newspapers with statewide coverage, Redfield tallied the incidence of homicide in the South from the Civil War to the late 1870s. "The number of homicides in the Southern States since the war," he concluded, "reaches the enormous aggregate of at least forty thousand. Continuing through a generation at the same rate, the destruction of life would equal that of a great war." Comparisons with the North, even rural portions of the North, drove the point home. "During the years 1877 and 1878, when we find two hundred and fifty-one homicides in South Carolina, there were but forty in Massachusetts, with more than double the population!" Homicide "is twelve to thirteen times more frequent in South Carolina than in Massachusetts."[4]

Ultimately, Redfield seemed mystified by southern violence, but nonetheless he offered a number of astute observations. Given the rural and agricultural nature of the South, plus the absence of a large immigrant population, one would expect, he thought, relatively fewer homicides in that region. "There is in the South," he noted, "precisely the condition of things which, in society properly organized and governed, would make murder exceedingly rare. . . . The occupations of the people are largely agricultural, the foreign element comparatively small, and there are no great cities and mining and manufacturing centres with attendant clashings of classes and interests."[5]

Why then were murders so frequent? Redfield's answer was that in the South the law was not vigorously enforced, at least not against whites.

5

When a black man kills a white man the law is enforced with rigor. He is not permitted to escape on technicalities. He is not released on a straw-bond or any other bond. He is not released from jail at night by a clan of his friends. When taken out unlawfully it is by a mob of the murdered man's friends, who hang him. For a negro to be acquitted of the charge of killing a white man requires the most direct and positive proof either of innocence or that it was clearly a case of self-defence, when no other alternative was left but to kill. If the killing of whites by whites and blacks by blacks was reduced to as low a per cent, as the killing of whites by blacks, the homicide rate in . . . the South would not reach such fearful proportions as now. It is the killing of whites by whites that swells the aggregate out of all proportion to that which prevails in well-governed communities.[6]

And how do these white-on-white killings come about? In the classic nineteenth-century manner, of course, through personal conflict, intensified by alcohol, not infrequently degenerating into a general melee or brawl.

In the larger towns, where the police regulations are measurably good, there are rarely such scenes of violent disorder, and the killings are usually the result of sudden "difficulties," which the officers cannot prevent. It is in the smaller towns and villages, of from one to seven or eight hundred inhabitants, that street-fights, and affrays, and difficulties most often take place. Sometimes these scenes of violent disorder utterly overpower the local authorities, and the contestants fight it out. Often these deadly difficulties arise from very trifling causes, and parties are drawn in to help their friends who had nothing to do with the beginning of the affray. Originating in whiskey, they usually end in blood. . . . Two men have a "difficulty," both draw weapons, and one falls while attempting to shoot or stab his adversary. He pleads "self-defence," and is acquitted by the jury and by public opinion. He has simply killed his man, and his status in society is not impaired.[7]

Redfield was writing about postbellum Dixie at a point when black violent crime was not yet a concern (a circumstance that would change dramatically a decade later) and white violence largely went unpunished. Had he conducted his study in the first half of the nineteenth century, before the Civil War, however, he would have found much the same situation, except of course that the blacks would have been slaves. And had he arrived instead in the first half of the twentieth century, conditions would have evolved as follows. White violent crime, while no longer committed with impunity, would still be disproportionately high compared to white crime in other states. And black violent crime, not infrequently ignored by the southern authorities, would have skyrocketed.[8]

Until recently, the South has been culturally unique, if not somewhat culturally isolated from the rest of the United States. In W. J. Cash's classic statement,

> There exists among us by ordinary—both North and South—a profound conviction that the South is another land, sharply differentiated from the rest of the American nation, and exhibiting within itself a remarkable homogeneity. . . . That is to say, it is easy to trace throughout the region . . . a fairly definite mental pattern, associated with a fairly definite social pattern—a complex of established relationships and habits of thought, sentiments, prejudices, standards and values, and associations of ideas.[9]

There is, in short, a distinctive southern culture, and violence certainly has been a major component of it. In Cash's words, violence "has always been a part of the pattern of the South."[10] The contours of southern violence have been described in great detail by historian Dickson Bruce, who devoted an entire book to its manifestation in the antebellum South. The chapter titles alone reveal much: "The Southern Duel"; "Child-Rearing and the Southern World View"; "Slavery and Violence"; "Militarism and Violence"; "Hunting, Violence, and Culture"; and so on.[11] Likewise, the *Encyclopedia of Southern Culture* devotes a full seventy-four pages to the subject of violence, including such evocative entries as "Cock-fighting," "Hatfields and McCoys," "Bonnie and Clyde," "Capital Punishment," "Chain Gang," and "Convict Leasing"—entries that could not have made Bruce's antebellum list.[12]

Violent crime in the South is a part of this picture and the evidence is great that southern cultural support for violence helps explain why violent crime has been so disproportionate in the South for so very long. The persistence of this penchant for violence can, in fact, be traced to some of the earliest white immigration to America, notably to the seventeenth- and eighteenth-century migrations of the so-called Scotch-Irish.

## ORIGINS

One might think that a study of violent crime from the late nineteenth century to the end of the Great Depression could profit little from examining the culture of seventeenth- and eighteenth-century immigrants. Once one accepts, however, that cultural characteristics may persist—even for hundreds of years—the notion no longer seems far-fetched. After all, haven't regional groups, such as the Basques and Catalans in Spain, or the Bretons in France, retained their distinctiveness for centuries?[13] Since a predilection for violence may be one of those persisting traits, the relevance of the early history of a regional group comes more sharply into focus.

This is especially true where, as was the case with American southerners, the group was relatively isolated socially. Before the late nineteenth century and the advent of mass transportation and communication technologies, interaction between North and South was limited. Southern culture, while sharing much with the North, developed independently, and the Civil War was in large measure a massive clash of differing cultures. Of course, a culture may be altered through conquest, and the South arguably was conquered in the 1860s. But, as Thomas Sowell has observed, many conquests have had little cultural effect because of the brief duration or limited aims of the conquerors.[14] It is noteworthy that within little over a decade after the Civil War ended, the South was left free to determine its own fate, albeit without slavery. By 1877, conservative whites had regained control of all southern state political machinery.

In addition to conquest, a second common instrument of "cultural diffusion," as Sowell called it, is migration. Here too the impact on southern culture was limited. To be sure, there was, as is shown below, a significant immigration effect on the American South—but that was due to British immigration in the eighteenth century. By contrast, the European immigrants to the United States of the late nineteenth and early twentieth centuries overwhelmingly settled in the North and left little cultural imprint on Dixie. Consequently, distinctive southern norms and values related to violence, crime, and law enforcement underwent but limited change for roughly two centuries.[15]

Everyone knows how America was settled by English colonists and how we imported myriad ideas, values, and institutions from Great Britain. Less well known are the *differences* among the early British immigrants to America and the varying impact these different groups had on what later became the United States. In the 1980s, historians became more sensitive to these differences. These historians noticed that certain of the British migrants, notably the "Scotch-Irish" from northern Ireland and the turbulent border region between England and Scotland, had customs and values that bore a striking resemblance to the customs and values of the Americans of the South. At the same time, these historians discerned, New Englanders or Yankees, descending from a very different group of British—Puritans from the southeast of England—shared very little culturally speaking with their fellow British immigrants or with the American southerner.[16]

The violence of the Scotch-Irish, the fact that they settled in the southern states and not the north, and the long history of violent crime in the South are inextricably linked. The historical evidence strongly suggests that cultural support for violence directly traceable to the initial (white) settlers in the region—the Scotch-Irish—helps explain the persistently high violent crime rates of the South throughout the nineteenth and most of the twentieth centuries.

Historian David Hackett Fischer, author of *Albion's Seed* ("Albion" being the Greek name for Britain in the sixth century BCE), identified four waves of British immigrants to America: 1. Puritans from the east of England who landed in the New England region between 1629 and 1640; 2. Royalists and indentured servants from the south of England who traveled to Virginia, 1642–1675; 3. migrants from the north Midlands of England and from Wales who arrived in the Delaware Valley roughly between 1675 and 1725; and most significantly, 4., from 1718 to 1775, an influx to the Appalachian backcountry of "English-speaking people from the borders of North Britain and northern Ireland."[17] These four immigrant groups, Fischer concluded, "carried across the Atlantic four different sets of British folkways which became the basis of regional cultures in the New World."[18]

The fourth group, the Scotch-Irish, shared much with the earlier migrants: a common language, the Protestant religion, English laws, and a belief in English liberties. But there were crucial distinctions—differences in their origins, in their "methods of doing much of the ordinary business of life," and in their place of settlement in America. While the Puritans and their descendants fled to and occupied New England in search of religious freedom, the Scotch-Irish, seeking economic betterment, landed first in Pennsylvania and Delaware, then drifted into the southern backcountry along the Appalachian mountain range. From the western parts of Maryland and Virginia to the Carolinas, Georgia, Kentucky, and Tennessee, these former borderland Britons established the dominant English-speaking culture in the South.[19]

Their culture had been formed in a region of the mother country wracked by turbulent violence. Lying in the contested territory between Scotland and England, the border region was for centuries aflame with dynastic wars. These were followed by vicious clan rivalries. "Borderers placed little trust in legal institutions," Fischer observed. "They formed the custom of settling their own disputes by the *lex talionis* of feud violence and blood money." "This incessant violence shaped the culture of the border region," creating a social system very different from that of the south and east of England from which the Puritans hailed. When, in the seventeenth century, the Scottish and English kingdoms merged, pacification (an ironic word) led to more bloodshed. Many were executed or exiled to Ireland, then often banished again to America. "The so-called Scotch-Irish who came to America," said Fischer, "thus included a double-distilled selection of some of the most disorderly inhabitants of a deeply disordered land."[20]

Once in America the Scotch-Irish continued many of their border ways. Alone on the frontier, surrounded by hostile forces—from Native Americans to bandits to rival clans—the ex-border Britons maintained their culture of self-help, including do-it-yourself justice. Fischer saw a pattern.

> There were official sheriffs and constables throughout that region, but the heaviest work of order-keeping was done by ad hoc groups of self-appointed agents who called themselves regulators in the eighteenth century, vigilantes in the nineteenth, and nightriders in the twentieth. This was not a transitional phenomenon—unless one wishes to think of a transition five centuries long. Nor was it the reflexive product of a frontier environment, for other frontiers experienced little or none of it. It rose instead from a tradition of retributive folk justice which had been carried from the British borderlands to the American backcountry.[21]

Vigilantism has a long history in the South. One of the earliest known outbreaks in North America involved the Regulator movements in the western Carolinas of the 1760s and 1770s. These occurred because the Scotch-Irish settlers, terrorized by bandit gangs in the near anarchy of the Carolina frontier, felt compelled to take law enforcement into their own hands. To be sure, the Regulator movements, unlike the post-Reconstruction lynchings over a century later, had nothing to do with race, and until they got out of hand, which eventually they did, were perfectly understandable. They may be seen, however, as the start of a pattern of unofficial law enforcement in the region. The success of the Regulators made vigilantism acceptable as a way of coping with crime wherever the lawfully constituted criminal justice system was perceived to be weak. There were subsequent surges of vigilantism in the antebellum South, for example, in Alabama and Mississippi in the early 1830s, and following Nat Turner's rebellion in Southampton County, Virginia, 1831, during which at least fifty-eight whites were murdered. The Turner rebellion triggered some of the bloodiest race-related vigilante violence in the South, a foretaste of the postbellum lynchings of the 1890s. Although authorities in Virginia and North Carolina charged ninety-one men and women with conspiracy and hanged thirty-five, including Turner, militant whites "went on a rampage, beating, burning, mutilating, and killing suspicious blacks and whites." Homicide historian Randolph Roth estimates that proslavery vigilantes killed between six and seven hundred people in the first half of the nineteenth century.[22]

The southern culture of private enforcement was not limited to mob violence. Killings quietly carried out, accepted by the populace, and rarely prosecuted were a feature of southern communities well into the twentieth century. William Lynwood Montell did an elegant study of a modern borderland—not on the boundary between Scotland and England, but the area around the state line dividing Kentucky and Tennessee. In this isolated region at roughly the midpoint of the line, he found small mountain farm communities with "a subregional culture that tolerated violence in all forms, including homicide." Montell counted fifty documented killings from the 1880s through the 1930s, while suspecting many more, with annual rates ranging from 41 to 114 per 100,000. These homicides were carried out "quickly and quietly in defense of property, family, and personal honor." "Interpersonal lethal violence," Montell concluded, "was an acceptable way of handling disagreements and tensions among residents."[23]

Blood feuds were yet another common feature both of the British borderlands and the South. "The custom of feuding," historian Fischer explained, "had been very common on the borders of North Britain. Bloody strife continued for many generations between families on both sides of the border."[24] Introduced to the southern backcountry in the eighteenth century, such feuding flourished for over two hundred years. Perhaps the most famous, though hardly an isolated instance, was the Hatfield-McCoy vendetta, which began with conflicts stemming from the Civil War and led over the next two decades to a series of deadly killings. The culmination was the cruel New Year's 1888 raid on McCoy's house, which the Hatfields set ablaze, killing two McCoy children. It took a sensational trial, in 1897, followed by the hanging of one Hatfield and the imprisonment of others to finally put an end to the warfare.[25]

In addition to the internecine violence of the blood feud the South also was known for its brutal one-on-one fighting—the "rough-and-tumble" as it came to be known. In such contests, common in the eighteenth and early nineteenth centuries, a man could do virtually anything he wished to his opponent provided it could be accomplished with bare hands.

> Honor dictated that all techniques be permitted. Except for a ban on weapons, most men chose to fight "no holts barred," doing what they wished to each other without interference, until one gave up or was incapacitated. The emphasis on maximum disfigurement, on severing bodily parts, made this fighting style unique. Amid the general mayhem, however, gouging out an opponent's eye became the sine qua non of rough-and-tumble fighting, much like the knockout punch in modern boxing.[26]

"Foreign travelers might exaggerate and backwoods storytellers embellish," historian Elliott Gorn reported, "but the most neglected fact about eye-gouging matches is their actuality. Circuit Court Judge Aedamus Burke barely contained his astonishment while presiding in South Carolina's upcountry: 'Before God, gentlemen of the jury, I never saw such a thing before in the world. There is a plaintiff with an eye out! A juror with an eye out! And two witnesses with an eye out!'" And while the rough-and-tumble was not unknown in the North, "men in the East and Middle West did not glorify mayhem and mutilation in practice and folklore to the same extent as did the southern backwoodsmen."[27]

Laws were passed to restrain the violence when, as often happened in the South, it veered toward the extreme, but such enactments proved ineffectual. Virginia, for example, made it a crime in 1772 to engage in "gouging, plucking, or putting out an eye, biting or kicking or stomping upon." The maiming nevertheless continued, reinforcing the acceptability of sadistic violence—cruelty that resurfaced in the next century when fear of blacks became overwhelming.

By the nineteenth century hand-to-hand combat began to be considered unseemly for a gentleman, and while brawling continued among lower-class males, especially in the backwoods, among the elite, the planter class, the duel with pistols became the most acceptable form of bloodshed.[28] Stylized though it may have been, the duel was nonetheless violent. As historian Bertram Wyatt-Brown observed, "whether the combat took a prescribed form or consisted of sheer unchecked fury, did not make too much difference, if one or both of the contestants died."[29] And many did die in these contests. One analyst tallied nearly nine hundred duels in the nineteenth century, 45 percent of which were fatal.[30] Dueling, in short, was the upper-class version of the rough-and-tumble, bullets taking the place of teeth and fingernails.

Edward L. Ayers, one of the leading historians of crime and criminal justice in the nineteenth-century South, said that "by 1830 dueling and the South became virtually synonymous." In the North, by contrast, revulsion over Aaron Burr's killing of Alexander Hamilton in 1804 had pretty much ended the practice. The duel, and to a certain extent all interpersonal violence in the South, was the product of a culture of "honor." Ayers explained.

Honor might be defined as a system of beliefs in which a person has exactly as much worth as others confer upon him. Antebellum northerners and most twentieth-century Americans have some difficulty understanding the idea of honor, for it runs contrary to what has come to be a national article of faith: each person regardless of race, class, sex, or religion, possesses equal intrinsic worth—regardless of what others think of him. Insult has little meaning to people who share such a faith, but if one takes honor seriously, insult from a respected person can cut to the quick. Accordingly, much of the violence in the South from the eighteenth century to the present appears to have been sparked by insult, by challenges to honor.[31]

As duel-related deaths began to increase, the southern states once again resorted to regulation by law. And once again the law was of little avail. South Carolina made dueling a crime in 1812, but there were only a small number of prosecutions and the conviction rate was just 40 percent.[32] There even sprang up in the major cities of the South antidueling societies, also without effect. Dueling had rules, the *code duello,* but southerners didn't always bother about them, and shooting a man down in cold blood right on the street became an everyday occurrence. While southern Christian ministers roundly condemned dueling, the culture of honor with its violent implications was deeply engrained and the practice continued until the Civil War.[33]

Among whites in plantation counties it is estimated that 67 percent of the antebellum homicides involved guns or knives. As weapon-carrying was commonplace in the South there began in the early 1800s a public debate over the legitimacy of concealed weapons, a debate with echoes in our own day. Defenders of the custom claimed that it facilitated self-defense and actually deterred assaults, while their adversaries pointed to the number of woundings and deaths occurring as a result of petty disputes. The proregulation side apparently had the better of the argument, and Kentucky and Louisiana passed the nation's first concealed-weapons laws in 1813. By the 1830s most states in the South had followed suit. Once again, however, legislation proved futile. "Despite their popularity," wrote homicide historian Roth, "concealed-weapons laws had no clear impact on homicide rates."[34]

Perhaps the major reason for the ineffectiveness of any laws to regulate violence was the South's refusal to severely punish violent misconduct. "The dictates of the legal code and the concerns of the jury," said Ayers, "ensured that property crime was dealt with more harshly than violence or disorder." Fewer than one-fifth of those convicted in southern courts—but about half the southern penitentiary population—were thieves or burglars.[35]

Ayers's study of the felony court in Chatham County, Georgia (essentially the city of Savannah), provides an excellent illustration of the southern nonchalance about violent crimes. Throughout the 1850s, fewer than 20 percent of the indictments were for property offenses, mainly larceny, whereas 43 percent were for crimes of violence (90 percent of which were assaults). The incidence of violence, judging by these figures, was relatively high. Two-thirds (64 percent) of these violent crime prosecutions resulted in convictions, as did 58 percent of the property indictments. While the conviction rate suggests foursquare disapproval of violence, the punishments tell a very different story. Whereas 54 percent of those convicted of property crimes were sentenced to prison, only 14 percent of the violent offenders were incarcerated; two-thirds (67 percent) of them were merely fined.[36]

Savannah sentencing practice was reflected in the population of the Georgia penitentiary: more than half the prisoners (52 percent) had done property crimes; only one-third had committed crimes of violence. This situation—much violence, little punishment—prevailed throughout the South, and not just in cities like Savannah. "Rural counties, like urban counties," noted Ayers, "treated property offenders much more harshly than those accused of violence." Ayers reported the following proportions of property and violent crimes for inmates in southern penitentiaries between 1850 and 1860.

TABLE 1.1. Percentage of property and violent crimes by inmates in southern penitentiaries, 1850–1860

| Offense | Ala. | Ga. | Miss. | Tenn. | Va. | Md. | La. |
|---------|------|------|-------|-------|------|------|------|
| Property | 46.5 | 52.1 | 54.1 | 52.0 | 48.6 | 54.5 | 40.4 |
| Violent | 30.0 | 32.5 | 24.9 | 27.3 | 29.0 | 26.7 | 42.9 |
| Other | 23.5 | 15.4 | 21.0 | 20.7 | 22.4 | 18.8 | 16.7 |

*Source: Ayers, Vengeance and Justice, 111, 75n13.*

These figures paint a clear picture. In every state prison except Louisiana's, many more inmates—in three states, twice as many—were serving time for theft-related offenses as violent crimes. Though violent crimes were common in the South the perpetrators were given mere wrist slaps. Indeed, one of the main reasons violence *became* common in the South is that it was treated so leniently.

The violence of the South was not just a matter of some general nineteenth-century insensitivity or coarseness. The levels of violence simply were much lower in the North. Michael Stephen Hindus compared criminal prosecutions in Massachusetts and South Carolina during the first half of the century.[37] In Massachusetts, crimes against the person (murder, rape, and assault) made up 17.8 percent of the cases, whereas in South Carolina they were a whopping 58.3 percent. "Concern about lawlessness in South Carolina," said Hindus, "was largely a concern about violence. Grand jury presentments, the most reliable source of public sentiment about crime in the state, complained about assaults, dueling,

and carrying concealed weapons." Nevertheless, violent crime—white crime—
"was not considered a vital social problem. Punishments were insubstantial, and
few resources were devoted to improving courts or jails."[38]

There were three reasons for this unconcern. First, as is now clear, southern
culture supported all types of violence, including violent crime. While the existence of laws against dueling and concealed weapons shows that significant
elements of the region were profoundly disturbed by all the mayhem, the general
ineffectiveness of such laws suggests that support for violence was stronger still.
Even more significantly, the failure to seriously sanction violent crime—despite
repeated grand jury indictments and presentments—betrays the South's deep-
seated ambivalence about violence.

Second, violent crime, though often deadly, was not random or indiscriminate. Southerners killed people who offended them, killed to defend their honor,
killed over property, slaves, and triflings. But they seldom killed total strangers.
Crime in the South was the emblematic nineteenth-century crime among acquaintances, often armed and drinking. Such crime posed little threat to community order; it did not affect ordinary social functions; it was not at all like the
big-city robbery-assaults of the twentieth century. "Robbery and skilful burglary
are exceptionally rare in the Southern States," observed Redfield, no southern
apologist, "and there is no more reason to arm for the protection of property than
in New York or New England."[39]

Third, violent crime cut across class lines. It frequently was committed by
young men from the middle class—one of the few examples of violent crime as a
middle-class problem. Historian Ayers found that in Savannah, half the prosecutions of merchants, professionals, and planters were for crimes of violence; one-
quarter were for property offenses. For poorer defendants it was the other way
around. Over half (51.4 percent) of the unskilled worker prosecutions were for
property crimes; 25.7 percent were for violence. The ability of better-off defendants to avoid incarceration was a major reason why the southern penitentiaries
were filled with poor property crime offenders, whereas violent crimes were so
often punished by fines.[40]

## SLAVERY

Many thought that slavery was instrumental in forming the southern culture of
violence. "Do we not know," asked Charles Dickens rhetorically, "that the worst

deformity and ugliness of slavery are at once the cause and the effect of the reckless license taken by these freeborn outlaws?"[41] There was good reason to think this. Slavery was, by the nineteenth century, unique to the South, and extreme violence was distinctively, even if not exclusively, southern. The very foundation of slavery, ultimately, was the lash. Why else would blacks toil? Fear of slave revolts sometimes led white militants to resort to ruthless use of force against slaves and white abolitionists. And setting aside the sporadic vigilante brutalities, which included burnings, beheadings, and mutilations, slaves were lawfully executed in high numbers, much higher than whites. Exact figures are wanting, but Hindus estimated that 296 slaves were executed in South Carolina alone between 1800 and 1855, a number he thought probably low. His figures for Massachusetts indicate only twenty-eight executions, though for a somewhat shorter time period, 1801–45.[42]

The brutalities of slavery surely must be counted as one of the consequences of the southern culture of violence, as well as a reinforcement of it. "Slavery had a brutalizing effect that fell on both the bondsmen and their masters." But it is difficult to accept slavery as the main *cause* of southern violence. As Ayers succinctly observed, "an explanation of Southern violence based . . . [on] slaveholding does not explain either the apparent violence of the great majority of Southerners who never owned slaves or the persistence of Southern violence for more than a century after the end of slavery."[43]

As for slave ownership, fewer than 5 percent of southern whites actually kept slaves, and less than one-third of the free population were members of slave-owning families.[44] Moreover, entire swaths of the South—the hills and mountains of the Carolinas and Georgia, for example—had very few slaves, but violence aplenty. This is demonstrated by Ayers's study of indictments for violent crimes in five southern counties for various years prior to 1860.[45] The overwhelming majority of these indictments were of whites, as few blacks were tried for violent crime in the antebellum South. These counties had very different populations: rural and urban, slave and no-slave. The highest proportion of violent crime accusations was in Shenandoah County, Virginia, a western mountain county with very few slaves. Nearly as high was Chatham County, Georgia (Savannah), where slaves were nearly half of the population, though most lived out of the control of their masters. The lowest was in Greene County, Georgia, a part of the Black Belt, where slaves were two-thirds of the population. There was, in short, no correlation between slavery and violent crime by whites.

TABLE 1.2. Proportion of indictments for violent crime, selected counties, antebellum South

| County | Violent Crime, % of Indictments | Description of County |
| --- | --- | --- |
| Greene (Ga.) | 24.3 | Black Belt county; 66% slave |
| Whitfield (Ga.) | 31.3 | Mountain county; 17% slave |
| Louisa (Va.) | 26.6 | Plantation county; 61% slave |
| Shenandoah (Va.) | 43.4 | Mountain county; 5% slave |
| Chatham (Ga.) | 42.9 | Savannah; 48% slave |

Sources: Ayers, *Vengeance and Justice*, 116n28; Superintendent of Census, *Population in 1860* (Washington, DC: GPO, 1864), Georgia, table 2; Virginia, table 2.

If additional proof is wanted, recall Montell's study of the central Tennessee/Kentucky border, where nary a black face could be seen and undesirables were quietly disposed of by plain folk, not "hardened criminals."[46]

No, slavery did not make the white southerner violent; it presented, rather, one of many opportunities to exercise violence, and was one of many violent behaviors supported by southern culture. The slave system itself would end with an even greater agony of bloodshed, brought on in part by the South's militarism (another manifestation of southern violence?)[47] and followed by the worst violence of all insofar as the African American was concerned—the fury unleashed by Reconstruction. From this point on—from the late 1860s through the next century—white southerners would engage in violent crime at rates well above those of other white Americans. A legacy of slavery? Certainly. But also a legacy of unruly British border dwellers, eye-gouging frontiersmen, sadistic vigilantes, an exaggerated sense of honor, dueling, clan feuds, and by century's end, a new, more virulent brand of racism. All of this was part of the southern culture of violence, a heritage shared by whites and blacks that would fuel high violent crime in the South for a century.

## CRIME POSTBELLUM

Devastated by the Civil War, the South entered into a period of turmoil with scant counterpart in American history. "Few people have been so buffeted by chaos and change as the blacks and whites of the South in the twenty years between 1860 and 1880," wrote Ayers. "The suffering of those twenty years, as inevitable as it may have been, left a bitter legacy—a legacy more damaging in its effect on crime and punishment, perhaps, than on any other facet of Southern society." Violent crime soared in the immediate postwar years, declined dramatically after the end of Reconstruction, and escalated once again in the depression of the late 1880s. Until roughly the last twelve years of the century, violent crime was overwhelmingly white and treated, as before the Civil War, with considerable indifference.[48]

During the war murder rates held steady wherever the Confederacy established control. Where it did not, such as in north Texas and the mountain areas of North Carolina, Tennessee, and Georgia, homicide rates soared. At the end of the terrible conflict, predictably, vengeance killings mounted. By the time they abated, in the early 1870s, hundreds had been sent to their graves. There even was an outbreak of theft killings—a rarity for the South—as the southern economy, reduced to shambles, drove people to desperation. But the biggest contributor by far to postwar homicide was the returning Confederate soldier, armed and embittered. "They killed blacks, white Republicans, and one another," said Roth, "at an alarming rate." Gun use, spurred by the war, was responsible for 80 percent of the postwar white homicides.[49]

Former Confederate officers helped organize the terror groups, like the Ku Klux Klan and the Knights of the White Camellia, which sought to dismantle Reconstruction governments and prevent or undo, at all costs, "Negro rule." Blacks and white Republicans were the targets of their wrath. In some areas homicide rates shot up. In three plantation counties in Georgia, for instance, rates went from 10 per 100,000, a rate that had held steady since the end of the War of 1812, to well over 20, where they remained until the end of Reconstruction.[50]

The amount of bloodshed in a locale depended on whether federal troops or an effective city police force was available to control the violence and on the willingness of southern elites to accept Republican rule. In rural Louisiana, for example, the Mississippi River Delta region in the northeastern part of the state had low levels of violence during Reconstruction—3.5 percent of the state's rural homicides—because the planters cooperated with the Republicans and accepted black political predominance. The Red River parishes in northwestern Louisiana, by contrast, with more than half of the state's rural homicides, were populated by whites "who stubbornly opposed the Federal government and its Reconstruction policy," bitterly resented federal troops, especially the black brigades, and would not shrink from anything, including murder, to resist the postwar changes. In addition, it was hard for federal troops to respond quickly to threats in an area as remote as this.[51]

Once Reconstruction ended, in 1877, and "Redeemer" or Conservative governments were installed, homicide declined abruptly. Roth reports that when Redeemers took charge in Louisiana (1877), rural homicide rates fell from 89 to 35 per 100,000; in New Orleans they went from 35 to 25. Likewise, in 1872, when former Confederates returned to power in Georgia, rates fell in the mountain counties 53 to 12, and in plantation counties 24 to 16.

Peace reigned in the South for roughly a decade, until the late 1880s, then economic catastrophe struck. The second greatest depression in American history, which officially began with the Panic of 1893, had started devastating the South several years earlier. America's agricultural economy—and despite the growth of railroads and cities, farming remained the predominant activity among southerners—was in crisis.

As the depression worsened in the early part of the 1890s so did the "anger, alienation, and bitterness." "The consequence of political upheaval and the reaction that followed was once again a rash of lynchings, vigilante killings, and," Roth thought, "everyday murders." Conservative elites played the race card, "regained ascendancy in the late 1890s and early 1900s and created a political regime that was more brutal, corrupt, and nakedly antidemocratic than any the nation had seen since slave times."[52]

The claim that political and economic turmoil caused "everyday murders" is not self-evident, but there is some evidence, hardly conclusive, that that was the case in the South of the 1890s. Homicide historian Randolph Roth reported the following increases in homicide indictments per 100,000.[53] (Of course, indictments are a feeble proxy for actual murders, as many murderers are never apprehended and many of those arrested are not prosecuted.)

- From 12 in the 1880s to 23 in the 1890s in Georgia mountain counties Gilmer and Rabun
- From 16 in the 1880s to 30 in the 1890s in Franklin, Jasper, and Wilkes, former plantation counties in Georgia

- From 27 in the late 1880s to 71 in the late 1890s in the state of South Carolina
- From 125 to 800(!) in the upper Cumberland of Kentucky and Tennessee (time frame unclear)
- From 6.5 in seven southern and border cities, 1877–87, to 9.0 from 1888 to 1911

Thanks to the research of John Hammond Moore, we have some statewide data for South Carolina, based, it appears, on reports of county solicitors (as prosecutors are called to this day in South Carolina). As indicated by figure 1.1, derived from Moore's data, there was a steady rise in homicides throughout the decade of the 1890s.

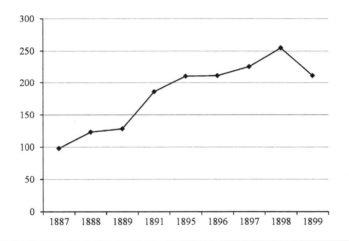

FIGURE 1.1. Murder and manslaughter indictments, South Carolina, 1887–1899. *Source:* Moore, *Carnival of Blood,* 130–31.

What is not clear from Moore's or Roth's statistics is the proportion of the increase in homicides attributable to whites. On one hand, black violent crime increased dramatically starting in the late 1880s, so we cannot be sure that white homicide drove the upsurge. On the other hand, in some areas, such as the mountain and Cumberland counties, where the African American population was low, whites probably were overwhelmingly responsible for the homicide increases.

Ayers's data on homicide arrests in southern cities (graphically depicted in figure 1.2) also show a steep incline in the late 1880s and early 1890s, as the economic crisis worsened.[54] Once again, however, these data don't differentiate white and black violent crime.

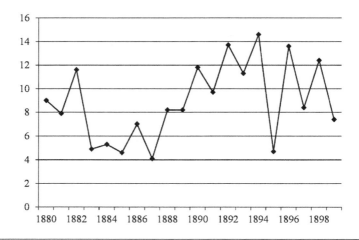

FIGURE 1.2. Homicide arrests per 100 million, southern states, 1880–1889. *Source:* Ayers, *Vengeance and Justice,* 250n56.

Prison data for the South in the 1890s indicate a sizable increase in white inmates (though nowhere near the increase in blacks), from fewer than 100 prisoners in 1893 to over 200 in 1895–97.[55] This points to more white crime, but these data present a different problem: we cannot be sure we are dealing with violent or property crimes.

There the matter must rest until researchers look more closely into crime at the end of the nineteenth century. Suffice it that violent crime most definitely rose in the South and the data imply contributions by both races. "The South was not as homicidal as it had been during the Civil War or Reconstruction," concluded homicide historian Roth, "but in these decades [between the late 1880s and World War I] the South surpassed the Southwest as the most homicidal region of the United States."[56]

As will be seen, blacks contributed considerably to this dubious honor, but white violence below the Smith and Wesson line (as sociologist H. C. Brearley dubbed it)[57] was higher than white violence almost every place else in America. Why should this be? The best answer is that southern culture, white and black, encouraged all sorts of violence, both within and without the law.

As will be made clear, southern white violence remained high for most of the twentieth century. It wasn't due to poverty since many nonsouthern whites were just as needy. It wasn't due to urbanization, which never was as significant in the South as in the North. It wasn't due to slavery, or to a frontier mentality. The violent crime of the South was a part of the "redneck" culture—a culture that only recently has begun to loosen its grip on the region.

# 2

# The Roots of Black Violence

## A VAST PROBLEM

When, in 1899, the renowned black sociologist W. E. B. Du Bois wrote his classic study *The Philadelphia Negro,* he devoted an entire chapter to "the Negro criminal." Du Bois characterized black crime as "a vast problem," one that "since 1880 . . . has been steadily growing."[1] Looking at blacks committed to Eastern Penitentiary, where Pennsylvania's serious offenders were confined, Du Bois discovered two notable facts. First, black violence was increasing. Of commitments from 1885 to 1895, he observed, convictions of robbery, burglary, and assault rose considerably (though homicide stayed the same and sex crimes decreased). Second, Du Bois found that nearly six out of ten of the black convicts had been born in the South, three times the number native to Philadelphia.[2]

Now this is curious. Why should black violence be high at the end of the nineteenth century? And why in Philadelphia, where, compared to the South, African Americans were relatively unmolested by whites? Why, too, were so many of these northern black offenders southern transplants? These questions invite two competing answers. First, that black crime, especially violent crime, developed in the North, where, despite relative freedom, the harsh conditions of urban life engendered violent misconduct. The second possibility is that those northern black criminals brought with them from Dixie a culture of violence that had developed below Mason and Dixon's line.

Roger Lane, who wrote a pathbreaking history of crime in late nineteenth-century Philadelphia, argues that black violence was a northern phenomenon.

Economic discrimination [against blacks] had helped to create the poverty and insecurity which led to underworld activities that were always rich in the potential for violence. The heritage of racial fear, inspired by a long history of white persecution, contributed to the growing popularity of handguns. Most important, exclusion from the urban industrial revolution meant that blacks were far more likely than whites, even Irish immigrants, to retain an older, or preindustrial social psychology, in which aggression was primarily directed outward, at others.[3]

According to this analysis, the then-new urban industrial economy, its schools and factory work serving to discipline the population, had the effect of reducing crime by taming bands of footloose, bellicose males. African Americans, however, locked out of the new economy by race prejudice, retained a "preindustrial" mentality, the kind of pugnacious and lawless mindset that characterized the Irish throughout most of the nineteenth century.

Assuming for the moment that Lane is correct about the "civilizing" impact of urban industrialization ("civilization" literally means "city-fication"), it still seems likely that black attitudes were forged in the South, since, as he acknowledges, a large portion of Philadelphia's blacks came from there. Moreover, there is evidence that southern blacks were violent *before* they came north. Subsequent chapters will have considerably more to say about black crime in northern cities, but for now, the focus is on the African American situation in the South at the end of the nineteenth century. For it is in the late 1880s and early 1890s, in the towns and cities of the South, that the pattern of black male aggressiveness and lawbreaking first took shape.

## A DREAM DENIED

When they were slaves blacks were not especially violent. Their transgressions mainly were property crimes. Slave offenses were tried by the landowner and punished—by whipping—on the plantation. Courtroom trials and imprisonment in the state penitentiary were reserved by and large for whites. Antebellum penitentiaries in Tennessee, Alabama, Georgia, Kentucky, and Mississippi were at least 90 percent white.[4] Georgia, for example, had 183 prisoners in its penitentiary in 1858, every one of them white.[5]

Some slave offenses, however—capital cases, for instance—were court-tried, even in the antebellum South. In addition to death penalty cases, it was useful to have courtroom proceedings for slave offenses that crossed plantation boundaries, illegal assembly by slaves, and crimes by free blacks.[6] A sampling of such cases for two South Carolina counties is revealing. Nearly 40 percent of the cases tried were for theft offenses, over twice the number of crimes of violence.[7] Even more startling is the contrast with white crime: roughly six of ten cases on South Carolina dockets in the nineteenth century were assault prosecutions.[8] A study of free blacks in antebellum Tennessee confirmed these results; 71 percent of the felony accusations involved property, whereas only 29 percent were crimes against persons.[9]

Jeff Forret, who analyzed slave-on-slave conflict in detail, contended that slaves had an honor culture that matched the white honor system and went hand in hand with violence. Slaves saw violence as appropriate when challenged, argued Forret; it was for them an expression of manhood. Black honor values, he added, explain "much of the violent conflict" among slaves.[10]

And yet, despite their honor code, slave violent crime rates were relatively low. Southern whites had higher homicide rates, and slave homicide rates never exceeded four per 100,000.[11] Each of the following probably contributed to the low rates: the regulation of slave life by masters and overseers; efforts by the Baptist church, which sought to control the morals of black and white parishioners; deterrence created by the risk of criminal prosecution; and conflict resolution by slave peacemakers.[12] In addition, the lack of guns—which slaves were forbidden to possess—made fatal assault more difficult and therefore less frequent.[13]

The take-away point is that the slave subculture of violence existed *along with* low rates of violent crime. Thus, while excessive rates of African American violent crime cannot be traced back to slavery, the violent subculture that supports it developed during bondage.

On the first of January, 1863, Lincoln proclaimed that all slaves within any state in rebellion shall be "thenceforward, and forever free." Since the Civil War still raged at the time, the Emancipation Proclamation was unenforceable. Two years later, in 1865, Lee's army surrendered at Appomattox, and scarcely a week afterward, the Great Emancipator himself was shot dead. Between 1865 and 1877, Reconstruction governance was imposed on the southern states, which had been devastated by the war. The Freedmen's Bureau, a federal agency, distributed food and clothing to destitute blacks (and even some whites); supported the first schools southern blacks ever had; helped establish eleven black colleges and universities, sixty-one normal schools, more than forty hospitals; and tried in vain to assure legal equality.[14] The bureau even maintained special courts for a few years to adjudicate minor civil and criminal cases involving freedmen.[15] But southern whites thwarted it at every turn.

Although most African Americans remained in rural areas after emancipation, turning to sharecropping, thousands fled to southern cities hoping to find work and a new life in freedom. Penniless, the newcomers poured into ramshackle cabins that they threw up on the outskirts of town. Unable for the most part to obtain any but the most menial jobs, the former slaves became dependent for subsistence on public and private charity, theft, and prostitution.[16]

From 1860 to 1870, southern cities were transformed by the black influx. The black population of Vicksburg, Mississippi, tripled; that of Natchez more than doubled. Black residents in the four biggest cities in Alabama increased over 57 percent. In Virginia, Richmond, Norfolk, and Lynchburg acquired near majorities of blacks, while more than half the population of Charleston, South Carolina, became African American.[17] It should be kept in mind that African Americans constituted nearly half of the population of most of the former Confederate states, and in South Carolina and Mississippi they formed absolute majorities.[18] The size of the African American population combined with assumptions about black inferiority go a long way toward explaining the extremism of the South. How else but by violence, terror, and systematic repression could a majority or near-majority population be controlled?

Many blacks were set adrift by emancipation. Some young men adopted the lifestyle of the urban hustler, working odd jobs and engaging in petty crime. Historian Joel Williamson vividly portrays the situation.

Separation and alienation from the white world loosened the threads of black life for a generation or more. . . . Walled away from the dominant white society, denied the order afforded by living in that relatively stable universe, and missing the protection of a black enclave, some black people were left to isolation, to self-denigration, and ultimately to self-hatred. . . .

Here and there individual Negroes fell entirely out of all society, white or black, and took to a roaming, reckless, and often enough violent existence. It was these that the whites most feared. . . . The strange black man, the "nigger in the woods," only glimpsed and seldom totally seen, like Edgar Allen Poe's "Raven" or William Faulkner's Joe Christmas, menaced whites in awful ways that only a mind that did not know him could create. It was especially bad in the rural communities where whites were few and policemen fewer.[19]

As reports of black crime, mainly petty theft and vagrancy, increased, whites became alarmed and fearful. In 1865–66 southern states adopted the Black Codes, under which blacks who were unemployed or without a permanent residence were declared "vagrants," subject to arrest and punishment. The sentences commonly were fines, but if the defendants were unable to pay, a white landowner might put up the money which the defendant then would have to work off on a plantation.[20] Or worse. In Greene County, Georgia, in 1866, twenty-one blacks were convicted of vagrancy under the Black Codes and given thirty-nine lashes apiece.[21] The codes soon were abolished by the Reconstruction governments, although elements would emerge later in the century as Jim Crow laws.

Demoralized and impoverished by the war, horrified by the thought of black governance—the Reconstruction governments enfranchised African Americans—whites were above all determined to reestablish their power. They were convinced that the ordinary courts and the Freedmen's Bureau tribunals were far too weak and ineffectual. Forceful action was needed to restore order. Secret vigilante groups were formed, the Ku Klux Klan being the best known (though not the most powerful). Loosely organized in 1867 as "The Invisible Empire of the South," they whipped and occasionally murdered unruly or "impudent" blacks, and hounded their white supporters. From the end of the war to 1871, in Jackson County, Florida, alone, approximately one hundred people were murdered by Klansmen, 90 percent of them blacks, the rest white Republicans.[22] The Klan was formally disbanded in 1869, and the federal government broke its back through prosecutions in 1870–71.[23] But that didn't prevent the terror that lay in store for blacks in the 1890s.

The Invisible Empire operated mainly in the rural South, where law enforcement was weak. In fact, ineffectual rural law enforcement was a spur to vigilantism and lynching throughout the United States, even (as in the West) where race was not the main motivation, as it surely was for the KKK.

Southern cities meanwhile, beset by thousands of migrating freedmen and increasingly apprehensive whites, had become social tinderboxes. Between 1866 and 1898 there were scores of race riots in the urban South, the peak occurring in the two years between the Panic of 1873 and the presidential election of 1876.[24] These outbursts were triggered by black efforts to obtain or assert their rights and white determination to block them.

Between 1869 and 1877, southern whites, organized as "Conservatives" or "Redeemers," recaptured from Reconstruction governments control of all southern state political machinery. Following the hotly disputed Hayes-Tilden election of 1876, the federal government withdrew the U.S. Army from the South. Nevertheless, for nearly two decades, up until the 1890s, race relations, while not exactly harmonious, seemed to be achieving a measure of stability.

There were legal advances for blacks during this period, although they proved illusory. U.S. Supreme Court rulings eviscerated the Civil Rights Act of 1875 and, more destructively, the Fourteenth Amendment itself. The Court held that even affirmative state action to require race segregation—Jim Crow laws—would not be considered violations of the Fourteenth Amendment, as later was made clear by the notorious *Plessy v. Ferguson* case.[25] Thus was born the "separate but equal doctrine," the final unraveling of constitutional protection for African Americans.

The Court's rulings, deplorable as they were, merely ratified the national political compromise of 1877 that ended Reconstruction and restored state governments to local rule—white rule. "More profoundly than Constitutional amendments and wordy statutes," wrote the leading historian of the compromise, "it shaped the future of four million freedmen and their progeny for generations to come."[26]

## ORIGINS OF THE GHETTO

Before the 1890s, those African Americans who had migrated to southern cities began to establish their own viable communities, with black churches, clubs, newspapers, and benevolent and mutual aid societies to help the sick and destitute and pay for burials.[27] While most blacks settled on the outskirts of town, not all were ghettoized. In 1880 Savannah, for example, blacks resided on practically every street. Many black men took advantage of expertise gained on the plantation to establish skilled trades as shoemakers, butchers, barbers, blacksmiths, carpenters, plasterers, and painters. Nevertheless, a large percentage of black males in Savannah were low-paid common laborers and domestic workers, and in 1880, blacks constituted 75 percent of the city's male unemployed. Sixty percent of Savannah's black women worked away from home, undoubtedly out of economic necessity, mainly as laundresses, domestic workers, and cooks. Three-quarters of African American families were male-headed.[28]

In other southern cities, predominantly black residential communities were developing in some of the worst sections of town, near contaminated streams or smelly slaughterhouses. As it was, southern cities, with their unpaved and poorly drained streets, inadequate sewage systems, and public garbage heaps, were notoriously unhealthy. The black sections were especially bad.[29] Sometimes the name of the district served to identify its inhabitants, for example, Nashville's Black Center and Black Bottom; Raleigh's Hayti Alley; and Atlanta's Darktown.[30] Whatever it was called, the forerunner of the "black ghetto" already was taking shape in the nineteenth-century South.

These black residential districts facilitated black crime in much the same way that they did (and would throughout the twentieth century) in northern cities. They provided the supply of lower-class young males and the (often illicit) recreation—sex, gambling, and drinking—that encouraged them to congregate. Needless to say, the potent mixture of young men in groups and freely available intoxicants was a recipe for trouble. Savannah, for example, near the close of the nineteenth century, had about a dozen "low dance houses, known as 'Free and Easies,' run in connection with saloons." According to W. E. B. Du Bois's associates, these were the setting for a "large percentage of the murders and other offenses against the person" in Savannah.[31]

Law enforcement was difficult in these black districts as white officers began to be afraid to enter, and there were, due to race discrimination, relatively few African American police on city forces. It also should be kept in mind that these were the days before radio communications within police departments, and even call boxes on streets, a new innovation at the end of the nineteenth century, were not yet universal. The police officer, reasonably well paid, but untrained, usually was on his own.[32]

In the 1890s, while most southern cities had all white police, some, such as Raleigh, New Bern, Greenville, and Wilmington, hired black officers. Typically, however, black officers had authority to arrest only other blacks. The paucity of black recruits exacerbated distrust and hostility between the police departments and African Americans.[33] When black crime rose, arrests naturally became more frequent. Sometimes they were based on vague charges ("suspicion") and occasionally they were carried out with violence and brutality.

As blacks grew resentful of the abuse they started resisting arrest, often aided by black mobs. At times they even recaptured and freed black prisoners. By the 1880s, black resistance to arrest was becoming common in southern cities. In 1888, in the predominantly black Yamacraw District of Savannah, blacks rioted when a white policeman shot and killed an escaping black suspect. A mob of several hundred, armed with clubs and rocks, and shouting "kill him," severely beat two officers.[34]

The *Atlanta Constitution* wrote in 1892 that it was dangerous for a lone officer to enter Elbow Bend, inhabited by "negro workmen of the lowest and vilest sort," where "more than once policemen have been attacked."[35] Some years earlier the same newspaper had complained: "When a white criminal is pursued and arrested, we never hear of the white people surrounding the officers of the law and attempting a rescue. But the conditions are all changed when the criminal is a negro. The moment that a negro steals, or robs, or commits some other crime, his person seems to become sacred in the eyes of his race, and he is harbored, protected, and deified."[36]

Here then, in the nineteenth-century southern city, lies the origin of black mistrust of the police. African Americans resented the refusal to hire blacks to serve as officers, the physical abuse of black arrestees, the dragnet arrests following raids of black social gatherings, and the frequent refusal of police to enforce the law at all when blacks were the victims.[37] The catalog of complaints will sound very familiar to twentieth- and twenty-first-century ears for they retained validity for many decades in urban settings north and south. Indeed, even when, nearly a century later, police abuses were reduced to occasional and isolated occurrences, not necessarily racially motivated, many black people, their hostility toward police engrained in their thinking, assumed the worst.

## IMPERFECT MEASURES

Historians by and large have neglected crime by African Americans in the nineteenth century, partly because of the focus on their subjugation. Certainly another factor is the less than perfect data for this period.

It would be too tedious to review all of the inherent shortcomings in the nineteenth century sources, but it is essential to consider some problems specific to the South toward the end of the century. These deficiencies are much more profound than the general weakness of the data as they cast doubt on virtually any conclusions about African American crime below the Mason-Dixon line. I refer, of course, to the notorious race bias of the southern criminal justice system. The southern justice system of the nineteenth century nowadays is seen as part of a general policy of race subjugation designed to keep African Americans in a position of subservience. It is assumed (though seldom proved) that every facet of the criminal justice system discriminated against blacks: that police in southern cities more readily arrested African Americans for conduct tolerated when engaged in by whites; that courts then eagerly convicted them and gleefully imposed harsh sentences, harsher certainly than those meted out to comparably culpable whites. The situation was neatly encapsulated by Edward Ayers, the leading historian of the subject: "The fundamental patterns of institutionalized Southern justice and injustice established during the 1860s changed little for generations. Southern blacks in 1900 no less than in 1870 found themselves singled out for arrest, indictment, conviction, hanging, and long sentences to the chain gang or convict lease system. The punishment for whites remained as lenient as ever."[38] I will examine each of these facets of the southern justice system, from arrest to sentencing, including the unofficial vigilante justice that rose to new heights in the 1890s.

There is no reason to doubt the race subjugation thesis, demonstrated by numerous, disturbing historical studies. Indeed, the view here is that racial oppression was a significant factor in the development and perpetuation of the black culture of criminal violence. Had African Americans been permitted to rise up the social ladder like other ethnic groups America's crime story might have presented a very different narrative. Nevertheless, there are compelling reasons to believe—reasons I will discuss momentarily—that black crime, including, significantly, violent crime, rose sharply at the end of the nineteenth century.

## BLACKS AND POLICE

Proof of widespread discrimination in arrests, as opposed to convictions and sentences, is difficult to come by, although contemporary observers insisted it was so. The principal complaint was not so much that blacks were being falsely arrested, but that white crimes were being ignored. Although we of the late twentieth and early twenty-first centuries associate African Americans with crimes of violence, for most of the nineteenth century it was whites who committed this type of offense and often got away with it. This white violence was the personal-dispute variety, not accompanied by robbery or rape. It was, therefore, less threatening to the average citizen.

Although there was an increase in black violence at the end of the century, most African American arrests were for theft, disorderly conduct, drunkenness, loitering, and the all-purpose "suspicion." When it came to assaults on white victims, other whites, not blacks, usually were responsible.

Regarding relations between late nineteenth-century southern police departments and African Americans we know the following. Deep hostilities developed between big-city police and black communities, no doubt exacerbated by discriminatory hiring which resulted in all or preponderantly white forces. The strain also may have been indicative of discrimination in arrests, brutality in effecting them, or both.

Black newspapers complained, sometimes bitterly, about police abuses. The *Savannah Tribune* in 1895: "Nearly every day we can hear of some brutality exhibited toward our people by the policemen." The Richmond *Planet* in the same year: "The police-officers of Richmond have generally been regarded with a distrust bordering on hatred by the colored people of this community," and "this feeling was reciprocated with compound interest by the officers."[39] Angriest of all, Atlanta's *Weekly Defiance* declared that it had "never seen a meaner set of low down cut throats, scrapes and murderers than the city of Atlanta has to protect the peace."[40] The police, for their part, viewed blacks as a problem class that they had the responsibility to control, although as we saw, white officers sometimes were afraid to enter black areas.

Perhaps most significantly, we know that African Americans were disproportionately arrested, which, of course, could be a sign of police prejudice, high black crime, or some indeterminate mix of the two. In Atlanta, for example, African Americans constituted about 40 percent of the city's population near the end of the century, but two-thirds of the arrests.[41] In Louisville, from 1890 to 1894, they were 18 percent of the population, but 45 percent of the arrests. And in Charleston, South Carolina, 1890–94, black males were two-thirds of all male arrests at a time when African Americans constituted 56.5 percent of the city.[42] These are exceedingly high rates, but it must be kept in mind that the principal grounds for black arrests were drunkenness, disorderly conduct, idling and loitering, and suspicion.[43] These are minor crimes for which the police had a great deal of discretion to arrest or look the other way, and discretion, of course, invites discrimination.

However, by century's end, arrests of blacks for more serious offenses, such as violent crimes, also were high. Table 2.1 presents figures for Charleston arrests from 1889 to 1894.

TABLE 2.1. Arrests, Charleston, SC, 1889–1894

| Violent Crime | Total Arrests | Black Arrests | % Black |
| --- | --- | --- | --- |
| Homicide | 67 | 55 | 82.1 |
| Rape | 18 | 17 | 94.5 |
| Assault | 942 | 765 | 81.2 |
| Domestic violence | 60 | 58 | 96.7 |

Source: Hoffman, "Race Traits," 227.

A recent analysis of Savannah for 1896 to 1903 corroborates the Charleston statistics. Three-quarters of the Savannah homicide arrests were attributed to African Americans.[44] It is highly unlikely that these arrests were a result of race prejudice, if only because they are consistent with the pattern of intraracial homicide. Of the 60 murders for which black males were apprehended, 54 of the victims were of the same race. It will be recalled that an earlier study of Savannah coroner's reports, for 1895–98, found that over 64 percent of the homicides involved black killers and 55 percent were black-on-black incidents.[45]

The clinching argument here are the figures for black arrests in northern cities. If anything, they are higher on a per capita basis than arrests in the South. The turn-of-the-century North was no mecca of enlightenment for black people, as urban riots and housing and job discrimination will attest. But compared to the South, with its lynch mobs and convict lease, northern cities were downright progressive. The high black arrest rates above the Mason and Dixon line—staggeringly so in Chicago—suggest that the rates below it were not purely a product of law enforcer malevolence. They tell us that black crime was excessive throughout the United States. Table 2.2 provides arrest rates of African Americans per 1,000 for cities in 1890, data, incidentally, published by an associate of W. E. B. Du Bois.

TABLE 2.2. Arrest rates of African Americans per 1,000 for selected U.S. cities, 1890

| Northern | Southern | Border |
|---|---|---|
| New York—82 | Charleston—70 | Washington, DC—166 |
| Philadelphia—80 | Savannah—75 | St. Louis—120 |
| Cincinnati—225 | Louisville—99 | |
| Chicago—387 | | |

*Source:* Work, "Crime in Cities," in Du Bois, ed. (1904), *Some Notes*, 20.

No doubt many arrests of African Americans in the nineteenth-century South—especially the low-level public disorder offenses—were driven by bias. These discretionary apprehensions were inflated by the unspoken police mission to control a "dangerous class." However, when it came to serious transgressions— murder, rape, robbery, and felonious assaults—the outsized numbers of black arrests were a product of high black crime and not bigotry. As in the twentieth and twenty-first centuries, most of the serious crimes with black victims were committed by African Americans, and this was reflected in the arrest patterns. It is not as if white police were under pressure to "frame" some innocent black man in order to protect a Caucasian killer. The virulent prejudice of the southern criminal justice system is indisputable, and I will have more to say about the convict lease system and the lynching, but the fact remains that everything points to a major black crime problem in the last decades of the nineteenth century.

## COURTS OF INJUSTICE

As for southern courts, their biases were widely decried even in the nineteenth century itself. They were as unduly lenient with whites as they were unfairly harsh with blacks. A white southern lawyer of that era candidly observed that for a white man, "conviction or acquittal is determined more upon his family connections, his business standing or his local political influence than upon the evidence in the case as applied to the law." Whereas a black, he continued, "has scant consideration before a jury composed entirely of white men, and is given the severest punishments for the most trivial offenses."[46]

It isn't just that white jurors were bigoted. Black defendants usually were unable to afford attorneys, there were precious few black lawyers available to defend them, and to uneducated laymen, court procedures must have seemed an impenetrable mystery. (In 1890, half of the African American population could neither read nor write and only a minority could obtain a public school education. Black offenders had even higher rates of illiteracy than the general public.)[47] As for black jurors, despite nineteenth-century Supreme Court rulings prohibiting exclusion from juries because of race, racial exclusion seems to have been near total throughout the South.[48] Booker T. Washington wrote in 1890 that "in the whole of Georgia & Alabama, and other Southern states not a negro juror is allowed to sit in the jury box in state courts."[49]

The extent of the discrimination depended on the location of the trial. Historian Edward Ayers provided revealing figures for the period prior to 1880. He examined verdicts in three Georgia counties: Chatham County, essentially the city of Savannah; Whitfield County, located in the northern mountains, where the black population was small; and Greene County, a part of the Black Belt, in which blacks outnumbered whites, as they had during slavery.

TABLE 2.3. Verdicts by race in three Georgia counties, 1866–1879

| County | Verdict | Black (%) | White (%) | Antebellum (%) |
| --- | --- | --- | --- | --- |
| Greene | Guilty | 80.3 | 60.4 | 74.7 |
| | Not guilty | 19.7 | 39.6 | 24.2 |
| Whitfield | Guilty | 69.4 | 44.5 | 51.0 |
| | Not guilty | 30.6 | 55.5 | 49.0 |
| Chatham | Guilty | 77.1 | 57.2 | 63.0 |
| | Not guilty | 22.0 | 41.8 | 33.9 |

Source: Ayers, Vengeance and Justice, 176.

After the war, as table 2.3 shows, the courts of all three counties became considerably more lenient toward whites and a lot harder on blacks. As between the races in the postbellum period, the treatment differentials are stark. In Savannah and the Black Belt (Greene County), there was a 20 percent greater chance of a black conviction than a white. African American defendants in Greene County were found guilty eight times out of ten, whites only 60 percent of the time. In other words, the bigger the black population, the greater the white fear and determination to control it, the more black convictions. In the mountains (Whitfield County), where the African American population was sparse, white defendants were the main beneficiaries; more were acquitted than convicted, a pattern rare for criminal prosecutions.

Although Ayers's study didn't extend to the last two decades of the nineteenth century it is highly unlikely that the situation changed. White political power had solidified by then and blacks were unable to organize effective protests against the injustices. Moreover, the southern states found a low-cost way of imprisoning offenders which actually created an economic incentive to punish African Americans: the convict lease system.

## PUNISHMENT

After the Civil War the South found an alternative to prisons—the convict lease system. This was the nineteenth century's version of "privatization." The lease was used mainly for blacks and provided a low-cost way of punishing large numbers of offenders. Ayers estimated that by 1890, some 27,000 convicts were performing labor in the southern states.[50] By the end of the century, however, there had been so many shocking revelations about the lease system that Mississippi, Tennessee, and Louisiana abolished it, and the other states with leasing (only three outside the former Confederacy) imposed new controls. Nonetheless, some southern states continued to lease into the twentieth century.[51]

Convict lease began largely for economic reasons. The war had destroyed southern penitentiaries and there was, at first, little money for rebuilding. As slaves, blacks had been punished on the plantation; as freedmen, the state was now responsible for them. At the same time, there was a major postwar labor shortage and few free laborers would accept jobs in dangerous swamps or mines. Consequently, the southern states began to lease convicts to businesses, primarily to planters, railroads, lumber and mining companies, all starved for labor. Convict lease seemed a perfect solution, controlling the rising black crime problem while providing a much needed workforce. What began as a stop-gap eventually began turning a profit. Alabama and Tennessee, both mining states, took in about $100,000 from leasing in 1886.[52]

The leniency toward white defendants of the postbellum criminal justice system meant that few ended up leased. In his 1882 report, for example, the principal keeper of the Georgia penitentiary stated that there were 1,101 black prisoners—89 percent of the total—and only 113 white. Nor did the keeper manage a penitentiary in the contemporary sense, that is, a facility housing inmates. Rather, Georgia had multiple work camps where prisoners mined coal and iron ore, quarried rocks, made brick, and laid railroads. Some were supervised by the Marietta and North Georgia Railroad rather than by state or county officials.[53]

For blacks, who were readily convicted—oftentimes of thefts or burglaries involving small sums—the lease system was a nightmare. Ayers offers a vivid description, worth quoting at length.

> The Ku Klux Klan or urban mobs might be explained away as local and temporary disturbances in otherwise benevolent race relations, but the death and suffering in the convict lease system went on for decades with the approbation of the South's "leading men." As a result, that system played a central role in the history of crime and punishment in the postwar South.
>
> For half a century following the Civil War, convict camps could be seen scattered over the Southern landscape. Thousands of Southern men and women, most of them black, passed years of their lives in the convict lease system, deep in mines or waist-high in swamps during the day, in wet clothes and filthy shacks during the night. Men with capital, from the North as well as the South, bought these years of convicts' lives. The largest mining and railroad companies in the region as well as small-time businessmen scrambled to win the leases. The crumbling antebellum penitentiaries, granite monuments of another social order, became mere outposts of the huge and amorphous new system of convict labor. Only a few white men convicted of murder, a few black men too sick to remain profitable at the work site, and a few women of both races remained in the dilapidated penitentiaries. Wardens had little to do; the state had become superfluous in the punishment and reclamation of its criminals.[54]

Most of the leased convicts were in their twenties, but a third were mere youth, not yet twenty years old, as the southern states were slow to develop separate juvenile justice systems. Although conditions in the convict camps varied considerably, some of the work was so brutal that it was tantamount to a death sentence. In 1870, 41 percent of Alabama's 180 convicts died. In Mississippi in the

1880s, the death rate was nine times the average northern prison.[55] In the United States as a whole the prison mortality rate was 25 per 1,000. In Texas, it was 49 per 1,000 for those leased to plantations, 54 for those sent to iron works, 74 for prisoners leased to railroads, "and 250 for those so unfortunate as to be rented out to the isolated timber camps in the swamps of eastern Texas."[56]

Developing alongside the lease system was the chain gang, which, because the prisoner was employed by the county rather than by the private sector, was used for labor on public roads and property. Most of the rural Black Belt convicts went to the lease, while prisoners in urban areas ended up on the chain gang. Surviving well into the twentieth century, the chain gang, with its "black convicts in striped uniforms laboring under the gaze of armed white guards[,] has endured as one of the most telling symbols of the American South."[57]

Under the lease system, unsurprisingly, black imprisonment escalated, while for whites, who were literally getting away with murder, imprisonment rates remained stable and relatively low.[58]

The blatant injustice of the convict lease deepened the alienation of African Americans to the point where the criminal justice system became more hated than the criminal. As Du Bois put it:

> When, now, the real Negro criminal appeared, and instead of petty stealing and vagrancy we began to have highway robbery, burglary, murder, and rape, there was a curious effect. . . . The Negroes refused to believe the evidence of white witnesses or the fairness of white juries, so that the greatest deterrent to crime, the public opinion of one's own social caste, was lost, and the criminal was looked upon as crucified rather than hanged.[59]

This antagonism to the "system," born of a deep-seated resentment of its blatant injustices, became another facet of black culture produced in the nineteenth century South and transported down through the generations.

## EVOLVING BLACK CRIME

No one can be absolutely certain that black crime rose substantially at the end of the nineteenth century, but all of the evidence, incomplete as it is, points in that direction. Certainly that was the conclusion of contemporary analysts, such as Du Bois, who were unqualifiedly committed to the welfare of African Americans. Even after taking account of southern white abuses, Du Bois concluded that "there can be no reasonable doubt but that there has arisen in the South since the [civil] war a class of black criminals, loafers and ne'er-do-wells who are a menace to their fellows, both black and white."[60] That black crime also was the favorite rejoinder of apologists for the South makes its occurrence no less true. Those apologists pointed to high black crime in the North as proof that the problem was race-based rather than regional.[61]

Horrified and angered though we may be by the brutalities of the southern system, the fact is that starting in the late 1880s, black crime, and not just petty, nonviolent crime, soared. One piece of evidence is that arrests of blacks actually were higher in the North, where there was little convict leasing and racism had much less of an impact on the criminal justice system. Table 2.4 compares the arrest rates of African Americans in the North and South.[62]

TABLE 2.4. Arrests of blacks per 100,000, 1880–1899, South vs. North

| Year | South | North |
| --- | --- | --- |
| 1880 | 6.9 | 8.6 |
| 1881 | 7.0 | 8.4 |
| 1882 | 7.2 | 8.0 |
| 1883 | 7.4 | 7.6 |
| 1884 | 7.6 | 7.3 |
| 1885 | 8.1 | 7.0 |
| 1886 | 7.9 | 6.7 |
| 1887 | 7.7 | 6.5 |
| 1888 | 7.3 | — |
| 1889 | 7.9 | 24.2 |
| 1890 | 8.0 | 18.0 |
| 1891 | 8.2 | 15.8 |
| 1892 | 8.2 | 13.3 |
| 1893 | 8.0 | 12.0 |
| 1894 | 7.9 | 11.1 |
| 1895 | 6.9 | 10.5 |

TABLE 2.4 *(continued)*

| Year | South | North |
|------|-------|-------|
| 1896 | 7.0 | 30.7 |
| 1897 | 6.7 | 16.7 |
| 1898 | 6.6 | 15.9 |
| 1899 | 6.1 | 11.9 |

*Source:* Ayers, *Vengeance and Justice*, 250n56.

One reason for the higher arrest rates in the North is the greater number of police in that region. In 1890, the major cities of the North had 6.2 police for every million people; the South had only 1.6. This no doubt explains why the average arrest rate in the South during the last two decades of the century was 7.4 per 100,000, whereas for the North it was 12.5.[63] But the fact remains, whether above or below the Mason-Dixon line, in the heavily policed North or the lightly policed South, it was the African American that was increasingly being arrested.

Significant as was the rise of black crime in the late nineteenth century, of equal importance was its changing nature. Violence, never associated with blacks during or in the immediate aftermath of slavery, was becoming a disturbing feature of black criminality. As slaves, blacks were seen as overwhelmingly nonviolent; their predominant crime was larceny. This was not considered a serious social problem, as slaveholders were far more worried about insurrection than petty pilfering. Even after emancipation, southern whites continued to associate blacks with theft, not violence. As a leading historian put it, "blacks and property crime were virtually synonymous in Southern courts."[64] Given the widespread destitution of the freedman during the turbulent postwar years, larceny probably was, at least in some cases, literally necessary for survival. Du Bois, curiously, did not make this claim. He attributed African American theft to the unfamiliarity of slaves with concepts of private property, accustomed as they were to communal plantation life.[65]

Whatever the explanation for it, black crime during slavery and Reconstruction was overwhelmingly nonviolent. And even after Reconstruction whites committed the vast majority of homicides. H. V. Redfield, writing in 1880, found that blacks were responsible for only 19 percent of the killings.[66] This raises considerable doubt that slavery was somehow responsible for subsequent African American violence, although such an argument is sometimes offered to explain why black violent crime rates exceed those of other ethnic or racial minorities.

Despite their apparent subculture of violence, developed over the centuries in the South, African Americans committed relatively little violent crime as slaves or in the fifteen-year period after emancipation. Nevertheless, their honor culture shaped the type of violent crime in which the freedmen engaged, viz., quick-tempered violence in response to perceived affronts. As Randolph Roth put it, African Americans (in postwar Georgia and South Carolina) "found it hard to bear any kind of insult."[67] In his study of rural Louisiana, 1865–84, Gilles Vandal found that 39 percent of black-on-black homicides, a plurality, were motivated by "personal" issues. African Americans, he noted, "killed each other over personal grudges, in self-defense, and as a result of minor disputes"—just the types of killings one associates with an honor culture.[68]

Postbellum black crime rates, though rising, remained modest. In postwar Virginia (1864–80), the black-on-black murder rate was 5.0 per 100,000, comparable to the white-on-white rate of 5.3.[69] In Edgefield County, South Carolina, the homicide inquest rate (undoubtedly lower than the actual murder rate) was 7.3 per 100,000 per year from 1877 to 1885.[70] In Louisiana, however, the homicide rates were higher than in Virginia or South Carolina. New Orleans (1866–76) had a black-on-black rate of 10.6 per 100,000, and in rural Louisiana it was 18.3.[71]

It is difficult to be certain about the factors that kept the levels of African American violent crime modest after emancipation. One obvious circumstance is that blacks still had few guns. Before 1880, African Americans in Virginia used firearms in only .08 percent of homicides; from 1881 to 1900 guns were used in 46 percent of the cases.[72]

A second consideration is that blacks had the Freedmen's Bureau, a legal and impartial mechanism for resolving disputes. Blacks saw in the bureau's agents and courts "their best hope for impartial justice in the postwar South" and brought to them many family and personal conflicts.[73]

In addition, many African Americans remained on or returned to the plantations on which they had been slaves and where there was no reason for them to change their behaviors and engage in increased violence.[74] Other freedmen migrated within the South and were perhaps too unsettled to engage in violent quarrels. (Following emancipation there was a near-obsession with traveling—

forbidden during bondage—resulting in, as earlier discussed, massive increases of blacks in southern cities.)[75]

Finally, blacks were often hounded and violently abused, if not outright murdered, by whites in this period. In Texas, 1865–68, there were 499 white-on-black murders compared with 48 black-on-black. For nonlethal assaults against African Americans, 548 whites were the perpetrators versus 107 blacks.[76] It would be understandable if blacks felt that they should limit their violence to self-defense against menacing whites rather than targeting their own kind.

In short, though a subculture of violence influenced the type of crime committed by emancipated African Americans, their violent crime rates were fairly low prior to the 1880s. Thereafter, the same subculture contributed to their disturbingly elevated rates.

It was not until the late 1880s that black violence began to grow to ominous proportions. Arrests more and more were for violent crimes, not just theft and drunkenness. Handguns, introduced in the middle of the century, had become cheap by the 1890s—around the price of a man's shirt—making them more available to poor whites and blacks. The Sears Catalogue of 1897 offered twelve different revolvers ranging in price from 68 cents to $4.70, seven of them available for less than $2 (plus postage up to 25 cents).[77] This was at a time when a southern farm laborer earned about 70 cents a day, and a common laborer in town took in 97 cents.[78] The three decades following the Civil War "saw a more widespread dissemination of arms among the populace in general than at any time before or since."[79] Black homicides in the South before 1890 involved weapons other than firearms, such as razors, knives, axes, and hoes. After 1890, guns became the instrument of choice.[80]

Homicide arrests were higher in the South than in the North for twelve of the twenty years that closed out the century. And significantly, starting in the late 1880s they rose at a fairly steady clip.

TABLE 2.5. Homicide arrests of blacks per 10,000,000, 1880–1899, South vs. North

| Year | South | North |
|------|-------|-------|
| 1880 | .90 | .24 |
| 1881 | .79 | .29 |
| 1882 | 1.16 | .71 |

TABLE 2.5 *(continued)*

| Year | South | North |
|------|-------|-------|
| 1883 | .49 | .26 |
| 1884 | .53 | .43 |
| 1885 | .46 | .54 |
| 1886 | .70 | .62 |
| 1887 | .41 | .57 |
| 1888 | .82 | 1.25 |
| 1889 | .82 | 1.56 |
| 1890 | 1.18 | 1.01 |
| 1891 | .97 | 1.01 |
| 1892 | 1.37 | .92 |
| 1893 | 1.13 | .84 |
| 1894 | 1.46 | .87 |
| 1895 | .47 | .98 |
| 1896 | 1.36 | .76 |
| 1897 | .84 | 2.10 |
| 1898 | 1.24 | 2.41 |
| 1899 | .74 | 1.87 |

*Source:* Ayers, *Vengeance and Justice,* 250n56.

The 1880s and 1890s were the crucial period for African American criminal violence, not just for murder, but for assault, robbery, and rape. The 1890 census of prisoners, a nationwide survey conducted at a time when black males over age fifteen were 10 percent of the population, found that 41 percent of the rape convicts, 40 percent of the males serving sentences for assault, and 24 percent of the male robbery inmates were African Americans.[81] Since southern whites were getting preferential treatment when they killed, the high proportion of blacks in prison is not conclusive proof of excessive African American criminality. While prison data is unhelpful as a measure of the incidence of crime by a group, it can be useful as an indicator of the *type* of crime in which the group engages. The commitment levels for crimes of violence by blacks were both new and disturbing.

Though imperfect in the nineteenth century, homicide mortality statistics, a mainstay of crime research, are more valuable than prison data. For one thing, homicide data (persons killed through human agency) rely on coroner or physician reports on the cause of death, not on criminal justice system processes (i.e., apprehension by police, charges by prosecutors, conviction and sentencing by courts). Consequently, the notorious leniency afforded white killers had little impact.

The Census Bureau pressed the states to collect and report cause-of-death statistics, including figures on homicides. By 1890, eight states plus the District of Columbia cooperated, but the southern states, where 90 percent of African Americans lived, failed to comply.[82] However, eighty-three cities, in the North and South, did forward mortality data to the Census Bureau in 1890. The data from these "registration cities," along with the figures from cities within the eight registration states plus Washington, DC, are revealing.

Aggregate data for the eighty-three cities report 266 white homicides in a population of 14,085,466, for a victimization rate of 1.89 per 100,000. Among "colored" persons (census terminology at the time), 84 of 872,788 were killed as a result of human agency for a rate of 9.6 per 100,000.[83] This puts the colored victimization rate at over five times that of whites. However, since "colored" encompassed "all persons of negro descent, Chinese, Japanese, and Indians," this is only a proxy for African American rates. A second problem is that these are figures for urban areas, where only 20 percent of the black population of 1890 lived; 80 percent were rural.[84]

A better sample of African Americans was provided by a census analysis of homicide in the nine registration cities with the biggest nonwhite populations. Here the victimization rates were 2.74 per 100,000 for whites, 8.88 for persons deemed colored, more than three times the white figure.[85] Once again, this is a proxy for the African American population alone. However, the African American portion of the colored population in the nine cities never fell below 92 percent.

As these are victim data we can't be sure of the race of the killers. The 1890s was the decade of black lynching, overwhelmingly by whites, so white-on-black killing was hardly a rarity. On the other hand, if Savannah, Georgia, was typical, black-on-black killing was far more common.

One investigation found that in 90 percent of black murders in Savannah in the 1890s the perpetrators were people of color.[86] The *Savannah Morning News* reported 70 assaults between 1889 and 1892. Despite the well-known violence of white southerners, 69 percent of these crimes involved black assailants and 77 percent of their victims also were black. While one justly might be suspicious of southern white newspaper accounts, the Savannah coroner's report provides corroboration. Of 42 homicides, 1895–98, the coroner stated that over 64 percent involved black killers and 23 of the 42, or 55 percent, were black-on-black incidents.[87]

This monoracial violence partly was a result of the tendency to associate with others of the same race and social standing. But other factors played a role, such as the severity of the punishment for black assaults on whites, including the significant risk of a lynching.

These mortality figures indicate significant black violent crime, at levels virtually unknown before the last two decades of the nineteenth century. In short, the late 1880s and early 1890s mark the precise point in history in which black violent crime became alarmingly elevated. Despite the fact that black crime mainly targeted black victims, the upsurge in violence alarmed whites and helped trigger an outburst of vicious, extralegal white violence—the lynch mob.

## LYNCHING

Before the 1880s, vigilante killing was by and large a white-on-white phenomenon, reserved for horse thieves, cattle rustlers, and murderers in the Far West. In Arizona alone, before statehood was granted in 1912, there had been sixty-nine lynchings.[88] Even in the South, during the worst period for black lynching, the practice was not exclusively racial in motivation. Whites provided 15 percent of the victims from 1882 to 1899.[89]

Urban lynchings were rare. Lynching overwhelmingly was a rural activity, due in part to the weakness, and perhaps more importantly, the perceived weakness, of law enforcement in the countryside. "Lynching served as a method of law enforcement in sparsely populated places," observed Ayers, "where white people felt especially insecure."[90] Rural Mississippi, for instance, had more black lynchings (248) in the late nineteenth century than any other southern state. Georgia, with 171 incidents, came in third, but only one atrocity took place in its biggest city, Atlanta, despite its high black population, significant black crime, and serious racial tensions.

The greatest number of lynchings occurred in the low population density areas of the Gulf plain (the Florida Panhandle, Alabama, Mississippi, and Texas, all lying just north of the Gulf of Mexico) and the cotton uplands (central Mississippi, northern Louisiana, southern Arkansas, and adjacent Texas). The counties in these areas that were "most likely to witness lynchings," said Ayers, "had scattered farms where many black newcomers lived and worked. Those counties were also likely to have few towns, weak law enforcement, poor communication with the outside, and high levels of transiency among both races. Such a setting fostered the fear and insecurity that fed lynching. . . . In those places most blacks and whites did not know one another, much less share ties of several generations. The black population often moved from one year to the next in search of jobs at lumber camps and large plantations."[91]

In the 1890s there was a sudden and dramatic increase in southern lynching, and African Americans were the special targets. More than eight hundred blacks (along with 123 whites) were murdered by mobs, usually small groups of whites, though in a few cases African Americans participated in the lynching of other blacks.[92] This little-known fact—that blacks occasionally lynched other blacks—further supports the conclusion that bias was not the only impetus. Lynching was for crime control *and* racial suppression.

The main explanation given by white southerners for the epidemic of black lynchings was the rise in the rape of white women, a crime considered particularly odious to white southerners, especially if committed by an African American. A study of black lynchings that occurred in the South between 1882 and 1930 found that sexual assault was the allegation in 29 percent of the cases, whereas 39 percent involved retribution for murder or murder-rapes. Over 28 percent of the black lynchings, however, were for noncapital offenses, such as assault, robbery, theft, arson, miscegenation, etc.[93] One might think that such excessive punishment was a mark of racism, except that nearly as many of the whites lynched in the South also had been accused of noncapital crimes.[94]

Historians are puzzled by the onset of the lynching epidemic. Why the 1890s? The special zeal for blacks by white southerners is readily explained by bigotry and the white determination to keep blacks subservient, but such views were in abundance in the South well before the 1890s. Ayers attributed the outbreak to "a sort of spontaneous combustion fed by racial and sexual fear," exacerbated by the speed and voyeuristic thoroughness of southern press accounts of lynching incidents.[95] Others have pointed to declines in the cotton economy or to economic and political competition between whites and blacks.[96] Indeed, economic developments in the early 1890s added significantly to the turmoil of the period.

It is unlikely that the farm crisis or the depression of 1893 caused lynching, but the anxiety and turmoil they created, coupled with the antiblack rhetoric of the southern politicians, set the stage. The final straw was an actual rise in black crime. This crime rise was blown totally out of proportion by angry, frightened, uneducated, and bigoted whites. But that doesn't mean it didn't happen.

Historians are understandably loath to credit southern claims that black crime was a cause of the lynching frenzy. It smacks too much of justification. But there is no need to go down that path. There was no justification for vigilante justice, not even in the rural areas. The southern criminal justice system may have seemed inefficient at times, but it had not broken down. Blacks were aggressively arrested and punished—too often unfairly—by the lawful mechanisms. There was no need and no excuse for lynching.

The lynching frenzy began at virtually the same time that black homicide arrests spiked throughout the South. From 1887 to 1894, African American homicide arrests rose 350 percent. Lawful executions of blacks by southern states, unsurprisingly, escalated as well, jumping from twenty-nine in 1888 to seventy-one in 1893. The trend lines for homicide arrests, executions, and lynchings of African Americans followed the same upward trajectory over the same time period. As I already observed, it is unlikely that the homicide arrests were a product of white bias. These were serious crimes, not discretionary minor violations; the police ordinarily would not ignore murders. (However, given that the victims usually were black there was no public pressure to solve the crime by pinning it on some innocent African American.) That the murder arrests, the executions, and the lynchings took place at roughly the same time strongly suggests that all three were responding to the same cause: a rise in serious black crime.

Here is additional evidence. John Hammond Moore's study of South Carolina violence from 1880 to 1920 uncovered a high correlation between murder and lynching. Rural communities like Aiken, Barnwell, Laurens, and Orangeburg, with nine or ten murder/manslaughter cases per year, "recorded a substantial number of lynchings." "At the other end of the scale, where authorities usually dealt with only three or four homicides per year, lynching was rare or even unknown. This latter group included, for the most part, heavily black counties, such as Beaufort, Fairfield, and Georgetown, and those with relatively few black residents, such as Chesterfield, Horry, and Pickens." Moore concluded that "communities that murdered also lynched." We do not know, unfortunately, whether these homicidal communities were experiencing a disproportionate increase in

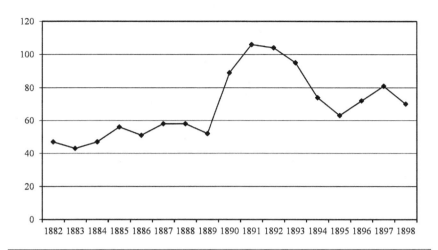

FIGURE 2.1. Lynchings of blacks in ten southern states, 1882–1899. *Source:* Hines and Steelwater, Project HAL, http://people.uncw.edu/hinese/HAL/HAL%20Web%20Page.htm #HAL%20History. Included states: Alabama, Arkansas, Florida, Georgia, Kentucky, Louisiana, Mississippi, North Carolina, South Carolina, and Tennessee.

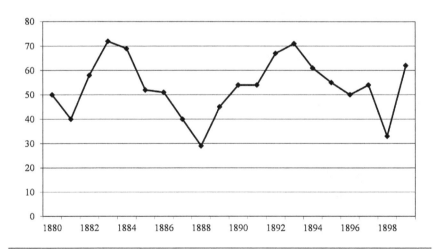

FIGURE 2.2. Executions in eleven southern states, 1880–1899. *Source:* Espy File, available at http://www.deathpenaltyinfo.org/executions-us-1608–2002-espy-file. Included states: Alabama, Arkansas, Florida, Georgia, Louisiana, Mississippi, North Carolina, South Carolina, Tennessee, Texas, and Virginia.

black murders, but this seems highly likely. Moore found that blacks were accused of two-thirds of the murders statewide in 1900.[97]

As Monroe Work, a black associate of Du Bois and a tireless campaigner against lynching, observed: "It is significant that the number of lynchings reached its highest point about the same period that Negro crime reached its highest point."[98] Indeed, for it is black violent crime—during a time of great fear, economic decline, and antiblack demagoguery—that stimulated the lynching frenzy.

The significance of black crime, however, extended far beyond the impetus it gave to lynching. Violence became a part of the lower-class black culture. As such, it would continue for over a century.

## CONCLUSION: A BLACK SUBCULTURE OF VIOLENCE

The first postslavery generation reached its most criminogenic years in the last two decades of the nineteenth century. With no memory of slavery, the war, or emancipation, these young black men would have known only the turbulence and violence of the post-Reconstruction years. Those who had moved to southern cities found themselves, as thousands of freedmen had, encamped in undesirable communities with few work opportunities. Barely literate, without marketable skills, many of them turned to drinking, loitering, and petty theft. This petty criminal lifestyle became the prototype for the lower-class black male. Historian Joel Williamson describes the situation:

> The black family might well have been at home on the land, but the deepening agricultural depression of the late 1880s and on through the 1890s drove large numbers off the land. . . . By the Victorian model the young men would leave first, looking for work. The search might prove endless and lead them to a perpetually marginal existence, hovering on the fringes of organized life. Ultimately, they might come to New Orleans, Memphis, or Atlanta, or one of the lesser cities. Loosened males tended to congregate in the cities, and Negro families in the urban situation tended to lose the form of family that farm life had supported. . . . Trapped in the city, young black men might sometimes take to a street-corner, pool-hall hustling, and petty criminal way of life.[99]

By the 1890s, these low-income young black men began fighting and killing one another in greater numbers. If the older generation of blacks, subject to the lash and then the terror, had grown submissive, their sons felt no such constraints. They "began carrying guns everywhere," homicide historian Randolph Roth observed, "even to church." "Older members of the black community," he added, "deplored the recklessness and viciousness of the new generation." Roth went on to describe the young man of the new generation.

Determined to win respect by being "bad," he cultivated a tough, menacing exterior and demonstrated repeatedly that he was willing to use violence. He and his contemporaries carried pistols and knives to protect themselves against white bullies and predators, but they were more likely to use those weapons on other blacks as they fought for scraps of dignity within their communities. Too many died trying to prove their manhood at each other's expense. A few of them gave vent to their frustrations by going on rampages against whites, which almost invariably ended in their own deaths.[100]

Assault, rape, robbery, and murder rose alarmingly. The criminal violence even began to be reflected in black folklore. "From the late nineteenth century," Lawrence Levine found, "black lore was filled with tales, toasts, and songs of hard, merciless toughs and killers confronting and generally vanquishing their adversaries without hesitation and without remorse."[101] The black culture of violence was now celebrated.

Was this culture of violence, as historian Roger Lane contended, a product of black exclusion from the urban industrial revolution? This seems tenable, because the cities of the South were not manufacturing centers like their northern counterparts. There was no great factory system to employ and tame the southern workforce and few schools were available to blacks to educate and discipline their children. Moreover, as Williamson pointed out, while black women could find work in southern cities as domestics, "Negro men and their labor, in contrast, were tangential to and increasingly expendable in the commercial and risingly industrial society."[102]

But as we saw, violence was not exclusive to African Americans. Both black and white crime in the South remained relatively high for decades, and this pattern would continue well into the twentieth century. In fact, it is plausible to conclude that both black and white violence were the products of a southern culture untamed by the industrial revolution. The black culture, it must be remembered, was quintessentially southern. Religion, dress, dietary preferences, speech patterns, values and temperament—including an acute sensitivity to slights and a hotheaded readiness to use a knife or gun—all were molded in the South and shared with white southerners. "Much of the cultural pattern of Southern rednecks became the cultural heritage of Southern blacks," Thomas Sowell wrote, "more so than survivals of African cultures, with which they had not been in contact for centuries."[103]

I conclude that five factors were crucial in the onset of black criminal violence. They were:

1. The uprooting of black slaves and their movement to southern cities after emancipation. This created a new urban African American, a black "rootless cosmopolitan."

2. The creation of a black petty criminal class (initially nonviolent) in southern cities.

3. The social and economic turmoil of the post-Reconstruction years, the formative years of the second or postslavery generation. This was capped by the bitter disillusionment of the rigid race segregation system established in the 1890s.

4. The violence of white southern culture, which blacks shared.

5. The availability of cheap handguns at the end of the nineteenth century.

What role did the Jim Crow system play? It would have been understandable if blacks, angrily resentful of their subordination, resorted to retaliatory violence against whites. By and large, however, that didn't happen. In fact, antiwhite violence by African Americans was greater in the North than in the segregated South. What the new segregation system of the 1890s did was to embitter African Americans. Historian Roth thought this the central fact in the black turn to violence.

The reversals they suffered, like the persecution and discrimination that minorities endured in the urban North and Southwest, fostered resentment and alienation, led them to divert their energies into criminal enterprises, and created a heritage of anger and violence that was passed down through successive generations. The growing homicide problem among black southerners was not caused by slavery or by the failure of Reconstruction to create a racially egalitarian society. It was caused by the hopelessness and rage that the political disaster of the 1890s and early 1900s engendered.[104]

But bitterness and alienation, crucial as they were in helping to mold black culture, would not necessarily have led to violence, especially against their own kind. One also must take into account the context: the acceptability of violence, even armed violence, in the South, the milieu into which they were born; plus the tumult and turmoil of those awful postwar decades. It was the combination of all of these conditions along with the resentment fostered by the establishment of the segregation system that created the criminal culture that would be associated with African Americans for a full century.

We can easily imagine a very different scenario. Had blacks been permitted alternative pathways to the middle class the black crime problem would have been considerably reduced and almost certainly shortened. If, after emancipation, they had received their twenty acres and a mule and remained in rural areas, as they dreamed, the freedman and his children might have lived much as the white farmer did, a precarious, but not an antisocial lifestyle. Had they been given public school educations and opportunities for decent jobs in the cities of the South, they or their children might well have "graduated," like the Irish and German immigrants of the time, into the respectable world of the middle class. Sadly, tragically, none of this happened. Instead, a black criminal lifestyle rooted, and if anything, became in the twentieth century more violent still.

# 3

# White Southern Crime in the Early Twentieth Century

If, therefore, an attempt is made to understand why the homicide rates of the United States are so much higher than those for other civilized countries, emphasis should be laid upon the presence in this country of influential folkways or culture patterns, most of them survivals of more barbarous days, when human life was little esteemed.
—H. C. BREARLEY

He reckoned that there were just more folks in the South that needed killing.
—ANONYMOUS SOUTHERNER

Southerners, black and white, have contributed more to violent crime in the United States than any other American subgroup. We already have seen that in the nineteenth century southerners had exceptionally high violent crime rates. For Dixie's whites this was the case for most of that century, at least from the 1820s on.[1] For black southerners, enslaved for over half the period, violent crime is of more recent vintage; it may be traced (as was shown in chapter 2) to the late 1880s. The remarkable thing, however, is the persistence of these elevated rates throughout both the nineteenth and twentieth centuries, and indeed, into the twenty-first. The southern states have had, during this period, the highest homicide rates of any region in the country, while African American violence has far exceeded that of any other racial or ethnic group.

Such continuity is prima facie evidence that southern violence is the product of a distinctive culture passed on from generation to generation. Whatever the problems with a cultural explanation for crime, the historical evidence for a link between southern culture and violent crime is quite strong. A distinctive southern culture, to a great extent shared by blacks and whites, was fostered by the regional isolation of the South for most of American history, right up to World War II. Likewise, African American southerners, even after their migration north and west, long remained a people apart, mainly due to the nation's thoroughgoing segregation system. For good and ill, migrating blacks maintained their unique brand of southern culture. As for white migrants from the South—who, as we shall show, far outnumbered the black southern migrants—the preservation of a distinctive culture outside of Dixie is not as apparent.

This chapter will examine the historical background to southern crime, followed by an analysis of crime by white southerners. The time frame is the first four decades of the twentieth century, that is, from about 1900 to the start of World War II. The next chapter focuses on the social and economic conditions of African Americans during the same period and the impact of the Great Black Migration on crime.

## THE SOUTH

There is a certain amount of ambiguity about the definition of the "South." I think all would agree that at a minimum it consists of the eleven states that had joined the Confederacy during the Civil War, viz., Alabama, Arkansas, Florida, Georgia, Louisiana, Mississippi, North Carolina, South Carolina, Tennessee, Texas, and Virginia. Most authorities would add Kentucky and Oklahoma, probably West Virginia too, for a total of fourteen states. The federal Census Bureau, using a more expansive measure, ends up with sixteen states plus the District of Columbia, but this seems a stretch.[2] The fourteen-state formula will be used here. Where departures are necessary the reader will be put on notice.

During the first four decades of the twentieth century the South was isolated and different from the rest of the country, or as one historian described it, the "poor stepchild in a well-to-do American family." By some common indicators of crime—dire poverty most notably—we should have expected lots of lawlessness in Dixie. But there were confounding factors too, especially the overwhelmingly rural nature of the southern states and the absence of great metropolitan areas. Nowadays we do not expect high rates of violence in rural areas, though as we saw in the earlier chapters, the nineteenth-century take on this was quite different. The soaring rates of southern violence challenge us to rethink our views on the relationship between urbanization and crime. A second consideration militating against outsized southern crime is the distinct absence from Dixie of violent European immigrants. Because of the lack of urban employment opportunities, immigrants such as the southern Italians scarcely went south at all.

The South was dreadfully poor. During the first four decades of the twentieth century, personal income never exceeded two-thirds of the average for the nation as a whole, and for much of the period it was little more than half.

TABLE 3.1. Personal income per capita as a percentage of the U.S. average, by region

| Region | 1900 | 1920 | 1930 | 1940 |
|---|---|---|---|---|
| Northeast | 137 | 132 | 138 | 124 |
| North Central | 103 | 100 | 101 | 103 |
| South | 51 | 62 | 55 | 65 |
| West | 163 | 122 | 115 | 125 |

*Source:* Grantham, *South in Modern America,* 5.

Nor was this poverty confined to black southerners, who during this time period made up between one-third and one-quarter of the region's population. Most whites who worked the land didn't own it. There were 2.3 million white-operated farms in the South in 1930, but 1.4 million landless white farm families—sharecroppers or tenant farmers. They often were forced by high debt and low wages to put their entire families, wives and young children included, to work, and the men commonly turned to nonagricultural labor in the slack season, in mills for instance, to supplement their meager earnings. Though backbreaking, cotton farming paid very little, and as I said, most farmers, white and black, were wage workers. The standard wage for picking cotton was 50 cents for 100 pounds, and an average adult could do only 150 pounds in a fourteen-hour day, children far less. By 1910, incidentally, the southern states had laws prohibiting child labor, but they were filled with so many loopholes, such as broad exemptions, that they were practically ineffective.[3]

The region was overwhelmingly agricultural, a situation that did not change radically until after World War II. At the start of the twentieth century, 82 percent of the southern workforce was in farming. And despite the ups and downs of the agricultural market in the 1920s, that figure still was at 50 percent in 1930. This doesn't fully capture the dominance of agriculture, however, as even manufac-turing in the South was tied to cotton, the biggest industry being textile mills. The Cotton Belt ran across a vast swath of the lower South, from the Carolinas to Texas, not coincidentally home to the region's Black Belt, as millions of blacks remained bound to the land they had farmed as slaves. Cotton was the region's mainstay, its principal cash crop, well ahead of tobacco, the number-two staple. But cotton also was the South's albatross. When production rose, in the South and worldwide, prices would fall, and the entire southern economy would suffer.[4]

In addition to farming and cotton mills, the South's main economic activity was the extraction and processing of natural resources: vegetable and seafood processing; coal, ore, and phosphate mining; turpentine production; sugar re-fining; lumbering and sawmills. These industries were not highly mechanized before World War II, and the labor-intensive work was both miserable and dan-gerous. Employers had to resort to forced convict labor—overwhelmingly black—to get men into the coal or phosphate mines. Starting in the mid-1920s, extractive industries went into a tailspin, spurring a major white migration out of the upper South—an outflow that ultimately exceeded by far the better-known black migra-tion of the period. Later, I will discuss the consequences of these migrations for crime. But one point should be clear: the southern migrant was not necessarily a farmer, and even when he was, he probably also had off-season experience in the industrial sector.[5]

Although the South was overwhelmingly rural, there was a steady growth in the number and size of southern cities in the first half of the twentieth cen-tury. The region went from 15 percent urban in 1900 to 32 percent in 1930, but one must keep in mind that the Census Bureau's threshold for "urban" was only 2,500 people. During the 1920s, which were in the main boom years, the larger southern cities grew at an impressive rate: Nashville, +30 percent; Atlanta, +35 percent; Birmingham, +45 percent; and Memphis, +56 percent. When it came to great metropolises, however, Dixie was far outpaced by the North and West. Not one southern city made the Top Ten population list for 1920. New Orleans, the biggest southern municipality, ranked seventeenth. Moreover, the metropolises of the South had neither the population diversity nor the manufacturing bases of their nonsouthern counterparts.[6] Despite the absence of the more violent of the European immigrants, however, southern cities, as will be seen, had some of the highest crime rates in the United States.

TABLE 3.2. Top ten U.S. and southern cities by population, 1920

| Rank | United States | | South | |
|------|---------------|---|-------|---|
| 1. | New York | 5,620,048 | New Orleans | 387,219 |
| 2. | Chicago | 2,701,705 | Louisville | 234,891 |
| 3. | Philadelphia | 1,823,779 | Atlanta | 200,616 |
| 4. | Detroit | 993,078 | Birmingham | 178,806 |
| 5. | Cleveland | 796,841 | Richmond | 171,667 |
| 6. | St. Louis | 772,897 | Memphis | 162,351 |
| 7. | Boston | 748,060 | San Antonio | 161,379 |
| 8. | Baltimore | 733,826 | Dallas | 158,976 |
| 9. | Pittsburgh | 588,343 | Houston | 138,276 |
| 10. | Los Angeles | 576,673 | Nashville | 118,342 |

Source: Bureau of the Census, "Population of 100 Largest Cities," Working Paper No. 27.

Levels of education were low in the South, illiteracy high. While spending per pupil more than quadrupled between 1910 and 1930, the South still lagged behind the rest of the country, which spent two and one-half times as much on each student. Black schools, of course, were separate and unequal; spending on them did not begin to improve until the late 1920s. Still, 22 percent of southern blacks were illiterate in 1930, but only 4 percent of southern whites. Even ten years later, a mere 62 percent of black youngsters were enrolled in school (and 66 percent of whites).[7]

To round out the picture, we need to discuss the beliefs and values of southerners. We already have seen (in chapter 1) that the nineteenth-century South was extraordinarily violent. This violence was attributed to a culture of honor, the violence-supporting value system commonly found in rural regions in various parts of the globe. Such value systems have been associated with the nineteenth-century Irish, and with southern Italians, and with Mexicans in the twentieth century.

For well over a century the South has been associated with a long list of violent behaviors. These include:

- vigilantism; lynching
- hand-to-hand fighting

- duels
- blood feuds (e.g., Hatfields and McCoys)
- sadistic violence, especially with some black lynchings
- hypersensitivity to slights and insults
- weapons carrying
- hunting
- militarism
- cockfighting; dogfighting
- underenforcement of laws against violence
- the slave system, enforced by whipping
- corporal punishment of children

Some of this violence, the slavery system obviously, is attributable only to whites. Some, such as dueling, is exclusive to the nineteenth century. But most of these behaviors were engaged in by white and black, continued well into the twentieth century, and were nourished by a culture perpetuated by the isolation of the South from the rest of America. "Violence," wrote W. J. Cash at the start of World War II, "has always been a part of the pattern of the South." And, of course, violent crime was a component of the violence.[8]

Important as it was, violence was only one element of the southern culture. Southerners also were (and to some extent still are) deeply religious and moralistic. A highly individualistic Protestantism has always dominated the southern landscape, primarily represented by Baptist and Methodist churches, separated of course by race. Writing about the 1920s—though he might have written the same thing at any point in the entire twentieth century—Howard Odum, who built a career studying the South, offered the following observations on religion in Dixie:

> Like politics, religion is closely interwoven in the fabric of southern culture. In its church membership, in its Protestant representation, in its church colleges, in the position which the church holds in the community, and in its general influence upon social policy, the Southeast outranks the other regions of the nation. In most of the indices relating to these factors, with the exception of Louisiana, the southern Baptist and Methodist bodies are to the Southeast what the Catholic Church is to certain subregions of the Northeast. This factor is a key to many of the general culture patterns of the region.

In 1926, the Southeast, with 20 percent of the adult population of the United States, had one-third of the nation's adult Protestant church membership. Church affiliation was even higher for blacks than it was for whites. Fifty-seven percent of the African American population in the South was affiliated with a black Protestant church, overwhelmingly the Baptists. Among whites, membership in Southern Baptist and Southern Methodist churches combined ranged from over half the population in South Carolina, Mississippi, and Georgia to only 19 percent in heavily Catholic Louisiana.[9]

The southerner's strong moral sense was very much bound up with his religion. Attitudes often took on a conservative, even reactionary hue. "Alarmed by the growing secularization of their society," wrote historian Dewey Grantham, "southern fundamentalists became more involved in the support of Prohibition, the anti-evolution movement, and the conservative Protestant opposition to Roman Catholicism."[10] A subsequent chapter (10) will discuss how the South gave more support to Prohibition than any other region.

As for evolution, the teaching of Darwin's theory was prohibited by law in five southern states in the 1920s. The 1925 prosecution of a biology teacher, John T. Scopes, for violating Tennessee's statute, riveted the country. The Scopes trial was portrayed by the media as a showdown between southern fundamentalists, who took literally the biblical story of creation, and the scientific community, which saw humans as the culmination of a process of animal evolution. Scopes was convicted, but the verdict was overturned, and he was never reprosecuted. The trial nonetheless shaped the image of the South as backward, anti-intellectual and superficial in its religiosity.[11]

The impression of a benighted South was reinforced by the rise (some say reincarnation) of a new organization, the Ku Klux Klan, which began in Dixie but by the 1920s had gained a national following. Though the secret order took the name and some of the trappings (robes, hoods, and cross burnings) of one of the post–Civil War terrorist groups, it was significantly different from its nineteenth-century counterpart. Most importantly, its methods were far less violent. The twentieth-century Klan was a populist reaction to social change threatened by immigration (associated with Catholicism), unions and labor radicals (associated with Jews), and blacks who sought more rights. Its members, 40 percent of whom were in the South, mixed social conservatism with ethnic, racial, and religious bigotry. After some political success in state and local elections in the early 1920s, the Klan faded from view and by the end of the decade became politically insignificant.[12]

Lynching remained a problem in the South, though much reduced from the nineteenth century. In the 1920s there were 315 incidents, all but thirty-four involving blacks. By the 1930s the total dropped to 128 (including nine whites). Though southern senators defeated an antilynching bill in 1938, the occurrences were dwindling on their own. Lynchings never again reached double digits after 1935, reflecting in part the decline in the murder rate. Meanwhile, the famous (or notorious) Scottsboro Case, involving interracial rape claims now commonly understood to be false, exposed the injustices of the legitimate criminal justice process in the South and inspired a major 1932 U.S. Supreme Court ruling on the right to counsel.[13]

## MIGRATIONS

The agricultural slowdowns during the 1920s, followed by the virtual collapse of the rural economy in the 1930s would have the most profound long-term consequences for the entire nation. The agricultural breakdown of the South triggered massive relocations. It set millions of southerners, white and black, onto the roads, both rail and automotive. Not only did they head to towns and cities in Dixie, but millions fled the South altogether. The black migration north, which spiked in the 1920s, when over 810,000 African Americans left, was in fact dwarfed by the southern white outmigration, which reached nearly 1.5 million during that decade alone. To this massive outflow must be added another million whites and roughly 400,000 blacks who migrated during the depression decade.[14]

The black migration and its repercussions for crime will be discussed in the next chapter. Much less is known about the white migrants. This may be because the white migration had fewer lasting social consequences, both for many of the migrants themselves and for the nation, than the black exodus. For one thing, the white migrants did not establish long-term communities the way African Americans did. Of course, the black ghetto communities in the big metropolises of the North and West were partly a product of race discrimination in housing, which the white migrants did not face. Whatever the cause, however, the creation of so many large-scale urban black districts profoundly changed the nation.

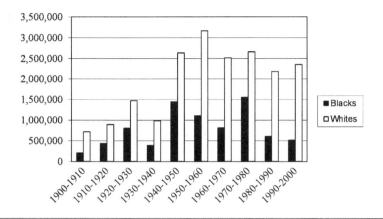

FIGURE 3.1. Twentieth-century black and white migration from the South, by decade. *Source:* Gregory, *Southern Diaspora*, 330.

There was a second factor. Despite their hardships up North, life there for African Americans must have been more appealing, or at least less distasteful, than it had been in Dixie since the black return rate was one-third of the white. White migrants, by contrast, often did not want to stay away from the South; they missed "home," and quite literally owned homes to which they returned as soon as their economic situation permitted. Migration historians estimate that over the course of the twentieth century there were 19.5 million southern white migrants and more than half of them returned. When they remained outside the South, moreover, whites did not seek communities of fellow southerners; they wanted to blend in, which of course the black migrants could not do.[15]

Although the white migrants by and large dispersed and became invisible, there nonetheless were several poor white southern migrant districts—"hillbilly ghettos" as they were derisively labeled. Included among these were San Joaquin Valley, California, the setting for *Grapes of Wrath,* John Steinbeck's angry 1939 novel depicting their plight. Other examples include some of the lumber towns of northern California, Oregon, and Washington; the Tennessee Valley and Uptown districts in Chicago; Lower Price Hill and Over-the-Rhine, Cincinnati; Bell Gardens in Los Angeles; San Pablo, across San Francisco Bay; towns and cities in the Miami Valley, Ohio; and Cass Corridor, Detroit. One would have expected high crime rates in these areas, at least in the low-income districts, for as we've seen repeatedly, migrants carry their cultural baggage with them, and southern white crime was, as will be shown, much higher than nonsouthern. But this population has been overlooked by scholars, and crime in the hillbilly ghettos has been grossly understudied.

Most of the white migrants in the 1920s came from farms, but by the 1930s, when the mills and coal mines in the South failed, the work experience of the migrants shifted to reflect the change. In addition, as southern agriculture collapsed during the depression and the World War many southerners, white and black, became urban migrants twice over, moving from farms to southern cities, and from southern cities to northern. While Yankees may have scorned them as "farm boys," the migrants of the 1930s and 1940s often came North with urban experience, though it was urban experience southern style.

There were two main routes for white migrants. Those from the Appalachian mining region and Dixie's northern tier headed due north. In Hamilton, Ohio, for instance, just forty miles north of Cincinnati, a paper company recruited Kentuckians starting in the late 1920s, spurring a regular migration to southern Ohio from Kentucky, West Virginia, and Tennessee—an outflow that continued for decades. Other southerners ventured farther, lured by corporate labor agents for tire manufacturers (Indiana and Akron, Ohio), automobile companies (Michigan), and steel mills (Chicago; Gary, Indiana; and Youngstown, Ohio). For the most part these migrants were economically successful; their 1939 median income was 91 percent of nonsouthern-born whites. As these industries contracted during the depression, however, the inflow of migrants tailed off and the return migration received new impetus.[16]

The second white exodus was from the western states of the South to the nation's West Coast. In the early 1930s, drought and soil erosion due to improper agricultural techniques destroyed millions of acres of farmland in the Oklahoma and Texas panhandles, terrible dust storms carrying off the now-eroded soil. The ensuing misery led hundreds of thousands of impoverished whites ("Okies") to flee to San Joaquin Valley, California, where they worked for subsistence wages as pickers in cotton fields and fruit orchards and on oil rigs. Steinbeck's novel captured some of the violence of the migrants (the young protagonist commits murder), but I know of no systematic study of crime in this area. This is especially unfortunate since southern culture prevailed here. Even as late as the 1950s it was estimated that southerners were close to one-third of the white population of the San Joaquin Valley, their presence making itself known through the drawled speech, the Baptist and Pentacostal churches, the country and western music in bars and the southern-style food in restaurants.

## CRIME BY WHITES IN THE SOUTH

Data on crime in the South for the first few decades of the twentieth century are difficult to come by. The most accurate crime figures, for deaths due to homicide, were not available for the majority of southern cities and states until 1919, and Texas declined to provide mortality data until 1933.[17]

Regional homicide data for cities in the registration area, compiled by the resolute Frederick L. Hoffman, who long championed the collection of homicide mortality statistics, presented figures that were typical for the era: southern rates of violence were excessive, the West wasn't far behind, the Northeast had the lowest rates in the nation, and the North Central states were somewhere in the middle. This was the pattern for 1901–10 and 1916–20. In 1901–10, for example, homicide mortality rates in thirty cities differentiated by region were examined. The southern rates were 14.7 per 100,000; rates for western, central and eastern cities were, respectively, 9.7, 7.8, and 4.3.[18] Rates for states, 1916–20, are shown in table 3.3. It must be kept in mind, of course, that these rates are racially undifferentiated and will not support generalizations about whites alone.

TABLE 3.3. Homicide rates per 100,000, by region, 1916–1920

| Region | Rate |
|---|---|
| New England | 2.7 |
| Middle Atlantic | 5.1 |
| South | 11.3 |
| Central | 6.2 |
| Rocky Mountain | 9.0 |
| Pacific | 8.4 |

Source: Hoffman, Homicide Problem, 56–57.

Lacking suitable mortality statistics, the next-best sources of national data for the early decades are the prisoner counts conducted by the Bureau of the Census. Imprisonment data do not accurately indicate the amount of crime or fluctuations in its incidence, as there are big gaps between the commission of an offense, apprehension of a suspect, conviction by the courts, and a sentence to imprisonment. Such data, however, could indicate the types of crimes that some groups committed, for example, whether or not white southerners engaged in more violent crimes than did whites outside the South. Even here imprisonment data are at best a proxy for crime commission figures.

There were three enumerations of prisoners: 1904, 1910 and 1923, and all three cast the South in a bad light respecting crimes of violence. In 1904, a higher percentage of southern prisoners were incarcerated for crimes against the person (including homicide, assault, robbery, and rape) than in any other section of the country.[19]

TABLE 3.4. Percent of prisoners committed in 1904 for crimes against the person, by region

| Crime Type | No. Atlantic | So. Atlantic | No. Central | So. Central | West |
|---|---|---|---|---|---|
| Against the person | 6.8 | 21.3 | 11.6 | *23.9* | 9.1 |
| Homicide | 0.4 | 4.3 | 1.4 | *9.2* | 1.5 |
| Assault | 5.5 | 14.9 | 8.1 | *11.7* | 5.7 |
| Robbery | 0.5 | 1.6 | 1.4 | *1.8* | 1.2 |
| Rape | 0.3 | 0.5 | 0.5 | *1.0* | 0.5 |
| Other | 0.1 | 0.1 | 0.1 | 0.2 | 0.1 |

*Source:* Bureau of the Census, *Prisoners and Juvenile Delinquents 1904*, table XIV.

*Note:* Italicized figures are the highest for each crime type.

In 1910, when rates of imprisonment (which take account of population size) were provided, the outcomes were similar. The South had the highest rates in the nation for homicides and assaults—five and one-half times the rates of the North for the most serious murders.

TABLE 3.5. Rate per 100,000 of prisoners and juveniles committed in 1910 for crimes against the person, by region

| Offense | North | South | West |
|---|---|---|---|
| Homicide-grave | 0.4 | 2.2 | 1.4 |
| Homicide-lesser | 1.0 | 4.1 | 2.2 |
| Assault | 21.5 | 30.3 | 25.2 |

TABLE 3.5 *(continued)*

| Offense | North | South | West |
|---|---|---|---|
| Robbery | 1.8 | 1.5 | 3.5 |
| Rape | 1.7 | 1.3 | 2.1 |

*Source:* Bureau of the Census, *Prisoners and Juvenile Delinquents 1910*, table 16.

And in the 1923 enumeration the situation remained unchanged; once again the southern states led all others in assaults and homicides.

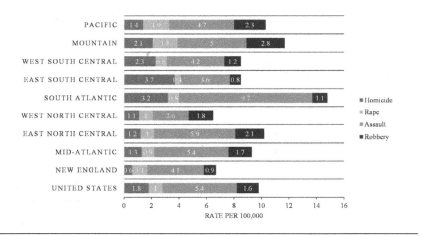

FIGURE 3.2. Prison commitment rates per 100,000, violent crimes, by region, January 1 to June 30, 1923. *Source:* U.S. Census Bureau, *Prisoners 1923*, table 15-C.

White southerners, not without some basis in fact, attributed the outsized violent crime rates to the high black population of the South. It should be kept in mind that African Americans, whose violent crime rates were, as I will show, considerably higher than those of whites, made up a majority of the populations of South Carolina and Mississippi, and over 40 percent of Georgia, Alabama, and Louisiana (1910 figures). What's more, blacks constituted a mere 2.3 percent of the northern population. But the notorious racism of the South undoubtedly made black criminality seem worse than it was and casts suspicion on some of the crime data for that region.[20]

Perhaps the best evidence for white southern offending in this early period is supplied by the 1910 prisoner survey, which presented violent crime rates by race and region. Table 3.6 presents the rates for whites only.

TABLE 3.6. White prisoners and juveniles committed for crimes against the person per 100,000, by region, 1910

| Offense | North | South |
|---|---|---|
| Homicide-grave | 0.3 | 0.8 |
| Homicide-lesser | 0.8 | 1.9 |
| Assault | 17.5 | 10.2 |
| Robbery | 1.4 | 0.6 |
| Rape | 1.5 | 0.6 |

*Source:* Bureau of the Census, *Prisoners and Juvenile Delinquents 1910*, table 82.

Notice the higher homicide rates for southern whites—from 2.4 to 2.7 times higher for lesser and greater homicides, respectively. However, the figures for assault, robbery, and rape are greater in the North. This is surprising for assault since the overall 1910 assault rate for the South (i.e., the rate without distinction as to race) was 29 percent higher than that of the North (30.3 to 21.5). The anomaly of higher white rates in the North may be an artifact of the greater number of police per capita in the northern cities and a more aggressive arrest policy for nonhomicide offenses. This explanation is bolstered by the higher incarceration rate for assault by blacks in the North: 231.7 per 100,000 versus 77.5 in the South. Murders, which are less sensitive than assaults to the vagaries of policing, are undoubtedly a truer measure of the crime situation.[21]

In sum, for the first twenty years of the twentieth century, the evidence for excessive violent crime in the South is compelling, whereas the data for white southerners alone is somewhat contradictory. Unquestionably, though, white southerners had significantly higher rates of incarceration for murder than northern whites: 2.7 times higher for the most egregious killings. As we will see, the white southerner's murder rates remained excessive for decades.

I now turn to the 1920s, a period in which mortality data, our most accurate measure, are more readily available. The data are not ideal, since the so-called death registration area did not yet include all of the states. But additional southern states cooperated as the decade progressed, and by the end of the 1920s every southern state was "in" except Texas. The result: as in the earlier decades the South had the worst record for homicides in the nation.

Criminologist H. C. Brearley conveniently collected homicide rates for registration area states for 1918 to 1927. He calculated the average rate of each state for the time period, ranked the states in order of the magnitude of their average rates, and then divided the list into four groups, roughly equal in size. It will come as no surprise that the South furnished nine of the top ten states, with Wyoming completing the list for the highest rate group.

TABLE 3.7. Ten states with the highest homicide rates, 1918–1927

| State | Rate |
| --- | --- |
| Florida | 29.55 |
| Mississippi | 20.57 |
| Alabama | 19.30 |
| Louisiana | 19.00 |
| Georgia | 18.13 |
| Arkansas | 16.4 |
| Tennessee | 16.27 |
| Kentucky | 13.02 |
| South Carolina | 12.93 |
| Wyoming | 12.78 |

Source: Brearley, Homicide, 19–20.

Recognizing that the South might have scored better had black homicides been excluded, Brearley proceeded to calculate white-only homicide rates for twelve southern states, comparing these to the rates (undifferentiated as to race) of the nonsouthern states. The results were that six southern states moved down in the rankings, that is, they dropped to the second worst list. Table 3.8 presents the two highest homicide groups of states, listed alphabetically within each group, as Brearley did not provide rates.

TABLE 3.8. Twenty-one states with the highest white homicide rates, 1918–1927

| Highest Rates | | Second-Highest Rates | |
|---|---|---|---|
| Arizona | Louisiana | Alabama | Mississippi |
| California | Missouri | Arkansas | Montana |
| Colorado | Tennessee | Delaware | Ohio |
| Florida | West Virginia | Georgia | South Carolina |
| Illinois | Wyoming | Michigan | Virginia |
| Kentucky | | | |

*Source:* Brearley, *Homicide,* 22–23.

Note that while the South no longer dominates the top ten list as thoroughly as it did when African American homicides were included, southern states continue to occupy four positions in the top grouping and four in the second group—a striking result.[22]

There is a shortcoming in Brearley's work that may have made southern whites seem less homicidal. Brearley did not compare southern white homicide rates to white rates outside the South, but rather, compared them to the overall rates for each nonsouthern state regardless of race. This methodology is perhaps understandable since the number of African Americans outside the South in the 1920s was relatively small. However, the population of blacks outside the South, as we saw in the discussion of migration, was growing, and it tended to be concentrated in certain states, such as Illinois, where its influence on the crime rate might be felt. Moreover, the nonwhite group in the states was augmented by Chinese, Japanese, and American Indians, all of whom along with African Americans were considered "colored." In short, Brearley wasn't comparing apples to apples.

To compensate, I examined homicides by state for one year, 1927, comparing white-only rates in the South with white-only rates above the Smith and Wesson line (as Brearley dubbed the South's boundary). One caveat: because white migration out of the South accelerated in the 1920s—nearly a million and a half would leave in that decade alone—the figures for some of the destination states (Ohio, for instance) may have been corrupted by southern migrant homicides. With the preceding limitation in mind, the results were as depicted in table 3.9.

TABLE 3.9. Homicide by whites per 100,000, by state, 1927

| State | White Homicide Rate | State | White Homicide Rate |
|---|---|---|---|
| Alabama | 9.9 | Nebraska | 2.4 |
| Arizona | 9.1 | Nevada | — |
| Arkansas | 8.7 | New Hampshire | 0.6 |
| California | 8.2 | New Jersey | 2.8 |
| Colorado | 4.9 | New Mexico | — |
| Connecticut | 1.7 | New York | 4.8 |
| Delaware | 5.2 | North Carolina | 4.3 |
| Florida | 14.4 | North Dakota | 1.7 |
| Georgia | — | Ohio | 5.2 |
| Idaho | 2.5 | Oklahoma | — |
| Illinois | 7.2 | Oregon | 3.3 |
| Indiana | 4.2 | Pennsylvania | 3.7 |
| Iowa | 2.3 | Rhode Island | 2.6 |
| Kansas | 3.1 | South Carolina | 5.9 |
| Kentucky | 11.6 | South Dakota | — |
| Louisiana | 10.1 | Tennessee | 8.5 |
| Maine | 1.9 | Texas | — |
| Maryland | 3.4 | Utah | 2.1 |
| Massachusetts | 1.9 | Vermont | 0.9 |
| Michigan | 5.9 | Virginia | 7.2 |
| Minnesota | 2.3 | Washington | 3.8 |
| Mississippi | 9.5 | West Virginia | 8.1 |
| Missouri | 6.8 | Wisconsin | 2.3 |
| Montana | 4.7 | Wyoming | 8.0 |

*Source:* Bureau of the Census, *Mortality Statistics 1927*, tables I A, 5.

This exercise casts white southerners in a considerably more negative light. The average rate for whites outside the South was 3.9 per 100,000; for the South it was 8.9, which is 2.3 times higher. Eight of the ten highest homicide states, including the top five, were in Dixie: Florida, Kentucky, Louisiana, Alabama, Mississippi, Arkansas, Tennessee, and West Virginia. Two western states, Arizona and California, complete the list. Even without black homicides the South remained the most violent region in the nation. The average rate for whites in the West, the second most violent section of the country, was 5.2; the white South was 1.7 times higher.[23]

Before examining the 1930s, there are three city-level studies worth discussing. An intriguing article by Jeffrey S. Adler, comparing Chicago and New Orleans in the first decade of the twentieth century, offers insights into the nature of southern crime in general and white crime in particular. New Orleans was in many respects an atypical southern city. The population was more heavily Catholic than other urban areas in the South, with sizable French Canadian and southern Italian/Sicilian populations. The Italian/Sicilian inhabitants had high homicide rates, though Adler did not say whether they were higher than the rest of the white population of New Orleans.[24]

But if New Orleans was more diverse than most southern municipalities it nonetheless was southern, with a large and segregated black population (27 percent of the inhabitants) and, at least before the 1920s, an economy tied to the importation and exportation of cotton. As for violent crime, Adler tells us that "white New Orleanians killed at almost double the rate of their Chicago counterparts—11.3 per 100,000 residents for the former and 6.5 for the latter." In both cities the principal types of murders were family quarrels (18 percent of the killings in New Orleans, 19 in Chicago) and drunken brawls (17 percent for New Orleans, 18 percent Chicago). What really distinguished the southern slayings was the relative absence of indiscriminate killings, such as the typical robbery-murder. There were, among whites, twice the percentage of stranger killings in Chicago as in the Big Easy, 20 percent to 10 percent. As regards murdered robbery victims and unsuccessful robbers killed, the difference between the cities was greater still: such incidents comprised 7 percent of New Orleans's homicides, but over 15 percent of Chicago's.[25]

The lessons seem clear. First, southern white violent crime was more common by far than the northern variety. Second, despite the greater frequency of southern crime it posed less danger to the community because the victims were acquaintances, not random selections. On the other hand, whites in New Orleans were more apt to kill with guns and to use them right on the streets, a practice hardly conducive to public safety. (Forty-three percent of white homicides occurred on New Orleans's public streets; fewer than 33 percent of Chicago's. Nearly eight of every ten homicides in New Orleans were carried out with firearms; under two-thirds of Chicago's.) Still, public fear is apt to be greater in a city in which perfect strangers are regularly targeted, as opposed to occasionally shot by accident.[26]

The preceding proves once again that southern whites were more violent than Yankees, and more apt to be armed as well. But it also shows that southern white crime was acquaintance-based; the southerner, in short, had more to fear from kin than strangers. Incidentally, and contrary to what one might expect, New Orleans was safer than Chicago for African Americans. The homicide victimization rate for Chicago's black populace was 54 per 100,000 compared with 34 in the southern port.[27]

A second study, this one on Memphis, Tennessee, reaffirms some of our conclusions about the nature of southern white violence. The study was prompted by Frederick L. Hoffman's charge, based on mortality statistics, that Memphis was America's "murder-town." To support his indictment, Hoffman pointed out that for five years, from 1912 to 1916, the city's average homicide rate was 74.9, and from 1917 to 1922 it was 54.9. He said it was "probably the highest rate for any civilized community in the world."[28]

To rebut Hoffman, Andrew A. Bruce and Thomas S. Fitzgerald published a comprehensive analysis of crime in Memphis. The authors examined police records and court documents, and they derived homicide figures that, while lower than Hoffman's, are hardly the basis for celebration. In essence, they conceded that the city's murder rate was high, but blamed it on African Americans, a sizable transient population and deaths in Memphis hospitals as a result of assaults occurring outside the city limits. Of special interest are their data on homicide in 1920 and 1924, for which white and black rates can be calculated. It should be recalled that in the 1920s southern cities were growing at a rapid pace, a reflection of the weakening agricultural economy. Memphis grew by 56 percent during the decade.

While I do not want to be diverted from my immediate concern with white southerners, I cannot help but comment on the shockingly high African American homicide rates, which lend credence to the apologia for the white South. It must be noted, too, that the overwhelming majority of killers of black Memphians were themselves African Americans: 79 percent in 1920, 86 percent in 1924. I will soon have a good deal more to say about black crime, but two other issues are more relevant to the present discussion.

TABLE 3.10. Homicides in Memphis, Tennessee, 1920 and 1924

|  | 1920 | 1924 |
|---|---|---|
| Population | 162,351 | 172,100 |
| Whites | 101,151 | 109,700 |
| Blacks | 61,200 | 62,400 |
| Homicides | 64 | 75 |
| Rate | 39.4 | 43.6 |
| White victims | 15 | 14 |
| White rate | 14.8 | 12.8 |
| Black victims | 49 | 61 |
| Black rate | 80.1 | 97.8 |

*Source:* Bruce and Fitzgerald, "A Study of Crime," 6, 13, 15, 17, 19, 23.

First, we have the exorbitant overall homicide rates for the city of Memphis: 39.4 in 1920 and 43.6 four years later. To better appreciate the magnitude of these figures compare the rates of other cities during the same time period. In 1920, Chicago's rate was 9.7, one-quarter of the Memphis rate. New York City's score was lower still; at 5.5 it was but one-seventh of the rate for the southern city.[29]

For 1924, we may compare Memphis to numerous American municipalities, the rates having been collected by Hoffman. Memphis would have been second on the high-rate list, below Jacksonville, Florida. Note that six out of ten of the cities on that enumeration, including the top five, were southern. As for the low-rate list, not one southern town appears, whereas six are located in New England.

TABLE 3.11. U.S. cities, ten highest and ten lowest homicide rates per 100,000, 1924

|  | *Highest* | *Lowest* |
|---|---|---|
| 1. | Jacksonville, FL—58.8 | Fall River, MA—0.8 |
| 2. | Nashville, TN—36.0 | Manchester, NH—1.2 |
| 3. | New Orleans, LA—32.5 | Grand Rapids, MI—1.3 |
| 4. | Louisville, KY—25.0 | Brockton, MA—1.4 |
| 5. | Savannah, GA—24.0 | New Bedford, MA—1.5 |
| 6. | St. Louis, MO—21.7 | Paterson, NJ—2.1 |

TABLE 3.11 (*continued*)

|  | Highest | Lowest |
|---|---|---|
| 7. | Pueblo, CO—21.2 | Milwaukee, WI—2.2 |
| 8. | Petersburg, VA—20.5 | Hartford, CT—2.6 |
| 9. | Chicago, IL—17.5 | Jersey City, NJ—2.6 |
| 10. | Detroit, MI—17.1 | Lowell, MA—2.6 |

*Source:* Hoffman, *Homicide Problem*, 97–98.

The conclusion is clear: Memphis's homicide rate was excessive even by southern standards, and southern cities generally were among the most homicidal urban locales in the United States.

A second noteworthy point may be gleaned from Bruce and Fitzgerald's work: the proportion of homicides caused by firearms is remarkably high. For 411 incidents occurring between 1920 and 1925, the authors found that 78.6 percent involved firearms and 70.6 percent handguns. Once again, Memphis was not a standout among southern jurisdictions. Criminologist H. C. Brearley collected data on state homicides from 1924 to 1926, recording the proportion attributable to firearms. A ranking of the states reveals that seven of the top ten were below the "Smith and Wesson line."

TABLE 3.12. Proportion of homicides by firearms, ten highest states, 1924–1926

| Kentucky | 86.1 | Montana | 76.7 |
|---|---|---|---|
| West Virginia | 80.6 | Tennessee | 76.6 |
| Wyoming | 79.8 | Idaho | 76.3 |
| South Carolina | 78.6 | Georgia | 75.2 |
| Mississippi | 77.9 | North Carolina | 75.0 |

*Sources:* Bruce and Fitzgerald, "A Study of Crime," 21; Brearley, *Homicide*, 70.

Finally, I note Bruce and Fitzgerald's insistence—unfortunately not backed up by data—that there were "comparatively few burglaries and street holdups" in Memphis and that the homicides were "mainly the result of sexual passion and jealousy and marital discord and not the wanton and premeditated acts of the hold-up man or the burglar." If true, this corroborates the inferences we drew earlier, in the discussion of New Orleans, about the nature of homicide in the South. That is, murder southern style was more about personal disputes, whereas up North it was more apt to involve strangers, theft, and indiscriminate selection of the victim.[30]

A final confirmation of the high white homicide rates in the South is provided by a third study, also prompted by Frederick L. Hoffman's attack on Memphis (obviously a nerve was struck). Homicide rates were calculated for four southern cities over a two-year period, 1921–22—Atlanta, Birmingham, Memphis, and New Orleans—and in each city, except for New Orleans, the rates were appallingly high (though nowhere near the astounding black rates, discussed in the next chapter). Using 1920 Chicago as a benchmark—and Chicago hardly was crime-free—we find an overall rate of 9.7 (not including automobile accidents, abortions, and infanticides). This is a bit over half the rate of New Orleans and a mere one-sixth that of Memphis.

TABLE 3.13. Homicide rates per 100,000, by race, in four southern cities, 1921 and 1922

| City | Year | White | Black | Total |
| --- | --- | --- | --- | --- |
| Atlanta | 1921 | 14.7 | 99.4 | 40.9 |
| | 1922 | 15.2 | 107.0 | 43.0 |
| | Avg. | 15.0 | 103.2 | 42.0 |
| Birmingham | 1921 | 29.2 | 86.4 | 51.6 |
| | 1922 | 26.7 | 108.0 | 58.6 |
| | Avg. | 28.0 | 97.2 | 55.2 |
| Memphis | 1921 | 35.6 | 94.3 | 57.3 |
| | 1922 | 23.6 | 139.2 | 66.3 |
| | Avg. | 29.6 | 116.8 | 61.8 |
| New Orleans | 1921 | 7.2 | 47.2 | 17.8 |
| | 1922 | 9.5 | 46.2 | 19.0 |
| | Avg. | 8.4 | 46.7 | 18.4 |

*Source:* Department of Health, City of Memphis, *A Study of Violent Deaths Registered in Atlanta, Birmingham, Memphis and New Orleans for the Years 1921 and 1922*, by J. J. Durrett and W. G. Stromquist (Memphis: Davis Printing Co., 1924?), 30.

More to the point of this chapter, if we compare the white-only rates we find that with the exception of New Orleans, urban white southerners were much more homicidal than white Chicagoans.

| | |
|---|---|
| Chicago | 8.5[31] |
| Atlanta | 15.0 |
| Birmingham | 28.0 |
| Memphis | 29.6 |
| New Orleans | 8.4 |

And, as table 3.14 shows, the big southern cities, excepting New Orleans, had many more murderous whites per capita than the nonmetro South.

TABLE 3.14. Average white homicide rates per 100,000 for selected southern cities and states, 1921 and 1922

| State | Rate | City | Rate |
|---|---|---|---|
| Alabama | 8.5 | Birmingham | 28.0 |
| Georgia | 8.0 | Atlanta | 15.0 |
| Louisiana | 10.3 | New Orleans | 8.4 |
| Tennessee | 11.1 | Memphis | 29.6 |

Source: Brearley, Homicide, 19–20.

Note: Rates for Alabama and Georgia unavailable for 1921 and 1922. Alabama figure is average for 1925–27; Georgia figure is average for 1922–24.

In short, southern metropolitan areas on the whole had the highest urban homicide rates in the United States, and whites in those cities suffered more deaths due to homicide (mainly at the hands of other whites) than whites in the North or the South.

## THE 1930s

The Great Depression began early in the South. Despite several boom years during the 1920s, cotton and tobacco prices fell in 1920–21 and 1925–26, the boll weevil continued to ravage the land, the Mississippi River flooded horribly in 1927, and a drought struck the Southwest in 1930–31. By that point the world-wide economic calamity had begun, making a bad situation infinitely worse.[32]

The depression was ruinous in the South as it was everywhere in America, indeed, over much of the world. By 1931, most southern textile mills were closed or operating just two or three days a week. Wages fell from $8 a week to $3. Cotton production was too high for demand, steadily driving prices down: from 12 cents a bale in 1929, to 8 cents in 1930, to a rock bottom 5 cents in 1931. Mortgage payments stopped, but the banks couldn't sell the land they had foreclosed, and they too went under. Credit dried up, and farm owners, unable to borrow, cut back operations, laying off farm workers.[33]

"Across the South it stretched," wrote Arthur Schlesinger, "an endless belt of dirt, drudgery, and despair, where worn-out people, whom disease made feeble and lack of hope made shiftless, scratched at life against the background of over-crowded shacks, rusting Model T Fords, children with hookworm, clothes falling into rags, tumble-down privies, the cotton patch and the corn cob." Historian Dewey Grantham added these specifics:

In Harlan County, Kentucky, 231 children died of malnutrition-induced disease between 1929 and 1931. . . . On one day in April 1932, a fourth of the farmland in Mississippi was sold at sheriff's sales, and between 1930 and 1932, 127 of that state's 307 banks failed. By early 1932, almost one-fourth of the Birmingham labor force was unemployed. In Arkansas 725 schools had been forced to close by February 1933, while 1,200 others had found it necessary to shorten the school year.[34]

The South, which had abandoned the Democrats in 1928, unable to stomach Al Smith (wet, Catholic, and very New York), returned enthusiastically in response to Franklin Delano Roosevelt's hopeful message. "No section of the country," observed W. J. Cash, "greeted Franklin Roosevelt and the New Deal with more intense and unfeigned enthusiasm than the South." FDR carried thirteen southern states in the 1932 election. Within a year, Congress passed much of Roosevelt's New Deal legislation, and the impact on the South, though not all positive, was substantial. The three major components of the New Deal, insofar as the South was concerned, were:[35]

1. The Federal Emergency Relief Act (1933), which allocated over $3 billion to the states for relief, aiding over 4 million unemployed southerners; succeeded by the Works Progress Administration (1935), which employed millions to carry out public works projects, including the construction of public buildings and roads.

2. The Agricultural Adjustment Act (AAA; 1933), which established production controls, government payments, price support loans, and marketing agreements in order to raise farm commodity prices for cotton, tobacco, and rice.

3. The Tennessee Valley Authority Act (1933), which established a regional program of flood control, navigation, agricultural regeneration, and cheap hydroelectric power.

New Deal employment and relief programs undoubtedly saved millions from hunger and despair, but they, along with the crop production restrictions of the AAA, pushed southerners off the land and into towns and cities, where crime became more of a problem. Works Progress Administration (WPA) jobs paid year-round wages for far less backbreaking labor than picking or hoeing cotton, which in any event was short-term work. Consequently, southerners flocked to nearby towns and cities with WPA offices to establish residency until jobs or relief payments could commence. Agricultural production restrictions likewise drove off farm workers as landowners cut back on their workforces. The sudden urban proliferation of males with lots of idle time had the predictable consequences insofar as theft and violence were concerned.[36]

The decade of the 1930s seems to have had little effect on the relative standing of southerners and northerners with respect to violence. The South retained its dubious status as No. 1 in violent crime. Evidence for this was enhanced by significant improvements in our ability to measure crime. As of 1933, the "death registration area" encompassed all of the states in the Union, affording researchers nationwide data on homicide. Moreover, the FBI, at roughly the same time, began collecting and assembling data from hundreds (later thousands) of police departments all over the United States, published in annual (initially, a monthly bulletin) reports of crimes known to the police—Uniform Crime Reports. These reports distinguished the most serious (Part I, or Index Crimes) from the less serious offenses. Despite obvious limitations—for example, not all police departments reported, not all that reported kept accurate records, many incidents went unreported and were not known to the police, definitions of offenses varied from state to state, etc.—these data greatly facilitated the analysis of crime on a national as well as a local level.[37]

Taking advantage of the FBI data, sociologist Stuart Lottier found for 1934–35 a pronounced sectional distribution for crimes, with murder and assault far more prevalent in the southeastern states. Lottier created an index for each crime in order to facilitate comparisons. Calculating the rate per 100,000 of each crime for each state (based on the FBI reports), he then determined the national average for the offense to which he assigned the number 100. Each state's rate for the offense was then expressed as a percentage of the average. So, for example, since New York state had murder rates that were 46 percent of the national average, that state was assigned a score of 46. Table 3.15 shows each state's index score for murder. Lottier ranked the states by score and placed them into six categories, eight states (octiles) per category. It is telling that southern states comprised all eight of the highest-rate octile and five of the second-highest-rate octile.

TABLE 3.15. States grouped by murder rates per 100,000 expressed as percent of national average, 1934 and 1935

| United States Average | 100 | | |
|---|---|---|---|

| Lowest-Rate Octile | 2%–21% | Second-Lowest-Rate Octile | 27%–45% |
|---|---|---|---|
| Maine | 2 | Minnesota | 27 |
| Vermont | 5 | Iowa | 30 |
| Wisconsin | 11 | Oregon | 30 |
| New Hampshire | 12 | Utah | 30 |
| Rhode Island | 12 | Michigan | 34 |
| Connecticut | 15 | Washington | 39 |
| Massachusetts | 18 | South Dakota | 44 |
| North Dakota | 21 | New Jersey | 45 |

TABLE 3.15 (*continued*)

| Third Octile | 46%–67% | Fourth Octile | 68%–98% |
|---|---|---|---|
| California | 46 | Indiana | 68 |
| New York | 46 | Nebraska | 69 |
| Pennsylvania | 46 | Illinois | 73 |
| Wyoming | 52 | Kansas | 73 |
| Idaho | 56 | Ohio | 79 |
| Maryland | 58 | Missouri | 91 |
| Montana | 66 | West Virginia | 94 |
| Colorado | 67 | New Mexico | 98 |
| *Second-Highest-Rate Octile* | 100%–202% | *Highest-Rate Octile* | 206%–364% |
| Delaware | 100 | Virginia | 206 |
| Oklahoma | 106 | Florida | 223 |
| Nevada | 120 | South Carolina | 225 |
| Arizona | 162 | Georgia | 229 |
| Louisiana | 174 | North Carolina | 265 |
| Kentucky | 185 | Arkansas | 269 |
| Texas | 189 | Tennessee | 323 |
| Mississippi | 202 | Alabama | 364 |

*Source:* Lottier, "Distribution of Criminal Offenses," table 1.

Lottier contended that regional culture drove the crime pattern. "It is culture," he claimed, "which distinguishes sectional regions"; and sectional culture, he concluded, determines the type of crime that predominates in an area. "Culture refers roughly," he explained, "to the social inheritance or the historical background which a group of people have in common." He recommended that crime control policymakers begin by "dividing the country into natural regions of crime . . . for areas of homogeneous culture would have common problems of crime control."[38]

Lottier's research covered the mid-1930s, but by the end of the decade little had changed. Table 3.16 presents a ranking of states for 1937 to 1939, prepared by sociologist Austin Porterfield and based on FBI Index Crimes coded in a manner similar to Lottier's study (i.e., with each state's score representing its percentage of the national average, which had been assigned the score of 100). Note that the entire bottom third of the list (sixteen states), with the exception of New Mexico and Arizona, was in the South.[39]

TABLE 3.16. Ranking of states by index crime scores, 1937–1939, in ascending order

*(100 = national average)*

| | | | |
|---|---|---|---|
| New Hampshire | 27 | United States | 100 |
| Wisconsin | 28 | Illinois | 101 |
| Vermont | 31 | Utah | 102 |
| Rhode Island | 33 | Ohio | 102 |
| Massachusetts | 47 | Indiana | 105 |
| Nebraska | 47 | Delaware | 106 |
| Maine | 49 | Washington | 110 |
| South Dakota | 50 | Maryland | 119 |
| Connecticut | 56 | California | 121 |
| New York | 56 | Nevada | 126 |
| Iowa | 58 | Oregon | 128 |
| Minnesota | 61 | West Virginia | 131 |
| North Dakota | 66 | Louisiana | 132 |
| Pennsylvania | 67 | Oklahoma | 134 |
| New Jersey | 75 | Mississippi | 136 |
| Wyoming | 76 | New Mexico | 146 |
| Montana | 84 | Texas | 168 |
| Colorado | 86 | Arkansas | 175 |
| Kansas | 87 | South Carolina | 178 |
| Michigan | 87 | Arizona | 182 |
| Missouri | 90 | Alabama | 190 |
| Idaho | 99 | Kentucky | 237 |
| | | Virginia | 240 |
| | | Georgia | 251 |
| | | Florida | 253 |
| | | Tennessee | 265 |
| | | North Carolina | 296 |

*Source:* Porterfield, "Decade of Serious Crimes," 49.

As neither of these studies was race-specific, I analyzed based on mortality data white-only homicides for all states in the United States for one year, 1935. (This was the same methodology I had used for 1927, discussed above.) The average rate for white homicides in the South was 8.5, which was 124 percent higher than the nonsouthern state average of 3.8, and 42 percent above the rate for the western states (6.0). Of the ten states with the highest rates, eight were southern.

TABLE 3.17. Ten states with the highest white homicide rates, 1935

| Kentucky | 14.5 | Arkansas | 9.2 |
| Nevada | 11.6 | Tennessee | 9.1 |
| Mississippi | 10.4 | South Carolina | 8.9 |
| Florida | 9.9 | Alabama | 8.8 |
| New Mexico | 9.3 | Texas | 8.4 |

Sources: Federal Security Agency, Vital Statistics Rates, population tables, table I; Bureau of the Census, Mortality Statistics 1935, table 5.

## CONCLUSION

For nearly four decades leading to the Second World War white southern murder rates soared.[40] They were consistently higher than the rates for whites in all other parts of the country. This violence was essentially quarrel-based, as opposed to the more predatory assaults of the North. Southern whites, in short, were committing the same type of crime they had been committing in the nineteenth century. This is consistent with the social isolation of the region, which was scarcely affected by the waves of immigrants entering the United States and staunchly resisted the social changes they fostered. Southern customs and the southern lifestyle, including a propensity to violence, simply hadn't changed that much from what they had been toward the end of the previous century.

While southern white violent crime was pervasive, it was, oddly, not threatening to the peace and orderly functioning of the community. That is because the victims knew their assailants and essentially voluntarily placed themselves in harm's way. Up north, by contrast, the victims were more likely to be strangers to the perpetrators, selected because they were tempting targets. The latter type of crime is more damaging to the community because it generates widespread fear, in turn jeopardizing public activities. Southern crime, in short, was less menacing despite the fact that it was more common.

But why should southern crime rates have been so high? And why so persistently elevated for so many decades? When a particular type of crime is committed by a distinctive and socially isolated group over a long period of time the suspicion must be great that the group's culture—its unique way of perceiving and acting in the world—is implicated. This conclusion seems especially apt in the case of southerners because their fondness for violence manifested itself in so many different ways, from blood feuds to weapons carrying to hunting, animal fighting, and so on through a very long list. Nor is the overwhelming rurality of the region inconsistent with high crime. As we have seen, rural adherents to a culture of honor, with their touchiness and extreme sensitivity to slights and insults, often have higher rates of violence than industrial populations. While cultures of honor are perhaps more a nineteenth-century phenomenon, the South, in its isolation and rurality, may be seen as perpetuating the older cultural pattern well into the twentieth century.

But what about poverty: wasn't it the case that white southerners were by general American standards impoverished? Of this there can be little doubt. A presidential report of 1938 found that 66 percent of tenant farm families and roughly half of the sharecroppers in the region were white, the latter "living under economic conditions almost identical with those of Negro sharecroppers."[41] Doesn't this impoverishment explain their elevated crime rates? Researchers have yet to closely examine the relationship between southern white poverty and crime during the first quarter of the twentieth century. But some points are worth bearing in mind. First, virtually all violent crime is a lower-class phenomenon, but it does not follow that all groups of poor engage in violence at the same rates. Second, it is not invariably the case that a group's propensity to violence is proportionate to the depths of its poverty or the size of its lower class. With southerners—white and black—it was their cultural milieu that prompted levels of violence unmatched by most other Americans.

# 4

# African American Crime, 1900 to 1930

Armed, angry, and drunk: This deadly combination accounts for more black lives lost in a shorter period of time than lynching and capital punishment combined.
—JAMES W. CLARKE

Nowadays we celebrate, and rightly so, the extraordinary migration of black people from the South to the rest of the country. A recent account described it as "a turning point in history." "It would transform urban America," the author effused, "and recast the social and political order of every city it touched. It would force the South to search its soul and finally lay aside a feudal caste system. It grew out of the unmet promises made after the Civil War and, through the sheer weight of it, helped push the country toward the civil rights revolutions of the 1960s."[1]

There is indeed much to celebrate. Before the migration blacks were relegated to a subordinate status with little hope for the future. Most were bound to the land, deep in Dixie, where they toiled in a lifelong cycle of debt and partial payment to landowners and the furnishers of their necessities. Even before the northward exodus considerable numbers of African Americans had moved to southern cities where they were mired in a nonagricultural poverty. They have been described as an American caste: a stratum determined by birth, or more precisely, by skin color and other physical characteristics. The migration, of course, did not change the subordinate status of blacks overnight. In the space of only three decades, however, it transformed African Americans from a rural to an urban people, from farmers to city laborers and from southerners to ex-southern migrants.

Ultimately, as the historians say rightly, the migration laid the foundation for the shattering of the caste system and an equality only dreamed of by the dedicated proponents of the great drive for civil rights. One cannot help note that these words were written not long after an African American served two terms as president of the United States.[2]

None of the above is gainsaid by this chapter. But the heart of this book—its entire raison d'être—is to discuss and analyze the history of violent crime: an inherently ugly aspect of any society. This story cannot be told, not honestly, unless we also chronicle black violent crime. Crime too was a part of the Great Migration. As I will show, twentieth-century black violence predated the migration, and as with the southern Italians at the turn of the century, and the Irish over one-half century before them, African Americans transported their rural violence to the great cities of America every bit as much as they conveyed their meager physical possessions.

This chapter will survey black life in the South in the three decades before the Great Depression, then segue into an analysis of black crime in that region. The focus will then shift to the cities of the North as the migration gathered steam in the 1920s. In those cities, sprawling, poor and sometimes dangerous black communities grew apace, early on dubbed "ghettos" to reflect the immense barriers to moving out. The discussion then will move from general conditions to crime in the northern cities. As will become evident, the migration, while emancipating African Americans from the stultification of black rural life, also transported black criminality from the South to the North, where it grew with the floodtide of migrants.

## IN THE SOUTH

At the dawn of the last century the African American population of the United States was concentrated in a broad swath of land across the deep South, the so-called Black Belt, which ran from the Carolinas to Louisiana. Although African Americans were roughly one-third of the population of the southern states, in South Carolina and Mississippi they were the majority, and in Georgia, Alabama, and Louisiana, over 40 percent of the inhabitants were black. This enormous concentration of population made no difference whatsoever in terms of political influence as blacks were disenfranchised and rendered totally powerless. What it does reveal is that African Americans overwhelmingly were southerners, not just geographically, but (as will be seen) culturally as well. Though segregated and subordinated, blacks shared with southern whites a range of values, including for example dietary and religious preferences, and most significantly, a readiness to use violence.

TABLE 4.1. Black population of the United States and the South, 1900–2000

| Year | Black Population of U.S. | Black Population of South | % of Blacks in South | Black % of South |
|---|---|---|---|---|
| 1900 | 8,833,994 | 7,922,969 | 89.7 | 32.3 |
| 1910 | 9,827,763 | 8,749,427 | 89.0 | 29.8 |
| 1920 | 10,463,131 | 8,912,231 | 85.2 | 26.9 |
| 1930 | 11,891,143 | 9,361,577 | 78.7 | 24.7 |
| 1940 | 12,865,518 | 9,904,619 | 77.0 | 23.8 |
| 1950 | 15,042,286 | 10,225,407 | 68.0 | 21.7 |
| 1960 | 18,871,831 | 11,311,607 | 60.0 | 20.6 |
| 1970 | 22,580,289 | 11,969,961 | 53.0 | 19.1 |
| 1980 | 26,495,025 | 14,047,787 | 53.0 | 18.6 |
| 1990 | 29,986,060 | 15,828,888 | 52.8 | 18.5 |
| 2000 | 34,658,190 | 18,981,692 | 54.8 | 18.9 |

Sources: U.S. Census Bureau, Historical Census Statistics (Working Paper No. 56); U.S. Census Bureau, Black Population: 2000.

Note: The Census Bureau defines the South as Alabama, Arkansas, Delaware, District of Columbia, Florida, Georgia, Kentucky, Louisiana, Maryland, Mississippi, North Carolina, Oklahoma, South Carolina, Tennessee, Texas, Virginia, and West Virginia.

Blacks, like whites, were principally employed in agriculture, cotton farming being the mainstay of the southern economy. In 1910, for instance, 56 percent of the African American male population worked on farms. Other occupations, primarily some type of manual labor, such as in construction, sawmills, or on railroads, employed the remainder. Black employment may even have been higher than white: nationwide in 1910, over 87 percent of black males age ten and older were gainfully employed whereas for whites the figure was less than 80 percent. (I'll say more about unemployment in a moment.) But the wages of black workers undoubtedly were much lower, and black women, even those who were married, had to work, as 55 percent of the black female population did. The magnitude of this latter figure becomes clear when we see that fewer than one in five white women held jobs. Fifty-two percent of the black female labor force also worked in agriculture; an additional 18 percent were laundresses, 10 percent cooks. Note, by the way, the expression "worked on farms." That isn't the same as *owning* a farm. Only 219,000 blacks owned their own farms (in 1910), compared with 3.7 million whites. The black farms tended to be relatively small, averaging 47 acres compared to 153 acres for whites. And when the cotton economy sank in the 1920s and 1930s, independent black farmers were nearly wiped out.[3]

Those who worked the land but did not own it, which is to say the overwhelming majority of blacks, were tenant farmers or sharecroppers. Starting in the late nineteenth century, more and more acreage in the South was dedicated to cotton, expansion that continued right up to the Great Depression of the 1930s, which meant, given the labor-intensive farming methods, more employment for blacks in the fields. In the Mississippi River Delta, vast acreage—plantations—owned by whites, was farmed by millions of black tenants. The Delta was, as Nicholas Lemann's widely read history of the black migration called it, "the capital of the sharecropper system."

We have no hard data on black income in this period because the Census Bureau collected none before the 1930s. But given that most of the better-paying jobs, such as supervisory positions, were foreclosed to blacks; that sharecropping, which employed a majority of African Americans, was an economic dead end; and that whites owned sixteen times as many farms, the conclusion seems obvious. It is further confirmed by scholarship comparing the assessed wealth of whites and blacks in the South around the turn of the century. Ratios of white wealth to black in 1910 ranged from six times greater for whites in Arkansas to twenty-five times as high in Louisiana.[4]

Surprisingly however, black unemployment was not higher than white, and there were periods before the Second World War in which it was lower. Economists have graphed black and white unemployment (figure 4.1). Note that the racial gap doesn't become significant until after World War II.

One plausible explanation for this employment parity is that before the Second World War blacks resided and worked mainly in the South, which had a shortage of labor in low-paying jobs such as cotton farming. In addition, prior to the 1930s, blacks found work in the expanding manufacturing sector of the

North, which also needed manual labor, and to which roughly 1.9 million blacks migrated. When the depression hit and the northern economy contracted it was, ironically, the South that kept black unemployment on a par with white. Evidence for this last point is found in a breakdown of unemployment rates by region.

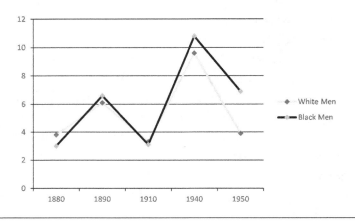

FIGURE 4.1. Male unemployment rates by race, 1880–1950. *Source:* Fairlie and Sundstrom, "Emergence," 255.

TABLE 4.2. Racial differences in U.S. unemployment rates by region, 1930

| Region | Unemployment Rate | | Nonwhite-to-White Ratio |
|---|---|---|---|
| | White | Nonwhite | |
| New England | 8.42 | 10.73 | 1.27 |
| Mid-Atlantic | 8.01 | 10.74 | 1.34 |
| East North Central | 8.01 | 14.97 | 1.87 |
| West North Central | 4.28 | 9.07 | 2.12 |
| South Atlantic | 4.21 | 4.41 | 1.05 |
| East South Central | 3.40 | 2.67 | 0.79 |
| West South Central | 4.36 | 4.46 | 1.02 |
| Mountain | 5.97 | 9.16 | 1.53 |
| Pacific | 7.32 | 9.37 | 1.28 |
| U.S. average | 6.59 | 6.07 | 0.92 |

*Source:* Vedder and Gallaway, "Racial Differences," 699.

Observe that black unemployment on the eve of the depression was lower than white nationwide but exceeded white in the northern manufacturing regions. In the South, however—home to 79 percent of the African American population in 1930—black unemployment was below or only slightly above that of whites. Southern employment, in other words, drove the relatively low black rates.

What is the relevance of this for black crime? One common explanation for crime is economic adversity as measured by such factors as high unemployment and low income or wealth. But if black crime was high before World War II, which as I will show momentarily it certainly was, then the unemployment explanation must be called into question. For the first half of the twentieth century there appears to be no correlation between black unemployment and violent crime. As we will see, black violence was elevated throughout the 1920s, when unemployment was low, and it declined in the 1930s, when unemployment escalated. On the other hand, since black wealth during this time period was considerably lower than white, a correlation between wealth and violent crime remains viable.

Nearly three-quarters of the black population lived in rural areas, many in plantation cabins provided by the landowner. Some lived in small towns, in rented housing on the "wrong" side of the tracks. A minority of these homes were well-built and well-equipped; many, however, if not most, were "tumbledown shacks with neither light, heat, nor running water, and often enough without a whole floor or a whole roof." They also lacked electricity and insulation—heat came from a wood stove—and of course there were no indoor toilets.[5]

For black children in the South education was considered optional, as they were needed to work the fields. A mere 44 percent of southern black youngsters were enrolled in schools in 1910, rising to 62 percent in 1940. Schools were one- or two-room buildings without heating or plumbing. All grades were taught together and no schooling was offered beyond the eighth grade. Little public money went to black schools until the 1920s; before that, the ratio of black to white education expenditures actually declined. The result was predictable: 36 percent black illiteracy in 1910, 22 percent in 1930.[6]

Increasing numbers of blacks relocated to big cities, at first in the South, but by the 1920s, to Chicago, New York, and other northern metropolises—the Great Migration. Even before the surge northward thousands of African Americans had moved to southern cities such as Atlanta, Birmingham, and Memphis. Indeed, as of 1910, eight southern cities (counting Baltimore and Washington, DC) each had forty thousand or more black residents.[7] Still, this southern metropolitan black population probably never exceeded one-half million people in total, less than 6 percent of all African American inhabitants of the South. These metropolitan blacks worked in domestic or personal service for whites or as laborers. Crime rates among blacks in these cities were higher than in the towns or rural hamlets, but it is possible that this was a by-product of the greater number of police in urban locales.

## BLACK CRIME IN THE SOUTH

Though no statistics are available as proof, the preponderance of black-on-black violence seems to have taken place on Saturday nights.[8] This was a time for partying, for letting off steam and shedding the cares of the workweek. In rural areas there were "hot suppers" in some farmer's field or gatherings at roadside taverns known as "juke joints." In towns "balls" were held in a schoolhouse or at a "disreputable roadhouse" (i.e., a brothel). In the big cities, taverns or illicit equivalents served as venues. Wherever the party was held, the scene was much the same: loud music and dancing, drinking and gambling lasting well into Sunday morning. Inevitably, there were quarrels, usually involving sexual jealousy or gambling disputes. Even the slightest offense could trigger a fight, culminating in a stabbing or shooting. Fox Butterfield told how one man killed another at a supper over some utterly trivial disagreement: "William Bosket's son, Mamon, killed a man named George Dozier over a bet of ten cents in a game of skin [a popular card game] at another hot supper. Dozier had refused to pay up and then challenged Mamon, saying, 'I'm not scared of you.' Mamon pulled his pistol and shot him."[9]

Whites told John Dollard, "really to understand what the Negroes are like, one should see the slum section after twelve o'clock on Saturday night. A constant series of cases of shooting, cutting, beating, and occasional murder, comes out of this area."[10] The racism of this statement aside, there was in fact, especially on Saturday nights, a steady stream of violent incidents in poor black areas. Accounts of such rowdyism, related by numerous observers, including those totally sympathetic to black advancement, corroborate one another. They tell us a great deal about black crime in the South.

Most southern black crime, like white crime, was minor and inconsequential. A disproportionate amount of it, however, was extremely violent. Assaults and killings were a frequent occurrence, and not only on Saturdays. Black women were continually in fear of violence at the hands of black men; and black women, as the data bear out, were themselves violent (compared with white women), assaulting other females, and when they caught them unawares, the black males who menaced them.[11]

Butterfield thought that the violence by black men was a product of southern male values. "It grew out of the old white southern code of honor," he explained, "an extreme sensitivity to insult and the opinion of others."[12] This view makes sense. African Americans were quintessentially southern. For hundreds of years, both as slaves and in freedom, nearly all blacks lived in the South, isolated from external cultural influences. It would be astonishing if under those circumstances they did *not* share southern values. And as demonstrated in chapters 1 and 3, white southern crime, driven by the male code of honor, was exceptionally violent.

Many questions remain. For instance, why was black violence so much greater than white, even low-income southern white violence? Second, what is the relationship of this honor code violence to economic adversity? Assaults motivated by sexual rivalries and petty gambling disputes had, by all appearances, nothing to do with pecuniary gain. They were about demonstrations of male ego—showing how "tough" and macho a young man could be, how no one was going to push him around or humiliate him, especially in public. To be sure, these were lower-class males with little opportunity for social advancement, and this status probably fostered a nothing-to-lose attitude. But not all lower-class groups were as "touchy" or aggressive as low-income African Americans. Finally, why did African American violent crime continue at high rates in the North, where conditions, though hardly a model of fairness and equal opportunities, were much better than those in the South?

## THE DATA

Perhaps the first question anyone will ask when African American crime in the South is the subject of analysis is: can we trust the data? This really is another way of asking whether black crime was little more than an artifact of white bias or whether it was a factual reality. It is an apt question, because race bias in the pre–World War II South was so deeply entrenched and so all-pervasive as to taint virtually every aspect of black life. Anecdotal information on disgraceful unfairness in the prosecution of crime abounds, and much of the data indicate blatant bias in adjudication and sentencing.

An example of the latter is offered by criminologist H. C. Brearley, who studied his native South Carolina. Brearley determined that for 1920–26, blacks accused of murder or manslaughter were found guilty in 64 percent of verdicts, whereas whites were adjudged guilty in only 32 percent, precisely half as many. Moreover, with respect to sanctions, from 1915 to 1927, fifty-three blacks but only seven whites were executed, which comes to one white executed for every 101 white homicides and one black for every thirty-eight black homicides.[13]

A second illustration of bias was provided by criminologist Thorsten Sellin for Alabama courts in the 1920s. Except for robbery and arson, the percentages of acquittals in serious offense cases brought to trial was much lower for African Americans than for whites. With murder, for instance, from 1920 to 1922, 24 percent of indicted and tried blacks were acquitted, but 45 percent of accused whites were—a 90 percent difference.[14]

TABLE 4.3. Outcomes in criminal cases tried before the Alabama Circuit Courts, by race, 1920–1922 and 1924–1926

| Offense | Race | 1920–1922 | | |
| --- | --- | --- | --- | --- |
| | | Tried | Acquitted | % Acquitted |
| Sex offense | Black | 71 | 20 | 28.2 |
| | White | 89 | 32 | 36.0 |
| Arson | Black | 23 | 7 | 30.4 |
| | White | 9 | 4 | 44.4 |
| Assault | Black | 317 | 25 | 8.0 |
| | White | 303 | 70 | 23.1 |
| Burglary | Black | 342 | 49 | 14.3 |
| | White | 134 | 39 | 29.1 |
| Forgery | Black | 65 | 6 | 9.1 |
| | White | 115 | 55 | 47.8 |
| Larceny | Black | 608 | 75 | 12.3 |
| | White | 296 | 64 | 21.6 |
| Manslaughter | Black | 86 | 4 | 4.4 |
| | White | 37 | 5 | 13.5 |

TABLE 4.3 (*continued*)

| Offense | Race | 1920–1922 | | |
|---|---|---|---|---|
| | | Tried | Acquitted | % Acquitted |
| Murder | Black | 273 | 65 | 23.8 |
| | White | 170 | 77 | 45.3 |
| Prohibition offense | Black | 822 | 163 | 19.8 |
| | White | 1,240 | 390 | 31.4 |
| Robbery | Black | 21 | 9 | 42.8 |
| | White | 18 | 4 | 22.2 |
| Total | Black | 2,628 | 423 | 16.1 |
| | White | 2,411 | 740 | 30.7 |
| All other offenses | Black | 521 | 157 | 30.1 |
| | White | 1,174 | 382 | 32.5 |
| Total | Black | 3,149 | 580 | 18.4 |
| | White | 3,585 | 1,122 | 31.3 |

| Offense | Race | 1924–1926 | | |
|---|---|---|---|---|
| | | Tried | Acquitted | % Acquitted |
| Sex offense | Black | 75 | 19 | 25.3 |
| | White | 129 | 43 | 33.3 |
| Arson | Black | 18 | 11 | 61.1 |
| | White | 16 | 5 | 31.2 |
| Assault | Black | 349 | 12 | 3.4 |
| | White | 306 | 21 | 6.8 |
| Burglary | Black | 220 | 19 | 8.6 |
| | White | 147 | 20 | 13.6 |
| Forgery | Black | 43 | — | 0.0 |
| | White | 79 | 8 | 10.1 |
| Larceny | Black | 432 | 54 | 12.5 |
| | White | 308 | 54 | 17.5 |
| Manslaughter | Black | 92 | 4 | 4.3 |
| | White | 41 | 6 | 14.6 |

TABLE 4.3 (*continued*)

| Offense | Race | 1924–1926 | | |
| | | Tried | Acquitted | % Acquitted |
| --- | --- | --- | --- | --- |
| Murder | Black | 240 | 68 | 28.3 |
| | White | 146 | 57 | 39.0 |
| Prohibition offense | Black | 832 | 108 | 12.9 |
| | White | 1,573 | 219 | 13.9 |
| Robbery | Black | 20 | 3 | 15.0 |
| | White | 23 | 5 | 21.7 |
| Total | Black | 2,321 | 298 | 12.8 |
| | White | 2,768 | 438 | 15.9 |
| All other offenses | Black | 590 | 89 | 15.1 |
| | White | 1,193 | 227 | 19.0 |
| Total | Black | 2,911 | 387 | 13.3 |
| | White | 3,961 | 665 | 16.8 |

*Source:* Sellin, "Negro Criminal," 58–59.

These numbers certainly are consistent with a profoundly biased criminal justice process. But the picture is not as clear as it might be. There also was a tendency for white southerners to ignore or downplay certain misconduct by blacks, especially where the behavior didn't adversely affect whites. The effect of this was to diminish the number of prosecutions of African Americans or afford them sentencing leniency. As an illustration we have a decade-long study for the 1930s of Richmond, Virginia, and five counties in North Carolina. In both jurisdictions when whites murdered other whites approximately one in four of those convicted got the harshest sentence: death or life in prison. But when blacks killed blacks fewer than 6 percent of the convicted received the harshest punishment. At the same time, convicted African Americans were between four and five times as likely as convicted whites to get a sentence at the lower end of the sentencing scale for murder, ten to nineteen years. Thus, if black defendants with white victims were "overpunished," black defendants with African American victims appear to have been "underpunished."[15]

TABLE 4.4. Percentage of indicted murder defendants convicted and percentage of convicted defendants given various sentences, by race of offender and victim, Richmond, VA, 1930–1939, and five counties in North Carolina, 1930–1940

|  | Convicted (%) | Life or Death (%) | 20–Life (%) | 10–19 (%) | Under 10 (%) |
|---|---|---|---|---|---|
| North Carolina |  |  |  |  |  |
| White on White | 68.9 | 23.8 | 19.0 | 4.8 | 52.4 |
| Black on Black | 81.4 | 5.9 | 18.9 | 22.9 | 52.2 |
| Richmond, VA |  |  |  |  |  |
| White on White | 75.0 | 26.7 | 20.0 | 6.7 | 46.7 |
| Black on Black | 72.7 | 5.7 | 21.9 | 30.5 | 41.8 |

*Source:* Johnson, "Negro and Crime," 99.

John Dollard, in his classic mid-1930s study of "Southerntown" (actually Indianola, Mississippi, a Delta town of 2,500, famous for its native son blues great B. B. King), confirmed that one must take into consideration the race of the perpetrator and the victim.

> White persons are held much more strictly to the formal legal code; Negroes are dealt with much more indulgently. It is not a question of different formal codes for Negroes and whites, but rather of differences in severity and rigor of application of the code that does exist. This is true only under one condition, however—when Negro crimes are committed on Negroes; when they are done on whites, the penalties assessed may rather be excessively strict.[16]

In short, race bias produced greater leniency for black criminal offenders, though at the same time, less protection for black crime victims.

As for the effect of race bias on the number of accusations against African Americans, this is harder to gauge, and the answer may depend on the seriousness of the crime. It is probably safe to assert that the graver the offense, the less likely it would have been ignored by the authorities. Murders, for instance, were taken too seriously simply to disregard, even if they were overwhelmingly intraracial and whites had no special reason to prosecute them.[17] With lesser offenses by blacks, however, enforcement was more unpredictable. Black-on-black assaults were seen by whites as a common and idiosyncratic characteristic of African Americans that the justice system might safely ignore. As John Dollard put it, white court officials "simply do not take it as seriously as they would the same offense by whites."[18] Given this perspective, the assault data for blacks—as measured by arrests in the case of misdemeanors, and by indictments for felonies—are undoubtedly an undercount, and probably a gross undercount, of actual incidents.

What does all of the above mean for our analysis of crime? The most prudent course is to rely primarily on homicide mortality figures, which are far less likely to be tainted by bias, and to consider the mortality data and the criminal justice data as mutually corroborative. That is, if all the data indicate high levels of offending by African Americans the obvious conclusion—despite the racism—becomes unavoidable.

I will review the data chronologically, moving from the early 1900s to around 1930. The arrest, conviction, and imprisonment data for the South are severely compromised by blatant race bias. They are, however, as I will show, corroborated by high African American rates for the non-South, as well as by the more reliable mortality data on homicides. Taken together, these figures support the conclusion that African American violent crime rates were exceptionally high in both the South and the North.

In 1904 the Census Bureau did the first of three enumerations of prisoners nationwide, the latter two occurring in 1910 and 1923. In the 1904 tally, an astonishing 64 percent of the prisoners committed in the South Atlantic states were African Americans, this at a time when blacks were 36 percent of the general population of those same states (1900 Census). Similar results obtained in the South Central states, where blacks were 30 percent of the residents, 59 percent of the commitments.[19]

Race bias certainly inflated these figures, but the question is, to what degree? By 1904, profits from convict leasing, which created financial incentives to convict African Americans and impose longer sentences on them, had begun to wane. But as some states had not yet abolished the lease (e.g., Georgia continued it through 1908), it may still have had an impact.[20] However, when I examined the ratio of black prisoners to the general black population I found, rather surprisingly, that they were much higher in the North.

TABLE 4.5. Ratio of Negro prisoners committed in 1904 to the colored general population in 1900, by region

| Region | % Negro Commitments | % Colored Pop. | Inmate to Pop. Ratio |
|---|---|---|---|
| No. Atlantic | 6.8 | 1.9 | 3.6: 1 |
| So. Atlantic | 64.3 | 35.8 | 1.8: 1 |
| No. Central | 12.7 | 2.1 | 6.1: 1 |
| So. Central | 59.4 | 30.3 | 1.9: 1 |
| West | 5.1 | 5.3 | 0.96: 1 |

Source: Bureau of the Census, *Prisoners and Juvenile Delinquents 1904*, Tables VI, XIX.

In 1910, the Census published commitment rates per 100,000 of each race, and from these data it becomes even clearer that black rates were higher in the North. Above the Mason-Dixon line the ratio of black-to-white commitment rates was 5.6: 1; below it was 3.4: 1. Especially revealing are the commitment rates for violent crimes, shown in table 4.6.

TABLE 4.6. Prison commitment rates of blacks and whites per 100,000 for violent crimes, by region, 1910

| | North | | | South | | |
|---|---|---|---|---|---|---|
| | White | Black | B/W | White | Black | B/W |
| Grave homicide | 0.3 | 5.6 | 18.7 | 0.8 | 5.4 | 6.8 |
| Lesser homicide | 0.8 | 12.6 | 15.8 | 1.9 | 9.2 | 4.8 |
| Assault | 17.5 | 231.7 | 13.2 | 10.2 | 77.5 | 7.6 |
| Robbery | 1.4 | 21.9 | 15.6 | 0.6 | 3.6 | 6.0 |

Source: Bureau of the Census, *Prisoners and Juvenile Delinquents 1910*, tables 78, 82.

Note: "B/W" is ratio of black to white commitment rates.

This table indicates that black imprisonment rates for violent crimes were high relative to whites in both North and South. For the most egregious murders ("grave homicides"), for instance, black commitment rates were nearly nineteen times the white rates in the North, almost seven times the white rates in the South.[21] Moreover, the black rates were higher in the North for each of the violent crimes. Since race discrimination was undoubtedly less pronounced in the northern justice system, the inference is that the figures reflect actual black crime and are not just a by-product of bias. Of equal importance, 1910 is well before the height of the Great Migration and the development of northern black ghettos; nevertheless, black violence already was excessive in the North. This demonstrates that the northern ghettos were not the starting point for black violence, a matter that will be addressed momentarily.

According to the 1923 census of prisoners, the last of the special prisoner enumerations (though there were annual prisoner tallies from 1926 on), high numbers of blacks continued to be incarcerated for violent crimes. For homicide, African Americans provided 41.5 percent of the prison commitments. The percentages were way out of proportion to the African American population, which was 9.9 percent of the national total (1920 Census).[22]

TABLE 4.7. Percent of prisoners committed for crimes of violence, by race and nativity, 1923

| Offense | Black | Foreign-born White | Native White | Total |
|---|---|---|---|---|
| Assault | 43.9 | 17.8 | 35.2 | 96.9 |
| Homicide | 41.5 | 13.4 | 43.6 | 98.5 |
| Rape | 17.8 | 16.8 | 63.3 | 97.9 |
| Robbery | 25.9 | 8.8 | 64.1 | 98.8 |

Source: Bureau of the Census, Prisoners 1923, table 36.

Before turning to the other data sources for the 1920s, I examine some arrest figures for 1908 for two southern cities, Charleston, South Carolina, and Birmingham, Alabama. Charleston, according to the 1910 Census, was a city of 58,833, of which 27,764 (47.2 percent) were white and 31,056 (52.8 percent) were black. With respect to homicide, white arrest rates exceeded black, 18 to 9.7, which was unusual, but the actual number of killings was very small: five for whites and three for blacks. Assault, together with aggravated assault, followed the more typical pattern. The black rate (293 per 100,000) was more than twice the white (144). These latter figures must be judged with the pervasive race bias of the South in mind, the precise impact of which remains unknown. It is entirely possible that, due to white indifference to black-on-black crime, the figures for blacks are an undercount.

Birmingham was more than twice as big as Charleston, with a 1910 population of 132,685, including 80,369 whites (61 percent) and 52,305 blacks (39 percent). The arrest rates for violent crimes show black rates many multiples of white. For murder, white rates were 8.7 per 100,000, while black rates were 38.2. For affray (fighting or brawling), the rates were 437 for every 100,000 whites and 681 per 100,000 blacks. And for criminal assault combined with an offense described as "shooting at another," the black rates were over three times the white: 84 to 25.[23]

Thus, in the first two decades of the twentieth century, when the overwhelming majority of African Americans lived in the South, black violence already was elevated. It is highly unlikely that racism alone could account for such high rates, especially for serious crimes of violence, most of which victimized other African Americans. This violence took place before the Great Migration reached its apogee and before the creation of large-scale black ghettos in the North. It occurred when black unemployment was low, probably lower than white, though income and wealth was considerably below white levels. Most important, this violence would continue for decades in the South and it would, starting in the 1920s, migrate North with the great trek to freedom. Black violent crime, in short, did not originate in the northern black ghettos, though it was magnified and modified there.

By the 1920s, with the so-called death registration area nearly complete, mortality data became the best measure of murder. The advantage of such data is that they are derived from coroner's reports on the cause of death, which, unlike arrest and adjudication data, were not tainted by race bias. If black homicide mortality rates were high—and they certainly were—then they cannot be dismissed as a mere by-product of bigotry.

For the entire decade, African American homicide rates nationwide, on average, were seven times white rates. In 1926, they were more than eight times as high.[24]

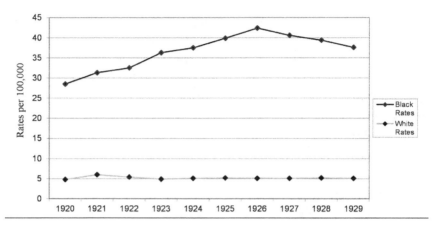

FIGURE 4.2. Homicide rates per 100,000, by race, 1920–1929. *Source:* Federal Security Agency, *Vital Statistics Rates,* mortality tables, table 16.

Additional insights may be gleaned from the work of criminologist H. C. Brearley, who collected homicide data for 1920 and 1925, organizing it by state, race, and urban/rural location. (Urban location here means ten thousand people or more.) Below are his figures for nine southern states. Although the race categories in Brearley differentiated white and "colored," in the southern states colored meant almost exclusively African Americans.

TABLE 4.8. Homicide mortality rates per 100,000 in the South, 1920 and 1925 combined, by state, race, and rural or urban location

| State | Total | | Urban | | Rural | |
|---|---|---|---|---|---|---|
| | White | Black | White | Black | White | Black |
| Alabama* | 7.4 | 34.4 | 15.4 | 81.1 | 5.8 | 23.5 |
| Florida | 12.5 | 62.9 | 16.8 | 102.4 | 10.9 | 49.1 |
| Kentucky | 8.7 | 49.1 | 9.6 | 72.1 | 8.4 | 38.5 |
| Louisiana | 8.7 | 35.4 | 14.4 | 78.0 | 6.0 | 23.6 |

TABLE 4.8 *(continued)*

| State | Total | | Urban | | Rural | |
|---|---|---|---|---|---|---|
| | White | Black | White | Black | White | Black |
| Mississippi | 8.3 | 32.2 | 17.0 | 82.2 | 7.4 | 28.7 |
| No. Carolina | 4.7 | 20.8 | 8.8 | 50.5 | 4.1 | 15.4 |
| So. Carolina | 8.6 | 18.5 | 20.8 | 57.9 | 6.8 | 15.0 |
| Tennessee | 8.0 | 48.8 | 14.9 | 103.2 | 6.5 | 24.7 |
| Virginia | 6.7 | 20.0 | 9.2 | 37.7 | 5.9 | 13.2 |

*Source:* Brearley, *Homicide*, 99.

*Note:* Alabama data for 1925 only.

The disparities between black and white rates within each state are dramatic, ranging from more than double white rates in South Carolina to over six times the white rate in Tennessee. Almost as eye-popping are the differences between urban and rural rates for African Americans; the former are quadruple the rural rates in most states. It is not entirely clear why the urban/rural difference is so great. Perhaps it involves the increased interaction between people in the city, the city's greater anonymity, or a breakdown of rural social constraints. (The additional police presence in cities, which contributes to higher arrest rates for a number of offenses, seems an implausible explanation for homicide differentials, as rural area killings were unlikely to go undetected.) These factors, of course, are relevant to urban crime generally, not just to African Americans.

The Census Bureau published mortality data for those municipalities that provided such information, and below are figures for some of the southern cities, which kept separate records for whites and blacks ("colored" in the Census publications). Several of the black rates are shockingly high, many multiples of the white rates, and this being the South, the white rates were not insignificant. Consider, for example, the race differentials for Memphis, Tennessee. For 1911 to 1919, the African American rate, a staggering 130 per 100,000, was five times the white rate. By the end of the 1920s matters got even worse: the black rate in 1929 was 144, over twelve times the white.[25]

TABLE 4.9. Homicide mortality rates for selected southern cities and selected years, by race

| City | 1911–19 Avg. | | 1920 | | 1928 | | 1929 | |
|---|---|---|---|---|---|---|---|---|
| | White | Black | White | Black | White | Black | White | Black |
| Atlanta | 12.3 | 76.3 | 9.3 | 106.2 | 16 | 88.4 | 14.1 | 109.8 |
| Baltimore | 4 | 23 | 3.3 | 23.6 | 5.2 | 27.8 | 4.7 | 37.8 |
| Birmingham | — | — | 17.1 | 92.1 | 9.2 | 116.8 | 17.8 | 89.7 |
| Houston | — | — | 4.6 | 45.5 | 11.8 | 80.7 | 13.5 | 77.7 |
| Louisville | 9.1 | 57.9 | 6.5 | 39.4 | 8.1 | 102 | 7.3 | 84.7 |
| Memphis | 25* | 130.2* | 20.6 | 132.4 | 21.6 | 115.7 | 11.8 | 144.2 |
| New Orleans | 10.8 | 60.3 | 9 | 36 | 11.2 | 62.2 | 11.1 | 64 |
| Richmond | 5.3 | 40.8 | 2.5 | 18.5 | 3.1 | 35.7 | 3.9 | 28.2 |
| Wash., DC | 4.5 | 21.7 | 5.8 | 24.2 | 4.6 | 33.3 | 6.5 | 28.2 |

Source: Bureau of the Census, *Mortality Statistics 1929*, table BH.

Note: Figures for Memphis, 1911–19, do not include 1916, which was unavailable.

## BLACK-ON-BLACK CRIME

Since this was the Jim Crow South one might think that the high number of black homicide victimizations was attributable to white aggressions. That was not the case. The overwhelming majority of African American homicides came at the hands of other blacks. Consider the following study of the Memphis, Tennessee municipal court records for the early 1920s. This court handled all arraignments following arrests, and the records enabled investigators to identify the race and gender of the alleged perpetrators and the victims. Table 4.10 presents the results for the years 1920 to 1925 combined.

TABLE 4.10. Homicide arraignments, Memphis, Tennessee, Municipal Court, 1920–1925, by race and gender of victims and perpetrators

| Victim | White Perp. | Black Perp. | Perp. Race Unknown |
|---|---|---|---|
| White male | 48 male | 9 male | 15 |
| | 8 female | 2 female | 0 |

TABLE 4.10 *(continued)*

| Victim | White Perp. | Black Perp. | Perp. Race Unknown |
|---|---|---|---|
| White female | 12 male | — | 1 |
| | 6 female | — | 0 |
| Black male | 50 male | 143 male | 13 |
| | — | 53 female | 0 |
| Black female | — | 40 male | 3 |
| | 0 | 9 female | 0 |

*Source:* Bruce and Fitzgerald, "Study of Crime," 20.

*Note:* "—" means no data provided.

Ignoring gender we find 295 black victims where the race of the killer was identified. Fifty of the perpetrators, 17 percent, were white, whereas 245, or 83 percent, were African American. If 83 percent of the race-unknown killers had been black (n = 13) and that figure were included in the overall tally then the proportion of black-on-black cases would rise to 88 percent. With or without this last calculation it is evident that white killers accounted for a small minority of black homicide deaths.

Was Memphis typical of the South in this respect? We have some, though limited, corroboration. In Washington, DC, Brearley reported that from 1915 to 1919, 87 African Americans were victimized by homicide, 92 percent (n = 80) by other African Americans.[26] Indeed, as will be shown, this pattern of intraracial killings continued when blacks migrated to the North and remains characteristic up to the present day.

Before discussing the migration, I need to consider the reason for the inordinately high black violence in the South, especially against other African Americans. I already enumerated several factors, primary among them the southern code of honor, augmented perhaps by a black sense of despair at the lack of opportunity, which in turn stimulated a kind of heedless risk-taking behavior. I now consider one additional possibility: that black-on-black violence is a surrogate for a suppressed desire to lash out at whites, a course of action too dangerous to pursue. Here is an analysis by John Dollard, who may have been one of the first to develop the point.

> The Negro individual occupies a socially stereotyped caste position in which he suffers certain systematic disadvantages. He is aware of these disadvantages because he knows the difference between his actual status in Southerntown and his theoretical status as defined by the dominant American folkways and mores. His situation, therefore, is one of frustration because he perceives the contradictions in his situation and prefers his theoretical role as an undifferentiated member of American society to his actual role as caste man. The usual human response to frustration is aggression against the frustrating object. In this case the frustrating object is the American white caste which maintains its dominance over the Negro caste in various ways. Our problem then becomes: what happens to the aggression which is inevitably germinated in this situation? . . . Aggressive tentatives [*sic*; tendencies?] by the Negro bring out marked counter-hostility in the dominant group; this puts the Negro in a dangerous situation. . . . There is another method of dealing with this aggression which is too dangerous to express; that is, to divert it from the provoking object to some other object. It will be argued in this chapter that some of the hostility properly directed toward the white caste is deflected from it and focused within the Negro group itself. There are two advantages to this procedure. First, it is expressive from the Negro standpoint; Negroes are able to react in a biologically satisfying manner. Second, it is safer than taking up the hopeless direct struggle against the white caste which is so severely sensitive to all hostile expressions from Negroes.[27]

In short, according to Dollard, black violence against other African Americans is the product of frustration over the all-encompassing racism of American society, a violence that would be directed at whites were it safer to engage in such behavior, but which, to avoid the lynch mob, must be redirected toward other blacks. Implicit in this view is the notion that black crime has a social or political content, that is, that it is an expression of profound discontent with the social order. This hypothesis is perfectly plausible under the circumstances, but it has two shortcomings. First, the offenders themselves certainly do not seem to have been motivated by such considerations. They were driven, or so it appears, by sudden anger over insults or sexual jealousy, or by seemingly petty gambling or property disputes, not some broader social goal. Perhaps such feelings of social discontent are too deep-seated to be expressed; perhaps they are hidden even from the actors themselves. Or maybe frustration over societal conditions produced general feelings of anger that were easily triggered by incidents that would be considered inconsequential by others. Still, some demonstration of a link between black violence and black feelings of frustration over racial repression would make Dollard's explanation much more credible.

A second issue is this: If black violence were a product of racial subordination one would expect a diminution in that violence as the repression eased. Consequently, one would have expected *less* black violence in the North, where the caste system was less pervasive and less entrenched. This, however, was not the case. As will be seen (and we already saw some evidence of it earlier) black violence was *greater* in the North. Furthermore, to think ahead momentarily, after the civil rights gains of the 1960s one would have expected a further decline in black violent crime; but that too did not occur (at least not before the mid-1990s).[28]

An alternative to Dollard's explanation is the southern culture of violence hypothesis, or what Thomas Sowell called the "black redneck thesis."[29] On this view, black criminal violence was the product of the southern male honor culture, which, among lower socioeconomic status blacks, manifested itself as a violent response to petty insults, sexual rivalries, etc. Since African Americans interacted socially with other African Americans much more than with whites, the victims of such "honor" culture assaults invariably were black. This violence would continue when African Americans migrated to the North. Indeed, it would escalate in the northern cities, where there was greater freedom and less oppression. The violence, in short, was an integral part of the southern culture of poor blacks, a culture transported by the Great Migration—the subject of the next section of this chapter.

## THE MIGRATION

Prior to World War II the biggest surge in black migration occurred during the 1920s, when over eight hundred thousand African Americans left the South. In 1900, only 10 percent of all African Americans lived outside of Dixie; by 1930 that figure had doubled to over 20 percent. The 1920s was crucial for the creation of the populous black communities—black ghettos to some—in the big metropolitan areas of the North. To fully understand black crime and the other social deficits of the "inner cities," one must examine the genesis of these communities.

Before the 1920s, long-settled northern blacks and recent black migrants lived in small concentrations scattered throughout the big cities of the North, often alongside recent immigrants from Europe. As long as the number of blacks remained small there was no serious disharmony between the races. Stimulated by the job openings of the First World War, however, the pace of migration accelerated dramatically, and this surge quickly disrupted the fragile racial equilibrium.[30]

TABLE 4.11. Black migration from the South, 1900–1940

| | |
|---|---|
| 1900–1910 | 204,382 |
| 1910–1920 | 437,154 |
| 1920–1930 | 810,614 |
| 1930–1940 | 391,641 |

Source: Gregory, *Southern Diaspora*, 330.

A quick look at the population figures for some of the destination cities will give a sense of the situation. Detroit, which had 5,000 blacks in 1910, tallied 35,000 by 1920. In Philadelphia, there were 40,000 newcomers between 1916 and 1919 alone, and another 85,000 in the 1920s. Chicago's African American population increased fivefold from 44,000 in 1910 to 234,000 in 1930. And New York went from 91,000 in 1910 to 327,000 in the course of two decades. Population increase, of course, isn't everything. Racial conflict and job and housing competition played big roles in the unfolding events. But the numbers shouldn't be ignored either; the sheer size of the black influx over such a relatively short time frame exacerbated the problems arising out of the migration.[31]

There is a consensus among historians on the reasons for the exodus, though they might not always agree on the order of importance. The big "pull" factor was the opening of jobs in northern factories during World War I, which the United States entered in 1917. While the number of factory jobs was increasing, the supply of labor was shrinking. The draft removed millions of young men from the workforce at the same time that the war cut off foreign immigration, which dropped from 1.2 million in 1914 to 110,600 in 1918. Consequently, manufacturers in the North and North Central states turned to southern labor, black and white, to fill the gap. For African Americans, whose unemployment rates (previously discussed) were low, it was the higher wages and the certainty of work that attracted.[32]

Among the "pushes" were the serious ups and downs of the cotton economy, on which the southern population totally depended. Cotton was buffeted by a confluence of pressures: dips in crop prices on the international market and the boll weevil infestation that tore through the cotton fields, doing substantial damage in the early 1920s. In subsequent years even more problems arose: massive flooding of the Mississippi River in 1927, and drought at the start of the 1930s. The resulting economic roller-coaster added to the luster of city jobs both in southern and northern urban areas. (It should be kept in mind that African Americans relocated in vast numbers to southern cities too, sometimes heading north after a sojourn in the urban South. Contrary to common assumptions, black migrants were not exclusively farmers; they had urban work experience too.)[33]

What about the South's racial oppression? How significant in pushing African Americans out of Dixie were the "inferior educational opportunities, behavioral restrictions imposed by Jim Crow laws, political disenfranchisement, and racial violence?"[34] Certainly these were part of the causal mix, but historians tend to rank them on the lower end of the scale. After all, the subjugation was worse in the 1890s, when the outward movement of blacks was a mere trickle. And the twentieth-century *white* exodus from the South was far greater than the black, suggesting that racism was a less potent factor in outmigration than one might think.

Unquestionably significant in the exodus was the word-of-mouth effect, which impacted African Americans the way it had earlier affected the European immigrants. Nicholas Lemann, in his aptly titled book *The Promised Land* (apt because it reflected a commonly held black view, though Lemann used the phrase with more than a touch of irony), described the scene in the Mississippi Delta.

There really wasn't any young black person in Clarksdale [Mississippi] who wasn't thinking about Chicago. During the traditional family reunion periods, July Fourth and Christmas time, people who had made the move would come home wearing dressy clothes and driving new cars. The mere sight of a black person, dressed as a businessman, pulling up to his family's sharecropper shack in an automobile—sometimes a Cadillac!—was stunning, a paradigm shift, instant dignity. . . . The land of milk and honey had finally materialized for black folks, after all these hundreds of years in the wilderness.[35]

This was, of course, an exaggeration, akin to the European immigrants thinking wishfully that the streets of America were paved with gold. The point, however, is that word-of-mouth was vital. "The presence of family or friends in the North," sociologist Stewart Tolnay summarized, "improved the flow of information about specific destinations to potential migrants, especially [about] the availability of jobs, and eased their transition upon arrival."[36] Nor were friends and family alone helpful in the transition. Black communities, with their churches, newspapers, and various other social supports, already were established up North, and they too facilitated the relocation.

A final factor was the ease of getting out. Leaving the land was straightforward. Sharecropping contracts were annual and landowners and furnishing merchants commonly wrote off the debts. Travel to the North had become cheap and easy. The interstate highway system was being developed to facilitate America's craving for automobile travel while Ford Motor Company was selling cars for only $300. If the would-be migrant couldn't afford a car there were always the trains. The Illinois Central Railroad provided inexpensive and relatively direct runs to Chicago from Louisiana and Mississippi, while blacks in Georgia and South Carolina could take advantage of the rail lines that ran to Philadelphia and New York. (This last point explains why Chicago's blacks usually hailed from the Delta, whereas African Americans in Philadelphia and New York were more apt to have come from Virginia, the Carolinas, or Georgia.)[37]

How were the migrants received? Not too well. "In virtually all destinations," Tolnay observed, "the southern migrants were greeted with suspicion and hostility by black and white northerners alike." Note especially the reactions of the "old" settlers, the blacks who had been in the city for several decades. They had good relations with whites—"stable equilibrium" sociologists Drake and Cayton called it—and were developing a middle class. They feared—and rightly so—that they would be overwhelmed by the massive influx of ill-educated and unskilled southerners, with their social problems and their violent crime. In fact, before the First World War the old settlers were more antagonistic to the black migrants than were whites, who were still obsessing over foreign immigration.[38]

Once the floodgates opened, however, everything changed. The war made factory owners so desperate for labor that they went south to recruit, sometimes offering free train tickets. Fearing loss of agricultural workers, the southern land-owners tried to discourage the recruitment, but to no avail. On arriving, the impoverished blacks moved into dilapidated housing in the poorest parts of the city, usually near the vice district; often their housing had been abandoned by old settlers who had prospered and moved out. Despite the rundown conditions, rents skyrocketed in response to the steadily increasing demand.

Attempts to move into "white areas" were blocked by legal impediments (such as deeds containing "restrictive covenants" barring sales to nonwhites), and when these seemed inadequate were met with violence. In Chicago, black residences that breached the color boundary and the realtors who helped broker such sales were bombed an average of once every twenty days between 1917 and 1921. None-theless, the borders of the black sections pushed inexorably outward. As old set-tlers fled to contiguous white neighborhoods whites moved out and new black mi-grants replaced them. Thus did the black community expand despite the hostility.

The tensions between old and new blacks and between African Americans and whites were highest in the first few years of the migration surge, but the re-sponses were different depending on the city. In Philadelphia, for example, where there were 40,000 newcomers between 1916 and 1919, and another 85,000 in the 1920s, the "old" African American settlers bitterly resented the new. "The south-ern migrants who flocked to this and other northern cities during the "Great Migration" of the World War I years and after," wrote Roger Lane, "were often in conflict with the so-called 'O.P.s,' or Old Philadelphians, already on the ground." In other cities there were fewer intraracial conflicts and ultimately growth and welcome became the dominant ethos of the black communities. But the influx altered them irrevocably. "The tone and look of every northern black community changed," diaspora historian James N. Gregory noted, "as southerners took over old institutions and built new ones." Soon the black communities reflected a mix of northern and southern ways.[39]

Thus the sprawling, virtually all-black inner cities of the North trace their origin to the Great War and its aftermath. That is when New York's Harlem and Bedford-Stuyvesant (in Brooklyn) were born; Chicago's South Side; and De-troit's Black Bottom. These neighborhoods soon became high-density, low-wage slums, notable for their violent crime. In the boom years of the 1920s, however, things still looked hopeful. A burgeoning black middle class brought new cultural vibrancy to the northern cities. The Harlem Renaissance was an international phenomenon. To the optimists who stressed the black-run enterprises, black churches, and the growing black middle class, African Americans were building the "black metropolis," a self-sustaining community independent of whites. But those who focused on the black lower class, ever-expanding due to the relentless inmigration, saw only high crime and the most profound social deficits. "Largely within the space of a single decade," historian Gilbert Osofsky wrote of New York City in the 1920s, "Harlem was transformed from a potentially ideal community to a neighborhood with manifold social and economic problems."[40]

## BLACK CRIME IN NORTHERN CITIES

I look first at Chicago during the turbulent First World War years. Chicago 1920 was a harbinger of things to come, a foretaste of twentieth-century America's greatest crime problem: indiscriminate urban violence with an undercurrent of racial conflict.

In Chicago during the second decade of the twentieth century crime took a striking turn for the worse. Violent crime—robberies and murders—escalated dramatically. For at least thirty-five years robbery-murders had been uncommon in Windy City, rarely exceeding ten per year. By 1920, however, there were forty such incidents. What's more, the victims of these assaults often were passersby targeted for their money or possessions, not, as in the old days, young saloon toughs asking for trouble. Twenty-nine percent of the perpetrators were African American, even though blacks, despite the steady stream of inmigration, were as yet no more than 3 percent of the city's population.

Numerous victims of the black assaults were white and the black-on-white crimes were "especially gruesome." "Many of the black predators," crime historian Jeffrey Adler found, "used clubs or other blunt instruments and beat to death older, white, neighborhood shopkeepers and pedestrians." The newspapers gave the shocking crimes prominent coverage: "Negro Brutally Murders Prominent Citizen" blared one headline. All of their many racial prejudices reinforced, whites began to lose control. In 1919, with the doughboys returning from war only to find jobs and housing scarce, and with black and white southerners having already migrated to the city in large numbers to fill wartime job vacancies, tensions were running high. Following a racial incident at one of the (segregated) beaches they boiled over. Four horrific days of rioting ensued. Whites were the aggressors but both sides engaged in acts of wanton cruelty. At the end of the disturbances 38 were dead, 23 of whom were black; 520 were injured.[41]

The Chicago riot was not the only violence to greet African American migrants during this period. White worker animosity set off race riots in Philadelphia and Chester, Pennsylvania, and an especially bloody conflict in East St. Louis, Illinois, which resulted in thirty-nine black deaths. These riots, we should point out, were not typical of the racial strife of the second half of the twentieth century. In the World War I incidents whites usually were the aggressors, the races battled one another, and the police often looked the other way or unofficially sided with the whites. In the 1960s and afterward, blacks rampaged, looting and destroying property, while white civilians fled as police and soldiers tried to quell the disturbances.[42]

If the nature of race riots changed, the Chicago crime surge accurately foretold the kind of violent crime that would plague America for much of the century. First of all, the setting was a big metropolitan area, most of which were in the North. This marked a change from the rural southern-based violence that had predominated prior to the 1920s. As we have seen, violent crime continued at elevated levels in the South. But big-city crime became a new point of focus starting in the 1920s and continuing for the rest of the century.

Second, this crime was impersonal and indiscriminate, motivated by material gain, not by personal conflict. This was different from the saloon brawls of the cities in the late nineteenth century or the interpersonal quarrels in the South. It was the kind of crime that made urban dwellers fearful of moving about the city and disrupted everyday activities.

Third, African Americans played an important role in the escalation, creating a racial undertone. In fact, most of the Chicago robber-murderers were white, but the percentage of African American offenders was way out of proportion to the size of the city's black community—ten times as great. Note too that whites had been singled out for attack, not necessarily because of their race, but because they had valuables and were unable to defend themselves. Nonetheless, the fact that the victims often were unoffending whites and the black assailants especially brutal exacerbated already simmering racial tensions. Such crime could raise suspicions that the acts were racially motivated, that is, that blacks were paying whites back for racial oppression, something that they could not do—ironically— in the more repressive South.

Finally, if we look at murders alone, as opposed to robbery-murders, we see another typical characteristic of the violence: three-quarters of the victims of the black perpetrated killings were African American. Intraracial and intraethnic crime was nothing new of course, but the persistently high black-on-black violence would come to be seen as typical of America's big cities, especially as the black migration turned African Americans into an urban population.

We have, due to the painstaking work of the Illinois Crime Survey (an unofficial body established by the city's civic elites), details on every homicide in Cook County for two full years, 1926 and 1927. These were obtained through an examination of the records of the Cook County Coroner, the police, the state's attorney (i.e., the prosecutor), and the courts. Excluding automobile deaths, abortions, and deaths which could have been classified as accidents, there were 1,045 homicides in that two-year period, an average of 523 per year. This translates into an overall homicide rate for Cook County of 13.1 per 100,000. African Americans, who were just under 7 percent of the city's population, were the victims in 71, or 13.6 percent, of these cases, which translates to an elevated rate of 30.4 per 100,000 black Chicagoans.[43]

Looking at murders alone, the Crime Survey offered insights into the race of the killers and the nature of the crimes. Taking males and females together, 181 of the killers (42 percent of all perpetrators) and 184 of the victims (43 percent of all victims) were black. One hundred sixty, or 87 percent, of the black victims were killed by other African Americans.

TABLE 4.12. Murders in Cook County, Illinois, 1926 and 1927, by race and gender of perpetrators and victims

| Victims | Male Perpetrators | | Female Perpetrators | | Total |
|---|---|---|---|---|---|
| | White | Black | White | Black | |
| White male | 136 | 20 | 20 | — | 176 |
| Black male | 20 | 104 | 1 | 17 | 142 |
| White female | 56 | 1 | 15 | — | 72 |
| Black female | 3 | 35 | — | 4 | 42 |
| Total | 215 | 160 | 36 | 21 | 432 |

Source: Lashly, "Homicide (in Cook County)," table 13.

Note: "—" means no data provided.

Police records enabled the Crime Survey to determine the nature of the murders in the largely African American residential areas, the so-called Black Belt of the city. Of 94 Black Belt murders in 1927:

- 54 (57.5 percent) were the result of altercations or brawls
- 14 (14.9 percent) involved robbery
- 7 (7.5 percent) involved domestic violence
- 7 (7.5 percent) were cases of jealousy not involving a spouse
- 6 (6.4 percent) involved revenge between acquintances
- 5 (5.3 percent) were for unknown motives
- 1 was a gang murder

Especially noteworthy are the high number of killings arising out of personal disputes, very much like the black violence in the South. What appears to be new (though we lack good comparative data here) is the incidence of robbery-murder, which was 15 percent of the total.

A breakdown of murders by police precincts ("police districts" in Chicago) also is revealing. The Crime Survey provided descriptions of the ethnic/racial backgrounds of Chicago's police districts along with the number and types of murders. A sample of districts of roughly comparable population size is reprinted below. The Third District, which was in the Black Belt, had a murder rate of 35.4. Ten of the city's thirty-four holdup murders (29 percent) occurred there.

TABLE 4.13. Murders in four Chicago police districts, 1927

| District | Population | Race/Ethnicity | Murders |
|---|---|---|---|
| 3 | 130,013 | Black | 46 |
| 13 | 130,671 | East European | 6 |
| 18 | 135,621 | E. Eur.; Jewish | 7 |
| 33 | 128,945 | Native white | 3 |

*Source:* Lashly, "Homicide (in Cook County)," table 10.

Though the ethnic/racial descriptions of the police districts are imprecise, and we do not know the socioeconomic status of these neighborhoods, the crime figures are accurate and the implication that violence was disproportionately high in the African American areas was undoubtedly correct.[44]

## 1920s MORTALITY RATES

In virtually every city to which they migrated African Americans committed an inordinate number of murders and other violent crimes, in the main victimizing other blacks. A history of the black ghetto in Cleveland, for instance, offers this account of crime during the peak migration.

> Crime had always plagued the Central Avenue area, but between World War I and the depression reports of fist fights, shootings, and robberies in that section of the city became almost a daily occurrence. At the peak of the Great Migration the city Welfare Department reported a sharp increase in the number of black prisoners committed to the county workhouse. Undoubtedly, the number of serious crimes (the workhouse was designed for lower-level offenders) occurring in the black community also rose in the wake of the migration. No statistics are available for earlier years, but in 1930 the Negro homicide rate in the city was many times that of the white rate.[45]

In fact, mortality homicide statistics are available for several states and cities, including Cleveland, and all point toward extraordinarily high black violent crime during the 1920s. And unlike the data from the police and courts, the mortality data are virtually untainted by race bias. The rates presented below are homicide victimizations per 100,000, and if Chicago was typical, between eight and nine out of every ten of these killings was black-perpetrated.

Criminologist H. C. Brearley collected homicide mortality data for states and cities, combining results for 1920 and 1925. Table 4.14 shows the homicide rates for urban areas in the northeastern and north central states, the principal destinations of the black migrants; southern and western states were omitted. The main caveat is that African Americans were considered part of a broader category called "colored," which also included Chinese, Japanese, and American Indians. These last-named groups, however, were, compared with African Americans, insignificant in population for the states on this list.[46]

TABLE 4.14. Homicide rates per 100,000 in urban areas of selected northern states, by race, 1920 and 1925 combined

| State | White Rate | "Colored" Rate | C/W Ratio |
|---|---|---|---|
| Connecticut | 4.0 | 15.6 | 4: 1 |
| Illinois | 9.1 | 76.2 | 8: 1 |
| Indiana | 6.2 | 72.6 | 12: 1 |
| Iowa* | 4.4 | 61.2 | 14: 1 |
| Kansas | 7.8 | 51.9 | 7: 1 |
| Massachusetts | 2.5 | 12.3 | 5: 1 |
| Michigan | 7.3 | 99.8 | 14: 1 |
| Minnesota | 5.3 | 69.6 | 13: 1 |
| Nebraska | 8.0 | 69.0 | 9: 1 |
| New Jersey | 4.4 | 24.1 | 6: 1 |
| New York | 5.0 | 30.9 | 6: 1 |
| Ohio | 7.3 | 81.8 | 11: 1 |
| Pennsylvania | 5.3 | 47.1 | 9: 1 |
| Wisconsin | 2.8 | 87.8 | 31: 1 |

Source: Brearley, Homicide, 99.

Note: Iowa data for 1925 only. C/W (Colored to White) ratios are rounded.

As is readily apparent, the ratios of black-to-white homicide rates were enormous, ranging from four times as great in Connecticut to a staggering thirty-one-fold spread in Wisconsin. While the African American rates were all exceptionally high compared with whites, the differences among blacks from state to state also were significant. There doesn't seem to be any explanation for these differences, however, and no pattern, such as in the relationship between white and black rates, presents itself. For instance, while black rates were relatively low in Massachusetts and Connecticut, states in which white rates were likewise low, they were high in Wisconsin, a state that also had low white rates.

Brearley also provided (again based on federal mortality data) homicide rates for cities in 1925. Table 4.15 presents rates for selected cities in the northeastern and north central regions.[47]

TABLE 4.15. Homicide rates per 100,000 in selected northern cities, by race, 1925

| City | White Rate | "Colored" Rate |
|---|---|---|
| Boston | 2.8 | 21.4 |
| Cairo, IL | 46.3 | 20.8 |
| Chicago | 10.8 | 102.8 |
| Cincinnati | 7.0 | 189.7 |
| Cleveland | 8.9 | 101.2 |
| Columbus, OH | 5.2 | 24.8 |
| Detroit | 12.6 | 113.7 |
| E. St. Louis, IL | 17.4 | 228.9 |
| Indianapolis | 6.0 | 56.7 |
| Kansas City, KS | 11.4 | 87.6 |
| Leavenworth, KS | 16.9 | 31.4 |
| Newark, NJ | 4.9 | 36.2 |
| Philadelphia | 4.6 | 61.2 |
| Pittsburgh | 7.2 | 54.8 |
| Springfield, OH | 5.0 | 36.6 |

*Source:* Brearley, *Homicide*, 218–19.

TABLE 4.16. Annual conviction rates per 100,000 for murder and non-negligent manslaughter, male defendants, by race, Detroit, Michigan, 1926–1929

| Year | Murder 1° White | Murder 1° Black | Murder 2° White | Murder 2° Black | Manslaughter White | Manslaughter Black |
|---|---|---|---|---|---|---|
| 1926 | 2.0 | 29.3 | 1.4 | 31.3 | 2.4 | 43.9 |
| 1927 | 0.7 | 19.3 | 0.4 | 19.3 | 1.2 | 25.1 |
| 1928 | 2.0 | 21.5 | 0.3 | 12.6 | 2.3 | 19.7 |
| 1929 | 2.4 | 16.8 | 1.4 | 16.8 | 1.5 | 31.8 |

*Source:* Boudouris, "Trends in Homicide," table 22.

Once again, the African American rates were shockingly high, way beyond the figures for whites, except noticeably in Cairo, Illinois, for reasons that are not apparent.[48] As for the mind-boggling black rates in East St. Louis—229 per 100,000—the terrible race riot in that city eight years earlier may somehow account for the subsequent crime wave, but it is not clear how.

With regard to particular cities we have some interesting figures on murder and manslaughter convictions in Detroit during the late 1920s. They also show a huge gap between whites and blacks.

Data based on convictions naturally raise concerns about bias, either by courts or by police. With respect to the courts, comparable acquittal rates for the races diminish these concerns. In Detroit, the acquittal rates were as shown in table 4.17.

TABLE 4.17. Percent of male defendants acquitted of criminal homicides, by race, Detroit, Michigan, 1926–1929

|  | White | Black |
| --- | --- | --- |
| 1926 | 47.8 | 31.5 |
| 1927 | 42.2 | 37.7 |
| 1928 | 36.0 | 37.1 |
| 1929 | 27.6 | 36.9 |

*Source:* Boudouris, "Trends in Homicide," table 22.

The results are mixed, with white acquittals significantly greater in 1926, less so in 1927, but with black exonerations exceeding those of whites in the last two years. Given the difficulty of convicting whites involved in bootlegger gang killings, the high white acquittal rates in 1926 and 1927 may not be surprising. If this expains the racial gap then, of course, race prejudice is not the issue. But even if gang killer acquittals do not account for the race gap there is insufficient evidence here to conclude that the Detroit courts were biased.[49]

Detroit also reaffirms the intraracial nature of murder. When the figures for all years are combined we find that 97.8 percent of the killers were black when the victims were of the same race. Likewise, with white victims, 92.6 percent of the perpetrators were white. Notice that whereas the killers overwhelmingly were the same color as the victims, blacks killed more whites than vice versa. This pattern would persist throughout the North for decades.

TABLE 4.18. Interracial and intraracial homicides, Detroit, Michigan, 1926–1929

|  | White on White | White on Black | Black on Black | Black on White |
|---|---|---|---|---|
| 1926 | 90 | 2 | 111 | 11 |
| 1927 | 58 | 4 | 74 | 7 |
| 1928 | 73 | 1 | 76 | 1 |
| 1929 | 68 | 1 | 92 | 4 |
| Totals: | 289 | 8 | 353 | 23 |
| % White victim cases | 92.6 | — | — | 7.4 |
| % Black victim cases | — | 2.2 | 97.8 | — |

Source: Boudouris, "Trends in Homicide," table 15.

Note: Accused listed first, victim second, e.g., "White on Black" means white killer, black victim. Figures extrapolated from Boudouris, table 15, which expresses each paired killing as a percentage of the annual homicides.

With respect to same-race killings it is worthwhile comparing Detroit with a southern city such as Memphis, statistics for which were examined earlier. For Memphis, 1920–25, 14 percent of those arraigned for killing whites were black; 86 percent were white. Where blacks were the victims, 19 percent of the accused were white; 81 percent were black. Memphis, in short, had many more interracial murders than Detroit. Moreover, a considerably higher proportion of white-kills-black offenses occurred in the southern city: 19 percent versus a mere 2 percent in Detroit. Based on this concededly tiny sample, it may be that there was more racial interaction in the urban South than in the metropolitan North. It also seems to be the case that African Americans in the North felt freer to kill whites, while whites down South felt less inhibited about murdering blacks.[50]

## EXPLAINING NORTHERN BLACK VIOLENCE

How can such extraordinarily high black homicide rates in the North be explained? It is difficult to point the finger at straitened economic circumstances or other social adversities. Nationwide, as discussed earlier, black unemployment was low, perhaps lower than white (although reliable unemployment data for the

1920s is hard to come by). If Chicago is any indicator, the black communities of the North were brimming with optimism. The years 1924 to 1929 were, in Drake and Cayton's phrase, Fat Years, "no doubt the most prosperous ones the Negro community in Chicago had ever experienced." Yet the black homicide victimization rate in 1925 Chicago was a stunning 103 per 100,000, more than nine times the white rate. And this was a time when the bootlegger wars were raging, bumping up the white murder count. Of course, the migration of poor blacks from the South continued at a torrid pace throughout the 1920s, making housing and living conditions in the black communities of the North a real problem. But all in all conditions must not have been worse than they had been in Dixie because relatively few African Americans went back. Moreover, it is unlikely that the black neighborhoods of the 1920s were any more rundown than the Polish or Jewish slums of the two preceding decades, where violent crime was conspicuously lower.[51]

A comparison of northern and southern homicide rates for African Americans indicates that, on average, blacks were considerably more homicidal in the northern states. If economic and social opportunity are the crucial causal factors for violent crime, then such a result is difficult to fathom. The North, despite black hopes and dreams, was no Promised Land. But it was a far cry from the utter despair of the southern caste system. If anything, black crime should have declined outside of Dixie. Indeed, if we compare only big cities, black violence does seem to be somewhat greater in the South—or so our nonsystematic sample indicates. But ultimately this regional comparison is beside the point, since black violence was shockingly high everywhere, from northern cities to southern towns.

TABLE 4.19. Homicide rates per 100,000 of African Americans in southern and northern states, 1925

| Southern States | | Northern States | |
|---|---|---|---|
| Alabama | 34.4 | Connecticut | 19.0 |
| Florida | 79.6 | Illinois | 93.3 |
| Kentucky | 67.6 | Indiana | 83.8 |
| Louisiana | 45.3 | Massachusetts | 19.0 |
| Mississippi | 32.6 | Michigan | 101.5 |

TABLE 4.10 *(continued)*

| Southern States | | Northern States | |
|---|---|---|---|
| North Carolina | 20.5 | Minnesota | 50.5 |
| South Carolina | 16.3 | Nebraska | 69.3 |
| Tennessee | 55.4 | New Jersey | 25.3 |
| Virginia | 20.1 | New York | 36.2 |
| | | Ohio | 86.9 |
| | | Pennsylvania | 55.5 |
| | | Wisconsin | 36.4 |
| Average | 41.3 | | 56.4 |

*Source:* Bureau of the Census, *Mortality Statistics 1925,* tables I A, 5.

TABLE 4.20. Homicide rates per 100,000 of African Americans in selected southern and northern cities, 1925

| Southern Cities | | Northern Cities | |
|---|---|---|---|
| Atlanta* | 100.7 | Boston | 21.4 |
| Baltimore | 39.3 | Chicago | 102.8 |
| Birmingham | 114.8 | Cincinnati | 189.7 |
| Charleston, SC | 18.1 | Cleveland | 101.2 |
| Houston* | 43.2 | Columbus, OH | 24.8 |
| Jacksonville, FL | 115.2 | Detroit | 113.7 |
| Louisville | 108.5 | Indianapolis | 56.7 |
| Memphis | 124.8 | Kansas City, KS | 87.6 |
| New Orleans | 111.7 | Newark, NJ | 36.2 |
| Richmond, VA | 38.4 | Manhattan (NYC) | 55.6 |
| Washington, DC | 38.1 | Philadelphia | 61.2 |
| | | Pittsburgh | 54.8 |
| | | Springfield, OH | 36.6 |
| Average | 77.5 | | 72.5 |

*Source:* Bureau of the Census, *Mortality Statistics 1925,* tables I A, 5.

*Note:* Atlanta and Houston populations are averages of 1920 and 1930 census figures.

The most obvious explanation for the high violent crime by black migrants is that it simply was a continuation of behaviors that had been occurring in the South. Or, to put the same thing differently: the roots of northern black violence may be found below the Mason-Dixon line. There was, however, one very significant change in the nature, as opposed to the magnitude, of African American crime in the North. Black indiscriminate crime for monetary gain and black crime against whites (often the same thing) were more frequent in the North. There are two reasons for this. First, predatory crime generally was more common in the urbanized North, where there were more opportunities to rob and steal. There were, to put it simply, more people more densely packed together with more portable valuables (such as cash and jewelry) and greater, metro-wide mobility. In short, there were, in the metropolitan areas to which blacks migrated, lots of tempting targets. Second, an assault on whites was far less risky outside of Dixie, where black-on-white aggression might be answered by a lynch mob. In the North, where race riots in which whites attacked blacks declined sharply after 1921, violent black lawbreakers may have been emboldened.

If, as I assert, African Americans transported a culture of violence to the North, then they were in this regard no different from those immigrant groups whose violence at their point of origin persisted at their destination. The Italians provide a suitable comparison (discussed in detail in chapter 8). They too were impoverished agricultural laborers in a socially isolated region. Their culture of honor gave them some of the highest violent crime rates on the Continent. Fleeing primarily out of economic desperation, they settled in slum housing on arrival in America, became low-status manual laborers, and continued their violent ways. Despite their encounters with bigotry and an initial failure to make the educational gains that enabled advancement, the Italians eventually rose to the middle class and abandoned violent crime. All of the preceding is likewise true of African Americans, except (so far) the happy ending. But the rise of African Americans to the middle class is presently well under way, and in the post–civil rights era is now virtually assured.

# FEEBLE JUSTICE

# 5

# The Wild West

The violence of the nineteenth-century West is the stuff of legend: Wyatt Earp, Billy the Kid, the Sundance Kid, American Indian wars, cowtown shootouts, and so on. But by the end of the century the West had by and large been pacified. Most of the violence and turmoil lasted for three decades, from the 1850s to the end of the 1870s. Around the 1880s and 1890s, however, the turbulence had pretty much abated. The Mexicans and indigenous peoples were defeated. The West was settled and occupied, carved into states plus two territories that soon would be. The lesser conflicts, between cattlemen and sheepmen, and between ranchers and farmers, had wound down. The remaining big social conflict was between labor and management, which in the West, meant mine owners and miners. Labor disputes, sometimes quite violent, persisted right into the twentieth century.

A major issue in discussing nineteenth-century crime is differentiating crime from broad social conflict. This is the first topic considered in this chapter. The other focal points are:

- types of crime in the Old West
- "honor" and the Code of the West
- cowtowns and boomtowns
- lynching
- labor conflict
- race/ethnicity and crime

## TYPES OF CRIME

Western crime fell into three categories. There was "ordinary" crime for mercenary purposes. Of this, there was surprisingly little. Armed robbery of individuals purely for their money and valuables was unusual. Theft of horses and cattle was the predominant Western offense in the crime-for-profit category. But this was crime by stealth, not violence.

The sensational train and stagecoach robberies—immortalized by cinema and television westerns—were relatively rare, flourishing mainly in the post–Civil War turmoil on the Kansas-Missouri border. Despite hundreds of trains and stage coaches traveling through the West during the decades after 1848, there were relatively few robberies or killings of drivers or passengers.[1]

The public seems to have had mixed views about these robberies, seeing them, at least in part, as economic protest against the big-money capitalists—the banks, railroads, and mine owners. The typical western farmer, who blamed the railroads and banks for exorbitant shipping rates and economic recessions, probably let out a secret cheer when these "trusts" and monopolies were hit. The robbers took advantage of this sentiment, portraying themselves as Robin Hoods who robbed from the rich—though they never gave anything to the poor. Jesse and Frank James, who headed a gang of successful robbers operating from the mid-1860s to the early 1880s, publicly proclaimed contempt for their monied victims. This undoubtedly was a ploy, but it worked. A jury of farmers acquitted Frank James despite abundant evidence of guilt.[2] The capitalists fought back, however. They retained private Pinkerton guards who firebombed the James's family home and helped break up the gang.[3]

The Jameses joined forces with the Younger brothers in the 1870s, together engaging in a string of bank, stagecoach, and train robberies. But they seldom robbed passengers, which contributed to their Robin Hood image. In 1882, Jesse was assassinated by a fellow gangster-turned-informant. The killer was indicted, convicted (by plea), sentenced to hang, and pardoned by the governor of Missouri—all in the same day.

The Jameses were succeeded by Belle Starr's gang (1880s) and the Dalton Brothers in the 1890s.[4] In the final decade of the 1800s, only certain chaotic locales, such as Oklahoma (former Native American terrritory, just opened to whites) and Texas remained gang-infested, though outlaw gangs continued to operate in Missouri, Kansas, Oklahoma, and Arkansas right into the first decades of the twentieth century.

The main points to be taken with respect to these crimes is that they were localized, not common throughout the West, and that they were a product of the turmoil and turbulence of these unsettled and under-governed areas. Furthermore, by targeting unpopular institutions and sparing ordinary citizens, the gangs posed little threat to the man on the street, who was more sympathetic to the criminals than to their victims. Finally, despite their social protest aura, these gangs were in fact motivated by plain old greed. They robbed banks, railroads, and coaches because, as Willie Sutton famously explained a half-century later, that's where the money was.

Historian of the West Richard White suggests that one must differentiate between "personal violence and crime on the one hand and large-scale social conflicts on the other."[5] He makes a good point, as extensive social conflicts, such as riots or a protracted series of violent clashes, like the American Indian wars, do not really fit within the ordinary definition of crime. But some of the personal crime in the West was driven, at least in part, by social conflict, such as between whites and Chinese, or between cattle ranchers and sheepherders. So the line between the categories is somewhat blurred.

Consider, for example, the indigenous raids on white ranches and the white raids on Native American villages. In California, in the rather brutal 1850s and 1860s, white gangs raided indigenous villages, kidnapped Native children, whom they later put to work, and killed their parents.[6] Crime? Unquestionably, and shocking crime at that. But these raids didn't happen in a vacuum. Indigenous peoples were conducting raids of their own, attacking white cattle ranches and killing the cattle grazing on Native lands.[7] They saw, and rightly so, that whites were a threat to the entire Native American way of life. And after the white marauders attacked their villages, the Natives retaliated, followed by tit-for-tat atrocities on both sides. In other words, these outrageous crimes can only be understood as part of the bigger conflict between whites and indigenous peoples. So our second crime category may be labeled "crime motivated by larger social conflict," with the caveat that differentiating the mercenary from the social may be difficult, and at times, impossible.

The third type of crime common to the nineteenth-century West was the kind of conflict associated with male ego and personal honor, inflamed by alcohol and made deadlier by the ever-present firearm. We saw these kinds of offenses in the South especially, but in truth, as Richard Maxwell Brown, an expert on Western violence, observed, all of nineteenth-century America "was obsessed by masculine honor—North, South, East, and West."[8]

Although two-man duels of the formal and informal variety are typical of this crime category, one must extend its boundaries to family and clan feuds, such as the Tonto Basin War (1887–88). This Arizona imbroglio, a stew of social, political, and even religious conflict, began as simple bad blood between the Tewksbury and Graham clans. By the time the vendetta ended, three Graham and three Tewksbury brothers were dead, joined by anywhere from twenty to fifty others depending on the method of counting.[9]

The obsession with masculine honor was made manifest by the so-called Code of the West: no duty to retreat; the imperative of personal self-redress; and "an ultrahigh value on courage."[10] The first of the code's guiding principles—no duty to retreat—refers to a legal doctrine used in self-defense cases, one which is still significant in American criminal law.[11] Repudiation of the so-called retreat rule helped rationalize the acquittals on grounds of self-defense that were common-place in nineteenth-century murder cases.

The gist of the rule is that the defender, on trial for having slain his assailant, forfeits his right of self-defense if, at the time of the confrontation, he knew that he could safely withdraw and avoid the deadly conflict. The rule puts a premium on averting violence, to the point where the victim of the assault will be guilty of murder or manslaughter simply for failing to back off. Such a rule, as would be expected, was repudiated in the West where "real men don't retreat." But even Justice Oliver Wendell Holmes, an Easterner through and through, famously observed: "Detached reflection cannot be demanded in the presence of an uplifted knife. Therefore in this Court, at least, it is not a condition of immunity that one in that situation should pause to consider whether a reasonable man might not think it possible to fly with safety or to disable his assailant rather than to kill him."[12]

Even if one rejects the Code of the West, the retreat rule is not without difficulty. Why should a defender against unlawful attack be punished for exercising his right of self-defense rather than withdrawing? Such a requirement penalizes the party in the right while emboldening aggressors. After all, the one attacked is the party aggrieved. On the other hand, where life itself is at stake, it seems reasonable to demand that armed men back off, when they can safely do so, rather than kill.

Whatever we may think today, the retreat requirement clearly was not aligned with standards of reasonable conduct in nineteenth-century America. In truth though, juries probably would have acquitted accused killers even if the retreat rule had been adopted. These cases, with two armed young men quarreling over some matter whose significance was blown out of all proportion by drink, were hard to sort out. Only one of the combatants was alive to testify, witnesses were scarce, forensic evidence nonexistent. Who could tell which had been the aggressor, which the defender? The public, speaking through juries, probably thought the defendant luckier, or perhaps a better shot, but no more or less blameworthy than the deceased. And, as I've frequently noted, neither the acts nor the actors posed a threat to ordinary law-abiding citizens. Had the jury been instructed by the judge to convict if they found that the defendant could have safely retreated it is unlikely that they would have done so. And, under double jeopardy rules, the jury's decision would have been final, as acquittals in American law may not be appealed.

## COWTOWNS AND BOOMTOWNS

As suggested earlier, the West, insofar as ordinary crime is concerned, was not dangerous for the common man. The most violent places were the cattle and mining towns, the dominion of the young, single, and not infrequently, drunken male. At least as early as 1842, when the Belgian sociologist Adolphe Quetelet wrote his classic treatise on crime, criminologists have noted the correlation between young men and lawbreaking.[13] And because mining and herding cattle were rough and dirty jobs they were decidedly young men's activities. With few "decent" women or social institutions in the cattle and mining towns to domesticate them, these hard-drinking, gun-toting males produced legendary violence.

The cattle towns—places like Abilene and Dodge City, Kansas, and Cheyenne, Wyoming—were, in the mid-nineteenth century, the southernmost terminals for the rail lines, and therefore the destinations for the massive annual cattle drives that brought the herds from Texas and Wyoming to market. Once driven north, the steers were loaded onto trains in the cowtowns and transported to the newly established meat-packing plants in St. Louis, Omaha, Kansas City, and Chicago. There the meat was processed and, with the advent of refrigerated railroad cars, shipped east. Every year after the Civil War, cowboys, many of whom were Confederate army veterans or Mexican vaqueros, herded thousands of head north, along trails like the Chisholm and the Pecos, grazing the cows on the abundant public grasslands. And each summer, dirty and travel-weary cowpunchers would descend on places like Abilene and Dodge, starving for rest and relaxation, liquor, sex, and entertainment.[14]

As with our modern-day college "spring break" destinations, there was more boisterousness and rowdyism than true crime. Job Number One for law enforcement was controlling and disciplining the inebriated. And also as in the modern day, the host towns were ambivalent about the transients, eager to make money off them, but anxious about the disorder. The merchants hired gunmen like the legendary Wyatt Earp and Wild Bill Hickok to restrain the roughnecks. They even enacted gun-control ordinances, apparently effective.[15] Wichita, for example, outlawed the carrying of handguns within the city limits. However, the punishments for those arrested were lenient, as the towns didn't want to drive business away altogether. In an age when the death penalty was much more common than in recent decades, only three capital sentences were imposed on cowtown killers—and all three were commuted.[16]

The cattle trade offered a financial incentive to crime. Without an effective banking system the livestock had to be paid for in cash, and there was enough currency floating around to attract an influx of outlaws and hoodlums. Some say that there were a lot of holdups in the cattle towns, but statistical data on this are hard to come by.[17]

The background of the cowboys was another factor in cowtown violence. A significant number were ex-Confederate soldiers, men who were armed, angry, and especially hostile toward blacks and Mexicans. "The Civil War and Reconstruction," said historian Randolph Roth, "left them bitter and alienated."[18]

Historians are at odds over the seriousness of the cowtown homicides. One leading expert, Robert Dykstra, pointed out that the sum total of all cattle town killings over a fifteen-year period, 1870–1885, was forty-five. And Dodge City, the most violent of the cattle communities, still averaged only 1.5 homicides per cattle-trading year. But Roth pointed out that the homicide rates in five major Kansas cowtowns were a whopping 60 per 100,000 a year in the 1870s—and that was a big decline from the period when there were no police or weapons ordinances. He concluded that the towns in Dykstra's study "had exceptionally high homicide rates."[19]

By the 1890s, the cattle drives were over and the cowtowns settled into the bourgeois tranquility of homes, families, schools, and churches. The trails had become nearly impassable, fenced by settlers using newly invented cheap barbed wire, or criss-crossed by recently laid railroad lines. Indeed, the extension of the rail lines to the south helped make the cattle drives obsolete. One of the final blows was the especially brutal winter of 1886–87, which caused the death of thousands of cattle on one of the last big drives.

The mining towns were more violent than the cattle towns, one reason being that mining went on all year round, not just seasonally. Many mining towns, established in the gold and silver rushes of the postbellum decades, went bust, usually after a few boom years followed by a depletion of their precious minerals. Famous examples are Aurora, Nevada, and Bodie, California, both of which, fortunately, have received, insofar as their crime activity is concerned, excellent scholarly treatment from Roger D. McGrath.[20]

Aurora had its boom in the 1860s; Bodie in the late 1870s, early 1880s. As McGrath summarized: "They had widespread reputations for violence, boasted populations of more than five thousand, and produced gold and silver bullion worth a billion dollars in today's money."[21] These early mining sites, more camps than towns, while not necessarily representative of the mining and mill towns of the 1890s, are worth discussing because of what they reveal about violent crime in the nineteenth century.

First, as to homicide, twenty-nine of Bodie's killings, 1878–82, were probably murder or manslaughter (as opposed to accident or justifiable homicide), which makes for a pretty scary rate of 116 per 100,000. Aurora's sixteen murder/manslaughters, 1861–65, gave it a rate of 64. Eastern cities of the day had much lower homicide rates (e.g., Boston's was 3.8 between 1880 and 1882), and cowtowns like Dodge City had rates of 50 per 100,000, which was 43 percent of Bodie's. In other words, the Northeast was far less homicidal than the West, and the mining towns more dangerous than the cattle towns.[22]

One must be cautious about crime rates where small populations are concerned. Rates are calculated by dividing the number of crimes by the size of the population, and where the population is very low even a small number of crimes will produce a high rate. A high rate, in other words, may be an artifact of the statistics. Nonetheless, twenty-nine murders in five years in a town of only five thousand—Bodie's numbers—is a lot of killing.

So why were the townsfolk not terribly exercised about all the mayhem? McGrath's answer is significant because it is applicable to a great deal of the criminal homicide of the nineteenth century.

Aurorans and Bodieites accepted the killings because those killed, with only a few exceptions, had been willing combatants. They had chosen to fight. Commenting on killings in Bodie the *Daily Free Press* said on January 7, 1880: "There has never yet been an instance of the intentional killing of a man whose taking off was not a verification of the proverb that 'He that liveth by the sword shall perish by the sword.'" The old, the weak, the female, and those unwilling to fight were almost never the object of an attack.[23]

Thus, mining town murder was born of personal quarrels, intensified by spirits and machismo. The general public, except in a few cases (see below for vigilantism) shrugged off this behavior.

What about other crimes, for example, robbery, theft, and burglary? According to McGrath, there were, in Bodie, during the five-year interval he studied, only twenty-one robberies and three attempted robberies, for a robbery rate of 84 per 100,000. Boston's rate, 1880–82, was 23. Eleven of the twenty-one robberies were of stagecoaches, which sometimes carried bullion worth millions of dollars. Actually, the bullion stages out of Bodie, guarded by two or three riflemen, never were robbed, and the regular coaches, while occasionally forced to surrender their strong boxes, rarely experienced assaults on their passengers.[24]

And individuals? McGrath insists that they were "very rarely" victimized. Those who were probably had been drinking, flashing a lot of cash, and staggering home from a saloon or brothel late at night. The sober citizen, armed and ready to fight, made for a much riskier target. As for female victims, while some suspect that sex workers may not have fared so well at the hands of these short-tempered males, there were no reported rapes in Aurora or Bodie, and "respectable" women seldom were victimized.[25]

With respect to burglary, Bodie's rate (1877–83) was 128 to Boston's 87. The theft rate was 180, while Boston's was a much higher 575. McGrath uncovered only forty-five incidents of larceny in Bodie, mainly of some firewood and blankets. There were few horse thieves or cattle rustlers, crimes taken so seriously in the West that perpetrators faced the gallows.[26] Of course, these thefts are not violent crimes and shouldn't inform our assessment of violence in the West.

The conclusion is that the nineteenth-century mining towns were far more violent than the big cities of the East, even than the cattle towns of the West, but certainly less crime-filled than our own day. Aurora and Bodie, McGrath concludes, "were remarkably free from most crime: robbery, theft, and burglary occurred infrequently and bank robbery, rape, racial violence, and serious juvenile crime not at all."[27]

As for the excessive number of murders, the causes were fourfold. First, these towns were male enclaves; females were outnumbered ten to one. Second, the population was disproportionately transient, coming and going with the opportunities for financial gain. Transients are more disposed to crime as they tend to be anonymous and indifferent to the norms of the community. Third, the population was diverse—Bodie's was roughly half foreign-born—and ethnic hostility makes for more interpersonal conflict. Fourth, guns and liquor were ubiquitous. Handguns were cheap; one could buy them through the Sears Catalogue for less than two dollars. And finally, the culture of rugged individualism, sensitivity to sleights, and don't-tread-on-me made for a combat-ready environment.

## LYNCHING

The western public did not have much confidence in the ability of the official justice system to administer justice. In the mining camps and throughout the West, vigilance committees (sometimes called "Regulators") were formed to impose extralegal, but not necessarily unmerited, punishment. The typical vigilance committee had 100–300 members. It would capture suspected criminals, try them, and hang them. Sometimes the capturing and the lynching were carried out by posses, deputized and organized by the town lawman. The line between lawful posses, however, and some extralegal squad of self-appointed law enforcers was not always clear. And while a posse has the authority to arrest, obviously it has no legal warrant to impose punishment (though they could lawfully kill a suspect who was physically resisting arrest).

The average citizen's perception, not unlike that in our own day, was that the courts were too slow, hamstrung by procedural requirements, too lenient, and too costly. In Bodie, for instance, around forty men were arrested for murder, of which only seven were tried. And of the seven put to trial, six were acquitted, usually—as one might expect—on grounds of self-defense.[28] This was an acceptable outcome for one of those willing combatant situations so typical of the day and time. But what if the killing were just a plain cold-blooded murder, unusual but not unheard of? Or suppose the victim were not some young tough, but rather, a (respectable) woman, a child, or some nonaggressive man?

In Bodie, the "601," as the vigilance committee was named, would take care of the matter, as it did in the case of one cold-blooded killing described by McGrath. In this case, the murder victim was shot in the back of the head by his wife's secret lover, one John DeRoach, as the two men met, at the behest of the killer, to talk over the matter. The 601 debated the suspect's fate while the legitimate court began to take testimony. Having decided that the law courts were too unpredictable, too lenient, or too slow, hundreds of armed vigilantes intimidated the sheriff into releasing DeRoach, who was taken to the scene of the murder and hanged.[29]

The lynch mob is so offensive to modern sensibilities that it is hard to imagine any persuasive justification for vigilantism. The modern American is convinced, and rightly so, that due process is a requisite of justice. The nineteenth-century American, especially the westerner, was equally convinced that a just outcome occasionally required departures from established process. The citizen of the Old West had a point.

The nineteenth-century West was an undeveloped region; its justice systems were primitive, often unable to cope with the lawless behavior. The lure of instant riches through mineral strikes and the open and frequent conveying of precious metals and cash made the West a magnet for aggressive young men, some of whom were intent on, if not practiced in, lawbreaking. The territory was immense, perfect for outlaws to go into hiding, and law enforcement agents were few and far between. The jurisdiction of the town marshals was strictly local, county sheriffs had to cover a vast expanse on horseback, and there were no statewide law agents to fill the jurisdictional gaps. Juries were unreliable, sometimes engaging in "nullification" (acquitting despite strong evidence of guilt) on behalf of some sympathetic defendant. Moreover, the murder cases often were difficult to adjudicate, as self-defense claims were plausible given the typical willing combatant scenario and the lack of testimony by one of the participants. Another source of uncertainty with the trial system was the high number of transients; a delay in a case could mean the loss of key witnesses. Last, and perhaps not least, was the problem of corruption. Bancroft's classic study, published back in 1887, insisted that in 1851 San Francisco, "money, if not directly, then indirectly, would buy acquittal or pardon."[30]

The data on jury trial outcomes, though spotty, support the average westerner's skepticism about the ability of the lawful justice system to do the job. Below are some largely nineteenth-century conviction rates for a sampling of western jurisdictions.

- Arizona, all serious crimes: 58 percent[31]
- Colorado, Las Animas County, homicide defendants: 30 percent for accused Anglos, 31 percent for Hispanics[32]
- California, homicide defendants: 43 percent for whites[33]

To appreciate how low these conviction ratios are, consider as a basis for comparison that in 2009, 66 percent of adjudicated defendants in the most populous U.S. counties were found guilty.[34]

Richard Maxwell Brown, in his seminal study, differentiated the "socially constructive" committee of vigilance from the "ephemeral" spur-of-the-moment mob. The well-run committees were directed by the local elite, the leading businessmen, and supported by the bulk of the citizenry. They were well-organized, with officers and a hierarchy; they even conducted trials, albeit illegal trials. And once opposition mounted—a growing body of westerners considered lynching offensive—they disbanded, usually after a few months. The paradigm was the San Francisco Vigilance Committees of the 1850s, much copied in California and throughout the West.[35]

On the other hand, western lynching wasn't entirely benign. Most of it consisted of private bands of relatives and friends of murder victims impatient with lawful processes. It has been estimated that three-quarters of the lynchings in California were by these private vengeance seekers, as opposed to established and publicly operating vigilance committees.[36]

Every western state, save Oregon and Utah, had significant vigilantism.[37] Peak activity was in the rough period from the 1830s through the 1860s. Though the pace of lynching slowed after the 1860s, Brown counted at least 210 vigilante movements in the West between 1849 and 1902, the greatest number occurring in violence-torn central Texas. Brown also tallied 729 known deaths nationwide at the hands of lynchers, more than 70 percent of them in the western region.

By the 1890s lynching had sharply declined in the West. Colorado, for example, had 50–60 lynchings per decade in the 1860s–1880s, but only ten in the 1890s.[38] Some of the other states took a bit longer, but within a decade of the new century, the practice had become infrequent.[39] Certainly a decline in crime had a lot to do with this. The wild days of the mid-1800s, with their boomtowns and influxes of aggressive males, were over. Mill towns and the more permanent mining towns, the scene of violent labor conflicts (discussed below), were the new source of turmoil, but these were, as one historian put it, "enclaves of violence."[40] Most of the West was pacified, dominated by families, churches, schools, and stable, organized governance. To offer but one example, by 1895, homicide rates in Oregon were half of what they had been in the 1850s and 1860s.[41] Even more dramatically, San Francisco rates between 1850–54 and 1890–94 dropped 80 percent.[42]

In addition to reductions in crime, the end of the century brought a more efficient and effective criminal justice system, with the establishment of state police departments, technological advances in policing, especially police communications, plus a better-functioning judicial system. Arizona provides an example of an improved judicial system. From 1865 to 1900, juries convicted a mere 51 percent of whites tried for serious crimes. From 1901 to 1920, the white conviction rate jumped to over 62 percent. The increase in guilty pleas was greater still: from around 15 percent (of indicted cases, white defendants) in the nineteenth century to nearly 40 percent.[43] While we associate pleas in the late twentieth century with leniency, in the early part of the twentieth century, as compared with the nineteenth, pleas increased considerably the guilt-adjudication capability of the criminal justice system. There was, as a result of all these improvements, far less of a need for private law enforcement.

By the 1890s, the culture of the West had been transformed. The "culture war" between the rural and working class "rough justice" crowd and the respectable, middle-class "due process" forces ended in a victory for the advocates of orderly procedure.[44]

## LABOR CONFLICT

At least one part of the West carried the tradition of criminal violence right into the twentieth century: the mining and mill towns. In the mining towns the workers formed militant unions (the Western Federation of Miners) and fought—quite literally—with private security guards (such as Pinkertons) hired by the owners. As the violence escalated, the owners sought and obtained court injunctions and military interventions by state militia or federal troops.[45] The sabotage and killings associated with these disputes fall into the large-scale social conflict category: most definitely crimes, but not ordinary interpersonal violence.

An infamous example of this labor unrest occurred in the 1890s, in the mining towns near the Coeur d'Alene River, Idaho. In 1892, striking workers attacked four mines, destroyed a mill and a $500,000 ore concentrator and took guards and strikebreakers hostage. Six died in the fighting. The owners obtained a declaration of martial law, and the National Guard made wholesale arrests of union members, local businessmen, and lawyers sympathetic to the union, all of whom were herded into crude stockades. This broke the strike, but the U.S. Supreme Court overturned the convictions of union leaders for conspiracy to violate the federal injunctions.[46]

Colorado was another scene of sustained labor violence, lasting in this instance for decades and leading historians to dub the conflict Colorado's "Thirty Years War." The clash, between repressive coal companies and radical miners, began in the mid-1880s, culminating in the bloody Ludlow Massacre of 1914, an event that shocked the nation. The massacre occurred following a day-long gunfight between striking miners and state militia. The militiamen set fire to the workers' tent city, erected when the companies evicted the miners from company-owned housing. Thirteen women and children, who had sought refuge in a pit beneath a burned-over tent, suffocated to death. Outraged miners rampaged throughout the coal counties and President Woodrow Wilson sent federal troops to restore order.[47]

In addition to the labor violence, these mining towns had crime rates that were atypically high for the West, and it is fruitful to examine the reasons. Historian Clare V. McKanna has given us a close-up view of one of the mining locales—Las Animas County, Colorado—scene of the Ludlow Massacre.[48]

Las Animas was a coal mining and ranching (cattle and sheep) county. The Atchison, Topeka & Santa Fe Railroad had run through Trinidad, the county seat since 1878, and it provided the other major source of employment. Trinidad was known for its saloons, gambling parlors, and, in McKanna's words, "a wide variety of misfits." The town population quadrupled from 2,226 in 1880 to 10,000 in 1910.[49]

John D. Rockefeller's Colorado Fuel and Iron Company owned most of the coal mines and virtually ran the county, dominating its courts, law enforcers (the county sheriff and the town marshals), and coroner's office. Colorado Fuel and a competitor, the Victor-American Fuel Company, created company towns, run like migrant worker camps. Workers were paid in scrip, redeemable only at a company store. Living conditions were rudimentary, unsanitary, and unhealthy. There were, as one would expect, plenty of saloons. Trinidad had thirty-seven in 1907, a remarkable number for a town of ten thousand.[50]

One more addition to the stew was ethnicity. These towns, in the vernacular of the late twentieth century, were multicultural—and the tensions between the ethnic groups did little for law and order. The mining companies recruited immigrants to work as strikebreakers, mainly from Italy and Greece, along with American blacks. Hispanics also were a part of the volatile mix, having been in the county since the end of the Mexican War (and some longer than that). The mine owners undoubtedly recruited the various ethnic groups in the hope that friction among them would undermine the union.

## THE ITALIANS

The Italians present an interesting case. Nowadays we think of Italian immigrants to the United States as big-city dwellers, and this image is substantially correct. But a fair number were directed by their *padroni* to the coal mining towns of West Virginia and Colorado. (The *padroni* were, in essence, employment agents, recruiting immigrants for jobs in the new world, and not infrequently exploiting them as well.) These men had come over without their families, sending money home and intending to return to the old country—though many never did.[51] By 1900 there were over 1,600 Italian-born in Las Animas County, overwhelmingly male, which of course, added to the crime toll.

Tensions with native whites were acute. In 1895, six Italians, blamed for the death of an American saloon keeper, were put to death by a pack of miners. The Italians did more than their share of killing. Over one-quarter of the county's homicide indictments (between 1880 and 1920) were handed down against Italians. And more than 30 percent of those killed by Italians were of a different ethnicity. (High interethnic killings were the norm in Las Animas, a reflection of the commingling of the various groups, especially in saloons. Thirty-two percent of those killed by American whites were nonwhite or recent immigrants.)[52]

Of course, most of the homicides were intraethnic. Among the Italians, vendettas to avenge personal or family honor were a common cause of bloodshed. But *omertà,* the code of silence, made convictions difficult, especially in an age before the availability of forensic evidence. McKanna found twenty-one apparent vendetta homicides, of which ten were unindicted, six resulted in dismissals, two in acquittals, and only three in guilty verdicts.[53]

Italian crime in San Francisco provides an interesting counterpoint, as it too was high when measured against crime by non-Italian whites. The first Italians to arrive in San Francisco were nonviolent immigrants from northern Italy who seem to have had no particular impact on crime rates. They were, however, followed by more aggressive Sicilians and Calabrians fleeing depressed economic conditions in the south of Italy. The result of this southern Italian influx was a spike in San Francisco homicides.[54]

By the 1890s a new and distinctive Italian crime emerged: extortion-murders carried out by secret criminal syndicates known at the time as the Black Hand, a crude American version of the Mafia, which had developed in nineteenth-century Sicily. By the twentieth century, San Francisco's Italian community rallied behind the police to help defeat the Black Handers, whereas, as I will show, Chicago and other eastern cities couldn't seem to cope with them.[55]

I pause here to ask why Italian immigrants—more precisely, southern Italian immigrants—had such high crime rates, not only in Las Animas County, but in San Francisco and the cities of the East as well. To some extent the gender imbalance is responsible as any group with an overwhelmingly male composition, as was the case with the early southern Italian migration, is bound to be more violent. But even after the sex ratios within the Italian population evened out their crime rate remained relatively high.[56]

One explanation for this lawlessness is the link between the southern Italian culture and crime. The common culture of violence of the southern Italian would explain why Italian immigrant crime was high everywhere in the United States, not just in the western mining towns. It also would explain why Italian violence exceeded that of other immigrant groups despite comparable levels of poverty. The impoverished Scandinavians who migrated to the North Central states, for example, had exceptionally low levels of violent crime. The conclusion that cultural differences are the key requires fuller development than is appropriate at this point and will be treated in detail in subsequent chapters. Suffice it for now to quote historian Rudolph J. Vecoli, an expert on Italian immigration: "Both the Black Handers and their victims were with few exceptions from the province of Palermo where the criminal element known collectively as the *mafia* had thrived for decades. The propensity for violence of the south Italians was not a symptom of social disorganization caused by emigration but a characteristic of their Old World culture."[57]

## THE CHINESE

Nowadays we think of the Chinese as the model immigrants: law-abiding, hard-working, intelligent (with special aptitude for mathematics and its applications), and successful. This most certainly was not the image of the nineteenth-century Chinese, branded by the California media as "murderous mongols." Although they were abused by bigoted whites, especially when they began to compete for urban jobs, which they would work at lower pay, the fact is that nineteenth-century Chinese did a lot of violent crime. Their homicide rate in 1890s San Francisco was more than four times the white rate (30.8 per 100,000 versus 6.75), nearly all of it directed at other Chinese.[58]

The Chinese first came to America in the Gold Rush of 1849 and numerous Chinese ended up working in western mines. They also were recruited by the Central Pacific Railroad, which brought in ten thousand Chinese to do the back-breaking work of laying the tracks for the transcontinental rail line. Eventually, the Chinese migrated to towns and cities, where they ran small businesses, such as laundries and chop suey shops, or did odd jobs.[59]

By the late 1860s and 1870s, when Chinese were pouring into San Francisco at a rate of fifteen thousand per year, a strong anticoolie movement developed in California. A "Caucasian League" agitated against the Chinese, and the state constitution was amended in 1879 to deny them the vote and prohibit their employment in public works jobs.[60] By 1882, Washington caught the anti-Chinese virus and Congress passed the first of several acts designed to cut off Chinese immigration, this one excluding Chinese laborers from entering the United States for ten years.[61] In the mid-1880s, as Chinese mine workers began to compete more intensely with whites, white mobs attacked Chinese in Eureka, California; Tacoma and Seattle, Washington; and Rock Springs, Wyoming. In the Rock Springs riot the Chinese section of town was burned and twenty-five Chinese were killed. Many Chinese returned to Asia, but as they couldn't be replaced due to immigration restrictions, the Chinese population of California fell by over one-third in the last decade of the century.[62]

The Chinese were well organized for protection in an alien and frequently hostile land, but that protection also extended to Chinese engaged in illicit activities, including prostitution, opium smuggling, and gambling parlors. Migration to America was arranged by the Chinese Six Companies, a private organization established with the encouragement of the Chinese government. The Six Companies provided immigrants to America with transport, jobs, housing, health care, recreation, and legal representation.

In nineteenth-century United States, Chinese immigrants became associated with opium smoking. A Chinese practice dating back to the late seventeenth century, opium smoking grew popular in China early in the nineteenth century and became widespread in the 1870s among the Chinese in California.[63] It is estimated that as many as 35 percent of the Chinese immigrants smoked opium fairly regularly.[64] It wasn't illegal to do so, however, until 1875, when San Francisco passed a city ordinance against smoking and the dens that facilitated it—a law that had little actual impact on use.[65] Opium consumption, though highly addictive, does not, like alcohol, cause aggressive misconduct, and the ordinance may be seen as part of the anti-Chinese crusade of the day. But organized support within Chinatown for opium importation and distribution—especially after it was made unlawful nationwide by the federal Harrison Narcotics Act of 1914—involved significant numbers of Chinese Americans in crime.[66]

A majority of Chinese immigrants came from the culturally homogenous Kwantung (also spelled "Guangdong") Province, which had a long history of secret "Triad societies" that engaged in criminal activities or sold protection to legitimate and illegitimate businesses.[67] Blood feuds also were common in China as clans and Triads avenged the killing of their members.[68] In the United States, the Triads morphed into the fraternal lodges and worker's guilds that came to be known as "tongs." For those Chinese immigrants who were not members of family associations (clans) or district associations (common dialect and district in China), the tongs served an invaluable function. But by protecting gambling, drug, and prostitution interests, the American tongs—"Mongolian Mafias" to the media—became closely associated with the vice industry.[69]

In crucial respects, Chinese crimes against the person were very different from the violence that typified the West. Though some Chinese homicides resulted from personal disagreements, most involved self-enrichment, that is, the killing stemmed from robbery, extortion, or debt disputes. Rarely was drinking a factor and seldom was the crime interracial. Whereas whites sometimes killed Chinese, few were the Chinese-on-white homicides. In his seven-county California study, McKanna found that 86 of 92 murders by Chinese (94 percent) were of other Chinese. The victim and perpetrator usually were from rival tongs or from some new tong that had challenged the established Chinese Six Companies.[70] These tong wars were turf battles for control of illicit business activities, not unlike twentieth-century cocaine gang rivalries in poor black urban areas.

In addition to tong rivalries, a significant social condition exacerbated the Chinese crime problem: America's Chinatowns overwhelmingly were male enclaves. In the mid-1870s, for example, men outnumbered women 20 to 1 in San Francisco's Chinatown, and most of the Chinese women residing in the city were prostitutes.[71] Even in the twentieth century, when the sex ratios evened considerably, they remained distorted. In 1920, the proportion of Chinese men to women in the United States as a whole was 3.5 to 1; in 1930, it was 3 to 1. The imbalance was, in part, a reflection of Chinese custom: Chinese women (other than sex workers) did not travel far from home. But matters were made considerably worse by American exclusionary laws which made female emigration difficult. The Page Law of 1875, which sought to curtail prostitution (the "Oriental slave trade"), effectively excluded from the United States countless Chinese and Japanese women.[72]

Despite white hostility, the Chinese had a low conviction rate in American courts in the nineteenth century. McKanna's California study found 103 murder indictments of Chinese between 1850 and 1900, of which only 40 percent were found guilty. For whites, the conviction rate was 43 percent, also low by modern standards.[73] Part of the explanation for the Chinese rate involves problems with Chinese witnesses for the prosecution. Most spoke little or no English. Others were intimidated by the tongs or perhaps mistrustful of white courts. In addition, Chinese defendants were given lawyers by the Six Companies, which gave them a real advantage in dealing with courthouse complexities.[74]

When they were convicted, however, the sentencing of the Chinese was harsher than for whites. In San Francisco, 64 percent of the Chinese found guilty of murder were hanged or given life imprisonment; only 35 percent of non-Chinese met the same fate. This enormous differential simply may have been a matter of race prejudice. But crime historian Kevin Mullen contended that Chinese murders were more likely to be treated with severity because, unlike the typical white perpetrator killing, they were motivated by greed and "were almost never committed in the heat of passion."[75] This explanation gains plausibility from the fact that American Indian and Mexican defendants, who were just as likely to be discriminated against, had far fewer life sentences than the Chinese.[76] Be that as it may, the race bias explanation certainly seems credible when it comes to incidents involving the killing of Chinese by whites. Of twenty-four such cases, not one white was convicted.[77] Perhaps California laws prohibiting Chinese from testifying against whites had something to do with that outcome.[78]

In the next century, Chinese crime declined markedly, enabling Chinese Americans to burnish their model immigrant image. But even the Chinese succumbed—if only temporarily—to the great crime rise of the late 1960s. More importantly, the distinctive pattern of Chinese crime established in the nineteenth century—with its secretive organizations and gangs, its emphasis on vice crime, and its operation exclusively within the Chinese community—would repeat itself over the next one hundred years.

## INDIGENOUS PEOPLES

By the end of the nineteenth century the Native peoples, whose conflict with whites accounted for a great deal of the violence of that era, no longer posed any threat to the social order. The twentieth-century indigenous population was small and dispersed, its crimes typically rooted in drunkenness, a corrosive Native cultural problem. How did such a momentous change come about? How is it that the proud warriors who once roiled the American West were reduced to such straits? The simple truth is that the indigenous peoples were overwhelmed by whites, both numerically and culturally. The traditional Native way of life was shattered by century's end. It was fundamentally incompatible with the dominant culture and ultimately unsustainable in a land increasingly peopled by Euro-Americans.

American Indian tribes lived off the land, which they held in common. The Plains Natives were hunters and gatherers, and nomads, moving as the shifting bounties of nature seemed to dictate. Some, like the Apache, were bellicose as well, provoking whites to punishing retaliation. Whites, by contrast, were conquerers of the land, which they sought to possess individually or in the capacity of a business entity. They invented extraordinary new technologies to rapidly travel vast distances, extract the earth's mineral wealth, raise crops and livestock even in forbidding conditions, clear trees, and build cities. The American Indians worshipped the land and sought to retain it undeveloped; the whites were equally determined to acquire and develop it. Unfortunately for the Natives, they and whites were competing for the same vast real estate.

Nowadays, the environmental movement looks with a jaundiced eye at land development, and there is much sympathy for the Native Americans, fired by romantic notions of a life at one with nature plus feelings of guilt over their mistreatment. We can, of course, bemoan the course of history and wax romantic over lifestyles untouched by modernity, but that cannot change the past. The Native-white conflict of the nineteenth century was the quintessential "clash of cultures," and it was not a clash that the indigenous peoples could have won.

Aside from the obvious technological advantages of whites, there was the population differential. In the middle of the nineteenth century, approximately 360,000 indigenous peoples occupied the land west of the Mississippi; white settlers there already numbered 1.4 million. By 1890, the indigenous population west of the Mississippi River was augmented by eastern tribes that had been displaced by whites. But the white population, flooding west in search of wealth and new opportunities, rose to a remarkable (frighteningly so to the Natives) 8.5 million.[79] The massive white migration to the West simply overran the Native peoples.

Another reason for the white conquest was the inability of the Native Americans to unite. The various indigenous peoples, despite many similarities, considered themselves different from one another, and indeed, had been fighting among themselves long before whites entered the scene. Of the 75,000 Native peoples roaming the Great Plains, from Texas to the British possessions that are now Canada, the most powerful included the Blackfoot, Assiniboine, Sioux, Cheyenne, Arapaho, Crow, Shoshoni, Pawnee, Kiowa, and Comanche. Twenty-five thousand more, mainly Lipan, Apache, and Comanche, lived in Texas. The Mexican Cession (later the states of California and New Mexico) contained another 150,000: Ute, Pueblo, Navajo, Apache, Yavapai, Payute, Yuma, Mojave, Medoc, and tiny tribes of so-called Mission Indians. And 25,000, including the Nez Perce, Flathead, Coeur d'Alene, and Spokane, resided in the Oregon Territory, subsequently the states of Oregon, Washington, and Idaho.[80] "Thus the wave of white migration did not wash against a wall of Indian opposition," wrote historian Robert Utley, "but rather broke over a congeries of scattered groups that had been fighting one another for generations and would continue to fight one another to the day of their final conquest by the whites."[81]

In addition to their disunity, the Native Americans, for all their courage, had no chance against superior white firepower and military organization. The Native culture produced fierce individual warriors, but few military leaders, and "the Indians could not come close to matching the discipline and organization of the [U.S.] army."[82]

In the end, however, the death knell for the western Natives was the slaughter of the buffalo and other wild game, the source of food, clothing, and the nomadic life—the cultural fulcrum of the indigenous peoples. For whites, the buffalo was a source of leather, nothing more. In the 1870s, hides hunters killed 3 million a year; by 1883, a scientific expedition could find only 200 in the entire West. "For the Plains Indians," lamented Utley, "the disappearance of the buffalo was a shattering cultural catastrophe," leaving no alternative but the reservation.[83]

While some nineteenth-century whites sought to exterminate the American Indians, others dreamed of reforms that would enable them, if not to integrate into American society, at least to live at peace within its borders. President Ulysses Grant, under the influence of the Quakers, announced a Peace Policy in 1869, "aimed at placing all Indians on reservations, where they could be kept away from the settlements and travel routes and where ultimately they could be civilized."[84] Moving the indigenous peoples to reservations—several of which were bigger than the state of Rhode Island—was a compromise. The policy was intended to facilitate development (laying railroads, ranching, farming, and mining) free of Native attacks, while protecting the indigenous peoples from eventual destruction by whites. The Natives, however, resisted efforts at relocation and Grant's Peace Policy produced seventeen years of warfare.

Grant appointed William Tecumseh Sherman (middle name ironically taken from the Shawnee chief) head of the Army, and Philip H. Sheridan commander of the Great Plains. The two Civil War generals doggedly hunted down the Natives, not always successfully. The 1876 rout of George Armstrong Custer at Little Big Horn, in eastern Montana territory, stunned all of America. Five companies of the Seventh Cavalry, including Custer himself, were annihilated. This brought a new flood of troop reinforcements, and by 1881, when Sitting Bull surrendered, the Plains wars were over. "All tribes of the American West save one had been compelled by military force to go to, or return to, their reservations." The one holdout, the Apaches, gave up in 1886 when Geronimo, who had been playing cat and mouse with the Army across the Mexican border, finally capitulated.[85]

When the various Indian Wars ended in 1886, the indigenous peoples were "beset by more or less cultural disintegration and by feelings of helplessness and hopelessness."[86] As often happens in human history, there arises among people faced with extreme social disintegration a charismatic figure who promises a glorious future ushered in by an apocalypse. The extremism of these movements usually frightens the authorities, who move forcefully against them. The leader, surrounded by his most fervent followers, makes his last stand, and not uncommonly, all die along with the cause that impelled them.[87]

So it was with the American Indians in 1890. Among the Paiutes of Nevada, a prophet named Wovoka, known as the Messiah, appeared, offering a vision of Native paradise: no whites, bounteous game, no sickness or want, and peace among all indigenous peoples. Wovoka's message and his prescribed "Ghost Dance" swept through the West. While the Native Messiah was a pacifist, some of his Sioux followers called for militant action to usher in the millennium. Three thousand armed Ghost Dancers, clad in what they believed were bullet-repelling Ghost Shirts, mobilized on a peak, called the "Stronghold," within the Pine Ridge, South Dakota, reservation. At the same time, Big Foot, a Sioux leader, led a group of Sioux, most of whom were women and children, toward Pine Ridge. At Wounded Knee Creek they were met by the Seventh Cavalry, which sought to disarm them, fearing that they were seeking to join the militants at the Stronghold. With tensions mounting, shooting began, resulting in the death of Big Foot and 150 of his followers. The Army lost twenty-five men. Wounded Knee would be "the last major armed encounter between Indians and whites in North America."[88]

The twentieth century had no monopoly on sympathy for the plight of the indigenous peoples. In 1881, writer Helen Hunt Jackson published *A Century of Dishonor*, documenting white treaty breaches and seeking to stir the public conscience. Two years later, at Mohonk House north of New York City (a grand old hotel still), the Native American reform establishment had its first annual meeting to formulate and promote a new policy. Sincere in their concern for the Natives and deeply imbued with a reformist Protestant ethos, the Indian Rights Association's vision, as historian Utley put it, was of "an 'Americanized' American Indian."[89] That is, tribal ties and customs would have to be dissolved, replaced by family units engaged in self-sufficient farming. The Natives would be brought to

Christianity, educated in progressive schools, protected and punished in accordance with U.S. law, and ultimately, mainstreamed.

Among those Mohonk House reformers was Massachusetts senator Henry L. Dawes, who pushed through Congress the Dawes General Allotment Act, signed by President Grover Cleveland in 1887. The Dawes Act was designed to carve the reservations into farm and ranchland, parceling out units to indigenous families: 160 acres to each head of family, eighty to each single male adult, forty to each child; up to double the allotment for grazing. Title would be held by the federal government for twenty-five years to protect the Natives from land grabs until they were expected to become astute enough to protect themselves. Native Americans who took allotments would get U.S. citizenship and become subject to the civil and criminal laws of the state or territory in which they lived. Any Native who, after four years, refused to accept an allocation, would have one made for him. By 1900, all Native Americans who remained tribal were settled on reservations. Significantly, surplus reservation land could be transferred by the Interior Secretary to white homesteaders.[90] This, as will be explained, led to the notorious land rushes in the so-called Indian Territory (modern-day Oklahoma), and a huge crime surge by white settlers.

Many Native Americans took the Dawes offer and became citizen farmers. Some refused on cultural grounds: farming was women's work.[91] And those who accepted the deal sometimes lost their land anyway through an inability to make a success of farming or ranching and the eventual relaxation of the trust provisions. One historian calculates that between 1887 and 1934, American Indians lost 66 percent of their allotted land.[92]

Note, by the way, that the Dawes Act offered citizenship as part of the package. Indigenous peoples were not citizens of the United States, even though the Fourteenth Amendment, ratified in 1868, said that "[a]ll persons born or naturalized in the United States" were citizens.[93] American Indians had a neither-fish-nor-fowl status in U.S. law. In the Constitution itself, they were acknowledged in the Commerce Clause, which gave Congress the power to regulate trade with them as with foreign nations.[94] Chief Justice John Marshall, writing in 1831 for the Supreme Court in *Cherokee Nation v. State of Georgia*, said that the tribes were "domestic dependent nations" whose "relation to the United States resembles that of a ward to his guardian."[95] The following year the Court, in *Worcester v. State of Georgia*, held that state criminal laws did not apply to Natives on American Indian land in the absence of tribal consent or treaty with the federal government.[96] Eventually, Congress, in 1924, granted U.S. citizenship to all Native Americans not already designated.[97]

Once the reservation system was adopted, control over the Natives passed to a federal bureaucracy, the Bureau of Indian Affairs. After the Indian Wars and the withdrawal of the Army, the bureau established indigenous police forces on most reservations, and these proved effective.[98] But jurisdiction over crimes on reservations has always been, and remains to this day, a confusion.

Congress entered the criminal jurisdiction thicket in 1883, when the Supreme Court ordered the release of one Crow Dog (Native name Kan-Gi-Shun-Ca) after his conviction and death sentence in federal court for the cold-blooded murder of Spotted Tail (Sin-Ta-Ge-Le-Scka). *Ex Parte Crow Dog* held that federal statutes, which made the criminal laws of the United States applicable to American Indian country, did not extend to crimes committed by one Native against another or to crimes for which a Native American was already punished by the law of his tribe.[99] Consequently, Crow Dog was entitled to release on a writ of habeas corpus. Two years later, in 1885, Congress passed the Indian Major Crimes Act,[100] which repudiated the *Crow Dog* decision and provided for federal jurisdiction over American Indians who commit certain enumerated offenses against other Natives on the reservation.

Over the next century, criminal jurisdiction over Native Americans got, as Alice in Wonderland said, curiouser and curiouser. The short of it is as follows. Offenses by non-Natives against non-Natives in American Indian country (that is, on reservations or other Native lands) are subject to state jurisdiction. Offenses by non-Natives against Natives within American Indian country, or vice versa, are subject to federal jurisdiction. Minor offenses by Natives against Natives on the reservation are a matter for tribal resolution. Major Indian-on-Indian offenses within Native territory also may be handled tribally, but due to sentencing ceilings that prevent the imposition of felony sanctions, such cases are usually prosecuted federally. Finally, Congress has given certain states both state and local criminal jurisdiction on reservations.[101]

Perhaps the saddest chapter in the American Indian saga is that of the Five Civilized Tribes, so called because, unlike the nomadic bison hunters of the Great Plains, the Cherokees, Creeks, Choctaws, Chickasaws, and Seminoles lived most like whites. They resided in the southeastern states, within "nations" with fixed boundaries, a constitution, and political institutions adopted from the American system. There they farmed (some even ran plantations with black slaves), established public schools, embraced Christianity and prospered.[102] In one of the most ignominious acts in American history, President Andrew Jackson had them forcibly removed from their homeland in Georgia to what later became Oklahoma, west of the Mississippi River. Forced to travel a thousand miles with little food or provisions during the harsh winter of 1838–39, it is said that four thousand died on that Trail of Tears.

Relocated to "permanent" new homelands in "Indian Territory" between Texas and Kansas, the Five Tribes began to flourish once again. But the steady migration of whites and blacks—constituting more than 70 percent of the Oklahoma population by 1890—was ominous for Native independence. Actually, the non-Native migrants to the area themselves faced considerable hardship. Tribal law did not apply to them, and a meager law enforcement apparatus of U.S. deputy marshals barely protected them from increasing crime by bandit gangs. Likewise, schools for their children and other state services were nonexistent.[103]

Nevertheless, these land "boomers" kept coming, lobbying for homesteads on real estate not assigned to indigenous peoples. In 1889, Congress opened the unassigned territory to homesteaders, triggering the first of the great land rushes. Thousands gathered on opening day in a mad dash to acquire the nearly 1.9 million acres "almost directly in the heart of the reserved Indian lands." The first person on the land got to homestead it, and within a single day, virtually every desirable parcel was claimed. The very next year Oklahoma was declared a U.S. Territory, encompassing most of the land just west of the Indian Territory, which contained the tribal reservations proper of the Five Civilized Tribes.[104]

That situation didn't last long. The Five Tribes were pressed by two federal commissions (the last one headed by Senator Dawes himself) to agree to cede more "surplus" land to settlers and then to apply an amended Dawes Act (which originally had exempted the Five Tribes) to tribal holdings, that is, to allot the land collectively owned by each tribe to indigenous families or individuals and open the remainder to homesteaders. This set off another series of land rushes, with thousands more storming the Oklahoma Territory. The next blow to Native American independence came in 1898, when all occupants of that territory, indigenous peoples and non-, were placed by act of Congress under the authority of federal law and courts.[105]

The Five Tribes reluctantly agreed to phase out their national governments altogether by 1906. At the last minute, their leaders pressed for a separate American Indian state to be called Sequoyah. But Congress and President Theodore Roosevelt were determined to create a single state of Oklahoma. The Enabling Act was passed in 1906, and Roosevelt signed the statehood proclamation in 1907.[106] Any conception of an independent indigenous nation within the territory of the United States was now dead.

During the chaotic period prior to statehood Oklahoma became synonymous with crime. The headlong rush of settlers simply overwhelmed the slender federal law enforcement machinery then in operation. As a result, "from the first opening to white settlement until statehood, outlaw gangs ruled supreme. They robbed banks, trains, stores, post offices, and Indians and homesteader alike. When some member left the stage, another took his place, to bask in notoriety and folklore for a time and then, in turn, be replaced. There were few who did not end their careers in prison or death."[107]

Especially notorious was the border between the Oklahoma and Native Territories, known as Hell's Fringe. "It had become infested with every class of criminal, from the most deadly and ruthless killer to the petty thief."[108] The U.S. Marshal's office, "with fifty deputies to police thousands of square miles, seemed unable to cope with the situation despite the fact that in three years time it had made nearly fifteen hundred arrests."[109] And, of course, there was no state or local criminal justice system prior to 1907, when statehood was established.

The local newspapers sounded alarms. The *Stillwater Gazette* of July 8, 1892, raged: "A tidal wave of criminality is sweeping the country. There is scarcely a county that is not the scene of bloodshed, suicide, rape, robbery or gigantic thefts at the present time. About one murder in fifty is brought to justice." Less than two years later (on April 21, 1894), the *Oklahoma Daily Press-Gazette* reported two lynchings: "For the first time in the history of Oklahoma, a vigilance committee has been formed and taken summary action on two disreputables. This is to be deeply regretted. But the fault is not to be placed with the settlers. In their five years of settlement the people have proved themselves to be law-abiding and capable of civilized life. But lately there has been a perfect devastation of crime."[110] For all the actual violence and press exaggeration, however, cattle and horse thievery was the most common complaint. And "despite the cries of outrage" over their depradations, most of the colorful outlaw gangs—Bill Doolin's Wild Bunch, the Daltons, and the like—"were secretly admired for one reason or another."[111]

Oklahoma was a classic example of crime caused by explosive, chaotic, and virtually unregulated migration that simply overwhelmed the existing law enforcement apparatus. The lesson seems clear: any sudden influx of people to an area, due to foreign immigration or, as in Oklahoma, migration within the United States, must be matched by an augmention of the criminal justice machinery; otherwise, crime control simply becomes unsustainable. In subsequent chapters we will see variations on Oklahoma in the big cities of the United States, cities that, in the twentieth century, were beset by vast and sudden influxes of immigrants and American migrants. The difference between Oklahoma and the urban immigrant/migrant situation is that in the former the state and local law enforcement structure needed to be built from scratch, whereas the urban systems, already mature, simply had to be reinforced to cope with the population and crime increase.

As for the indigenous peoples, penned up in reservations, or (as with the Five Tribes) besieged by white migrants, they became less violent as the twentieth century progressed. This especially was the case with the more bellicose tribes, like the Apache. American Indians were, as mentioned earlier, separate peoples with distinctive cultures. There were, to be sure, commonalities, such as their attitudes toward the land, but there also were marked differences. The warlike Apache were a far cry from the "civilized" Cherokees in the East, or the nonaggressive Pueblos out West. We would expect the more violent indigenous cultures to manifest in more violent crime. But we also would expect violence to diminish in the twentieth century as Native American cultures crumpled and the Natives adopted white ways.

The Apache are a case in point. From 1883 to 1889, according to U.S. Department of the Interior figures, the western Apache had an annual average homicide rate of 165 per 100,000, and that does not not include killings of whites.[112] (By comparison, from 1976 to 2005, the African American homicide rate, considered disturbingly high, was 30 per 100,000.) The Interior Department's figures were corroborated by a study of an Arizona county which, in the late 1880s, produced an Apache homicide rate of 178. Thereafter, as the study showed, the rate declined dramatically, and by 1905 it fell considerably below the white rate.[113]

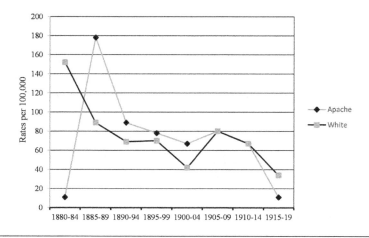

FIGURE 5.1. Apache and white homicide victimization rates per 100,000, Gila County, AZ, 1880–1920. *Source:* McKanna, *Homicide, Race, and Justice,* 41.

During the time that the Apache homicide rate of the 1880s was soaring, it is notable that other tribes, with very different cultures, were peaceable. The Eastern Pueblos were reported to have had a rate (Native victims only) of 1.9, and the Navajos, 5.88.[114] These tribal differences in crime seem to have persisted into the twentieth century. In 1968, at Nambe Pueblo, the arrest rate was 5.1 per 1,000; at the Mescalero Apache Reservation it was 2,151.[115]

A close scrutiny of American Indian crime is revealing. In general, it is unusual, due to infrequent contact between races, to find interracial murders in significant numbers. Nevertheless, nineteenth-century data suggest that a fair number of Native murder victims were whites. A California study documented 106 Indian-perpetrated killings from 1850 to 1900, 37 percent of which were of whites.[116] (Again, comparing modern data, we see how high this 37 percent figure is. From 1976 to 2005, black-on-white homicides never exceeded 9 percent of all homicides; and white-on-black killings never surpassed the 3.5 percent mark.)[117]

But white murders of Natives (killings of the criminal kind, as opposed to collective acts of violence) were surprisingly infrequent. Of 791 white-perpetrated homicides in California, 1850 to 1900, only 35 (4.4 percent) involved American Indian victims. The interracial homicide data suggest that in the nineteenth century, Natives had higher crime rates than whites, but without additional evidence it is not clear that such a conclusion is warranted.[118]

The nineteenth-century justice system, at least in California, was far less friendly to Native Americans than to white defendants. Of the thirty-five suspected white killers, only four (11.4 percent) were indicted and one convicted. By contrast, 47 of 106 (44 percent) suspected Native American killers were indicted, and 80 percent of these were convicted. Historian Clare McKanna attributed the unfavorable outcomes for indigenous suspects to their lack of familiarity with the legal process plus an inability to retain counsel—problems that did not afflict white defendants. (Nor, interestingly enough, Chinese, as their close-knit community organizations paid for lawyers.) McKanna also thought that white hatred of Native Americans played a role, which certainly is possible.[119]

American Indian criminals were, as a rule, marginal types, accepted neither by their own people nor by whites. They would leave the Native homeland to work as ranch hands or farm laborers, drinking heavily and getting into frequent scrapes. Typically, the white murder victim was found in some isolated rural area, his Native assailant, already under the influence of liquor, having targeted his money and valuables. Robbery was a motive in 62 percent of the cases, and three-quarters of the defendants knew the victims. The data also indicate that 68 percent of the indigenous killers had been drinking before the crime.[120]

The most significant characteristic of American Indian crime was, and still is, its association with alcohol, which historian Utley has dubbed "one of the white man's most destructive gifts to the natives." Indigenous peoples first obtained alcohol from white traders early in the seventeenth century, and by the time of the American Revolution their susceptibility to its effects was dramatic. It ravaged the tribes like an epidemic. "Indians believed that liquor contained a hidden spirit or demon that took possession of the imbiber. The perpetrator of injury or even death inflicted while drunk could hardly be held responsible for actions caused by evil spirits."[121]

For the Natives, as for some white cultural groups, notably the nineteenth-century Irish, alcohol abuse became both a part of the culture and the kind of social disinhibitor that fosters crime. The American Indian liquor problem first developed in the late eighteenth century and it persisted right into the twenty-first. In the late nineteenth century, for example, the Apaches would hold tiswin (corn liquor) parties that frequently culminated in violence and homicide. A study of nineteenth-century San Diego County found that 68 percent of the Natives who killed whites were under the influence.[122] And in the lower courts of San Bernardino County, from 1870 to 1900, the "vast majority" of American Indian cases involved drunk and disorderly behavior. The defendants nearly always pled guilty, the males getting five days in jail, the females one or two days.[123]

Some, no doubt, would prefer to see American Indian drinking and crime as by-products of the destruction by whites of the traditional Native culture. But the facts don't bear this out. Both drinking and crime were frequent among Native peoples in the nineteenth century well before they were completely subjugated. Even in the twentieth century, anthropologists found the greatest use of alcohol "among the most traditional and least acculturated Indians," and the lowest usage "in the most acculturated off-reservation group."[124] It is, of course, true that interaction with whites led to the introduction of alcohol into indigenous culture. But it is not correct to say that the disintegration of indigenous culture made American Indians turn to drink. Nor, for that matter, did the erosion of Native culture cause an increase in crime. As the traditional indigenous cultures weakened in the twentieth century Native American crime declined. Recall that Apache homicide rates had far exceeded white rates prior to 1905, but were lower in subsequent years.

Drinking, however, did not diminish. It remained in the twentieth century the quintessential Native social problem and the key to understanding Native crime. As one expert put it: "Native Americans do not have high crime rates, but rather high rates of alcohol use and misuse which leads to minor involvement in the criminal justice system."[125] Whether the involvement in criminality can fairly be characterized as "minor" is debatable, but that alcohol is at the root of the problem seems beyond challenge.

## HISPANICS

People of Spanish descent lived in the American Southwest long before it was American. Spaniards established settlements along the Rio Grande in the early seventeenth century, entered present-day Texas and Arizona by the latter part of that century, and settled coastal California at the end of the eighteenth.[126] As elsewhere on the North American continent, however, it was aggressive nineteenth-century settlement by whites of non-Spanish heritage—"Anglos"—that had a long-range impact on the region. In fact, the Mexican government, having won independence from Spain in 1821, promptly encouraged Americans to settle Texas and make it more productive, thereby sealing their fate. By 1830,

Anglos, three-quarters of whom were southerners, outnumbered Mexicans (or *Tejanos*, Spanish for "Texans") six to one. The Texans rebelled against the corrupt, ineffectual Mexican government in 1835, won their independence, and within a decade, Texas was annexed by the United States.

California was next. Sparsely populated by Spanish ranchers with slender ties to Mexico City, California attracted more and more Americans each year. War between the United States and Mexico seemed inevitable, and when it ended in 1848 with Mexico's utter defeat, the prize of California went to the victor, along with New Mexico, which included all or parts of modern New Mexico, Arizona, Nevada, Utah, Colorado, and Wyoming. By 1850, Mexicans in Texas and California made up less than 10 percent of the total population as the non-Spanish inhabitants increased rapidly. East Texas was the new western frontier for southern settlements, and the discovery of gold in California in 1848 attracted Anglo hordes into the central and northern portions of that state. Only in New Mexico, southern California, and Texas south of San Antonio, did the Hispanic population continue to dominate.

The worst of Hispanic crime in the nineteenth century occurred during the tumultuous 1850s. In California, Hispanic robber bands preyed on Anglo miners. Aside from American Indians, Hispanics had the highest interracial homicide rate in the state: 27 percent of their victims were white.[127] Newspaper accounts of 1854 ascribed 16 percent of all California homicides to Latinos, who were 10 percent of the population. San Francisco saw twenty criminal homicides by Latinos from 1849 to the end of the 1850s.[128] And in Los Angeles, there was a near race war in the first half of the 1850s. Los Angeles County, population under 2,300, had an astonishing 44 homicides in a fifteen-month period.[129] Vigilante organizations promptly formed and a number of Hispanics (along with quite a few whites, many of Irish descent) were hanged. In 1850s San Francisco, five of thirty-two (15.6 percent) hanged or imprisoned for homicide were Latino, who were 6 percent of the city's population.[130]

The other flashpoint for Hispanic-white conflict was south Texas. Under the Treaty of Guadalupe Hidalgo, which ended the Mexican War in 1848, the Texas side of the Rio Grande became part of the United States. However, the residents were overwhelmingly Spanish-speaking and of Mexican extraction and an enormous cultural, political, and legal gulf separated them from the Americans. Mexican rancheros had their long-standing land titles reaffirmed by the above-mentioned treaty, but as the territory was now under American law, aggressive Anglos used that law to divest the Mexicans of their holdings. The criminal law was no more evenhanded. If a Tejano injured an American he faced the rope; but if a Mexican died at the hands of a white man it usually was deemed justifiable. As a Texas historian put it: "The humbler classes of Mexicans were finding that they were treated with contempt, and that the American law would not protect their persons; now the upper class felt that American courts were not upholding their ancient [property] rights."[131] The situation was ripe for violence.

In 1859, the so-called Cortina War erupted when Juan Cortina (some sources call him Cheno Cortinas), born to a well-to-do ranchero family, shot the city marshal of Brownsville after protesting the lawman's beating of a drunken Mexican. A few months later, Cortina rode back into town with one hundred vaqueros, shot a Mexican and three Americans "notorious for their misdeeds among the people," and emptied the jail of its prisoners. To the Texans, the "Red Robber of the Rio Grande" was a mere bandit—nowadays he'd probably be called a terrorist—but to the Mexican border residents he was a hero. The Texas Rangers, and even the U.S. Army, pursued Cortina unsuccessfully for years, with a high toll in lives: 15 Americans, 150 Cortinistas, and 80 Tejanos.[132]

Perhaps because of the failure to capture Cortina, but certainly because of ongoing tensions between Anglos and Mexicans, the Texas-Mexico border was the scene of skirmishes between bandidos and Texas lawmen right into the twentieth century. Men like Gregorio Cortez (1875–1916) and Catarino Garza (1859–1902) became legends. To Hispanic sympathizers these border warriors were "social bandits," motivated by opposition to American encroachments. To most Anglos they were just bandits.[133]

Insofar as Hispanic crime in the early twentieth century is concerned, the most significant event was not the border war, but the socioeconomic changes in the Mexican-American population. The rancheros lost much of their holdings and sank into the laboring class. The vaqueros (cowboys), put out of work when the long cattle drives ended, were reduced to farm laborers. It is these marginal Hispanics—moving from job to job as sheep shearers or day laborers, drifting from the Spanish world to the white, drinking heavily in local saloons—who were responsible for Latino crime, for violence, and occasionally, death.[134]

Commercial farming, which began in Texas in the late 1880s, would become the principal employer, not only of the poorer Tejanos, Texans of Mexican heritage, but of the Mexican immigrants who, in the twentieth century, would flood across the border. "By the turn of the century," as one historian put it, "the pro-letarianization of the bulk of the Hispanic community, continuously reinforced now by impoverished Mexican immigrants from across the border, was complete."[135] The crucial point is that low-income Mexicans became ever more numerous in the United States, and would be, as disadvantaged people often are, a source of violent crime in the twentieth century.

Aside from Texas, the other hot spot for Hispanic crime was New Mexico. New Mexico retained its Spanish population through the end of the nineteenth century. Indeed, according to geographer Richard Nostrand, one could speak of an "hispano homeland" stretching over parts of five states, two-thirds of which consisted of residents of Spanish descent ("hispanos") born in New Mexico, as distinguished from recent Mexican immigrants or their children. The north central portion of New Mexico (a U.S. Territory until statehood in 1912) was the "stronghold" of the homeland, with an overwhelmingly—97 percent!—hispano population, mainly farmers and sheepherders, living in widely scattered villages.[136] "Rarely in twentieth century America," declared Nostrand, "has so large an area been so uniformly populated by a single ethnic group."[137]

By the late 1880s, Anglo and wealthy hispano cattle rancher efforts to enclose grazing lands began to threaten the integrity of the communal lands used by the small hispano sheepherders of northern New Mexico. A new, secret, group—known as Las Gorras Blancas, the "White Caps," for their distinctive headgear—began tearing down fences, burning barns and haystacks, scattering livestock, and terrorizing Anglos. Their nighttime raids and white caps—some wore white masks—were evocative of, and may have been influenced by, the Ku Klux Klan. Gorras Blancas's objective was to prevent the partition of communal lands by Anglos into separate, fenced ranches. By 1890, they were estimated to have around seven hundred members. But the movement died out soon thereafter, partly because the most objected-to fences had been cut down. Ultimately, in the late 1890s, the New Mexico territorial legislature passed laws to protect some of the most prized communal lands.[138]

Getting a fix on "ordinary" Hispanic crime in the nineteenth century is difficult, in part because little research has been done on the subject, and what work there is has been stymied by incomplete population reports. It is impossible, for instance, to determine crime rates without accurate population figures. Nonetheless, from what can be gleaned from the few investigations that have been conducted, Hispanic crime seems to have been low.

A random sample of male inmates in the New Mexican territorial penitentiary from 1890 to 1909 found that 57.6 percent were Hispanics, which the analyst thought in line with the Hispanic population of the Territory. The Anglo prisoners constituted 33.6 percent of the total.[139] More ominously for the twentieth century, recent Mexican immigrants made up approximately one-fifth of the Hispanic prison population. This probably was considerably more than their share of the New Mexico population in 1900.[140]

Also revealing are the crimes of the prisoners. Forty-three percent were in for murder, but when I broke this down by race, I found that 67 percent of the Anglo inmates were murderers and only 36 percent of the Hispanics. Judging by these figures, and given that Hispanics were a clear majority of the state population, one must conclude that the Anglos were much more violent. It should be kept in mind, however, that the American migrants to New Mexico, unlike the well-settled hispanos, "were likely to be young males with scant social or community attachments" and ready access to guns and alcohol.[141]

More startling still, a full 41 percent of the Hispanic prisoners, and 16 percent of the Anglo, were convicted of adultery![142] The explanation for the adultery prosecutions is the federal government's antipolygamy campaign, culminating in the Edmunds-Tucker Act of 1887, which not only disincorporated the Mormon Church and banned polygamy, but also made adultery a federal offense.[143] Apparently many Anglos thought that Hispanic moral standards were low despite the fact that the Roman Catholic Church and both Mexican and Spanish law had long prohibited adultery. One must suspect that these aggressive adultery prosecutions were just reflections of anti-Hispanic and anti-Catholic prejudices so rampant at the time.[144]

Anglos, however, certainly did not control the New Mexican criminal justice system. They did predominate among the judges, which, given that this was a federal territory, were presidential appointments (as was New Mexico's governor, its three supreme court justices, and some dozen additional territorial officers). But Hispanics were so numerous in the general population that witnesses commonly testified in Spanish; Hispanics served as bailiffs in the courtroom; and most important, Hispanics held around half of New Mexico Territory's county sheriff's positions and were the preponderance of grand and petit jurors.[145]

A study of crime in San Miguel, an overwhelmingly hispano county in north central New Mexico, is revealing. The 1880 Census tallied twenty thousand people in the county, 89 percent of Spanish descent. If one counts only adult males, the Hispanic figure falls to 79 percent, non-Hispanic white males comprising 20 percent. The sheriff, most of the deputies, and most of the jailers of San Miguel were Hispanics.[146]

This study examined 598 cases brought to the territorial District Court in San Miguel over a seven-year period, 1876 to 1882. Two-thirds of these cases were dismissed, mainly by the prosecutor. The predominant offense, involving 40 percent of the cases, was gambling. Two-thirds of these gambling cases were dismissed; the rest were resolved by guilty pleas and light sanctions, which implies plea bargaining. Property crimes were 20 percent of the total, and violent crimes made up only 16 percent. Three-quarters of the gambling law violators were Anglos, whereas 60 percent of the property crime defendants were Hispanics. Violent crime was split 50–50 between Hispanics and Anglos.[147]

These figures suggest, first, that violent crime must not have been terribly vexing in San Miguel, since it was a relatively small portion of the total docket and since gambling accounted for the biggest chunk of prosecutorial efforts. Second, gambling was mainly an Anglo problem and it was not taken very seriously, judging by the dismissals, pleas, and wrist-slap sentences. Finally, given that Hispanic males were 79 percent of the population, their 50 percent violent-crime-commission incidence indicates underrepresentation among the violent offenders, whereas non-Hispanic males, at 20 percent of the inhabitants, were considerably overrepresented. In short, San Miguel confirms that Hispanics— more precisely, *hispanos*, those long-term residents of New Mexico, not the recent Mexican immigrants—did not add significantly to violent crime in the West.

One last piece of evidence, thin though it is, is from neighboring Arizona Territory. A study of Arizona indictments and prosecutors' informations from 1865 to 1900 found only one-quarter attributable to Hispanics. Unfortunately, we do not know the size of the Hispanic population, which, in 1880, ranged from 4–15 percent in the north to 25–45 percent down near the Mexican border. We may eke out a bit more evidence by focusing on Pima County, which in 1890 was over 50 percent ethnic Mexican. Of all cases to come before Pima grand juries, 54 percent were Mexican, which seems to be precisely in line with the population. Incidentally, the author of the study found considerable bias by white juries against Mexican defendants, a diminishing phenomenon as plea bargaining increased at the beginning of the twentieth century. In other words, juries were more prejudiced than prosecutors.[148]

## CONCLUSION: THE NOT-SO-WILD WEST

While the South was recovering from the Civil War and reestablishing white rule, the West had yet to establish the rule of law. The nineteenth-century West is best understood as an underdeveloped region in a developing country. Its land and mineral riches were abundant and there for the taking, impeded by fierce indigenous peoples and immense natural hardships. The adventurous entrepreneurial spirit of Americans augmented by that of thousands of newly arrived European immigrants eventually would overcome all obstacles, but it wouldn't be pretty nor easy. Downright bloody, in fact.

The reason for all this bloodshed was not just an abundance of strong-willed, aggressive, and armed males, although that was a big part of it. The West was wild because it lacked the political/legal machinery to restrain those armed men and peaceably resolve conflicts. As political scientist Samuel Huntington once observed, "The primary problem of politics is the lag in the development of political institutions behind social and economic change."[149] This was precisely the situation in the American West for most of the nineteenth century: it lacked the political institutions to maintain order and resolve disputes without bloodshed. Historian Randolph Roth, referring to the western grasslands, declared: "the violence was primarily due to one factor: the absence of effective government."[150]

In short, the West was lawless, not just in the sense that frontiersmen commonly disrespected the law, but rather in that there was no law to respect, or more precisely, no administrative mechanism, no criminal justice system, with the capacity to enforce the law over the vast tracts of territory recently opened to exploitation. Vigilantism in the West, setting aside the contentious racial animus issue, can best be understood as a means of coping with the lawlessness, notwithstanding the irony that it was itself outside the law. In short, the West was, in the economic, political, and legal sense, an underdeveloped region, much like parts of Asia and Africa in the twentieth and early twenty-first centuries.

As historian Richard Maxwell Brown has argued, the "incorporator" forces— one might call them the forces of development—gradually imposed order on this wild land, motivated largely by visions of wealth, or at least better economic prospects.[151] These agents of development understood, at least intuitively, that property had to be protected by courts, law, and law enforcement, from the depredations of marauding American Indians, Mexican bandidos, and militant organized labor.

Thus, violence in the nineteenth-century West largely was a product of the unmediated disputes between the forces of economic development and those whose lives were disrupted or whose lifestyles were destroyed by that development: big ranchers versus small ranchers and homesteading farmers; railroad and mining capitalists versus militant labor unionists; whites versus Native Americans, Mexicans, and Chinese. Although ethnic-cultural differences magnified the enmity of the last-named disputants, there usually was an economic motivation as well. Indigenous peoples held (roamed on, to be more accurate) rich farmland or grazing land for cattle, or they threatened cross-continental railroad travel, while whites killed the bison and natural plant and animal life that provided Native Americans' food and clothing. Whites thought Chinese were stealing their jobs. Hispanics were uneasy with the Pueblos, but positively loathed the *indios bárbaros*. In New Mexico, Anglo cattlemen engaged in violent conflict over land with Hispanic sheepherders. And on the Texas-Mexico border, bandidos raided Anglo ranches and stores, then played cat-and-mouse with the Texas Rangers.

There were ethnic conflicts aplenty in the nineteenth-century West, especially between whites and Chinese, Mexicans, and American Indians. Racism was in no short supply in western America either, and the openness of Americans to immigrant labor frequently exacerbated the bigotry. Hostility to African Americans was not significant, however, undoubtedly because blacks were relatively few in number, the black western exodus occurring mainly in the twentieth century.

But what was crime like in this underdeveloped West? Ordinary crime for economic gain was surprisingly infrequent. Armed robbery of individuals purely for their money and valuables was unusual. Even theft was relatively uncommon, a kind of rough-hewn respect for property prevailing. Rape and juvenile crime were virtually unknown. The sensational train and stage robberies of legend were carried out by criminal gangs, but only in limited places and times, places wracked by turbulence. An example is Oklahoma of the late 1880s and early 1890s, roiled by huge unregulated land rushes onto territory "liberated" from the Native peoples.

Then there was the archetypal nineteenth-century killing by drunken young males in or around saloons, triggered by some affront to their personal honor. Guns, ubiquitous in the West, frequently turned a fistfight into a fatality.

Crimes motivated by ethnic hatred were numerous, and sometimes it is difficult to distinguish such offenses from broader social conflicts turned violent. Assault and killing on a large scale probably are best seen as riot or even (in the case of the American Indians) as a military engagement in a long-term war. There also were numerous "raids"—essentially guerilla attacks motivated by a combination of ethnic hatred and economic conflict—which straddled the line between personal violence/crime and social conflict.

Finally, some of the labor disputes near the end of the century got particularly ugly, as labor unions grew more militant and management hired private armies of detective agency employees to suppress the workers. This violence too was criminal, though sometimes closer to riot in scale.

On balance, the West surely was violent, though far less so in the 1890s than in the turbulent 1850s and 1860s. By century's end, however, the West wasn't nearly as menacing to the average American as crime would be in the big cities in the late twentieth century. It may seem odd, if not ironic, that the wild, wild West was safer than the civilized East. But in terms of personal security, one would have been far better off on a western farm in 1890 than in Manhattan in 1980.

What impact did the violence of the West have on crime in twentieth-century America? The main effect was to neutralize certain issues and certain groups. The violence driven by social turmoil quieted when the source of the conflict—whether land or labor—abated. The crime attributable to cultural differences among the races or ethnic groups was significantly altered in the nineteenth century. The indigenous peoples, confined to reservations, their cultures marginalized, were pacified, and they ended up no more menacing (except to one another) than the town drunk. The Mexicans became a greater problem, crime-wise, in the twentieth century, when a vast influx of young impoverished males came north to labor on American farmlands. But this was less a legacy of nineteenth-century North America than a reflection of the weakness of the Mexican socioeconomic system in the twentieth. The Chinese established their distinctive cultural pattern of crime in nineteenth-century San Francisco, a pattern that resurfaced in late twentieth-century New York City. But twentieth-century Chinese crime was localized in a handful of Chinatowns, and as the victims were other Chinese, whites by and large were indifferent. By the end of the twentieth century, the Chinese came to be seen as model immigrants. Italian crime was limited to the mining boomtowns, and would be more significant in Chicago and New York than in the far west.

Some thought the frontier itself left its imprint on Americans. Most famously, historian Frederick Jackson Turner, writing in 1893, noted that the frontier, defined in geographical terms, had been eliminated, but not without the most profound influence on the American spirit. "This perennial rebirth, this fluidity of American life, this expansion westward with its new opportunities, its continuous touch with the simplicity of primitive society, furnish the forces dominating American character. The true point of view in the history of this nation is not the Atlantic coast, it is the Great West."[152]

Others say the lasting effect of the frontier was not, as Turner put it, "the expansive character of American life," but rather its violence, or at least the myth created around violence. Contemporary writer Richard Slotkin: "What is distinctively 'American' is not necessarily the amount or kind of violence that characterizes our history but the mythic significance we have assigned to the kinds of violence we have actually experienced, the forms of symbolic violence we imagine or invent, and the political uses to which we put that symbolism."[153]

Insofar as American crime is concerned, however, the West is significant neither because of its frontier spirit nor because of its contribution to mythic violence. Rather, it is important as an object lesson in the relationship between violent crime and political underdevelopment. The lesson is that government without effective administrative machinery will be unable to control crime.

By the 1890s, crime was having a diminishing impact on the West. Most of the vast terrain had become law-abiding. The boomtowns and cowtowns were finished (although labor unrest in the mining regions remained a problem). The in-migration of lawless young males was replaced by peaceable families gone west to farm or otherwise better their economic lot. The indigenous peoples were neutralized and the Mexican bandidos soon would be. Even Oklahoma was becoming tame. A solid criminal justice structure—law enforcers, prosecutors, courts, and prisons—was taking shape. Until the last third of the next century, crime would be far less of a problem in the West than anywhere else in America except New England.

# DOES URBAN POVERTY CAUSE CRIME?

# 6

# A Multicity Crime Tour

Given the extraordinary growth of its biggest cities at the end of the nineteenth century, one would have expected a huge increase in crime in the United States. The urban population surge was nothing short of explosive. By 1900, nearly 40 percent of Americans lived in an urban setting, up from a mere 26 percent in 1870.[1] New York City, the nation's biggest metropolis, had over 1.5 million people in 1890, and after the merging in 1898 of Manhattan with Brooklyn and the other "boroughs," the total population was 3.4 million.[2] This was equal to the entire urban population of the United States in 1850. Chicago, if anything, grew even faster, its population increasing 568 percent in those last three decades. Table 6.1 lists the top ten U.S. cities, population-wise, in 1890.

TABLE 6.1. Top ten U.S. cities, 1890, by population

| | |
|---|---|
| 1. New York | 1,515,301 |
| 2. Chicago | 1,099,850 |
| 3. Philadelphia | 1,046,964 |
| 4. Brooklyn | 806,343 |
| 5. St. Louis | 451,770 |
| 6. Boston | 448,477 |
| 7. Baltimore | 434,439 |
| 8. San Francisco | 298,997 |
| 9. Cincinnati | 296,908 |
| 10. Cleveland | 261,353 |

*Source:* Bureau of the Census, "Population of 100 Largest Cities," Working Paper No. 27.

If cities breed crime, then the late nineteenth-century United States should have experienced a crime tsunami. Not only did America's urban population soar, but the living conditions in those cities were, by contemporary measures, petri dishes for criminality. The new urban masses were poor, often desperately so. They were densely packed into the most appalling housing, when not forced by impoverishment to sleep in public places or police station barracks.[3] Urbanites below the middle class were unable to support their children past age twelve, leading city youth to drop out of school to work long hours, or to join street gangs and steal for survival.[4] The cities were governed by thoroughly crooked municipal regimes, such as the notorious Tammany Hall in New York. The police, essentially a security force for the corrupt city governments, were untrained, incompetent, and abusive—free with their nightsticks, especially in dealing with the "dangerous classes" of poor immigrants. The immigrant groups, moreover, along with the African Americans who were just beginning their northward migration, were routinely discriminated against because of their nationality, their religion, or their appearance and socially isolated from the city's middle class, who fled to less menacing suburbs.

If one were to ask a contemporary criminologist to identify all the causal factors associated with crime, surely poverty, homelessness, extreme population density, inadequate housing, police abuse, discrimination, social isolation, and so on, would be on nearly every list. In other words, the list would constitute a virtual catalog of conditions in the big cities of nineteenth-century America. So, did crime soar in the cities in the last decades of the nineteenth century? The answer very much depends on the particular city and the kind of crime one is interested in.

Certainly one type of offense, vice crime—prostitution, illegal gambling, illegal sales of alcohol—increased appreciably, as did "public order" offenses, such as loitering and public intoxication. Larceny, too, must have risen as impoverished children and youth, virtually living on big-city streets, stole as needed to get by. But serious violent crimes against the person—robbery, rape, felonious assault, and murder, the kinds of crimes that frighten the general public—are another matter. The best evidence is that these crimes increased in *some* cities, but not in others. Region seems to have been significant here. Chicago and other midwestern cities, along with some of the far western municipalities, experienced an upsurge in violent crime. Eastern cities, such as Boston, Philadelphia, and

New York, by and large did not. Race and ethnicity also had salience, as not all groups, despite their common social deficits, were violent. And notwithstanding the increased violence, U.S. cities were far safer than they would be in the two and a half decades that began in the late 1960s.

If it is true that a substantial number of burgeoning cities of the late nineteenth century did not experience a surge in violent crime, then we may have to rethink our most fundamental assumptions about cities and crime. Criminological theory, derived from *fin de siècle* German sociology, assumes that cities cause crime and that cities crammed with the underprivileged virtually assure it.[5] But as the old Gershwin tune says, it ain't necessarily so. Our nineteenth-century cities grew tremendously, and much of the growth was in the terribly poor, disadvantaged sector of the population. That violent crime didn't rise in several such cities, including some of our most populous, raises serious questions about some of criminology's most basic assumptions.

This chapter provides a tour of late nineteenth-century American cities, focusing not on their amazing growth and vitality, though that certainly is part of the picture, but on their crime and violence. We begin our travels with New York, then move on to Chicago. We then head West to Los Angeles, concluding our journey in San Francisco. The portrait of New York will be especially detailed because it was America's biggest city and we have lots of information about it. Moreover, some of the characteristics of New York, for example, its huge immigrant population, were shared by many late nineteenth-century American cities.

## NEW YORK CITY

By the 1890s, New York was America's most crowded, dynamic, and vibrant metropolis, a city seemingly in a state of perpetual growth. It was already the nation's financial center and one of the world's great seaports. The arc of its expansion—in population, through its immigrants; upward, via its skyscrapers; outward through relentless development and incorporation of its surrounding real estate—was well in place as the century waned. A look at photographs from the period reveal many of the characteristics associated with the twentieth-century Big Apple: the skyline of tall buildings, the brick housing tenements lining the streets, electrical and telephone wires (laid underground after the Blizzard of 1888 leveled the poles), commercial signs everywhere. Conspicuous, too, were the throngs of people, milling about, buying and selling goods, working on some new construction project, or driving (horse carts) through the densely packed streets. Thousands of immigrants poured into New York in the 1890s, pulled by the lure of prosperity (or at least a fair chance at life's necessities), pushed out of Europe by fear of economic ruin or death at the hands of persecuting mobs. Ellis Island, the immigrant clearinghouse, which opened in 1892, already had processed a million and a half people by 1897.[6] Hundreds of thousands more were yet to come.

### German and Irish Immigrants

In 1890, America's biggest cities were already filled with foreign-born. Over 80 percent of New York City's population was of foreign extraction.[7] At this point in its history, New York was dominated by the Germans, who, though a minority (around 28 percent), were the most powerful group in the city by dint of their political clubs, fraternal organizations, and newspapers.[8] Many Germans arrived with craft skills already honed in the old country and they readily moved into middle-class occupations in the professions and manufacturing. By 1890, however, 45 percent were laborers or servants, perhaps reflecting changes in the American economy, which, with mass production, had less need for skilled workers.[9] The 1890s marked the peak of German influence in New York. Early in the next century German immigration declined, as did its numbers and power.[10]

The Germans had a reputation for nonviolence and their violent crime rates apparently were very low. A chronicler of gang crime on New York's west side declared that the Germans were regarded as the most orderly, least violent, of all the Hell's Kitchen groups.[11] There is, unfortunately, little by way of hard data to verify this. Crime historian Eric Monkkonen once estimated ethnic/racial homicide rates for New York City during the turbulent 1860s as follows: Irish, 37.5 per 100,000; blacks, 32; Germans, 15.7. While this suggests that the German American culture was less homicidal than the Irish American or the African American, it is a thin reed on which to base judgments about subsequent and very different eras. On the other hand, there is nothing to suggest a rise in German crime in the 1890s, and the strong likelihood is that it declined by the time New York entered that more peaceful time period.[12]

If the Germans were known for their lawabidingness, the same certainly cannot be said for the "wild Irish," the other major ethnic minority in the 1890s. New Yorkers of Irish descent, numbering around 410,000 in 1890, constituted

27 percent of the city.[13] More importantly, they governed the city, through the Democratic Party organization, the fabled Tammany machine, a political ascendancy that lasted until the Great Depression of the 1930s. In truth, the Irish were the dominant players on *both* sides of the law. "The Irish came to run the police force *and* the underworld; they were the reformers and the hoodlums; employers and employed."[14]

The Irish can trace their New York roots back to the seventeenth century, but it was an influx of Irish Catholics at the beginning of the nineteenth that touched off significant ethnic conflict. A historian of mob violence in the city noted that the Irish arrivals, who brought with them a "violent tradition," "injected a more virulent strain of violence into the popular disorder of New York City." "The Irishman," he added, "seemed all too ready to pick up his shillelagh and brutally assault his opponent."[15]

Midcentury brought an even greater influx of Irish. Between 1846 and 1850, the great potato famine drove nearly 134,000 wretched souls to New York.[16] "No ethnic group in the later nineteenth or early twentieth century," wrote crime historian Roger Lane, "neither the Jews fleeing pogroms nor the Italians devastated by cholera, was as desperate as the midcentury Irish, or as collectively pugnacious."[17] Murder in New York City rose substantially in the wake of the Irish immigration, from a low of three homicides per 100,000 in the late 1820s and early 1830s to over seven per 100,000 in the 1850s, leaping above 15 in 1863 and 1864.[18]

Examining city homicides from 1852 to 1869, Eric Monkkonen found that where their identity was known, 81 percent of the killers and 83.5 percent of the victims were foreign-born, in either Ireland, Germany, or England. Native-born white killers and victims were each under 10 percent. Since the figures for foreign killers/victims were double the proportion of foreign-born in the city at the time (which was about 41 percent), Monkkonen concluded "that young Irish and German males were slaughtering each other in New York City, [and] that at midcentury homicide was an ethnic problem."[19]

Monkkonen's comment gives the Irish and Germans equal billing, but recall that in the same book he estimated the Irish homicide rate "during the decade centered on 1860" at 37.5 per 100,000, more than twice that of the German Americans. Of note, too, is his finding that Irish spouses were responsible for 59 percent of the husband/wife killings in the nineteenth century, more than four times that of any other group.[20]

The Irish also provided the shock troops for the bloodiest riot the city ever knew, the Draft Riot of 1863. Measured by number of deaths caused, the Draft Riot was not only the worst mob violence in the city's history; it probably was the deadliest ever in the United States. Historians aren't sure of the actual toll, said to range anywhere from 105 to 500, but even the lower figure will suffice to top the record books.[21] "A vast majority of the rioters were Irish," reported Herbert Asbury in his colorful account, "simply because the gangsters and the other criminal elements of the city were largely of that race."[22] Less than a decade later, the Irish again were the principals in New York disturbances, this time in the so-called Orange Riots, which left over sixty dead, more than one hundred injured.[23] Most of the victims were Irish Catholics, protesting efforts to hold an Orange Day parade commemorating the Protestant Irish cause.

Following the big spike in New York homicides in the 1860s, the rate declined fairly steadily until 1900. By the 1890s, two generations after the potato famine immigration, there is evidence that Irish aggressiveness had toned down. In Philadelphia, for instance, Irish murder indictments fell below the overall rate for the city.[24] In New York, the huge Irish gang wars—pitched battles between grown men (and even some women)—already were reduced to legend.

Not that gangs were defunct. To the contrary, in poor neigborhoods all over lower Manhattan young men and boys eagerly joined gangs, described by one account as "the basic unit of social life among young males in New York in the nineteenth century."[25] From the 1860s to the 1870s, some of the bands turned from street warfare to a potentially more lucrative activity, bank robbery, but gang feuds and brawls continued. The biggest rivalry was between the Bowery Boys and the Dead Rabbits, and each of the adult gangs had juvenile "farm teams," such as the Little Dead Rabbits and the Little Plug Uglies, that replenished senior gang membership for years. The Plug Uglies and their juvenile counterparts operated out of the notorious Five Points neighborhood in the south of Manhattan, probably the roughest area in New York City in the mid-nineteenth century.

Perhaps the most powerful gang in the post–Civil War period was the Whyos, "a huge group who ranged all over Lower Manhattan."[26] By the mid-1890s, the Whyos, last of the old-era gangs, were fading, their leaders succumbing to imprisonment or death. They were succeeded by four huge gangs, the biggest of which, the Five Pointers, was said to have 1,200 members and close ties to Tammany Hall.[27] These end-of-century gangs engaged in street fights that threatened bystanders and broke store windows, but the days of out-and-out warfare in the streets were over. While some of the late nineteenth-century gangs remained "dedicated to violence for its own sake," others became preoccupied with theft.[28]

The Irish at this time lived mainly on the west side of Manhattan, in the Hell's Kitchen slum. The exact boundaries of Hell's Kitchen are a matter of debate, but the borders were roughly 8th Avenue to the North River (as the Hudson was then known), and 23rd to 59th Streets. There, the Gophers, one of the four gangs to succeed the Whyos, reigned. Stealing from freight cars and the New York Central Railroad depot seems to have been the favorite Gopher activity. The railroad ran at street level on 11th Avenue, through the heart of Hell's Kitchen, to the depot on 30th Street. (Given the danger to pedestrians, 11th Avenue came to be known as "Death Avenue." It was not until the 1930s that the New York Central placed the tracks below ground.) The railroad eventually organized a private security force (of ex-cops), which roughed up gang members. At the same time, the advent of reform administrations in City Hall ended Tammany protection and freed the city police to move in on gang leaders. By 1910, so many Gopher chieftains were in prison that the gang was forced to disband.[29] World War I (1914–18) marked the end of the mass gang era in New York City. And with the breakup of the big gangs, the streets were said to have become "considerably safer."[30]

## Slums

Hell's Kitchen typified the New York slum, its impoverished residents densely packed into tenement housing. The brick tenements actually were an improvement over the wooden shanties that frequently burned to the ground in nineteenth-century cities, or the earlier generation of tenements, many without indoor lighting, plumbing, or heating. Still, life in the "improved" 1890s tenements was hard, almost unimaginably so today, as over one hundred people were jammed into a building on a tiny 25 × 100–foot lot.

A typical tenement was four to six stories tall, six being the maximum allowed without an elevator, with one or two toilets, one water faucet, and four apartments per floor. The building was dumbbell-shaped, with a courtyard in the center. The outer wings were indented down their middles to provide air and sunlight to more apartments. The tenements were packed together as closely as possible, and two dumbbells side by side created a narrow shaft, sometimes used as a garbage dump by occupants, with the consequent stench and vermin.

With immigration swelling New York's population in the last two decades of the nineteenth century, it wasn't uncommon for more than one family to occupy an apartment. The result, in places such as the Lower East Side, was a population density greater than most cities in the world. A single block in lower Manhattan frequently housed anywhere from 2,500 to 3,500 people. The Tenth Ward alone, heart of the Lower East Side, had 57,596 people in 1890, which comes to 522 persons per acre. For all of Manhattan, the density was 114; for the whole of New York City (eight years before the merger with Brooklyn) it was 60 per acre. The steady flow of immigrants made crowding worse each year. Within five years, in 1895, the Tenth Ward population jumped from 57,596 to 70,168, and by 1900, the population density was 700 per acre, highest in the world.[31]

As might be expected, the crowding and filth had serious health consequences. Seventy percent of the deaths in New York City involved tenement dwellers, who died at a rate two to three times that of residents of other urban areas.[32] Despite the construction of thousands of tenements throughout New York, the housing stock was inadequate to shelter all who flooded into the city. Some lived in boardinghouses, but as these cost roughly $24 a month, many of the poor could afford to sleep only in a flophouse (25¢ a night for a cot, locker and screen; 10¢ for cot only; 7¢ for a wall-hung canvas hammock; 5¢ for a spot on the floor). Others slept in the streets, avoiding the harsh winter by overnighting in police station barracks.[33]

The lodgers must not have found the police station experience very pleasant; photographs show men crammed into rough wooden bunks. Jacob Riis complained bitterly about his maltreatment as a police lodger shortly after his arrival in the United States. He wrote in his famous 1890 exposé, *How the Other Half Lives,* that most station house "beds" were the soft side of a plank, and that each year nearly 150,000 New Yorkers felt compelled to accept such police hospitality, including more than 9,000 homeless young men nightly in the Bowery district.[34]

The 1890s were the waning years for police departments undertaking such social welfare functions as lodging and sometimes feeding the homeless, or caring for lost (or abandoned) children. The movement to professionalize policing had begun and police reformers were eager to concentrate on law enforcement (and later, with the advent of the automobile, traffic control). In 1896, Theodore

Roosevelt, then a commissioner of police in New York, ended the practice of lodging, which couldn't have made life for the homeless any easier.[35] Nor did it suddenly transform the New York police into professional crime fighters; as will be seen, they were abusive and corrupt and remained so for decades.

As for the children, private reform groups, such as the Society for the Prevention of Cruelty to Children, formed in the late 1800s, relieved the police of responsibility for their care. Riis said that from 1875 to 1890, the society intervened in nearly 139,000 cases, protected more than 25,000 children, and obtained around 16,000 convictions for child-beating and abuse. He estimated that in 1890, 15,000 dependent children were in New York's asylums and institutions.[36]

## Poverty

The level of indigence in late nineteenth-century America was much greater than anything imaginable in our own day. Robert Hunter's 1907 book, simply entitled *Poverty*, considered the "well-to-do" to be anyone earning between $5,000 and $50,000 annually, the "middle class" to make between $500 and $5,000, and the "poorer classes" to earn under $500 per year. In 1890, Hunter reported, 44 percent of all U.S. households fell into each of the bottom two categories. In other words, 44 percent of American households were on the lowest rung of the social ladder, scarcely earning $500 a year.[37]

A 1907 survey of New York City "workingmen's families" gives a sense of the standard of living of the poor in that era. Among those taking in less than $600 a year, according to the survey investigators, three-quarters were underfed, 88 percent were underclothed, and over two-thirds were housed in overcrowded apartments. Half of these families had to gather their fuel from the streets.[38]

Even allowing for massive inflation of the currency, contemporary America is an incomparably more affluent country. Today's bottom rung, those considered "below poverty," has shrunk to roughly 12 percent of American households earning nearly $20,000 per annum.[39]

In 1890s New York City, Hunter estimated that the numbers in poverty "rarely fell below 25 per cent of all the people." This is far less than his national calculation of 44 percent, which would have included the impoverished rural South, but still roughly twice today's figure. He offered, however, little solid evidence for his estimate. While I have no particular reason to doubt any of Hunter's figures, they are, as he recognized, only fragmentary. Among the few solid numbers he provided were data collected by the New York State Board of Charities on the number of statewide residents who received public or private assistance. For 1897, the Board of Charities tallied about 1.3 million people, or 19 percent of the state population.[40]

It should be noted that 1897 was one of the worst years of a severe depression that struck the country in 1893, second only to the catastrophic slump of the 1930s. Production and wages sank; 156 railroads went into receivership; over 800 banks failed; bankruptcies soared. As jobless men roamed the streets urban tensions were heightened. Things got so bad during the downturn that in the dead of winter 1894, the mayor of New York ordered the police to do a house-to-house survey of conditions; they found about 70,000 unemployed.[41]

Naturally, much of the poverty of the Gilded Age went hand in hand with unemployment, since there was no social safety net to make up for a lost job. The 1890 Census, conducted before the depression, estimated at 15.1 percent the number of workers nationwide over age ten (!) who were gainfully employed but out of work part of the year. In the 1900 Census the figure increased to 22.3 percent, but for the male population, 39 percent were said to be idle from four to six months in the year.[42] Obviously, all-year-round employment was not yet universal in the United States. The census figures, however, are not considered reliable. Contemporary economists estimate the average unemployment rate for the 1890s at a modestly high 8.9 percent, but during the depression years of that decade, the average rate was said to be 11.89 percent.[43]

Better-off New Yorkers increasingly were finding "white collar" jobs in the city's burgeoning finance, banking, newspaper, and publishing industries. For the poor and immigrant, however, light manufacturing, such as metal working, food processing, clothing finishing (a specialty of the Jewish tenement "sweatshops"), and construction labor were the main sources of employment. Such work was especially attractive since knowledge of English was not required. Italian and Irish immigrants took most of the physical labor jobs, on the docks as longshoremen and constructing roads, subways and the city's many new buildings. These jobs were dangerous and safety regulations were ignored. Hunter estimated the fatal accident rate for the United States at 80 to 85 per 100,000 people, roughly double today's rate.[44] It's fair to say that New Yorkers of this period had far more to fear from accidents, both on and off the job, than from assaults. Municipal employment, such as in the police department, also provided steady work, but this was basically an Irish monopoly.[45]

## Police

Few writers have anything good to say about nineteenth-century police. They did do a fair amount of what nowadays would be called "order maintenance." That is, "they often intervened in brawls, quieted family quarrels, escorted drunks home, . . . admonished careless drivers" and untangled traffic snarls in the days when there were few traffic lights or rules of the road that actually were obeyed. Much of this was accomplished without arresting anyone, a sign that street peace rather than strict enforcement of the law was the objective.[46] Moreover, fighting crime was low on the list of priorities, as police were expected to inspect boilers, clean streets, and, as we already noted, provide for the care of the homeless and lost or abandoned children.

Another point sympathetic to the police is that a patrol officer was pretty much on his own on the streets, as call boxes weren't installed in Manhattan until the early twentieth century, and of course, cars and radio communication were an even longer time coming.[47] As slum toughs were not above attacking a lone officer, the job required street smarts, muscle, and a fair amount of grit. It didn't require much else, however (aside from a payoff to get appointed in the first place), and the benefits were considerable, making it very attractive to uneducated immigrants. For the Irish, who controlled New York City's political apparatus and the patronage that went with it, the police department was a source of steady employment for decades, and few non-Irish need apply.

This, unfortunately, completes the positive side of the portrait of nineteenth-century police, as the rest of the tale is, as Luc Sante put it, one of "corruption, complacency, confusion, sloth, and brutality."[48] What's more, as crime increased and took new forms, it was clear that the old model of policing was ineffectual as well. Eventually—but not with any great impact before 1920—the "professionalized" police force model, with its focus on expertise and training in pursuit of the goal of fighting crime, became the accepted standard.

Nineteenth-century police work was the antithesis of professional. The New York City policeman's motto, attributed to Chief William S. "Big Bill" Devery, was

Hear, see and say nothin',
Eat, drink and pay nothin'.[49]

The corruption was endemic and systematic. The police, essentially, served as middlemen between the city's illegal vice operatives and its politicians, part of a system overseen by the Tammany Society, operating out of its famous 14th Street Manhattan hall. The bosses of Tammany—ten successive Irish-Americans from 1872 on—chose all of the Democratic Party nominees to political office, which meant, as a practical matter, nearly all city officeholders.

The city was divided into legislative districts, used to elect both members of the state legislature and the City Council. (Districts had replaced wards in 1857, but ward boundaries were maintained for administrative purposes, and in the 1890s, the term was still commonly used to refer to various locations in Manhattan.) The district politicians picked election precinct captains to turn out the vote for the Democrats, in exchange for which the captains would arrange for various benefits to the largely immigrant population, including help with family emergencies, jobs, and the resolution of legal problems. The local politicians also appointed the police precinct captain, who in turn selected the detectives and patrolmen in his precinct. Even after 1883, when New York adopted a civil service system, ostensibly mandating merit hiring, the politicians retained control over police appointments.[50] In short, Tammany controlled virtually every New York City politician and municipal employee, which of course included the police department.

New York's politicos routinely received bribes and kickbacks from municipal contractors, real estate developers, political aspirants, and various lawyers and insurance agents. They also profited from "honest graft" (as state senator George Washington Plunkitt, a long-time Tammany bigwig, dubbed it), essentially taking advantage of insider revelations to purchase real estate in locations where city construction projects were imminent.[51] But the corruption most directly implicating the police involved the payoffs by the gambling parlors, saloons, and brothels that lined the streets of lower Manhattan. The vice laws rendered these operations illegal, so a tribute paid to the district politicians and the police captain became the price of staying in business. Collecting that levy was a police function. The other crucial police task, insofar as Tammany was concerned, was to see to it, by force or fraud if necessary, that the Democratic candidates won the elections. The police apparently carried out their assignments with relish, as their jobs and their outside incomes depended on it.

A New York City patrolman's salary was between $1000 and $1,200 a year, in addition to which, he could count on free services from the brothels, taverns, and betting parlors on his beat. Patrol officers also collected petty graft, both "clean" and "dirty." The latter involved shakedowns of gamblers, pimps, prostitutes, liquor dealers and saloonkeepers. A state legislative committee investigating police corruption wrote in 1894: "The poor, ignorant foreigner residing on the great east side of the city has been especially subjected to a brutal and infamous rule by the police, in conjuction with the administration of the local inferior courts, so that it is beyond a doubt that innocent people who have refused to yield to criminal extortion, have been clubbed and harassed and confined to jail."[52] The clean variety of graft had no victims. It consisted of "donations" from businessmen for overlooking violations, checking on shop door locks, or guarding upscale gambling parlors.

The patrol officer's job was attractive enough that applicants were expected to pay in order to get it, the amount escalating with one's rank. They also had to pay for their own uniforms and equipment, as well as contribute to police associations and politically favored charities.[53] Law enforcement historian David R. Johnson described the system:

By the late nineteenth century politicians had established a standard fee for every appointment, from patrolman to captain. An applicant for the lowly job of walking a beat had to pay $300, aspiring captains $15,000. These fees provided an additional incentive, if any was needed, for profiteering. New York's precinct captains occupied the best positions to exploit their offices. Each captain was, for all practical purposes, the master of his domain. He selected one of his detectives to be his personal bagman. Once a month this officer made the rounds of every saloon, gambling house, and brothel in the precinct to collect their tribute. Each business paid a fee which varied according to its size and receipts. At the turn of the century the police assessed poolrooms between $100 and $300 a month; whorehouses between $50 and $150; and gambling houses $50 to $300 a month. The city's saloons contributed an estimated $50,000 to $60,000 a month to the police and politicians. Most of this money went to the commanders and their political sponsors. Bagmen kept perhaps 20 percent of each month's collection and turned the remainder over to their superiors.[54]

The 1890s police station was like a frat house, with a 40-bed dorm for reserve officers, necessitated by the absence of the three-platoon system, adopted in 1902. An arrestee would be taken to a holding pen in the station basement or annex, adjacent to the precinct homeless shelter, then transferred to the city's jail, the Tombs (so called because it was modeled after an Egyptian mausoleum). The Tombs complex, located in lower Manhattan, included men's and women's detention facilities, a jail for boys, courtrooms, a vagrant and drunk tank ("Bummers' Hall"), and six cells for wealthy arrestees. Accused felons were held at the Tombs until sentenced, then sent upstate to Sing Sing or Auburn prisons. Convicted misdemeanants served out their sentences on Blackwell's Island.

Blackwell's, nowadays Roosevelt Island, held a complex of buildings, including a penitentiary, which, in 1892, took in about 3,000 misdemeanants per year. But the island's workhouse, which was limited to drunk and disorderly cases, received over seven times the number sent to the Penitentiary, around 22,000 yearly. This is a good indication of the high proportion of arrests for public inebriation. Blackwell's also had an almshouse, which received over 3,000 paupers annually (mainly the blind, terminally ill, paralyzed, or otherwise disabled), an insane asylum, and various hospitals. Some of the treatment in the penitentiary was quite rough ("cooler" cells, high-pressure hoses, water torture) and there were occasional prisoner riots.[55]

The police also were rough, "[i]ndiscriminate use of the nightstick" their hallmark. The career of Alexander S. Williams, nicknamed "Clubber," is emblematic. Williams began as a patrolman in the late 1860s, assigned to cleaning up the gangs. He eventually advanced to inspector, with responsibility for the Tenderloin district, in the northern part of Hell's Kitchen, one of the roughest spots in Manhattan. His maxim, like his nickname, says it all: "There is more law in the end of a policeman's nightstick than in a decision of the Supreme Court." Charges were brought against Clubber eighteen times, but the Board of Police Commissioners always acquitted him. By 1887, he had 358 formal complaints against him and had been fined 244 times. The end came in the 1890s, when two investigative committees exposed his corruption, revealing that he owned a house in a posh New York neighborhood, an estate in Connecticut, and a steam yacht—all on a police inspector's salary. Forced to resign, Williams lived "in comfortable disgrace" and died a multimillionaire in 1910.[56]

Clubber's demise was hastened by reform efforts, which, in the 1890s, culminated in two investigations by Republican-led committees of the New York State legislature, the Lexow Committee of 1894, headed by Senator Clarence Lexow, and Assemblyman Robert Mazet's investigation of 1899. The moving force behind these exposés, which were fully, even gleefully, reported in the media and captured national attention, was Presbyterian minister Charles H. Parkhurst, head of the New York Society for the Prevention of Crime. Parkhurst launched his campaign in 1892 with a thunderous sermon, accusing "the Mayor and his whole gang of drunken and lecherous subordinates" of manufacturing criminals. As for New York's police, he called them "the dirtiest, crookedest, and ugliest lot of men ever combined in semi-military array outside of Japan and Turkey." Although Parkhurst understood that the problem went far beyond corrupt police and really involved the entire city government, the police became the immediate focus of attention.[57]

Throughout 1894, the Lexow Committee heard 678 witnesses and took over 10,000 pages of testimony, 9,500 of which were about police corruption, which embarrassed some high-ranking officers like Clubber Williams into retiring. In addition, around seventy indictments were filed against police brass, but only a small number were convicted, and many of the convictions were reversed. Of potentially greater significance, Tammany was defeated in the mayoral election of 1894, and the new mayor, William L. Strong, named Theodore Roosevelt to the four-man Board of Police Commissioners.[58]

Roosevelt, elected president of the board, set about reforming the force. He fired some officers, broke ethnic barriers by appointing Jews, named a women as his secretary (a department first), created a bicycle squad, set up a telephonic communications system, established training for new recruits, demanded politeness in dealing with the public, and sought to base promotions on merit. And, as we already know, he ended the practice of lodging the homeless in police stationhouses. Despite all this, which incidentally gave him a national profile, T.R. lost public support when he began aggressively enforcing Sunday blue laws, and by 1897 he resigned to take a Navy Department position in Washington.[59]

More significantly, despite the sensational attacks on police corruption, the media attention, and aroused public sentiment, and despite Commissioner Roosevelt's considerable efforts, the reform movement was unable to effectuate fundamental and lasting changes in the city. Reform administrations in City Hall alternated with Tammany restorations, and the "attempt to change law enforcement policies and eliminate vice came to nothing."[60]

## Crime?

If one sums up all of the relevant conditions in New York City in the 1890s, one has, it would seem, the perfect recipe for a crime wave:

- a tradition of ethnic violence and gang warfare
- large and growing immigrant populations, most without English, some with a history of violence
- extensive ethnic and racial prejudice
- massive slums
- enormous overcrowding, filth, and disease
- widespread poverty and homelessness
- serious economic depression from 1893 to 1897
- corrupt and abusive police
- corrupt city government.

There was, in fact, plenty of crime in late nineteenth-century New York, but it was vice, not violent crime. Vice crime—selling liquor, gambling, and prostitution—was the obsession of the reformers. One would expect, however, that if, in the 1890s, street violence was perceived to be a significant social problem there would be a concerted effort to do something about that too. After all, middle-class Americans at the close of the nineteenth century were not shy about organizing to reform.

For instance, in the 1890s, over one hundred cities had charity organization societies, on behalf of which thousands of "friendly visitors," usually middle-class female volunteers, visited slum families (apparently without threat of assault) to encourage them to adopt more morally upright lives. In addition, the first American settlement house, intended to provide various services to the immigrant poor, began in 1886 New York City with Stanton Coit's Neighborhood Guild. Three years later, Jane Addams organized the famous Hull House in Chicago. By the end of the century, over one hundred settlement houses had been established in the immigrant sections of most big cities.[61]

Not only were middle-class Americans eager to throw themselves into volunteer efforts to reform the poor; they also used their political influence to enlist the coercive power of the state. As noted earlier, Reverend Parkhurst's New York Society for the Prevention of Crime galvanized the state legislature into a sensational exposé of the city's police. As a result, a reform mayor was elected and reformist laws and policies were adopted, though sometimes with limited effects (such as Roosevelt's police reforms).

Indeed, some reform laws made the vice crime problem worse. A good example is the Raines Law of 1896, a state liquor licensing law revision, aimed at cutting back on Sunday sales. The law provided an exception, plausibly enough, for hotels selling drinks with Sunday meals. Suddenly, taverns and even so-called low dives, rented rooms in the overhead floors, declared themselves "hotels," and became in reality brothels and saloons combined. Raines Law hotels even spread to well-to-do neighborhoods, arousing "a storm of indignation."[62]

The failure of the Raines Law notwithstanding, reformist elements had public and media support as well as the organizational drive and skill to tackle all the social problems of the late nineteenth century, naïve and ineffectual as their remedies may have been. And yet there was no major effort by private organizations or public authorities to stamp out violent crime, not at least in New York. There didn't seem to be much public discussion of the matter either, though all sorts of publications offered shocking stories of violent, but apparently isolated, incidents.

The evidence we have, imperfect as it is, indicates that New York City did not experience a violent crime wave in the 1890s.

Eric Monkkonen's laborious research found that the New York City homicide rate—our best crime indicator—declined by 45 percent, from an average 5.8 per 100,000 in the early 1870s to 3.2 in the first half of the 1890s. In the mid-1890s, as the depression pummeled the economy, the rate rose a bit to near 4, where it finished the decade. For the entire ten-year period, the average was a mere 3.34. Taking a more comprehensive view of the matter, the homicide rate of the 1890s was, in fact, among the lowest in the city's history, lower even than the "Golden Age" late 1940s, early 1950s. To give a sense of how extraordinarily positive the 1890s figures were, consider that from 1972 to 1994, the city's rates only once dipped below 20 per 100,000, and in 1990 the rate topped 30.[63]

Arrest statistics for homicide and other crimes of violence seemingly tell a somewhat different tale. These figures can be read as suggesting that there was an increase in violent crime, or (more likely) an increase in police attention to violent crime. New York City arrest data for homicide in the last decade of the nineteenth century show a fairly steady increase, from 91 arrests in 1892 to 213 in

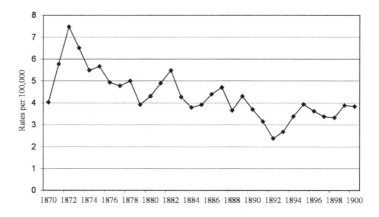

FIGURE 6.1. Homicide rates per 100,000, New York City, 1870–1900. *Source:* Monkkonen, "Homicides in New York City," https://doi.org/10.3886/ICPSR03226.v1.

1897, the year before the merger with Brooklyn. The homicide arrest rate, which takes into account the city's growing population, also rose, from 5.69 in 1892 to 13.85 in 1900. Similar rate increases in other crimes of violence occurred over the same time period. Robbery arrest rates, for instance, nearly doubled from 13.01 in 1892 to 24.53 in 1900. And the ratio of homicide arrests to drunkenness arrests increased in that same period by a factor of over three.[64] All of this indicates increasing attention by the police department to violent crime as the century waned. But this doesn't necessarily prove that violent crime, as opposed to violent crime *arrests,* rose.

At the end of the nineteenth century, most arrests in New York, and, for that matter, in cities throughout the nation, were for public drunkenness. In Manhattan and the Bronx, for example, from 1892 to 1900, 57.6 percent of all arrests were for being drunk or disorderly (the two offenses often were charged together), whereas only 6.6 percent were for felonies. In our own day, by contrast, roughly half of Gotham's arrests are for felonies. Turn-of-the-century concerns with violent crime must have been pretty muted if the police took into custody nearly nine times as many drunks as felons.[65]

The fact remains that there were fewer murders in New York City in the entire last decade of the nineteenth century than there were in *any one year* between 1970 and 1990. From 1890 to 1899 there were, all told, 675 murders; in 1970 alone there were 1,117, and that was the best year of the modern period.[66]

In short, the historical evidence along with the best quantitative proof we have suggest that New York City—despite all of the socioeconomic red flags—did not experience an upsurge in violent crime as the nineteenth century passed. After examining several other big cities—Chicago next—we will ask why crime *didn't* rise.

## CHICAGO

Of crime in Chicago during the last decades of the nineteenth and on into the next century we know, thanks to meticulous recordkeeping by the city's police, a great deal. It seems that the Chicago Police Department kept records on every homicide in the city, and when scholars matched these records with newspaper accounts and coroners' reports, they found them to be "remarkably complete."[67]

Crime historian Jeffrey Adler examined these documents and he has given us a detailed account of Chicago crime. He found, in a nutshell, that yearly zigzags notwithstanding, murder rose more than 300 percent between the late 1870s, when it was a bit over three per 100,000, and 1915 to 1919, when it was nearly ten per 100,000. As for the 1890s, our focus here, rates averaged 5.55 per 100,000, which, while hardly alarming by contemporary standards, was around 40 percent higher than the New York City rate. Why should this be? What was it about Chicago that made it, as Adler put it (quoting muckraker Lincoln Steffens), "first in violence, deepest in dirt?"[68]

Chicago in 1880 had 0.5 million people, double that (1.1 million) by 1890, and 1.7 million by the 1900 Census count.[69] Much as in New York, immigrants flooded to the city. Over one-third of the metropolis was foreign-born, and an amazing 78 percent of Chicago's population was of foreign parentage—and that was in 1890, *before* the massive foreign influx of the next two decades.[70] Twenty-nine percent of 1890 Chicagoans were of German ancestry, 15 percent of Irish, 9 percent of Scandinavian.[71] The African American, Jewish, and Italian populations of the 1890s were still too small to play a significant role in the overall crime picture. Between the Great Fire (1871) and the 1893 World's Fair, the black population had tripled, but African Americans still comprised under 2 percent of the city's total population throughout the last decade of the century. Russians (mainly Jews), were 1 percent of Chicago in 1890, Italians only 0.7 percent.[72] In poor inner-city areas, home base for crimes, Germans predominated (36 percent), with Scandinavians (20 percent) and Irish (19 percent) next most numerous.[73]

Examining the crime rates of these low population groups can be instructive, if only as a harbinger. Despite the modest impact of their nineteenth-century crime, blacks and Italians already exhibited the behavior that would so greatly contribute to Chicago's twentieth-century crime problem. Before the twentieth century, Italian homicide rates never fell below 20 per 100,000, running four to five times the citywide rate.[74] As for African Americans, from 1875 to 1890, their homicide rates were more than six times the level of white rates, leaping to over 80 per 100,000 in the middle of the last decade.[75] There is every reason to believe that these groups brought their crime cultures with them, as their rates were high from the time they arrived in the city.

By contrast, other groups, landing in Chicago at roughly the same time and in similarly distressed circumstances, had much lower rates. Take Scandinavians, for example. Over 100,000 lived in Chicago in 1890, making it the biggest Scandinavian enclave in the United States. Yet Norwegian-born Chicagoans murdered at only half the citywide rate, while Swedes killed at less than one-quarter of the rate for the city as a whole, less than one-twentieth of the black rate.[76] German immigrants provide another contrast to blacks and Italians. Between 1890 and 1910, Germans were 12.5 percent of Chicago and 36 percent of the central city, but were responsible for less than 5 percent of the total homicides.[77]

## THE VILEST SLUM IN CHICAGO

At the end of the nineteenth century, center Chicago was surrounded by seven miles of factories and workers' cottages, "an intensely centralized, economically segregated city with a belt of despair rimming the Loop."[78]

The epicenter of that despair was Packingtown, or the "Back of the Yards"—"the vilest slum in Chicago." In 1893, twenty-five thousand people worked in Chicago's stockyards and packing plants, processing almost 14 million animals a year. The meat-packing industry was built by two brilliant organizers whose products are known to this day: Gustavus Franklin Swift and Philip Armour. Armour and Swift's business acumen, along with that of the other Chicago commercial elite—George Pullman, of railroad car fame; Richard Warren Sears and Aaron Montgomery Ward, inventors of the hugely successful mail order business; and Marshall Field, the department store mogul—created "the Chicago production and exchange engine that had powered the city's spectacular recovery from the fire, built the new downtown business area, and given the city the 1893 Columbian Exposition."[79] But it also created Packingtown.

Packingtown housed over thirty-five thousand people in cottages or two-story tenements. (Chicago, unlike New York, didn't build many five-story tenements.) Many of its denizens were Poles and Slovaks, lured to the packing companies by labor agents. These east Europeans were, in fact, supplanting their more highly skilled immigrant predecessors, the Irish, Germans, and Bohemians, who, thanks to Swift and Armour's assembly line, no longer were needed to work the plants. The ethnic tensions that arose between the new, unskilled, and lower-paid immigrants and their better-paid forerunners were a real obstacle to union organizers, foreshadowing the racial conflicts at the time of the First World War when blacks were brought in as strikebreakers.

To the east of the slum lay the yards; to the west, the largest municipal dump in the city; south, a conglomeration of railroad tracks; to the north, Bubbly Creek, the massively polluted arm of the Chicago River. Packingtown, in a word, stank—even more than the rest of the city, which was no bed of roses. Rubbish was piled in alleys, sometimes a full story high. Rotting wooden streets were filled with horse manure, decaying garbage, and dog and horse corpses. Uncovered garbage boxes, overflowing and rat-infested due to infrequent pick-ups, decorated the plank-board sidewalks. For many years there were no sewers in this part of the city; garbage and drain water collected in ditches beside the roads. In-dwelling bathing facilities were virtually unknown in the slums, and residents simply did not bathe in winter. Is it any wonder that Chicago had the highest death rate from typhoid of any big city in the nation and that Packingtown's tuberculosis rates were among the worst?[80]

Between 1875 and 1900, Chicago's homicide rate per 100,000 people rose from an average of 3.1 in the 1870s to 5.6 in the 1890s, a 79 percent increase.[81] As the graph shows (fig. 6.2), the upward trend began in the late 1880s and climbed steadily to the end of the century. Compared, however, to our era, the last decades of the twentieth century, Chicago of the late 1800s was a veritable peaceable kingdom, with myriad peoples coexisting in relative harmony. In the early 1990s, Chicago's homicide rate seldom dipped below 30 per 100,000—more than five times the rate a century earlier.

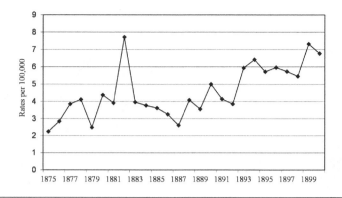

FIGURE 6.2. Homicide rates per 100,000, Chicago, 1875–1900. *Source:* Prepared by the author based on adjusted homicide rate data supplied by Jeffrey S. Adler.

Comparing murder in Chicago and New York City during the final stages of the nineteenth century is interesting, but a bit puzzling. Overall, America's two urban giants seemed quite similar. From 1875 to 1899, New York's homicide rate was 4.1 per 100,000 while Chicago's was 4.5, only a 9 percent difference. But when we break out the last decade of the century it becomes clear that Chicago's violent crime problem was becoming more serious than New York's. From 1890 to 1899, Chicago's rate had risen to an average 5.6, 40 percent higher than Gotham's 3.3.

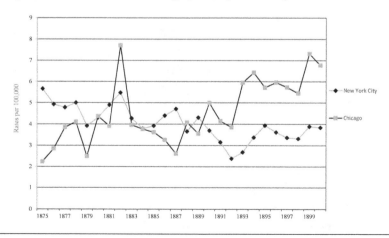

FIGURE 6.3. Homicide victimization rates per 100,000, New York City and Chicago, 1875–1900. *Source:* Chicago data supplied by Jeffrey S. Adler. New York data from Monkkonen, "Homicides in New York City," https://doi.org/10.3886/ICPSR03226.v1.

What accounts for the difference between the cities? The answer is not clear, as both municipalities seemed to face the same social problems: widespread poverty, ethnic tensions, massive population increases, corrupt police, major economic depression, and so on. It is possible that the answer never will be known. Nor may it matter terribly. For in the end, the most significant facts are that violent crime was, in both cities, quite low compared to the late twentieth century, and that the nineteenth-century violence was different not only in magnitude, but in quality, that is, it was acquaintance-based rather than indiscriminate.

In Chicago, as virtually everywhere else in nineteenth-century America, violent crime between strangers was less common than it would become in the 1900s. As Chicago crime historian Jeffrey Adler explained, "the participants were young, tough, and poor, and they knew each other."[82] He might have added "male" to that portrait since few women were involved, except as casus belli or victims of spousal rage. There also is evidence that a disproportionate number of the combatants were Irish, which accords with other indicators of Irish violence as well as the size of their population in the inner city (which was 19 percent Irish in 1900).[83]

The typical Chicago murder scene was a saloon—the center of social intercourse in American cities—or its immediate environs. Taverns, both legal and illegal, were ubiquitous; in 1895 there was one for every 232 Chicago residents. From 1875 to 1890, these saloons accounted for one-fifth of the homicides in the city, and over two-thirds of the tavern homicides were a result of drunken brawls. In fact, brawl homicide topped the list of causes of murder, accounting for 1 of every 4. Forty-two percent of the brawl deaths involved guns; nearly all involved alcohol (though not always intoxication). The vast majority of the remaining killings—quarrels over money, fights between coworkers, neighborhood feuds, disputes between relatives, lovers and spouses—also were acquaintance-based.[84]

Chicago, at this time, had a disproportionate number of young men, 112 for every 100 females, and a majority of the males in their twenties were unmarried. A surfeit of young males, of course, would be expected to swell the homicide count. New York City, by contrast, had more females than males, 103 to every 100, and the female imbalance was greater still for the crucial crime-prone ages twenty to twenty-five, hitting 119:100. Could this gender disparity explain the crime differential between the two cities? Undoubtedly it contributed, but just how much is difficult to say.[85]

The homicide perpetrators shared what Adler called a "plebeian culture," a lower- or working-class set of attitudes. For aggressive and impulsive men such as these, their inhibitions lowered by alcohol, "only a few words or seemingly trivial actions transformed revelry and camaraderie into brutality and homicidal rage." These young, uneducated, hot-headed males provided the overwhelming majority of the victims as well as their killers. The remaining fatalities were, by and large, their wives, but spouse-killing accounted for less than one-half of the brawl deaths.[86]

The killings typical of the nineteenth century seem especially tragic to us, as the victims were relatively young and the anger that destroyed them appears to have been completely out of proportion to the provocation. On the other hand, as I've noted before, these acquaintance-based homicides are in one crucial respect far less socially destructive than their twentieth-century counterparts. Acquaintance-murders create much less generalized fear in a community than murders of people who are strangers to one another. Taverns, after all, are avoidable, and even if violent husbands are not, victimization is at least limited to the home of the murderer. But those who kill indiscriminately—robbery-murderers, for instance—impose a fear tax on the entire community.

In nineteenth-century Chicago, seven out of ten robbery-homicides involved strangers, and this proportion rose in the twentieth century (to 94 percent). But robberies were exceptional. "Robberies, and particularly robbery homicides," Adler stated, "had been rare in nineteenth-century America."[87] In the late 1870s, when Chicago had around 400,000 people, there was, on average, less than one robbery-homicide per year. So unusual were these crimes that when they did occur they rated front page coverage in the newspapers. An 1875 killing of a saloonkeeper elicited this page one headline in the *Chicago Tribune*: "WELTERING IN BLOOD. *Murder of an Inoffensive Old German. He Is Discovered in the Morning Lying Dead in His Saloon.*" The article explained: "There had been nothing to provoke the attack; it was a deliberate cold-blooded slaughter for robbery, and in this light stood distinct from most of the Chicago murders which have generally been the result of brawls in which murder and murdered had been participants."[88]

With each passing decade, however, instances of robbery and accompanying murder increased. In the 1880s, there were only 13 robbery-murders (compared to 71 brawl-murders). By the 1890s, that figure jumped to 66, and in the first decade of the new century, 103. (Note the spike in the graph at 1893, just the time when the Chicago police established a special plainclothes antirobbery unit.) The trend was ominous.

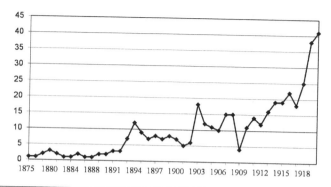

FIGURE 6.4. Robbery-homicides, Chicago, 1875–1920. *Source:* Adler, *First in Violence*, 243, and data provided by Adler.

I now continue our nineteenth-century journey with a peek at two West Coast cities—Los Angeles and San Francisco.

## LOS ANGELES

One of the great metropolises of contemporary America, Los Angeles was little more than a backwater for most of the nineteenth century. It wasn't until 1900 that the city broke the 100,000-residents mark, though Los Angeles County already had reached 170,000. The levels of violence in Los Angeles in the middle of the nineteenth century were little short of staggering. Crime historian Eric Monkkonen found L.A. County homicide rates for the 1840s and 1850s that topped 300 killings per 100,000. For the late 1850s, historian John Boessenecker tallied 90 homicides in the county, which comes to 18 a year in a place with no more than 10,000 people. It must be borne in mind that midcentury L.A.'s denizens were rootless, young, aggressive, males, armed and lusting for gold—the archetype of the saloon brawling, quick-triggered roughneck.[89]

By the end of the century there is little question that Los Angeles had mellowed considerably. Farming families and eastern transplants in search of a mild climate and gentler lifestyle (yes, even then) had moved in, the Southern Pacific and Santa Fe railroads easing travel from the rest of the continent. Oscar Winther, a historian of the city, described its new arrivals as "respectable and conservative . . . God-fearing, frugal Easterners and Middle Westerners who, influenced by promotion advertising, decided to seek semi-retirement in or near Los Angeles."[90]

The population growth, as a consequence of migration, was enormous. The city went from 11,000 in 1880, to 50,000 in 1890, to 102,000 at the end of the century. But compared to East Coast and Midwest cities, relatively few of the new Angelinos came from Europe. In 1900, 18 percent of Los Angeles County was foreign-born, whereas over 34 percent of Chicagoans had been born abroad. Among the foreigners in Los Angeles, the greatest numbers came from Germany, England, Canada, and Ireland; few were from Russia, Poland, or Italy. Likewise, in 1890, when more than three-fourths of Chicagoans had parents from another country, less than half of Los Angeles (48 percent) was of foreign descent, a figure that actually declined a bit (to 45 percent) by 1900, despite a decadal doubling of the city's population.[91]

Racially, Los Angeles was overwhelmingly white (which, as then defined, did not include Mexicans). For L.A. County, the 1900 Census tallied 163,975 whites (96 percent of the county population), 2,841 African Americans (1.7 percent of the population), 3,209 born in China (1.9 percent), and 1,613 born in Mexico (0.9 percent).[92] The vast influx to Los Angeles of African Americans and Mexicans would not occur until the twentieth century.

The great population gains notwithstanding, crime was down—way down compared to the middle of the century—proving once again that city growth and urbanization are not invariably linked to rising crime. Los Angeles County, which had been the most violent locale in midcentury California, underwent the most precipitous homicide decline. Los Angeles's 1890s homicide rate was not low, however, compared with other American cities. The county rate was 10.9, while the rate for the City of Los Angeles was 16.8 per 100,000. By contrast, Chicago's 1890s average was 5.6 and New York's was 3.3.[93]

Notice that murder rates seem to get higher as one moves west. It is no coincidence that nineteenth-century western cities also had a superabundance of males. All other factors being equal, the more young males in a locale, proportionally speaking, the higher the levels of violence. Table 6.2, which arrays cities from east to west, shows that as a general proposition, the farther west the municipality, the higher the male-female ratio. This reflected the tendency of the West to attract unattached, transient males seeking their fortune (as with the gold rush), rather than, as in the East and Central states, entire families permanently emigrating from Europe. "Late-nineteenth-century Boston and Philadelphia had plenty of young, unmarried men strutting around with guns and flasks," observed historian David Courtwright, "but they made up a much smaller proportion of the total municipal populations, ensuring . . . much lower rates of murder."[94]

TABLE 6.2. Ratio of males to 100 females, selected U.S. cities, 1890 and 1900

| City | 1890 | 1900 |
|------|------|------|
| Baltimore | 90 | 92 |
| Philadelphia | 95 | 96 |
| Chicago | 107 | 103 |
| St. Louis | 102 | 100 |
| Denver | 132 | 99 |
| Seattle | 167 | 177 |
| Portland | 168 | 142 |
| Los Angeles | 109 | 97 |
| San Francisco | 131 | 117 |

*Source:* Fogelson, *Fragmented Metropolis,* 64, 82.

The table also shows that, as a rule, the masculine tilt diminished by 1900. In late nineteenth-century Los Angeles, nearly three out of four inhabitants were born in the United States, many from California. And the newer arrivals were more apt to be families, not lone male fortune hunters.[95]

Another possible explanation for the high West Coast murder rates is the ubiquitousness of handguns in the region. But handguns were cheap at the end of the nineteenth century and common everywhere in the United States, so it is not clear that this explains very much. In Los Angeles County, an average 63 percent of the homicides between 1894 and 1900 involved firearms; in Chicago, from 1875 to 1890, 58 percent. The difference does not account for the near-doubling of the murder rate.[96]

A third reason for the relatively high murder rate may have something to do with the racial/ethnic factor. In his study of seven California counties in the last half of the nineteenth century (not including Los Angeles), Clare McKanna found a high incidence of homicide by American Indians, Chinese, and Hispanics (mostly of Mexican extraction), though whites murdered twice as many as these three groups combined. Unfortunately, McKanna made no attempt to calculate homicide rates, so we cannot say which of these groups was the most homicidal.[97]

Kevin Mullen, whose study of San Francisco will inform the discussion below, likewise found high murder rates for Hispanics and Chinese. Studies such as Mullen's and McKanna's suggest that these racial/ethnic minority groups also had high crime involvement in Los Angeles. But even if that inference were justified, their small numbers in the Los Angeles population—nonwhites comprised 6.3 percent of the city in 1890, 4.3 percent in 1900—create doubt that they were responsible for the city's elevated homicide rate.[98]

The take-away point here is the decline in crime. The more Los Angeles grew, the less violent it became, proving that the nature of the migration to a city is much more important than its population trajectory.

Now I discuss another West Coast city—San Francisco—where we have some intriguing data on ethnicity and crime.

## SAN FRANCISCO

As a result of the great California Gold Rush, San Francisco grew even more rapidly than Los Angeles, some 350 miles to the south. When gold was discovered in 1848, fewer than one thousand people lived in what had been Yerba Buena, a tiny settlement wrested from Mexico as a result of the Mexican-American War. Word of the discovery quickly spread, and that sleepy little settlement, which had now become the American town of San Francisco, grew to five thousand within only one year. By 1870, the population had reached almost 150,000, a figure that would double again in two decades. The 1890 Census count was 298,997; in 1900, it was 342,782, which was, at the time, roughly twice the population of Los Angeles County.[99]

In nineteenth-century San Francisco the Irish were major contributors to the high homicide rate; the Germans, by contrast, played a more pacific role. Kevin Mullen's data reveal that in the 1870s, when 14.7 percent of the city's population had been born in Ireland, that same immigrant group comprised 19.6 percent of those imprisoned or hanged for murder. In addition, at a time when Irish immigrants and their children totaled 35 percent of the population, 53 percent of the murder victims had ostensibly Irish surnames. (Because homicides are invariably disproportionately intraethnic it is highly likely that most of the Irish victims were killed by other Irish, but Mullen does not offer evidence on this. He concedes, moreover, that relying on surnames to identify ethnic Irish is risky, as many so identified could as easily have been English, Scots, Welsh, or Scotch-Irish.)

Another piece of evidence comes from coroners' records for 1879 through 1885, according to which 17.6 percent of the homicide victims were born in Ireland, a population that, at the time, made up 11.5 percent of the city's total. Finally, in the 1890s, when whites overall had homicide rates of 6.8 per 100,000, 1.8 points *below* the city average, Irish rates, which had declined significantly from earlier decades, were still at 11.1.[100]

These data, while perhaps not overwhelming, certainly point to high violent crime by San Francisco's Irish. There is corroborating evidence as well. San Francisco was hardly the only nineteenth-century American city with high Irish crime. In New York City, for example, the estimated 1860 Irish homicide rate was a scary 37.5 per 100,000. And New York's frequent riots along with its vicious gang warfare only burnished the image of the "wild Irish." "No ethnic group," observed crime historian Roger Lane, "was as desperate as the midcentury Irish, or as collectively pugnacious."[101]

It is interesting to note that homicides peaked in Ireland during the 1840s famine years, suggesting a cultural affinity for violence transported across the Atlantic. But Irish violence was much greater in America than in the homeland, for reasons that remain unclear.[102]

While the Irish were becoming less violent, the German element of the population—San Francisco's second biggest ethnic group—was contributing, as it seems to have done everywhere in late nineteenth-century America, to the peacefulness of the community. Nowadays Germans probably are not even thought of as a part of America's immigrant tradition. In truth, however, the Germans, along with the Irish, were the most important of all groups flocking to the nineteenth-century United States, the former comprising about 27 percent of the total immigrants in the last half of the century.

I now address the precipitous decline in San Francisco's crime rates from the middle to the end of the century. The explanation lies in the behavior of the city's key ethnic groups. Irish immigrants committed the bulk of the midcentury crime, but the Irish immigrant became less aggressive as the century progressed, and those who put down roots in San Francisco took advantage of its opportunities for betterment and became less dependent on violence to achieve their ends. At the same time, increasing numbers of German immigrants—already committed to nonviolent ways—helped transform the ethos of the city. In addition to the ethnic change, the gender factor also was crucial. As more women arrived in town and families replaced unattached male fortune-seekers, crime rates nose-dived. As in Los Angeles, feminization was one of the principal reasons for the downturn in violence.[103]

Now a second question: Why were San Francisco's homicide rates so much higher than those of the East Coast cities? A possible answer—by no means a certainty—is the high homicide rate of the Chinese. Over the decade of the 1890s, the Chinese were 6.1 percent of the population, but they committed 27.2 percent of the city's murders, mainly because of conflicts between Chinese community organizations, family feuds, and labor disputes. The average Chinese annual homicide rate for this period was a disturbing 30.8 per 100,000, a rate that would remain excessive until the 1920s. This was overwhelmingly intraracial murder; killings of Chinese by whites had dwindled to insignificance. Certainly, a major contributing factor was the gender imbalance of the Chinese American community, which, in 1890, was an overwhelming 90 percent male. Nonetheless, when Mullen calculated the homicide rates of Chinese males and white males he found that the Chinese ratio was substantially higher—2.4 times the white rate.[104]

While the Chinese obviously raised San Francisco's 1890s homicide rate, even if that rate were commensurately reduced by the full 27 percent attributed to the Chinese—which would lower it from 8.6 to 6.3—it still would be higher than Chicago's 5.6 and far worse than New York's 3.3. Aside from the gender imbalance factor then, we have no fully persuasive answer to this question.

What is beyond doubt, however, is that late nineteenth-century San Francisco's crime was far less frightening than its late twentieth-century violence. Setting aside the indiscriminate nature of recent crime, which of course makes it more disturbing to the average citizen, the homicide rates were dramatically higher in the recent period. In the early 1890s, the rate was 7.88 per 100,000; in 1990 it was 13.95, 77 percent higher.[105]

On entering the twentieth century, San Francisco suffered one of the most cataclysmic disasters in the history of the United States. In 1906, a massive earthquake, followed by even more devastating fires, destroyed an estimated 25,000 buildings, rendered between 200,000 and 300,000 people homeless, and killed, depending on the source, anywhere from 478 (the official death toll), to well in excess of 3,000.

In the face of such a catastrophe, one might imagine looting and other disaster-related crime on a mass scale, but according to contemporaneous accounts, there was very little. A respected history professor of the period, who maintained a large archive of accounts of the calamity, stressed the "remarkable freedom of the city from crime." Reports by officials and private citizens with first-hand experience of the events agreed that looting was insignificant. But Kevin Mullen thought that in the immediate aftermath of the disaster, the city "experienced a major crime wave." He calculated a 1907 city homicide rate of 15.4 per 100,000, the highest since the 1870s, and not equaled again until the 1960s.[106]

San Francisco provides the last stop for our crime tour of American cities. The next chapter ponders the implications of the nineteenth-century urban crime situations discussed above. As I will show, many of the contemporary assumptions about crime are not borne out by the realities of the late nineteenth century.

# 7

## Rethinking Cities and Crime

Suicide is much more urban than rural. The opposite is true of homicide.
—EMILE DURKHEIM

Our tour of American cities in the late nineteenth century is profoundly instructive, indeed, a revelation. This was an era of enormous urban population growth, truly the birth of the modern metropolis in the United States. It was driven by the rapid inmigration of millions of impoverished peoples, some with few if any modern work skills, many without an ability to speak English. Crammed into dilapidated housing, ghettoized, abused by police who lacked any professional training, governed by thoroughly corrupt municipal politicians, buffeted by economic recessions (in the 1870s and 1890s, the latter second only to the Great Depression of 1929), the American immigrant, it would seem, was on a path to social disaster. And yet nothing of the sort occurred. From the standpoint of violent crime these were "good years." Not only did violent crime not skyrocket, but measuring from a midcentury baseline, it actually declined—markedly. Indeed, compared to the last decades of the twentieth century the late nineteenth was positively peaceful. Rape and robbery were unusual, and murder accompanying such crimes was a rarity. Few feared to walk in impoverished immigrant districts; solitary female "friendly visitors," forerunners of the modern social worker, did it all the time.

The paucity of violent crime in the late nineteenth century demands a reassessment of some of our twenty-first-century theories about crime. Present-day assumptions and convictions about the relationship between crime and urbanization or crime and poverty are, it turns out, inapplicable to the late nineteenth century. First, with regard to population, neither size nor growth seemed to matter. The cities that grew the most in nineteenth-century America were not necessarily the most burdened by crime. Boston and Philadelphia grew by around 24 percent each decade, while homicide rates remained relatively low, at 3.5 and 2.1 per 100,000, respectively. Chicago, however, with a 54 percent population increase in the 1890s had a decadal homicide rate of 5.6, higher, to be sure, than the East Coast cities, but not frightening by twentieth-century standards.

Nor did the biggest cities necessarily have the worst crime rates. New York had less crime per capita than Chicago; Los Angeles, then tiny, had more than heavily populated Philadelphia. Even the truism that cities are more violent than suburbs, and suburbs more crime-prone than rural locales, had little validity in the nineteenth century. The rural South and sparsely populated West were more dangerous than the big cities of the Northeast. Renowned nineteenth-century sociologist Emile Durkheim believed that homicide was a rural phenomenon. "Suicide is much more urban than rural," he flatly declared; "the opposite is true of homicide."[1]

Second, not only are nineteenth-century urbanization and population growth unrelated to high crime, but even the most severe social deficits, considered individually or collectively—poverty, slum housing, overcrowding, filth and disease, economic stress (including high unemployment), social turmoil, corrupt and abusive police, and homelessness—did not invariably produce high violent crime. Virtually all of the immigrants suffered these woes, but their levels of interpersonal violence varied with the group. Among the midcentury Irish and the end-of-century Chinese immigrants, lethal violence was frequent if not commonplace. Among the Germans, Scandinavians, and Poles, it was not. And as we will see in the next section of this book, Jewish and Italian émigrés, both groups destitute and desperate, had very different rates of violence.

With respect to violent crime in the nineteenth century two questions must be addressed. First, why did violent crime decline as the century progressed? Why was violent crime so high at midcentury, only to fall dramatically as the century came to a close? Second, why was indiscriminate violence—the bane of the late twentieth century—so uncommon in the nineteenth? Why didn't big-city residents of the 1890s rob their neighbors or rape and kill total strangers at anywhere near the levels for these crimes one century later?

Ted Robert Gurr charted the overall rise and fall of violent crime in the nineteenth century. He noted a surge in the 1850s, a lull during the Civil War, when young men were diverted into the military, and a renewed increase in crime after 1865 and through the 1870s. From the 1880s to the end of the century, Gurr observed, violent crime subsided.[2] This accords with my findings. As table 7.1 shows, each city, except for Chicago, had diminished homicide rates as the century progressed.[3]

TABLE 7.1. Homicide rates, selected cities, by decades, 1850s–1890s

| Time Period | City | Homicide Rate | Notes |
| --- | --- | --- | --- |
| 1850s | Boston | 7+ | 1855–59 only |
| | Los Angeles | 221.1 | Los Angeles County |
| | New York City | 7+ | 15+ in 1863 and 1864 |
| | Philadelphia | 3.3 | 1839–59 |
| | San Francisco | 31.9 | |
| 1870s | Boston | 6.0 | 1869–71 only |
| | Chicago | 3.1 | 1875–79 only |
| | Los Angeles | 36.0 | Los Angeles County |
| | New York City | 5.8 | 7+ in 1872 |
| | Philadelphia | 2.8 | 1860–80 |
| | San Francisco | 13.2 | |
| 1880s | Boston | 1.5+ to 3.5+ | |
| | Chicago | 4.1 | |
| | Los Angeles | 11.0 | Los Angeles County |
| | New York City | 4.4 | |
| | Philadelphia | 2.8 | 1860–80 |
| | San Francisco | 9.3 | |
| 1890s | Boston | 3.5 | |
| | Chicago | 5.6 | |
| | Los Angeles | 9.8 | Los Angeles County |
| | New York City | 3.3 | |
| | Philadelphia | 2.1 | |
| | San Francisco | 8.6 | |

Sources: Jeffrey S. Adler, private communication (Chicago data); Ferdinand, "Criminal Patterns," 86; Lane, Violent Death, 71; Monkkonen, "Homicide in Los Angeles"; Monkkonen, "Homicides in New York City"; Mullen, Dangerous Strangers, 47.

To address my initial question—why did crime wane in late nineteenth century America—part of the answer is that Irish violence, which had soared at midcentury, declined by the end of the epoch, driving crime rates down across American cities. The Irish penchant for violence grew weaker over a half century and Irish-Americans became more peaceable and lawabiding. Four factors, it would seem, drove this cultural change: (1) the disciplinary impact of the industrial workplace and (2) public schools; (3) the widespread Irish involvement in police work; and (4) the passing of the hyperaggressive famine immigrants. The other piece of the explanation for the crime decline was the influx of millions of other peoples—Germans, Jews, Poles, English, Scandinavians and various other eastern Europeans—with relatively nonviolent cultures. These groups, added to the newly tamed Irish, created a much less violent America.

Compared to the United States of the mid-nineteenth century, 1890s America had indeed become peaceable. Compared to late nineteenth-century Europe, however, the United States still seemed wild and dangerous. While Philadelphia boasted homicide rates of about 2 per 100,000, and New York and Boston had historically low rates (for those cities) hovering around 3.5, London had turn-of-the-century homicide rates of 0.8 per 100,000, Stockholm under 1.0, and Berlin only 1.4. In other words, "peaceable" New York was still more than four times as homicidal as London.[4]

The explanation for this seeming anomaly is that the American culture—an amalgam of various cultures from Europe and China, along with the input of its former slave population—was more violent than the more homogenous cultures found in late nineteenth-century London, Stockholm, Berlin, and most other European cities. Ted Robert Gurr elucidated:

> North America was or became different in social composition from England in ways that fundamentally affected the American way of crime. England had no counterpart of Afro-Americans, first slave and then free, whose experience of crime as victims and perpetrators has been radically different from that of Anglo-Americans. And from the 1840s until 1919 American cities absorbed tens of millions of immigrants from Ireland, Germany, Scandinavia, Italy, and eastern

Europe. These groups had their own lifeways that only gradually were reduced in the American melting pot: turn-of-the century Italy . . . had the highest homicide rate in Europe. Moreover many of the immigrants were rootless young men, a group with a very high propensity for getting into trouble.[5]

In other words, America's receptivity to millions of foreigners, while helping to *reduce* violent crime as measured by midcentury American standards, also kept violent crime high by end-of-century European standards. There is no inconsistency here, simply two different bases for comparison.

Some European analysts offer a different explanation for high American crime vis-à-vis Europe, and they may see, as foreigners often do, crucial aspects of American life that we ourselves overlook. Peter Spierenburg, for example, argues that European societies accepted centralized control over the use of force long before they established democracies, whereas the Americans created democratic governance before they came to accept a centralized, governmental monopoly over the use of force. This led to "stagnation in the spread of more 'civilized' standards of behavior in some areas of social life—in the case of the United States, the area of conflict and aggression."[6] "In the United States as a whole and throughout most of its history, the social pressures favoring a monopolization of force have been weak in comparison with those in European national societies. This tendency, which originated in the precocious emergence of democracy and continues into the present, may go a long way toward explaining America's high homicide rates."[7]

This monopolization-of-force argument has especial validity in explaining high crime in the nineteenth-century West and South, where governmental controls were weak and communities were, essentially, on their own in maintaining law and order. Vigilantes and armed detective agencies, as Spierenburg correctly observed, were in "competition with the state's monopoly of force." This theory, however, cannot explain the decline in crime as the nineteenth century wound down, the relatively low crime rates of the northeastern cities, or the widely differing propensities toward violent crime among the various immigrant groups or between whites and blacks.[8]

Compared to Europeans, Americans are, no doubt, less willing to accept that government and government alone has the rightful authority to use force. Recurrent debates over the Second Amendment to the U.S. Constitution—establishing "the right of the People to keep and bear arms"—make this abundantly clear.[9]

Such debates and the rights claims that fuel them are unimaginable in Europe or the United Kingdom. But the fact is, despite the ubiquitousness of guns in nineteenth-century America, and the insistence on the legal right to possess them, violent crime declined dramatically by century's end, and as shall be discussed below, posed little threat to most of the citizenry.

Randolph Roth has offered yet another explanation for American violence, emphasizing the stability and legitimacy of government, especially the federal government, "fellow feeling arising from racial, religious, or political solidarity," and a "belief that the social hierarchy is legitimate."[10] Political legitimacy as an explanation for violent crime also was stressed by Gary LaFree, who contended that "the rapid growth of street crime in the 1960s and 1970s coincided with major increases in levels of political distrust."[11]

With respect to the 1890s, there may have been high levels of confidence in the federal government since this was a period of general optimism about the future of the United States, but it is difficult to assess with any certainty public opinion from that era given the lack of scientific surveys.

There are other problems with the governmental legitimacy thesis. The theory would be more convincing if the federal government had principal responsibility for crime control. In that case we could understand why ineffective governance would produce more crime. This in fact happened in the nineteenth-century West when the criminal justice apparatus, administered prior to statehood by the federal government, was perceived to be (and often was) ineffectual, and partly as a result, violent crime increased. But the nineteenth-century West was exceptional in the history of the United States in that under the federal system of governance municipalities almost always have had the lion's share of responsibility for criminal justice. Consequently, the legitimacy of the federal government would not seem as relevant to crime as the legitimacy of city government, which after all administers the police, prosecutors, and criminal courts. Indeed, one may plausibly argue that the focus should be narrowed even further to confidence in the criminal justice system itself. The extent to which the populace believes that the apparatus of criminal justice can deal fairly and effectively with crime should, at least theoretically, have a greater impact on lawlessness than attitudes toward the governing institutions in Washington, DC.

Additionally, for the purpose of understanding violent crime, the attitudes toward government of the upper and middle classes would seem less pertinent than the perceptions of the lower class, which is overwhelmingly the source of the violent crime. Political science scholarship has demonstrated a significant relationship between social class and political engagement, with both political knowledge and activity increasing with the income and education of the subjects.[12] Consequently, we would expect lesser levels of support for governmental institutions among those parts of the population that furnish the bulk of the violent offenders. The question, however, is not whether these levels of support are relatively low, but whether they rise or fall with the crime waves. This issue remains unresolved and ripe for scholarly exploration.

The Roth-LaFree hypothesis seems especially relevant to crime in the nineteenth-century West and South, where confidence in American governmental institutions was shaky. Whether it also can account for the decline in violent crime in the big cities of the United States at the end of the century is doubtful but unclear. While there probably was at this time rising esteem for such institutions, the relationship between these attitudes and violent crime over the course of the century remains to be proven.

This brings us to our second major question: why was there, in nineteenth-century America, relatively little indiscriminate violence, that is, robbery, robbery-murder, assault and rape of strangers? It is precisely this type of violence that made crime in the late twentieth century so disturbing. Because it is random (using the word in its colloquial, not its scientific sense), indiscriminate violence creates a lottery effect, generating fear out of proportion to the actual threat of victimization. Even after the crime rise of the 1960s, the real odds of a white, middle-class person being assaulted were low. Nevertheless, the sheer unpredictability of the attack, the difficulty of the ordinary unarmed citizen in defending against it, the volume of lawlessness generally (e.g., drug crime, quality-of-life offenses), and the daily drumbeat of media coverage with vivid television images of lurid crimes produced an angst in the general populace that affected virtually all public activities. Whenever he left his home, and sometimes even when remaining in it, the late twentieth-century city dweller had at least a bit of anxiety. The nineteenth-century urbanite, by contrast, had much more to fear from errant horsecarts and trains or trolleys operating at street level than from thugs.

Eric Monkkonen, who scrupulously recorded and analyzed New York City homicides, estimated that in the entire nineteenth century, murders by strangers totaled 3 percent of all of the city's killings, although he had some unease about the validity of this figure. For Philadelphia, however, Roger Lane found that 30 percent of all homicides, 1839 to 1901, were committed by strangers, 22 percent by a family member, 48 percent by an acquaintance. The discrepancy between the two northeastern cities, not that radically different from one another, is puzzling. Why should Philadelphia have had ten times more stranger-murders than New York? Moreover, the percentage of murders committed by strangers in Philadelphia is high even by contemporary standards. From 1976 to 2005, nationwide data show 21 percent of killings were by strangers, 23 percent by family, 56 percent by acquaintances.[13]

Given the high proportion of murders by strangers, a twenty-first-century analyst would expect lots of armed robberies. After all, aren't robberies usually committed by strangers and weren't guns widely available in late nineteenth-century Philadelphia? Guns indeed were, as Lane pointed out, cheap and easily obtained, but surprisingly, their use in crimes was relatively low; firearms were involved in only about 25 percent of the city's murders. Even more astonishing, armed robberies were rare. "Sober, respectable Philadelphians ordinarily had little cause to fear criminals in the starkly physical senses *[sic]*," Lane insisted, "simply because armed robbery was for unclear reasons virtually unknown then in the urban east."[14]

If armed robberies were a rarity then robbery-murderers must have dispatched their victims with their bare hands or some blunt object that the premeditated killer carried with him or that the impulsive one found readily at hand. This does not, of course, explain why it didn't occur to more robbers that firearms were an effective way to carry out their predations. Maybe the poor quality of nineteenth-century handguns had something to do with it; Lane was astonished at the number of people who simply walked away from shootings, not seriously harmed by underpowered bullets that were unable to pierce human bone.[15]

Be that as it may, however, the crucial point is that there were, compared to our own times, very few robberies at all, armed or unarmed. Stranger-homicides, whether 3 or 30 percent of the total murders in a city, were in the main motivated by personal disputes such as tavern flare-ups, as with most other nineteenth-century homicides. In short, even crimes by strangers were born of interpersonal conflict, arising out of chance meetings in public places, such as saloons. Unlike in the late twentieth century, crime by strangers was avoidable if one didn't frequent roughneck taverns.

The conclusion that robbery was uncommon, robbery-murders more so, is bolstered by Jeffrey Adler's incisive work on nineteenth-century crime in Chicago. Even though Chicago had much more violent crime than Philadelphia, Adler found that for the period 1875 to 1889, only 1 out of 21 homicides, a mere 4.8 percent, involved robbery. And nearly one-third (31 percent) of these robbery-homicides were between people who knew one another. "Robberies, and particularly robbery homicides," he too concluded, "had been rare in nineteenth-century America."[16]

That was most assuredly not the situation in late twentieth-century America. Each year, from 1976 to 2005, there were on average nearly 20,000 murders nationwide (19,811 to be exact) and around 18 percent of them (3,606) were contemporaneous with felonies, the preponderance of which were robberies. During that same time period the annual robbery rate was, on average, a scary 506 per 100,000. In 1992, the death rate from robbery, that is, the number of people killed during the commission of that crime, was 340 per 100,000 robberies. If robbery-homicides account for 15 percent of all modern day murders that would be more than three times Chicago's nineteenth-century robbery-homicide rate (4.8 percent).[17]

In the 1890s, Chicago crime began to change, taking on the trappings of modern street violence. Robbery spiked around 1893, the time of the city's world's fair, and after leveling off (despite a devastating depression), it started climbing steadily upward through the first decades of the new century. In the 1890s there were 66 robbery-murders; in the 1900s, 103; 194 from 1910 to 1920. Furthermore, the nature of the offense was changing. From a crime between acquaintances, robbery was fast becoming an offense between total strangers. Having been 31 percent of all robbery-homicides between 1875 and 1890, robbery-murders by acquaintances dropped to a mere 6 percent of the total between 1910 and 1920. What's more, robbery moved from saloons and homes to streets and stores. "Local streets became the most violent location in the city," Adler noted, "supplanting bars and private residences." Store homicides tripled between 1875 and 1920, and nearly half of the store murders, 1910–20, occurred during robberies. Worse still, the robbers were becoming vicious. Running in small packs, the predators would rob and shoot their victims—increasingly respectable middle-class pedestrians or shopkeepers—or club them to death. These were planned and mercenary assaults, designed to wrest money and valuables from those Chicagoans most apt to be carrying them. "Vicious, gratuitously violent, and predatory, such robbers were far more frightening to respectable Chicagoans than late nineteenth-century saloon toughs or turn-of-the-century wife beaters."[18]

Chicago's expanding African American population increasingly was involved in the attacks; though only 3 percent of the city, blacks committed 18 percent of robbery-homicides between 1910 and 1920. Moreover, 86 percent of black robbery-homicide victims were white, generating great fear among white Chicagoans. "In Chicago's Black Belt and at the southern fringes of the city's Loop," Adler explained, "African-American robbers stalked, preyed on, and brutally murdered older, vulnerable, white storekeepers, peddlers, and pedestrians, providing a new and enduring rationale for white racial antipathy and concern about street crime."[19]

Thus, as Chicago entered the twentieth century the crime picture became very different from that of the nineteenth—and very recognizable to those familiar with the last decades of the twentieth. In a word, "street crime" had arrived, and the new street crime—robbery at the hands of a stranger—became the prototype for the American city. The disproportionate black involvement would be another hallmark of the new urban crime problem. Chicago may or may not have the dubious honor of being the first major city to be menaced by the new style street predators, but it certainly was among the pioneers. Between 1890 and 1920, Chicago's population rose 146 percent, homicides increased 376 percent and robbery-homicides leaped a staggering 1,950 percent![20]

Adler attributed the rise in robberies to four factors, all products of the industrial revolution: 1. more valuable goods to steal and the new consumerism; 2. greater predictability in the distribution of money, such as regular pay schedules for workers; and 3. new technology, enabling the production of firearms and (in the twentieth century) the automobile.[21]

Broadening the analysis beyond Chicago to encompass the nineteenth-century city generally, it becomes clear that the change in the city itself, a gradual transformation over the second half of the century, created new opportunities for crime, and ultimately changed its very nature. By 1900, American cities had more people, more wealth, more goods, and greater mobility of both population and merchandise than ever before in the young country's history. Theft and violence were, as a consequence, more tempting and better facilitated than even a few decades earlier. All that was missing—and would through migration be supplied in abundance—were groups of people with violent subcultures, ready, willing and able to take advantage of the new opportunities.

To fully appreciate the change one must have a picture of the American municipality at mid-nineteenth century. The radius of the city was only two miles, often tightly packed around a seaport dotted with warehouses. Communication was face-to-face as there were no telephones, and movement on foot was the predominant means of human locomotion. Horse-drawn streetcars, traveling at four to seven miles per hour, served an area 2–3 miles from the city center, but the poor person didn't need and wouldn't have spent his meager earnings on such a mode of travel. The wealthy lived in the central city while the immigrants of that time— German and Irish—occupied shantytowns on the periphery. These early immigrants worked on the waterfront or in small factories dispersed around the city.[22]

Violent crime for most of the century was a product of conflict between acquaintances and relatives; strangers were most in danger of assault in the saloon, or on the streets nearby, where youthful male ego and alcohol combined in a volatile brew. There were few places of mass entertainment, few reasons to travel about the town, little means to buy consumer goods and few such goods to buy. One met one's needs through purchases from general stores located around the city; the downtown business district did not exist. In these conditions, robbery and armed robbery were rather rare, as human interactions were circumscribed, wealth was extremely limited, and there was little of value to steal. In short, the small, face-to-face, pedestrian city of the mid-nineteenth century offered neither incentives (few valuables, little cash in public places) nor opportunities (limited human interaction) for widespread robbery. All this would change rather rapidly near the end of the nineteenth century.

Starting in the 1870s, and accelerating in the last two decades of the century, the urban scene was dramatically transformed. Industrialization and the new technologies, especially electricity, enabled the city to expand in area, while new immigrants—6 million per decade starting in the 1880s—poured in to meet the growing demand for labor. The wealthy class began to leave the central city for more desirable environments on the periphery, pushing ever outward over time. The new immigrants—eastern Europeans, Scandinavians, and southern Italians, along with black migrants from the South—first occupied the abandoned central city housing of the wealthy, much subdivided, then moved into wooden shanties and cheap, closely packed tenements with tiny rooms, all within walking distance of the waterfront and the factories in which they worked. As the older immigrants, the Germans and Irish, entered the ranks of the middle class, they too sought less crowded, smelly, and unattractive living arrangements in nearby suburbs.[23]

The increased wealth generated by business and industry enabled the formation of a middle class, while the new transportation technology—especially the electric streetcar—made it possible for that new middle class to relocate to the suburbs. Within one year of a demonstration of the first electric transport system in Richmond, Virginia, in 1887, most American cities of any size started developing their own such system. With speeds more than double the horsecars, the new electrics enabled the upper and middle classes to work in the central city and commute from suburbs. In Chicago, for example, horsecart routes extended four miles from the downtown Loop until 1880; by the early 1890s the electrified transit system reached 8–10 miles from the Loop. At the same time, the central downtown was morphing into a business district, with specialized stores to sell merchandise to the general public and offices to manage industry, finance, and commerce. A new emphasis on consumerism both led to and was reinforced by the latest retailing innovation, the giant department store, a cornucopia of various goods made into "objects of desire" through advertising.[24]

Thus, in only three decades, the walkable, two-mile city of the midcentury was transformed into the modern metropolis, with boundaries ten miles or more from its center. This didn't happen overnight, of course, but the change was steady and inexorable. The expansive, dynamic, impersonal industrial metropolis, filled with migrants from the far-flung reaches of America and the world provided unheard-of opportunities to rob and steal. Middle-class or wealthy people commuted six days a week to downtown workplaces, carrying with them cash, jewelry, and other valuables. More and more costly goods were made available through downtown shops, attractively displayed for the benefit of customers (and crooks). Living nearby and within walking distance of these temptations were the new migrants, poor and, in some cases, violent, eager to acquire what they could not afford.

A modern criminological theory developed by Marcus Felson and Lawrence E. Cohen—they called it "routine activities theory"—makes clear how the late nineteenth-century American metropolis provided unprecedented opportunities for robbery. Focusing on "direct-contact predatory violations," Felson and Cohen observed that "one can analyze how the structure of community organization as well as the level of technology in a society provide the circumstances under which crime will thrive." "Routine activities (especially legitimate activities)," they continued,

> separate relatives and neighbors from one another and from some of their property as they go about their daily business. In addition, these processes bring together during various times of day or night persons of very different backgrounds, some of whom are suitable targets and others of whom are likely offenders. Thus the spatio-temporal structure of work, school, leisure, and other activities will tend to influence the rate at which direct-contact predatory violations occur in the community.[25]

Felson and Cohen also focused on the value and portability of goods and their presence in public places or in unguarded premises. The suitability of a crime target, they explained, depends on its value (its desirability for potential offenders), visibility (likelihood of discovery by potential offenders), access (suitability for criminal contact) and inertia (obstacles to criminal contact).

This theory neatly applies to the rising robbery problem of late nineteenth-century American cities. A new and burgeoning middle class began commuting to central cities for work, carrying with them cash, pocketwatches, rings, and other valuables, but probably not firearms. With rising income levels and more valuable goods in their possession, the value of the "targets," in the language of routine activities theory, increased manyfold. Additional targets, highly visible and not well guarded, were provided by the newly developed downtown stores, offering unprecedented numbers of goods. The new consumer mentality, fueled by advertising, made these goods more desirable than ever, increasing the motivation of potential offenders. Meanwhile, the would-be offenders, motivated by their desire for these goods, but without sufficient means to obtain them lawfully, resided near enough to the downtown area to enter on foot, giving them ready access to the targets.

It now becomes clear why robbery was uncommon for most of the nineteenth century but began to increase as the century concluded. The preindustrial city, with its dearth of valuables, relative scarcity of wealth, and limited opportunities for human interaction, provided insufficient targets to make robbery attractive. The modern, industrial metropolis, however, supplied all the ingredients: greater wealth, more and more valuable consumer goods, and unprecedented mobility via the new transport technologies.

Of course, some features of the modern, industrialized city served to tamp down crime, not increase it. America's accelerating economic expansion made possible a broad middle class, and that class, while providing a handy target for criminals, didn't engage in interpersonal violence itself. In addition, the older immigrants, the German and Irish, demonstrated that newcomers to the United States could move up the socioeconomic ladder, and this gave hope to the new immigrants that through hard work and thrift, as opposed to indolence and crime, they too could advance into the middle stratum. Moreover, as Roger Lane argued, the industrial system imposed a discipline on the working class male that the preindustrial economy did not, reducing over time the number of wild, drunken, barroom brawlers who had been responsible for the bulk of the era's criminal violence. Nevertheless, and at the same time, the new middle class, and the wealth that accompanied it—both creating it and being created by it—invited a new type of crime for a new century.

This analysis solves another mystery related to the city, which has been seen by some as a cause, and by others as a constraint, on crime. To Durkheim, the city meant less homicide, the countryside more. To contemporary criminologists just the opposite is assumed to be incontrovertible truth. In reality, both were correct. The late nineteenth-century industrial city was a place in transition insofar as crime was concerned. While reducing the old-style crime, the interpersonal dispute offense, it invited the new style, the depersonalized robbery-assault. The urban industrial system was responsible for taming the lower-class male while at the same time creating the middle-class target and the mobile, consumer-oriented city. The new city thus provided unprecedented opportunities for robbery and assault. All that would be needed were the groups who were prepared to take advantage of those opportunities. As the twentieth century unfolded, some of the immigrants from abroad and the African American migrants from the American South would fill those ranks.

# IV

# IMMIGRANTS AND CRIME

# 8

# The European Immigrants
*Italians and Jews*

They were despised by New Yorkers. They were filthy and illiterate. They stank of fish and garlic. They had running sores. They had no honor and worked for next to nothing. They stole. They drank. They raped their own daughters. They killed each other casually. Among those who despised them the most were the second-generation Irish, whose fathers had been guilty of the same crimes.

—E. L. DOCTOROW

The massive movement of European peoples to the United States that began in the nineteenth century with the Irish and the Germans shifted in the early twentieth to Italy and what was then the Russian and Austro-Hungarian Empires, the latter two the source of 2 million Jewish emigrés. In the 1880s, most immigrants to America had been coming from Germany, Ireland, and England. But by the last decade of the nineteenth century and up to the 1920s, when the United States began closing the golden door, the Germans and Irish had become the old immigrants.[1]

Along with the influx of Mexicans to the Southwest and the northern migration of African Americans, no event in the new century would have a greater impact on violent crime than the influx of Italians. This chapter tells the story of the Italian migration to America at the turn of the last century, focusing, of course, on violent crime. It also discusses the Jewish migration at the same time, and to a great extent, to the same place. It makes a nice point of contrast, these two desperate peoples, arriving at the same shores in the same era—but with very different rates of violence.

In terms of sheer numbers the Italian migration was remarkable. From 1900 to 1910 alone, the decade of maximal exodus, over 2 million Italians arrived, but so many returned home that the 1910 Census counted only 1.3 million (which still represented 10 percent of America's enormous foreign-born population).[2] A sojourner mentality, soon replaced by a more permanent commitment, contributed to higher Italian crime rates by creating in the *colonia* a disproportionate number of unattached males, invariably a recipe for violence. The place of settlement itself contributed to crime. The Italian immigrants gravitated to cities, somewhat surprising perhaps, given that they were largely rural folk from the agricultural south. But in light of America's prodigious industrial expansion and the economic disaster that was southern Italy at the time, it is no surprise that they went where the jobs were. And, of course, as with most other immigrants, the Italians settled in communities in which their *paesani* (countrymen) had already established a beachhead, easing the adjustment to the new world. These Little Italies were rundown big-city neighborhoods with slum housing, tenements abandoned by the Germans and Irish. Given their lack of money, skills, or English, it was all the latest occupants could afford.

Nearly 60 percent of the Italian immigrants settled in the mid-Atlantic states, mainly in New York, and roughly two-thirds of the Empire State Italians took up residence in New York City. They came by steamship, crowded into steerage class for the ten-day ocean journey. Fares had been reduced and legal restrictions on emigration were minimal, making relocation more appealing than ever. New York City was the principal destination where at the famous Ellis Island processing center millions were admitted to the golden land. Indeed, few were turned back—well under 2 percent—partly because some of the steamship lines screened passengers in Europe since the expense of returning rejected entrants would have to be borne by the companies.[3]

Most of the Italian arrivals remained in New York City. There they established the most famous of the Little Italies in lower Manhattan, eventually adding satellite communities in Greenwich Village, the Bronx, and Brooklyn. The city, with its half-million Italians (1908), had eight times the population of the next biggest colony, but Italians also settled in significant numbers in New Orleans, California (mainly San Francisco), and Chicago. Some even journeyed to remote mining towns in states like Colorado and West Virginia where their *padroni* (labor contractors) had gotten them jobs.[4]

The motivation for this huge migration was above all the abysmal state of affairs in southern Italy—*la miseria*. While the first nineteenth-century Italian immigrants were from the north, the twentieth-century flood tide was overwhelmingly from the *mezzogiorno* (southern Italy), where the agricultural economy, a mainstay for 80 percent of the population, was near collapse. Of 2.3 million Italian immigrants to the United States, 1899 to 1910, 1.9 million (83 percent) were from the south, either Campagnia, Basilicata, Calabrese, or the island of Sicily.

## MEZZOGIORNO VIOLENCE

Conditions in the south by the end of the nineteenth century had deteriorated badly. There were few schools in the region, and the population, viewed with contempt by northerners, was largely illiterate. Most of the southern workforce was involved in some way with agriculture, many as farmers, more as mere farm laborers. Farming methods were primitive, and due to deforestation, rains often washed away the topsoil. In fact, Mother Nature seemed to be conducting her own vendetta against southern Italy in the late nineteenth century, pelting it with earthquakes, volcanoes, and floods. Phylloxera blighted the grape vineyards while malaria epidemics plagued the humans, killing thousands each year. Nor was Italy doing well in the new international agrarian marketplace. Imported grain and fruit (much from America) drove farm prices down, while protective tariffs abroad, especially in France, hurt Italian exports, such as wine. Rents, imposed by absentee landlords, and taxes, levied by a remote national government, were high. Wages, meanwhile, were low, certainly by American standards. An agricultural laborer could earn 50 to 60 cents a day at harvest time and only 16 to 30 cents a day for the rest of the year. Miners took home a mere 30 to 56 cents per diem.[5]

The Italian peninsula, united in 1870 into a single state for the first time in its history, was governed by a parliament and a figurehead monarch. Italians didn't identify with the nation, however, seeing themselves more in regional than in national terms. As one of the leading statesmen remarked shortly after the formation of the Italian kingdom: "We have made Italy. Now we must make Italians." The national identification problem was even more pronounced in the south, where the population felt greater attachment to the village than to the surrounding region. "*Campanilismo*" the Italians called it; meaning that one's concerns extended no further than the campanile or village bell tower. As a result of this local orientation, immigrants to America tended to settle in neighborhoods populated by *paesani* from the same village. Neighborhood festivals in Little Italies celebrating the patron saints of the former village helped to reinforce the parochial orientation, and some speculate that campanilismo inhibited ethnic solidarity among Italian Americans. With the growing Italian nationalism of the twentieth century, however, these parochial attitudes gradually faded.[6]

Unchanged though was the famous Italian loyalty to family, what historian Luigi Barzini called "their true patriotism." The family was the focal point of the honor culture that drove much of the violence of the southerners, both at home and abroad. "Fathers, brothers, sons, grandsons (mostly from the south and the islands, but frequently also from the more advanced north)," Barzini noted, "daily risk death to protect their women from outrage and themselves from dishonour." The family also was the basic building block of the Mafia and the Camorra in the mezzogiorno, and later, of American organized crime, the latter more family business than national conspiracy. In the south, Barzini explained, "the family extracts everybody's first loyalty. It must be defended, enriched, made powerful, respected, and feared by the use of whatever means are necessary, legitimate means, if at all possible, or illegitimate."[7]

The similarities between the mezzogiorno and the American South are striking. Both were in geographically isolated southern sections of their countries, both more rural and agricultural than their industrial northern neighbors, both viewed as "backward" educationally and in terms of high culture, and most important for crime history, both were honor-driven and violent, especially in defense of wives and daughters. One must not, of course, push the parallels too far; the linguistic and religious differences, the overpowering Italian emphasis on the family, to say nothing of the historical accretions from centuries of Italian history, mark the American and Italian southerners as very different peoples. Nonetheless, both the Italian and American South are vivid illustrations of high rural crime rooted in an exaggerated sense of personal honor.

In the mezzogiorno, or at least certain parts of it, viz., western Sicily and Naples, the culture of honor came to be known as the "way of the mafia." As Barzini described it, it was

a state of mind, a philosophy of life, a conception of society, a moral code, a particular susceptibility, prevailing among all Sicilians. They are taught in the cradle, or are born already knowing, that they must aid each other, side with their friends and fight the common enemies even when the friends are wrong and the enemies are right; each must defend his dignity at all costs and never allow the smallest slights and insults to go unavenged; they must keep secrets, and always beware of official authorities and laws.[8]

This "mafia" culture took the form of a "loose network of secret criminal groups that existed from at least as early as the 1860s." The word "mafia" is properly used in three different senses. First, one may speak of a lower-case mafia culture, a form of culture of honor, described in the immediately preceding Barzini quote. Second, there was the Mafia with a capital "M" (Mafie in the plural), referring to the criminal organizations that developed in southern Italy in the nineteenth century. The mafia culture or culture of honor, was brought to America by the southern Italian immigrants where, as shall be shown, it manifested in violent crime, extortion (the Black Hand), and subsequently, during the Prohibition years, as large-scale organized crime, or what one might call the American Mafia—the third usage of the term.[9]

To return to the original Mafia, these criminal organizations flourished in western Sicily, but oddly, not in the eastern parts of the island. The resulting differences in violent crime across Sicily will be demonstrated in a moment. Comparable organizations operated in Calabria, where they were known as the *Fibbia*, and in Naples as the *Camorra*. The Sicilian Mafia was less a single, tightly organized structure than a loosely bound set of groups, each built on family alliances, and each operating as a shadow government in its own town or district. The Mafie, as well as the Fibbia and Camorra, were organized by economic activity, controlling cattle and pasture, citrus groves, water supply, construction, wholesale fruit, vegetable, flower, and fish markets, etc. They would fix prices, arrange contracts, and occasionally punish violators of their "laws." The first commandment for all of these crime groups was *omertà*—thou shalt not squeal. This would play out in America as a refusal to help police when they investigated crimes by (and usually against) Italian immigrants.[10]

The structure of the Sicilian Mafia operation was as follows. "The first nucleus of the Mafia," wrote Barzini, "is the family." Fathers passed down their domains—henchmen, vassals, property, relations with landowners, police, businessmen, politicians—to their eldest sons. These families frequently quarreled, killing one another, in some cases years after the original cause was all but forgotten. (Once again, the similarity to the clan vendettas in the American South is obvious.)

The next layer was an alliance of families (a "cosca") in the same district, each pursuing similar or related activities. An association of several *cosche* was known as a *consorteria*. "All of the *consorterie* in Sicily finally form the *onorata società*, or the Mafia." The Mafia was headed by one man, "acknowledged as the most respected, trusted, and revered of all," the one "who can generate more fear than anybody else." From the end of the nineteenth century until the late 1920s that man was Don Vito Cascio Ferro, who organized all crime on the Palermo end of Sicily.[11]

In urban Naples, the Camorra maintained similar operations, specializing in smuggling and selling protection. As early as the 1860s, camorristi controlled customs and imposed a "tax" on anyone who brought produce to market. It was not until the 1920s, when the Fascists were empowered, that the Camorra finally was suppressed.[12]

In Sicily, the ruthlessness of the mafiosi was the underpinning of their power. In *The Business of Crime*, Humbert Nelli describes the role of violence: "There were *mafiosi* in every class, and they were involved in the full range of illegal activities, including crop burning, fraud, robbery, extortion, and murder. While they engaged also in non-violent and non-criminal activities, their legal operations, and, in fact, the immense power they wielded, rested on the widespread knowledge that they could and would use violence and any type of crime necessary to gain their ends."[13]

Violent crime rates in Italy were among the highest in all Europe, following the same regional pattern in the nineteenth-century United States. In the industrial north, where it was accepted that the state should arbitrate disputes, we find low murder rates. But in the agricultural south, where custom and tradition demanded that the paterfamilias avenge insults, the killing was excessive. As a French analyst put it, acts of honor, sacred familial duties in an agricultural society, were seen as criminal homicide and crimes against the state in industrial civilization.[14]

Thus, in southern Europe (1880), we find the following homicide conviction rates per 100,000:[15]

| | |
|---|---|
| Serbia | 10.5 |
| Italy | 9.9 |
| Spain | 5.5 |
| Romania | 5.3 |

Contrast the much lower rates in northern Europe:

| | |
|---|---|
| France | 1.49 |
| Germany | 0.94 |
| Scotland | 0.68 |
| England | 0.60 |

European crime historian Manuel Eisner reported lesser homicide rates for Italy for the period 1875–99—5.5 per 100,000 population—but these rates still were six times those in Scandinavia and two and one-half times those of Switzerland and Germany.[16]

Within Italy, divided, like the United States, between the industrial north and the agricultural south, the murder rates, as expected, reflected the cultural-economic split. All of the southern regions, including Campagnia, Basilicata, Calabrese, and Sicily, had late nineteenth-century homicide rates in excess of 9 per 100,000, whereas the northernmost regions, such as Lombardy, Venezia, and the Veneto, had rates between 3.1 and 5.0.[17]

Equally striking is the apparent role of the Mafia in elevating crime rates. The figures in table 8.1 show the murder and robbery/extortion rates for different provinces within Sicily. Catania, Messina, and Syracuse—all with relatively low rates (for Sicily)—are in the eastern part of the island where the Mafie were not active.

TABLE 8.1. Murder and robbery/extortion rates per 100,000 for Sicilian provinces, 1902–1906

| City/Town | Murder Rate | Robbery & Extortion Rate |
|---|---|---|
| Caltanissetta | 44.5 | 41.4 |
| Catania | 13.9 | 24.8 |
| Agrigento | 38.8 | 46.8 |
| Messina | 8.1 | 7.2 |
| Palermo | 29.0 | 33.7 |
| Syracuse | 8.2 | 10.3 |
| Trapani | 26.1 | 76.8 |

Source: Nelli, *Business of Crime*, 11.

Once again, as we shall see, the violence of the Old Country would reproduce itself in the new. Perhaps this is to be expected. Why would a culture of violence suddenly become peaceful, especially in an environment as strange and open to aggressiveness as early twentieth-century America? Barzini explained why the Italian culture of violence was exported.

> Sicilian immigrants to the United States found themselves surrounded by an alien and hostile society. They had to cope with an incomprehensible language, puzzling customs, rigid laws, and what they considered an oppressive régime. They felt cut off, for reasons they did not quite understand, from access to the good things in life, wealth and authority. They clung to what could give them protection and comfort, the Church, the family, and their ways. They soon discovered that the arts their people had developed in the old country to neutralize alien laws were also useful in the new. . . . In fact, they discovered that the ancient arts were far more useful in America and went farther. The Americans were generally trustful, unprepared to defend themselves from guile, often unwilling to fight for what they considered small stakes. All Sicilians in the United States, among whom the criminals were a small minority, followed the same old rules, the only ones they knew anyway, a sharpened version of those all Italians follow. . . . In order to beat rival organizations, criminals of Sicilian descent reproduced the kind of illegal groups they had belonged to in the old country and employed the same rules to make them invincible.[18]

## ITALIANS IN AMERICA

Before 1910, many, perhaps most, Italian males came alone to America, looking to find work, make money, and return to the homeland. Their travel and jobs were arranged by *padroni*, essentially labor contractors, who also provided housing, handled their finances (often skimming some off for themselves), and in general helped the immigrants adjust to the strange new land. It is through the *padroni* that Italians ended up in such remote locations as Colorado and West Virginia, where mining jobs were plentiful. Their primary destination, however, was New York and the Northeast, along with a handful of big cities elsewhere.[19]

Despite a high rate of return—some say half of the Italian emigrés—hundreds of thousands came to America with wives and children, forever abandoning *la miseria*. With no English or skills, the Italians moved heavily into construction work, especially railroad construction. By one estimate, they were at the turn of the century three-quarters of New York City's building workforce. Italians also established themselves in barbering and with the New York City sanitation department. A study of southern Italian occupations in New York City, 1899 to 1910, found that 77 percent were laborers, 15 percent held skilled jobs, and 0.4 percent were professionals. Occupational mobility from the first to the second generation was slow for Italian Americans, perhaps due to their dislike of schooling. This may have prolonged their violent crime activity as it delayed advancement to the middle class.[20]

Regarding crime by Italian Americans, we have, despite the usual shortcomings in data for the nineteenth and early twentieth centuries, several indicators of high violence. I first examine national crime indicators, then local, mainly big-city. For nationwide conditions one can learn a fair amount from imprisonment statistics.

Prison data can tell us about the type of crime associated with a social group, but (because many offenders are never imprisoned) not about the amount of crime. In 1904, 1910, and 1923, the Census Bureau carried out special enumerations of prisoners in the United States; from 1926 on prisoner enumerations were conducted annually. Each enumeration measured the "flow" of inmates from the courts for a full year (sometimes six months) and the "stock" of prisoners on a date certain. Several of these enumerations showed a disproportionate number of violent crimes by Italians.

The census surveys ordinarily noted birthplace, not ethnicity, so second-generation Italians (born here to immigrant parents) could not be identified. The 1904 enumeration showed that Italy-born prisoners admitted to a penal institution during that year were 6.1 percent of all foreign-born admissions, but 14.4 percent of all foreign-born major offenders.[21] More noteworthy, 57 percent of Italian prisoners were incarcerated for crimes against the person. For no other nationality was the proportion so high. The next-highest percentage was for Austrians, 40 percent of whom were incarcerated for such crimes, followed by Poles, 36 percent. When crimes against the person are broken down into their components we find that Italians had the highest percentage of commitments for each offense: for homicide (16 percent), for assault (30 percent), for robbery (5 percent), and for rape (4 percent). When it came to minor crimes, however, Italians scored low. Italian prisoners had the lowest percentage of arrests for drunk and disorderly offenses (28 percent); unsurprisingly, prisoners born in Ireland had the highest percentage (64 percent).[22]

The preceding figures did not take account of age or gender, and since the Italian immigrants were disproportionately youthful and male, those characteristics may well have magnified the results. As we know, persons in their twenties and early thirties commit more violent crime than older populations, and likewise, males do more such crime than females. For true indicators of the relative number of offenders, therefore, one should compare equivalent age and gender groups.

Two economists, Carolyn Moehling and Anne Morrison Piehl, recently analyzed the early twentieth-century census data on crime and made adjustments for age. As they observed, the earlier immigrant Germans and Irish were aging by 1904, with nearly half of their population having reached age fifty or older, whereas the bulk of the new Italian immigrants were still in their twenties and thirties. To account for the difference the authors developed a "predicted" commitment rate for each immigrant group, a rate that took account of age. They then compared the predicted rate to the "actual" commitment rate, which did not account for age. If the actual rate were *higher* than the predicted rate, that would indicate a greater incarceration rate than one would expect given the age of the group. Likewise, if the actual rate were *lower* than the predicted rate this would suggest a lower-than-expected incarceration rate. Table 8.2, prepared by Moehling and Piehl, depicts the predicted and actual rates for each foreign-born group.[23]

TABLE 8.2. Actual and predicted prison commitment rates per 100,000, by national origin, 1904

| Country of Origin | Total Commitments | | Major Offenses | | Minor Offenses | |
|---|---|---|---|---|---|---|
| | Actual | Predicted | Actual | Predicted | Actual | Predicted |
| Austria | 329 | 572 | 72 | 90 | 257 | 482 |
| Canada | 582 | 544 | 86 | 69 | 496 | 474 |
| Denmark | 212 | 559 | 36 | 66 | 176 | 493 |
| England | 557 | 514 | 64 | 58 | 493 | 455 |
| France | 432 | 479 | 85 | 54 | 347 | 425 |
| Germany | 299 | 501 | 47 | 52 | 252 | 449 |
| Hungary | 383 | 589 | 62 | 102 | 321 | 487 |
| Ireland | 1,503 | 487 | 60 | 52 | 1,448 | 435 |
| Italy | 579 | 588 | 162 | 97 | 408 | 491 |
| Mexico | 1,092 | 553 | 420 | 79 | 673 | 475 |

TABLE 8.2 (*continued*)

| Country of Origin | Total Commitments | | Major Offenses | | Minor Offenses | |
|---|---|---|---|---|---|---|
| | Actual | Predicted | Actual | Predicted | Actual | Predicted |
| Norway | 226 | 538 | 34 | 68 | 192 | 470 |
| Poland | 340 | 578 | 63 | 94 | 278 | 483 |
| Russia | 382 | 584 | 89 | 98 | 293 | 485 |
| Scotland | 729 | 510 | 72 | 59 | 657 | 451 |
| Sweden | 282 | 562 | 28 | 73 | 254 | 489 |
| Switzerland | 251 | 540 | 33 | 64 | 218 | 477 |
| Others | 576 | 559 | 121 | 87 | 455 | 473 |

*Source:* Moehling and Piehl, "Immigration, Crime, and Incarceration," 758.

For Italians, the predicted rate for major crimes was 97, the actual rate, 162. The ratio of actual to predicted rates, 1.67, was higher for Italians than for any other major immigrant group except Mexicans, which indicates that their incarceration rates were excessive regardless of their youthfulness. For other immigrant groups, such as those from Russia, Austria, Germany and Poland, the ratio of actual to predicted rates was less than 1.0, meaning that the actual rates were *lower* than might have been expected given their ages. The actual-to-predicted ratios for the various groups as calculated by Moehling and Piehl are displayed in table 8.3.[24]

TABLE 8.3. Ratio of actual to predicted prison commitment rates for major offenses per 100,000, by national origin, 1904

| Country of Origin | Ratio of Actual to Predicted Commitment Rate |
|---|---|
| Mexico | 5.32 |
| Italy | 1.67 |
| France | 1.57 |
| Canada | 1.25 |
| Scotland | 1.22 |
| Ireland | 115 |
| England | 1.10 |

TABLE 8.3 (*continued*)

| Country of Origin | Ratio of Actual to Predicted Commitment Rate |
|---|---|
| Russia | 0.91 |
| Germany | 0.90 |
| Austria | 0.80 |
| Poland | 0.67 |
| Hungary | 0.61 |
| Denmark | 0.55 |
| Switzerland | 0.52 |
| Norway | 0.50 |
| Sweden | 0.38 |

*Source:* Moehling and Piehl, "Immigration, Crime, and Incarceration," 759.

It appears, however, that Moehling and Piehl did not take account of gender in the construction of these ratios, and as I said, gender is a factor that might have further diminished the Italian rates given the tendency of male Italians, at least in the early years of their migration, to come over without families. The 1910 enumeration provided incarceration figures by both country of birth and gender (but not by age), and the results are more favorable to the Italians, although they still show an outsized proportion of violent crimes. Table 8.4 shows the violent crime commitment rates for foreign-born male prisoners per 100,000 males born in the same foreign country. I compare Austrians, Russians, Italians, and Mexicans, all of whom in 1910 probably would have been youthful recent immigrants. As is evident, the Italians had the second-highest murder and assault commitment rates, and the highest robbery and rape commitment rates.[25]

TABLE 8.4. Commitment rates per 100,000 for violent crimes, male prisoners, by country of birth, 1910

| Offense | Country of Birth | | | |
|---|---|---|---|---|
| | Austria | Russia | Italy | Mexico |
| Grave homicide | 1.7 | 0.2 | 3.5 | 8.0 |
| Lesser homicide | 4.8 | 2.3 | 12.0 | 19.0 |

TABLE 8.4 *(continued)*

| Offense | Country of Birth | | | |
|---|---|---|---|---|
| | Austria | Russia | Italy | Mexico |
| Assault | 105.8 | 68.6 | 101.6 | 174.9 |
| Robbery | 2.7 | 1.9 | 7.2 | 5.9 |
| Rape | 2.9 | 2.5 | 9.0 | 8.0 |

*Source:* Bureau of the Census, *Prisoners and Juvenile Delinquents 1910*, table 148.

Iffy though they may be, the national data suggest that the Italian immigrants were responsible for a great deal of violent crime in the early twentieth century. This conclusion is bolstered by local crime studies for New York City and other places with significant Italian settlements.

## Italian Crime in New York City

It is unfortunate that no scholar has looked at Italian-American murders in New York City using Eric Monkkonen's meticulously developed database, especially since New York was home to more Italian Americans than any other place in the world. Monkkonen's aggregate New York data indicate that homicides rose during those crucial first three decades of the twentieth century, a time period in which, given their massive migration to the city, one would expect an Italian-American impact on homicide rates.

FIGURE 8.1. New York City homicide victimization rates per 100,000, 1900–1930. *Source:* Monkkonen, "Homicides in New York City," https://doi.org/10.3886/ICPSR03226.v1.

Note that in the first decade, when over 2 million Italians came to America, most of them settling not far from Ellis Island, New York City homicides rose steadily, from 3.8 per 100,000 in 1900 to 6.3 in 1907, an increase of 63 percent. I also note that there was a brief depression in 1907–8, which threw thousands out of work. Not only did New York City murders hit their peak in 1907, but so too did homicide arrests in twenty-three cities nationwide.[26]

Following a decline at the end of the decade, homicide rates climbed again until—due perhaps to the draft for World War I, 1917–18—they dipped once more. In the 1920s, rates zig-zagged a bit, but moved generally upward, averaging 5.4 for the decade. The upward-trending rates for these three decades, while no doubt disturbing at the time, cannot be considered alarming when one compares the rates of the post-1960s era, which were the highest by far in the history of the city. In fact, as Monkkonen pointed out, the city's rates were *lower* than national rates for the entire first half of the twentieth century, a situation that did not begin to change until 1959.[27]

While we lack definitive proof that the Italian influx accounted for the escalation, there is New York City and State evidence that suggests it. The principal source of this evidence is the Dillingham Commission report, a massive, forty-two volume work on immigrants, covering everything from their role in various industries to the performance of their children in school. The commission consisted of three U.S. senators, three congressional representatives, three presidential appointees, a staff of over three hundred people, and a budget in excess of $1 million. Created in an atmosphere of mounting public pressure to restrict immigration, the commission has been sharply criticized for assuming that the "new" immigrants from eastern and southern Europe were essentially different from and inferior to the old, as well as for paving the way for subsequent immigration restrictions.[28]

An entire volume of the commission's report, devoted to "Immigration and Crime," collected valuable data and drew by-and-large cautious conclusions about its subject. "Immigrants are less prone to commit crime than are native Americans," the report stated, but it added that "the American-born children of immigrants exceed the children of natives in relative amount of crime" and that "juvenile delinquency is more common among immigrants." The commission, for the most part, recognized the limitations of its data, conceding that it was unable to say whether immigration increased crime, and if so, which specific immigrant groups were responsible.

Significantly, however, the report also concluded that immigration had changed "the character of crime in the United States," mainly by increasing the volume of violent crime. This development was attributed to the Italian new-comers. "The increase in offenses of personal violence in this country is largely traceable to immigration from southern Europe, and especially from Italy. This is most marked in connection with the crime of homicide." These words were a bit incautious. While the thrust of the commission's conclusion was correct—Italian immigrants did play a significant role in the increase in violent crime in early twentieth-century America—the extent of that role could not be determined with certainty. The commission would have needed nationwide violent crime data over a long enough time period to discern an increase, plus data on the proportion of violent crimes attributable to persons of Italian heritage.[29]

Criticisms of the commission notwithstanding, the data it gathered on crime were significant. The commission collected crime data from felony and misde-meanor courts in New York City and New York State, the most important of which came from the New York City Court of General Sessions. That court (abol-ished in 1962), which had felony jurisdiction in New York County (Manhattan), was monitored for nine months, 1908–9, during which time the commission recorded the "race" (today we would say "ethnicity") of every convicted offender (n = 2,262). The commission also gathered birthplace data on every offender convicted from 1907 to 1908 in the New York State County Courts and Supreme Courts (n = 12,897), tribunals with jurisdiction outside New York County over felonies and certain misdemeanors.[30]

Although these data might have shed light on the violent crime rates of Ital-ians and other racial/ethnic groups in New York, the commission did not pres-ent such rates, perhaps because it lacked accurate general population counts or gender and age figures for each group, or perhaps because it thought that conviction data are poor indicators of actual crime. Given the deficiencies in the data, the commission did the next best thing, calculating the proportion of each ethnic group's offenses in each of five categories of crimes. The five crime categories, as defined by the commission, were: Gainful Offenses, Offenses of Personal Violence, Offenses against Public Policy, Offenses against Chastity, and

Unclassified Offenses.[31] Thus, while the commission could not say, for example, that Italians had the highest violent crime rates in New York, it could say that Italian offenders in New York committed proportionally more violent crime than other ethnic groups.

The results of the commission's study of the Manhattan felony court are presented in table 8.5.

TABLE 8.5. Percentage of convictions in each crime category for selected groups, New York City Court of General Sessions, October 1, 1908, to June 30, 1909

| Group | Gainful | Violent | Pub. Policy | Chastity |
|---|---|---|---|---|
| Native | 79.7 | 9.8 | 8.9 | 0.7 |
| English immigrants | 84.6 | 2.6 | 5.1 | 7.7 |
| English 2d generation | 79.3 | 13.8 | 6.9 | 0.0 |
| German immigrants | 75.2 | 10.4 | 9.6 | 0.8 |
| German 2d generation | 85.7 | 8.9 | 3.6 | 0.0 |
| Hebrew immigrants | 85.0 | 8.5 | 4.9 | 0.4 |
| Hebrew 2d generation | 89.6 | 5.2 | 4.2 | 1.0 |
| Irish immigrants | 60.5 | 29.1 | 3.5 | 0.0 |
| Irish 2d generation | 78.0 | 12.3 | 6.0 | 0.7 |
| Italian immigrants | 43.8 | 37.4 | 17.0 | 0.0 |
| Italian 2d generation | 72.0 | 17.1 | 9.8 | 1.2 |

Source: U.S. Immigration Commission, *Immigration and Crime*, 69.

Note: "Native" refers to persons born in the U.S. to U.S.-born fathers.

Reading across the rows, a higher proportion of Italian defendants, 37.4 percent, were convicted of crimes of violence than was the case with any other group. The violent crime ratio for the next-highest group, immigrants from Ireland, was 29.1 percent, which was 29 percent lower than the Italian figure. The violent crime figures for immigrants, especially for the Irish and Italians, also were higher than for natives. For instance, whereas 37.4 percent of Italian offenses were violent, only 9.8 percent of native offenses were. These figures undoubtedly fed the commission's conclusion that Italians were responsible for an increase in violent crime.[32]

Note that compared with the native-born, the violent crime ratio also was higher for the second generation of Italians (defined as born in the United States to a father born in Italy). On the other hand, the second generation's ratio was far lower than it had been with the generation born overseas, as was the case with four of the five ethnic groups. This supports the contention that violent crime declines with the so-called second generation. The commission concluded that immigrant crime became more like native crime—that is, less violent, more "gainful"—in the second generation. "The movement of second generation crime is away from the crimes peculiar to immigrants and toward those of the American of native parentage."[33]

The New York City data were confirmed by a second commission study, this one based on convictions in New York State County Courts and Supreme Courts over a two-year period, 1907 and 1908. This study recorded birthplace, as opposed to ethnicity, so conclusions about second generations were impossible. Also, these courts were located throughout the state, but not in Manhattan, the main area of Italian residence. The results nonetheless reaffirmed the outsized violence of the Italian defendants. Thirty-nine percent of Italian crime was violent, whereas the next most violent group, Austro-Hungarians (probably overwhelmingly Jews), weighed in at 18.6 percent, less than half the Italian rate. See figure 8.2.

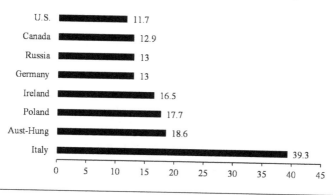

FIGURE 8.2. Percentage of convictions of offenses of personal violence in New York County Courts and New York Supreme Courts, 1907–8, by country of birth. *Source:* U.S. Immigration Commission, *Immigration and Crime,* 26.

The Italian violence is further illustrated by their relatively low proportion of "gainful" or theft crimes. For every other ethnic group such offenses constituted at least two-thirds of the convictions in the County and Supreme Courts, from 66 percent for Poles to 77 percent for Russians (again probably mainly Jews). For Italians, however, theft offenses were a mere 38 percent of the total.[34]

I end this part of the discussion with the Immigration Commission's final piece of New York data, this time from the New York City Magistrates' Courts, which at the time had jurisdiction over minor offenses, mainly public drunkenness and related violations. Indeed, so-called public policy offenses comprised 87 percent of the sample. As for violence, simple assaults rather than serious crimes of violence likely would have been on the magistrates' dockets.

The commission collected eight years' worth of data, 1901 to 1908, on all cases in which the defendant was committed to a penal institution or held for trial (n = 771,670). Once more, as shown in table 8.6, Italian defendants had the highest percentage of violent crimes among their total convictions.[35]

TABLE 8.6. Violent crime convictions as a percentage of total offenses, New York City Magistrates' Courts, 1901–1908, by birthplace

| Birthplace | Violent Crime |
| --- | --- |
| United States | 3.9 |
| England | 3.5 |
| France | 1.6 |
| Germany | 4.3 |
| Ireland | 3.7 |
| Italy | 7.3 |
| Russia | 3.3 |
| Scotland | 2.6 |

Source: U.S. Immigration Commission, Immigration and Crime, 90.

While one cannot say that the commission proved that Italian immigrants caused the increase in violent crimes in New York, there certainly are some striking signs that they did. Homicides were increasing in the city, and Italian immigrants, who made up about 7 percent of the population (1910 Census), seem to have been responsible for a goodly number of them—11 of 26 (42 percent) in the General Sessions study, albeit a tiny sample. Clearly, though, Italians were doing more violent crime in proportion to their total offenses—far more—than any other group, and this suggests that they almost certainly added to the rising tide of violence in New York. Precisely how much they added remains unknown.

One other piece of evidence for New York is from a small study of admissions to Sing Sing Prison. The study involved 683 consecutive admissions between August 1, 1916, and April 30, 1917. Of these 683 admissions, 213 were foreign-born, and of the 213 foreigners, 68, or 32 percent, were from Italy. It is noteworthy that more than half—53 percent—of the Italian offenses were crimes of violence, while 35 percent were deemed "acquisitive." By contrast, Russian prisoners (69 percent of whom were Jews) in the study group—58, or 27 percent, of the 213 foreigners—were involved in far less violence. Nineteen percent of their crimes were violent, 76 percent acquisitive.[36]

## Italian Violent Crime outside New York

Massachusetts, Philadelphia, Chicago, San Francisco, and Colorado had substantial Italian settlements, and as best we can determine, significant Italian crime. In 1910, over 85,000 Italian-born immigrants lived in Massachusetts, the fourth largest *colonia* in the United States.[37] While we have little indication of the extent of criminal involvement of the Massachusetts Italians, we have some evidence, once again from the Dillingham Immigration Commission, of the nature of their crimes.

Relying on state prison records, the commission created a database of one year's admissions, from October 1, 1908, to September 30, 1909 (n = 28,330), to all of the penal institutions in Massachusetts. The commission then determined the proportion of each type of crime committed by each immigrant group in the prison population. Nearly one-quarter of the Italian prisoners (24 percent) had committed crimes of violence, a higher percentage than any of the eleven other nationalities listed. (However, at 22.8 percent, Austro-Hungarians weren't far behind.) It is also interesting to see the relatively low proportions of Italian public policy offenses. Together, these figures suggest that Italians were violent, but seldom drunk and disorderly in public.

Italian violence, more than for any other Massachusetts group, was apt to be homicidal. With homicide accounting for over 5 percent of their violent crimes, the Italians were nearly eight times more likely to kill than the next nationality.[38]

Crime historian Roger Lane, who studied Philadelphia in detail, was convinced that "the presence and in-migration of both Italians and blacks had a truly dramatic impact on murder rates" in the early twentieth century.[39] His examination of Eastern State Penitentiary records for the period between 1899 and 1928 found 1,107 prisoners from Philadelphia who had been convicted of murder or voluntary manslaughter. Of the 1,107, 463 (42 percent) were black and 213 (19 percent) had been born in Italy. Together, these two groups—never more than 10 percent of the city's population—supplied an extraordinary 61 percent of its convicted killers.

The homicide imprisonment rates (per 100,000) for Italians actually exceeded those of African Americans, though they declined after World War I, which had sharply reduced Italian immigration. This suggests that the second generation of Italian Americans were more law-abiding than their immigrant parents. And indeed, Lane found that only 1.6 percent of the 1,107 convicted killers (n = 18) were descended from immigrants with Italian names.

Italian homicide rates in Chicago seemed to rise in proportion to Italian immigration to the city—a steep rise indeed. Chicago's Italy-born population, around 18,000 in 1900, tripled by 1910. At the same time, Italian homicide commission rates went from the high twenties per 100,000 to the high fifties just before World War I, then, as the war choked off Italian immigration, fell back toward the 1900 rate. From 1900 to 1910, Italians, around 2 percent of Chicago, were 7.5 percent of its killers; in the next decade that figure rose to 13 percent. While Italians were murdering at five times the citywide rates in 1910, their Scandinavian immigrant neighbors were demonstrating the difference culture can make. Nearly 25,000 Norwegian-born Chicagoans committed homicide at half the rate for the entire city, while 63,000 Swedes killed at less than one-quarter of the municipal rate. The Cook County Coroner found that Italian homicide deaths between 1910 and 1913 exceeded the combined totals of Bohemians, Greeks, Poles, and Russians, even though these groups were six times more numerous than the Italians.[40]

The first Italians to settle in San Francisco in the late nineteenth century were from northern Italy. Unsurprisingly, as their crime rates had been low in their homeland, their crime in the New World had no significant impact on murder rates. But by the mid-1890s, the situation changed as Italians from the south streamed in. Homicide rates for Italian immigrants in San Francisco doubled in the second half of the decade, from just short of seven per 100,000 to nearly 14. Moreover, the southerners brought a new type of crime: Black Hand extortion violence first emerged in San Francisco in the 1890s. As the new century dawned, non-Italian white homicide victimization held steady between six and seven for every 100,000 persons, while Italian rates were on average twice as high.[41]

Clare McKanna studied Las Animas County, a mining region in Colorado, and found high rates of Italian homicide. Though they were, in the first decade of the twentieth century, between 7 and 16 percent of the county's general population, Italian immigrants were named in over one-quarter of the homicide indictments. At least 30 percent of those killed by Italians were of a different ethnicity—an usually high proportion, especially for a group known for its intraethnic crime. With respect to homicides involving only Italians, McKanna found twenty-one apparently involving vendettas, typical of the honor-motivated killings associated with southern Italians. Also typical was the refusal to cooperate with the authorities. Ten of the killings were unindicted, six of the eleven indictments led to dismissals, two resulted in acquittals, and only three in guilty verdicts. On two occasions in the 1890s, perhaps out of frustration with the failure of the authorities, mobs lynched two Italians suspected of murder.[42]

### "Honor" and the Black Hand

This is a good place to take a brief look at the nature of Italian violence. A turn-of-the-century commentator on Italian crime observed that "affrays in which knives and pistols are used by Italians are in the great majority of instances confined to their own nationality. These grow largely out of jealous defence of wives, sisters, daughters or sweethearts, or resentment of rivalry. Often the exciting cause is covered up by trivial pretences and a quarrel flames up for no reason apparent to ordinary observers."[43] Contemporary historians have likewise concluded that Italian violence "rarely extended outside the ethnic community" and that it was intended by and large to protect the reputation of women. "Italian men killed in the defense of family honor," declared historian Jeffrey Adler, when "behavior toward women violated cultural norms and impugned the respectability of the family."[44] How much this sounds like the honor culture violence of southern Italy, or for that matter, the southern United States!

A second aspect to Italian violence was much more sensational—the "Black Hand" killings. In essence, these were extortion threats backed up not infrequently by actual violence: bombings, arsons, stabbings, shootings, kidnappings, and horse poisonings. From the early years of the new century to the 1920s, American newspapers were filled with stories of violence and intimidation marked by threatening letters signed "Black Hand" or imprinted with its symbol. While there is scant evidence of a single overarching organization, an American Mafia, the extortionate violence, the refusal of would-be witnesses to cooperate with the police, and the overwhelmingly southern Italian involvement were redolent of the Mafie organizations notorious in Sicily and southern Italy. "What seems clear from all of the evidence," wrote Francis A. J. Ianni, "is that the *Black Hand,* which lasted about 15 years (from the turn of the century to the first World War) was a cultural but not an organizational offshoot of *Mafia* and was completely Italian in origin and character." The cultural link is just too plain to be contested.[45]

It is significant, however, that most of the victims of the Black Hand were terrified Italian immigrants or their offspring, so that this aspect of Italian violence, like the honor killings in defense of women, was not as much of a threat to the greater community as say, indiscriminate street crime. But, though it is practically a cliché of multiculturalism to say so, extortion and violence within any ethnic group should be seen as a problem for the larger community, which owes every people the opportunity to live and do business in peace. Moreover, some of the Black Hand crime spilled over, so to speak, to the wider community by occasionally doing violence to the law enforcement authorities themselves. This occurred most dramatically with the New Orleans police chief killing of 1891 and the murder of NYPD Italian crime investigator Giuseppe (Joseph) Petrosino in Palermo, 1909.

One of the most shocking lynching of whites in American history occurred in New Orleans in 1891, when eleven Italians were shot to death by a mob entering the parish jail following a trial for the murder of the superintendent of police. The chief, David Hennessy, had been assassinated after launching a crackdown on Sicilian crime in the city. In a citywide atmosphere of near-hysteria hundreds of Italians were arrested. Nine were tried for the murder, but a jury acquitted six and reached no verdict on the other three. A mob broke into the jail and brutally attacked and killed the six acquitted Italians, along with five not yet tried.[46]

Fast forward twelve years. Joseph Petrosino, born in southern Italy, had risen up the ranks of New York City's police department, earning appointment by Chief Theodore Roosevelt to headquarters detective in charge of major Italian cases. He caught one of the most sensational such cases in 1903, when a woman discovered the mutilated body of a murdered man in a barrel on a street in the Lower East Side. The stiletto wounds had all the earmarks of a Sicilian gang killing and

Petrosino connected the victim to one of the more notorious such gangs. New York's newspapers had a field day with the Barrel Murder, and the widespread publicity didn't help the reputation of the NYPD or that of Italian immigrants when a trial of the suspected killers ended in an acquittal. The notorious case "solidified the image of Italians as ferocious criminals."

Petrosino's reputation as a dedicated crime fighter remained untarnished though, and six years later he was dispatched to Italy to ferret out evidence against suspect Sicilians in New York in an effort to have them deported. Shortly after his arrival in Palermo in 1909, Petrosino was shot to death on the street. No one ever was charged, but many years later, Don Vito Cascio Ferro, the aging head of the Sicilian Mafia, took credit for the crime.[47]

These dramatic events seared into the American consciousness the association of Italians (or perhaps southern Italians) with violent crime, a linkage reconfirmed by the organized crime that developed around Prohibition in the 1920s.

But this is to get ahead of the story. The reality is, as the evidence collected here attests, early twentieth-century Italian immigrants and second-generation Italian Americans (though considerably less so for the latter) committed a disproportionate amount of violent crime. Whether honor-related or extortion-related, this crime was a cultural import from southern Italy, part of the dark side of America's generous immigration policy.

## CRIME BY JEWISH IMMIGRANTS

It is instructive to compare in detail the crime of New York's Jewish population with that of its Italians. The two groups arrived at roughly the same time and took up residence in the same place—but with very different types of crime involvement. Despite the similarities of circumstance—impoverishment, squalid overcrowded housing, social and economic segregation, profound divergence with the host country's culture—the crime of the Italians was much more violent than that of the Jews. Accurate determination of Jewish crime rates, however, is as problematic as it was with the Italian. Even determining the size of the Jewish population is difficult since early censuses usually recorded birthplace, not religion, and Jewish identity was not precisely aligned with a particular country of origin.

The great wave of Jewish migration that began in the 1880s, and continued unabated until World War I and the immigration restrictions of the 1920s, was driven by flight from eastern Europe. Jews mainly fled the Russian Empire, secondarily Austria-Hungary (itself an empire before the First World War) and Romania, eventually supplying around one-quarter of the population of New York City. Relying on language, not just birthplace, the 1910 Census counted 861,980 Yiddish- or Hebrew-speaking residents in the city, 18.5 percent of the total white population (including whites who were foreign-born or natives of foreign descent). At the same time, the tally of Italians in New York totaled 549,444, or 11.8 percent of the whites. Taking the first few decades of the twentieth century as a whole, the Jews and Italians, in that order, ranked one and two among the city's enormous foreign-born population.[48]

One big difference between the New York Jewish and Italian immigrants was the proportion of young men. Between 1899 and 1910, only 21 percent of Italian immigrants were female, whereas among the Jewish immigrants women were 43 percent. After 1910, the Italian ratio started swinging toward normalcy, but clearly this gender imbalance needs to be controlled for when calculating the crime rates of the respective groups—a difficult task.[49] The gender gap may have played a pivotal role in creating the most significant difference crime-wise between Jews and Italians—the resort to violence.

Though the proud but sensitive New York Jewish community of the early twentieth century did not want to believe it, the contemporary view was that Jews had high criminal involvement. Jews were stunned and dismayed when New York Police Commissioner Theodore A. Bingham, writing in the 1908 *North American Review*, estimated that half the city's criminals were Jews and at least 85 percent of the Jewish offenders were foreign-born. Although Jewish involvement in crime was not insignificant, Bingham's estimate exaggerated. One modern study found that 50 to 60 percent of those arraigned in Magistrate's Courts in Manhattan and the Bronx, 1900–1914, were foreign-born, and of these, Russians were one-third of those arraigned; Italians and Irish, each around 20 percent. Of course, this being the lowest-level court, the offenses were overwhelmingly petty, like obstructing sidewalks or improper disposal of garbage. But even at the felony level, though Jewish involvement was high, it probably was not out of proportion to their numbers in the general population. Jews were 21 percent of a sample of New York County (Manhattan and Bronx) felony arraignments, 1900–1914.[50]

For Jews, as for Italians, the crime culture in the old country was a good predictor of behavior in America. Despite desperate conditions in Europe, Jewish crime, especially the violent type, was extraordinarily low. Before examining this crime in greater detail, I will look at the background conditions leading to Jewish migration.

Eighty percent of the Jews who migrated to America had lived in the northwestern regions of the Russian Empire, within the Pale of Settlement, a vast area that would later in the twentieth century become Poland, Lithuania, and western Ukraine. About 20 percent of the migrants had lived in Galicia, a province of the northeast Austro-Hungarian Empire, or in Romania, at the time an independent kingdom. There were several reasons for the massive departure for America. First, the czarist governments imposed severe economic, political, and residential restrictions on Jews, part of late nineteenth-century attempts to Russify the empire's myriad nationalities. The mass of Jews, in large measure because of these restrictions, was poverty-stricken. A second driver was fear of conscription into the Czar's Army, which, when the Russo-Japanese War (1904–5) broke out, meant service in harsh Siberian conditions. Third were the periodic pogroms—attacks by peasants or townfolks on Jews and their property, often instigated by authorities to divert attention from political or economic problems, and largely ignored by local police. The most notorious of the pogroms was the Kishinev Massacre of 1903, a three-day assault on the Jewish quarter which resulted in the deaths and injury of hundreds along with massive destruction of homes and property. Kishinev roused worldwide condemnation. This was followed two years later by a wave of pogroms stimulated by the Russian Revolution of 1905, the Jews being associated with the revolutionists in the mind of the average Russian. Over six hundred Jewish communities were attacked and approximately one thousand Jews were killed.[51]

While the draft and the pogroms spurred the migration of tens of thousands, some think the economic and residential restrictions were even more significant. Jews were forbidden to take up residence in certain towns and cities, and where they were permitted to live—small cities and villages (shtetl)—they were subject to government surveillance and barred from voting for city council (duma) representatives. Keeping Jews out of big cities, with their dynamic and growing populations, further stifled the Jews' economic advancement. Other major limitations included the following: Jews were unable to buy or lease land in rural districts; they were subject to admissions quotas in secondary schools and universities; they could not practice certain professions, including law, without government permission; they were subject to limits on the purchase of stocks in corporations; nearly all governmental positions were foreclosed to them; and they were effectively barred from admission to the officer corps of the military.[52] One result of these various restraints is that Jews were limited to certain types of work, such as retail merchandizing or banking. A turn-of-the-century study of Jewish occupations in Austria found 44 percent in business and trade, 29 percent in industry.[53]

Crime had been "a very real part of European Jewish life," but in the old world as in the new that crime was mercenary, not violent. Theft, embezzlement, fraud, dealing in stolen merchandise—these were the typical Jewish offenses both there and here. "The eschewal of violence among the Jews," observed Jena Joselit, "seemed to be a conscious decision, indeed a kind of cultural inheritance, transmitted from one generation to the next."[54] A study of Jewish crime in Austria, 1898, showed that Jews engaged in more minor crimes, but fewer serious crimes, than Christians.

TABLE 8.7. Convictions per 10,000 of serious and minor crimes, Austria, 1898, by religion

| Gravity of Offense | Catholic | Protestant | E. Orthodox | Jews |
|---|---|---|---|---|
| Serious crimes | 13.4 | 12.0 | 19.0 | 10.7 |
| Minor crimes | 2.7 | 5.3 | 9.2 | 10.1 |

Source: Wassermann, Beruf, Konfession, 73.

Rates for those Austrian districts with high Jewish populations were similar.

TABLE 8.8. Convictions per 10,000 of serious and minor crimes, Austria, 1902–1903, by religion and district

| District | Gravity of Offense | Catholics | Jews |
|---|---|---|---|
| Galicia | Serious crimes | 13.5 | 8.3 |
| | Minor crimes | 4.2 | 9.1 |
| Bukowina | Serious crimes | 15.8 | 8.0 |
| | Minor crimes | 8.9 | 20.2 |

Source: Wassermann, Beruf, Konfession, 78.

Note: Bukowina is now in northern Rumania and western Ukraine.

In Austria, as in America, for offenses involving violence, Jewish conviction rates were lower than for non-Jews; but for theft, fraud and business crimes, Jewish rates often were higher.[55]

TABLE 8.9. Convictions of selected violent and nonviolent offenses per 100,000, Austria, 1898, by religion

| Violent Crimes | Jews | Others |
|---|---|---|
| Forcible assault | 6.4 | 9.8 |
| Extortion | 1.2 | 1.8 |
| Rape, sex crimes | 1.8 | 5.1 |
| Serious bodily injury | 6.5 | 20.1 |
| Unintentional killing | 2.5 | 2.2 |

| Nonviolent Crimes | Jews | Others |
|---|---|---|
| Theft with accomplices | 39.4 | 62.7 |
| Embezzlement with accomplices | 5.6 | 2.6 |
| Fraud | 38.2 | 10.9 |
| Bankruptcy laws | 21.5 | 2.7 |
| Foreclosure laws | 3.1 | 1.1 |
| Draft laws | 3.5 | 1.2 |
| Credit laws | 6.5 | 0.1 |

*Source:* Wassermann, *Beruf, Konfession,* 73.

Turning to America, we find that the Jewish ghetto on the Lower East Side of Manhattan was riddled with crime, and yet, because violent offenses were exceptional, the average person could walk through it night or day without fear. In one square mile the New York authorities found 200 "disorderly houses," 336 youth gang hangouts, over 200 pool hall betting establishments, a dance hall in which pimps and procurers were active every two and one-half blocks, and a plethora of gambling parlors. What's more, as was common knowledge, the Jewish owners and operators of these illegal establishments bribed the police and their Tammany superiors to keep their operations running, thereby contributing to the corruption of the city government. There also was a fair amount of extortion and fraud. Jews ran a pallid version of the Black Hand, shaking down mainly Jewish businessmen by threatening to poison their horses. Another common swindle involved arson of businesses followed by fraudulent fire insurance claims—"Jewish lightning" as it came to be known. Joselit found that Jews were implicated in 44 percent of the city's arson cases in the 1890s, though this dropped to 15 to 18 percent from 1900 to 1910. "Vice and crime were not only widespread on the Lower East Side," she concluded, "they were also highly visible."[56] Nevertheless, as I said, muggings, rapes, and murders were rarities. "The Lower East Side was a horror," declared Albert Fried, historian of the Jewish underworld, "but its streets were safe even at night. Fear of physical harm was absent in the community."[57]

Overwhelmingly, the Jews committed property crimes, whereas the Italians engaged in crimes of violence. Joselit found that Jews accounted for 20 to 25 percent of all felony arrests (Manhattan and the Bronx, 1900–1915), but 30 percent of the grand larceny and fully half of the receiving stolen property arrests. Of defendants born in Russia, many of whom, of course, were Jews, Joselit found that over eight in ten of their offenses were property crimes—burglary, larceny, arson, horse-poisoning, receiving stolen goods, etc.—whereas 18 percent were crimes against the person or a mix of personal and property crimes (which included robbery). Italy-born defendants in the same sample had a very different distribution. Two-thirds of their accusations involved violent and mixed offenses, and only 28 percent were property crimes.[58]

Was there a *cultural* difference between Jews and Italians that played itself out in different levels of violence? Given the respective cultural support for violence of the two groups in their European setting this conclusion seems irresistible—especially since we have no reason to believe that crime in southern Italy was distorted by disproportionate numbers of young men. On the other hand, because the New York data don't readily permit adjustments for gender and age, we cannot be certain how much of the Italian violence in Gotham was attributable to the outsized young male population.

## RECAPITULATION

Wherever they settled, the pattern of crime among Italian immigrants was clear and it was consistent. Violent crime was considerably higher than among native-born whites, the victims overwhelmingly were other Italians, and cooperation with law enforcement and the courts was minimal, meaning that much of the crime was committed with impunity. The killings frequently were a result of honor-based conflicts arising from perceived insults to the murderer or his family. In addition, especially before 1920, a significant amount of Italian violence was extortion-related, attributed rightly or wrongly to the Black Hand.

Homicide rates increased in virtually all of the states, cities, and counties that hosted significant numbers of Italians, and while these increases had various causes, Italian immigrants clearly contributed disproportionately to the escalation. As murder rates had been, at the time of peak immigration, extraordinarily high in the *mezzogiorno,* and as these rates had been accompanied by Mafia extortion along with a strong culture of honor, the behavior of the immigrants seems to be readily explained by their unique cultural attributes. The southern Italian culture supported high levels of violence in Europe; transported to America, that culture helped push crime rates up in the United States. As historian Rudolph J. Vecoli concluded: "The propensity for violence of the south Italians was not a symptom of social disorganization caused by emigration but a characteristic of their Old World culture."[59]

The contrast with Jewish immigrants is striking. Both arrived in the same place at the same time in comparably impoverished conditions, and both moved into equally squalid and overcrowded New York neighborhoods. But Italians and Jews committed very different types of crimes. The stereotypes of Jews engaging in vice, theft, and deception had some basis in fact, while their resort to assault, murder, and robbery was a relative rarity. Italians, on the other hand, evinced high rates of violence.

The similarity of circumstances between Italians and Jews along with the striking dissimilarity in their violence give force to the cultural explanation for their behavior. Nevertheless, due to the excessive youth and male composition of Italian immigrants, especially during the first decade of the twentieth century, there remains uncertainty about the amount of Italian violent crime. As a result, one cannot say precisely how much of the high Italian violent crime rates were due to cultural and how much to demographic factors.

## CURTAILING IMMIGRATION

The "new" European immigrants—Italians, Jews, Greeks, and Slavs—were hated and scorned much as the Irish had been in the nineteenth century. But if one may speak of degrees of prejudice, their treatment was less bad than that of the

Chinese or certainly than African Americans. Difficult as it was for the Europeans, blacks and Chinese faced the insuperable skin color obstacle, and whites never let them forget it.

If, as is sometimes contended (though rarely defended in any sustained way), bias and discrimination cause violent crime, then one should have expected the most crime from blacks and Chinese, less from Italians and Jews. But the correlation is imperfect. Italian crime was as high as for blacks, higher in some places (e.g., Philadelphia). Chinese crime was exceptionally high during certain periods, far lower at other times, especially with arrivals from different and less violent parts of China. Jewish crime, as we just saw, never was very violent, though vice and theft ran high.

The bias or racism theory of violent crime fails to explain crime in the "old country." Southern Italians had high levels of violence in their homeland, where they were neither a minority nor the victims of prejudice. (This isn't to deny that they were disdained by northerners and suffered grievously due to the failure of the agricultural system.) Jews, however, were a minority group in Russia and Austria-Hungary, and they certainly felt the sting of discrimination. Yet their violent crime rates were low. So in one case we have crime without bias; in the other, bias without crime.

Prejudice and discrimination did affect violent crime in the United States, but only obliquely. First, where it delayed the movement of a group to the middle class—notably in the case of African Americans—racism perpetuated and prolonged the antisocial excesses of its lower-class elements. This is a major reason why, as will be seen, black crime remained persistently high throughout the twentieth century. More commonly—and this was especially the situation with Italian, Jewish, and Chinese immigrants—where bias led to restrictions on immigration it reduced the flow of young males into the immigrant community, thereby shrinking the supply of new recruits to crime. The effect was to give the group some breathing space to advance up the American ladder without the drag of new immigrants to assimilate. In this respect, the anti-immigration legislation, despite its validation of ethnic bias, actually helped the immigrants who were already here.

World War I stimulated a great deal of xenophobia in the United States, while simultaneously making overseas travel, and therefore immigration, extremely difficult. The figures for Italian immigration reflect this. In 1914, nearly 300,000 Italians entered the United States. By 1918, that number had dwindled to 5,200, and in the following year it was under 2,000. For America, the war lasted less than two years, "but the nativist feelings aroused during the conflagration did not die quickly. Americanization drives during the war turned into anti-foreign debaucheries," and support for limits on immigration soon carried the day in Congress.[60]

Religious (anti-Semitic and anti-Catholic) bias along with racial bigotry helped fuel the immigration restrictions. But support came too from those who were fearful that the recent Bolshevik revolution would be part of the immigrant's baggage. And labor unions, including the ethnic rank and file—themselves recent arrivals—were anxious to shut out foreign competition for jobs. Samuel Gompers, head of the American Federation of Labor, an immigrant and a Jew, supported the restrictions.

Congress passed two major laws, in 1921 and 1924, based on a quota system which limited entry by each nationality to a proportion of their numbers already in the United States. The first bill restricted each European nation to 3 percent of that country's total U.S. population as counted in the 1910 Census. The Immigration Act of 1924 superseded the 1921 law and reduced the quota to 2 percent of each nationality as measured by the 1890 Census, which, since it predated the bulk of the Italian and Jewish immigration, further reduced the inflow of those groups. This latter formula was in turn replaced in 1929 by a more complicated and even more restrictive allocation. In addition, the 1924 Act practically shut off Asian immigration altogether, forbidding entry to persons ineligible for naturalization, a category that encompassed all nonwhites, including, of course, Chinese and Japanese. The 1924 law (modified in 1952) effectively established U.S. immigration policy for forty years, until the liberalizations of the Immigration and Nationality Act of 1965.[61]

The effect of the quotas on Italian immigration appeared to be dramatic. From 1900 to 1910, Italians averaged around 195,000 entries per year. From 1925 to 1930, however, the average was fifteen thousand annually. But this drop-off wasn't just a result of the new immigration laws. The Great Depression took its own toll on immigration. Increasingly then, as the inflow of Italians and Jews wound down, immigrant crime would become a second- and even a third-generation issue. Meanwhile, in 1920, Congress passed a law prohibiting the sale of alcoholic beverages—a law that created perverse incentives for these hyphenated Americans to engage in new and ever more lucrative criminal activities.

# 9

## North of the Border
*Mexicans in the United States*

While the bootleggers were battling it out on big-city streets up north and southerners were slaying one another at frighteningly high rates, a new immigrant group was crossing America's southern border. Escaping from the turmoil of their revolution-wracked land, desperate for work in the surging economy of América del Norte, a massive influx of Mexicans flooded into southern California and Texas, then fanned north to Chicago and other alien climes. Once again, the United States would play host to wretched refugees, and once again the crime toll would uptick another notch. While average Americans held the Mexicans in contempt, the expanding U.S. economy was dependent on their labor, especially in the 1920s, when the door to European and Asian immigration was closed. For their part, the new immigrants suffered the sting of discrimination on top of miserable living conditions, low pay, and backbreaking work. The obvious question is why did they put up with it, and the simple answer is that the situation was even worse in Mexico.

### THE MIGRATION
The 1910 Census estimated the Mexican population of the United States at only 162,000, though this probably was an undercount. A decade later the total exceeded 700,000, and by 1930, this had doubled to 1.4 million. The 1920s were the biggest migration years for Mexicans, the "push/pull" factors being optimal during that decade. The immigration quota laws of the 1920s exempted Mexico and Canada, a situation that suited both the agriculture lobby and the State Department, which sought improved relations in the Americas. Nonetheless, a lot of the Mexican migration was illegal, abetted by the absence of any border

patrol prior to 1924, and an ineffectual one before 1930. Of course, as we've seen in recent decades, patrolling a two-thousand-mile boundary, even with a well-organized and trained force, is no easy task.[1]

As to the push factors, Mexico's political and economic disarray began in 1910 with a rebellion against the dictator Porfirio Díaz, who had ruled since 1876. Within one year the Porfiriato collapsed, but that hardly ended matters. The Revolution continued for nearly a decade, "punctuated by coups, countercoups, executions, bloody fighting, and more fighting." An estimated 1 million Mexicans died during this period, either from armed encounters, famine, or disease. The main battleground was the north central region of Mexico, especially the states of San Luis Potosi, Zacatecas, Jalisco, and Guanajuato.[2]

These areas were devastated, as regular armies and armed revolutionary bands occupied the haciendas, or large estates, that had for centuries been the mainstay of the rural economy. Historian James Sandos and Harry Cross described the impact.[3]

These armed men destroyed property, carried off and sold or personally consumed most of the area's livestock, and pillaged sugar mills and mescal [an alcoholic drink] manufactories. As a result, by 1917, operations had come to a halt on all large *haciendas*. This in turn meant a drastic loss of employment for the rural masses. Many peasants migrated to other parts of Mexico during those years, some emigrated to the United States, but most simply attempted to eke out an existence by hunting, gathering, and subsistence farming. Living conditions deteriorated disastrously. The price of maize rose tenfold; living standards, in terms of real wages for those still fortunate enough to be employed, declined by some 75 percent between 1913 and 1916.

A survey of Mexican immigrants in the Chicago area in the 1920s revealed, unsurprisingly, that two-thirds of the sample came from the states of Guanajuato, Jalisco, and Michoacán—all in the strife-torn north central region.

Even in the 1920s, well after the Revolution, blood continued to be shed, notably in the so-called Cristero War, or Cristiada, of 1926–29. This series of violent confrontations was sparked by peasant resistance to the extreme anticlerical policies of Plutarco Elías Calles, elected president in 1924. The rallying cry of the rebels, hence the name of the conflict, was "Viva Cristo Rey!" ("Long Live Christ the King"). Once more, north central Mexico, and especially Jalisco, was thrown into turmoil. By the end of the Cristiada, 70,000 people were dead, agricultural output had declined 38 percent, 200,000 people had fled to Mexico's cities, and even more significantly for our story, 450,000 people left the country altogether, most escaping to the United States.[4]

By the twentieth century, the differences between Mexico and the United States in terms of economic development and social well-being had become striking. "While the United States flourished," historians L. H. Gann and Peter Duignan wrote, "Mexico became more impoverished." In 1905, an agricultural laborer in Jalisco earned 13 cents and some maize for an entire day's labor, whereas an American truck laborer made $1.25 for ten hours' work. A Mexican family migrating to Texas to pick cotton could earn $5.00 a day, nearly forty times their pay in Jalisco. By the 1920s, when Mexican migration reached its apogee, the average wage for unskilled agricultural and industrial work in Mexico was 57 cents per day (1927); in the United States the pay for comparable labor was six times greater. Given the social turmoil and economic disaster south of the border, is it any wonder that nearly 10 percent of the entire adult population of Mexico crossed to the north between 1900 and 1930?[5]

Who were these Mexican migrants? They were disproportionately male, young, uneducated, and unskilled, with little interest in the United States except as a source of subsistence. Unlike most other immigrants, few Mexicans sought American citizenship, considering themselves temporary sojourners. Their lives in North America were nomadic, moving to farms at harvest times, to cities when recruited for unskilled railroad or factory labor. Living conditions were harsh, the work grueling, the pay low by U.S. standards. Mexicans were willing to work for less than other immigrants whom they replaced at the low end of the labor market. For instance, the Southern Pacific Railroad, in 1908, paid Greeks $1.60 per day, Japanese $1.50, and Mexicans $1.25.

Here are some additional facts and figures. As of 1930, one-third of all Mexican immigrants were less than twenty-five years old, and half were under age forty-five. Fifty-three percent were males, the sex ratios normal near the border, but male-predominant in the northern areas of settlement. In Illinois, for example, 63 percent of the Mexican population was male. Few of the migrants had skills, or were proficient in English, making advancement in the United States difficult. To illustrate, a 1928 survey of workers in two big steel plants in Calumet, south of

Chicago, found that 79 percent of the Mexicans were unskilled, 19 percent were semiskilled, under 2 percent skilled. A survey of Mexican prisoners in Illinois revealed that 21 percent had only five years of schooling; 35 percent had none. Forty-six percent spoke no English whatsoever.[6]

In the United States the Mexicans naturally gravitated to the Southwest, given the proximity to the Mexican border and the great demand for agricultural labor. But a surprising number ended up in urban areas, Chicago being a major destination. As already noted, Chicago had nearly twenty thousand Mexicans in 1930. In fact, by the Census definition of "urban" (towns and cities over 2,500) more than half the migrants lived in urban areas. This was mainly a by-product of the American economy, which needed unskilled labor on railroads, in steel factories, and in meatpacking plants. Employers in these industries recruited and often transported Mexicans from Texas. Other Mexicans came to Chicago (and, to a lesser extent, Denver, St. Louis, and Pittsburgh) from the sugar-beet fields of Wisconsin, Minnesota, or Michigan, where they worked the harvest, then moved on to cities in the off-season. Still others migrated to the Northwest on the advice of friends or relatives already there. This occurred in spite of the dilapidated housing, freezing winters, police abuse, constant clashes with European ethnics, and the discouragement of the Mexican educated class, which considered emigration a betrayal of the Revolution. Mexican newspapers repeatedly published stories of abuses north of the border, including riots and occasional lynchings, but the migrant workers' grapevine was more powerful than the media.[7]

The top three destinations for Mexican immigrants were California, Texas, and Arizona, where they worked as farm, mine, smelting, and railroad laborers. The expansion of agriculture, made possible by massive irrigation projects stimulated by federal legislation, created a huge fruit and vegetable industry, especially in southern California, which by 1929 was producing almost 40 percent of the U.S. total. The need for stoop labor to harvest the crops was expanding just at the time that the Mexican economy and political system were collapsing and the doors to Chinese and European immigration were slamming shut. Three southwestern cities—San Antonio, El Paso, and Los Angeles—became major Mexican settlements. Los Angeles, with over 90,000 Mexicans, mainly in East L.A., had the biggest Spanish-speaking population in North America save Mexico City itself. Los Angeles County had 167,000 Mexicans, 45 percent of the Mexican population of the state. In Bexar County, Texas, where San Antonio predominates,

Mexicans (98,901) comprised one-third of the population. In El Paso County, they were 59 percent of the inhabitants (77,389 of 131,597).[8]

Despite hardships in the United States, the flow of Mexicans did not stop until the Great Depression of the 1930s, whereupon Mexicans began to return to their homeland. Some were forcibly repatriated, as Americans, concerned about losing scarce jobs to aliens, approved state and federal repatriation laws. The exact number deported is unknown, but estimates are in excess of 200,000 for the years 1929–35, "by far the largest number of aliens of any nationality ever forced to leave the United States." Within a decade, however, with labor shortages growing due to World War II, the United States reversed course and established a contract worker (bracero) program with Mexico. Though much criticized on both sides of the border, between 1942 and 1947 the program brought about 200,000 braceros to the United States, more than half to California farms. Illegal migration also rose during this period, topping 1 million by 1954.[9]

## VIOLENT CRIME IN MEXICO

Not unlike other rural people, such as southern Italians and American southerners for that matter, Mexicans had a strong culture of honor. Much of the criminal violence in Mexico—and as will be seen, the rates were very high—was motivated by the defense of honor. Until the end of the nineteenth century, the Mexican upper classes engaged in duels, the archetypal honor-driven behavior. Lower-class Mexicans, though not expressly invoking honor, and not engaging in formal duels, followed strict rules of confrontation to satisfy collective notions of fairness. To ensure public approbation, fights had to be one-on-one and held in a neutral public location; police could not be summoned; and there could be no complaining about wounds. Even the types of knife wounds that were inflicted (knife fights being ubiquitous)—whether to abdomen or face—had significance. "It did not matter so much who prevailed in a fight, nor who was accused by the police," observed historian Pablo Piccato, "what mattered was demonstrating one's bravery and loyalty—those virtues that educated people called 'honor.'"

The very Penal Code itself reflected honor norms. Blows that caused no injury were not considered crimes under the Code of 1871—unless inflicted "publicly" or in circumstances "that public opinion would regard as dishonoring." (In the United States, assaults are graded by the extent of physical injury without any consideration of public opinion.) "Honor was a right that had to be defended daily," maintained Piccato, "against many threats, and at a very high cost."[10]

The Revolution and the Cristiada displaced rural Mexicans by the thousands. Many flocked to the capital and other cities, bringing increased theft and violence. Much of the violence was associated with drinking, and Mexico City had, in 1902, an estimated 2,423 alcohol outlets. Also, with the Revolution guns became cheaper and more abundant. They were said to be "readily available" in Mexico City and probably were one of the principal causes of the increase after 1916 in the proportion of homicides among crimes. Violent crime by strangers also escalated. The official crime count undoubtedly understated the problem. An unknown number of violent encounters went unreported because the participants, notwithstanding their degree of culpability, feared punishment. In addition, many assaults, dismissed by the authorities as mere *riñas* (fights), never were entered into the official statistics.

Crimes against persons were a substantial portion of serious offenses. According to Piccato, battery "constituted more than half of the felonies brought to trial" in Mexico City. And homicide rates, he noted, "were very high compared to other contemporary urban areas and were on the rise." In 1900, in the Federal District, which encompassed Mexico City and surrounding municipalities, the homicide sentencing rate was 13.3 per 100,000. By 1909, the year before the Revolution, the rate had jumped to 31.5 for every 100,000 people. By 1930, it was 37.2.[11]

## MEXICAN VIOLENCE IN THE UNITED STATES

As we have seen with other national and ethnic groups, the Italians for example, high levels of violence in the home country commonly travel with the immigrants to the new land. This was, as best we can tell, the case with the Mexicans who came to the United States. One must be cautious here because the data are less than perfect. But data seldom are as complete or reliable as researchers like. And where multiple data sources all point in the same direction one must pay heed: corroboration counts.

There was an effort, especially in the 1920s and 1930s, to rebut the arguments of nativists who pointed to immigrant crime in order to bolster support for their campaign to shut off foreign immigration. The debate was largely rendered academic by the Great Depression, which wiped out much of America's allure as the land of opportunity. In 1931, the well-known Wickersham Commission (officially the National Commission on Law Observance and Enforcement), famous for its exposure of police brutalities, devoted several volumes to immigrant crime, seeking for the most part to downplay any association of the recent arrivals with criminality. Three studies of Mexican crime were presented in the commission's report, covering California, Texas, and Illinois, respectively, areas of high Mexican concentration. The studies, apparently completed prior to the 1930 Census, were handicapped by lack of population data, but below I compensate for this by plugging in those census figures. The results, as shall be seen, are far less favorable to the Mexican immigrant than the rather benign conclusion drawn by Edith Abbott, dean of the school of social work at the University of Chicago, who prepared a summary of the commission's work. Abbott wrote: "Thoughtful reading of these three reports dealing with the Mexican tends to lead to the formation of an opinion that the lack of fairly exact population data which would permit corrections for sex and age makes it impossible to determine whether or not Mexicans commit more crimes than do the native white, but that there is reason to doubt that the popular belief as to excessive criminal behavior among Mexicans is justified by the facts." Abbott went on to cite by way of rationalization for Mexican crime the conflict between Mexican customs and U.S. laws. In addition, she blamed racial prejudice against Mexicans, especially by American police. An example of the former was offered by Paul Taylor, the labor economist, author of the commission's study on Mexican crime in California. Taylor pointed out that carrying knives, an offense in the United States, was no violation south of the border, and that Mexicans "wear knives so habitually as to regard them practically a part of the dress."[12]

As for American law enforcement, Mexicans were the victims of especially rough treatment. Prior to the 1920s, the Texas Rangers were notorious for brutality against them, killing an estimated one to five thousand over a multidecade period. A Mexican government study of Mexican immigrants killed by police between 1910 and 1920 concluded that the majority took place in Texas. This is partially explained by the proportion of Mexican migrants to Texas, by 1910 roughly two-thirds of the total.[13]

Starting in the 1920s, bad publicity for the Rangers plus a change in Mexican migration patterns considerably reduced the violence against Mexican migrants in Texas. At times, the Rangers even protected the Mexicans. When Ku Klux Klan–inspired violence spiked during the recession of 1921, the Rangers "secured the safety of Mexicans assaulted by masked men."[14]

In the 1920s, young males from the violent interior of Mexico migrated to the American Midwest in search of higher-paying jobs. There they met hostility from the residents (despite the fact that most of these were themselves recent immigrants) and brutality at the hands of the police. Historian Francisco Rosales estimated that 20 percent of the homicides of Mexicans in Chicago, 1922–27, were attributable to police. This was a higher percentage than for any other group; for African Americans, for instance, the estimated proportion was 10 percent. Nevertheless, the vast majority of the Mexican victims had been assaulted by their own countrymen. Sixty percent of the homicides were, in Rosales's words, "same-group passion killing." Mexican-on-Mexican violence, in other words, took three times as many lives as law enforcement killings.[15]

In recent years, two economists, Carolyn Moehling and Anne Morrison Piehl, published important work on immigrant crime in the early decades of the twentieth century. They relied on prison commitments, which though dubious for determining crime rates, have considerably more validity as indicators of relative amounts of crime by racial and ethnic groups.

Moehling and Piehl obtained data from special Census Bureau prisoner counts. The first of these special enumerations was conducted in 1904, followed by tallies in 1910 and 1923. These enumerations covered federal and state prisons, penitentiaries, and reformatories, along with county and municipal jails and workhouses. In 1926, the Census Bureau began annual prison enumerations, but these did not include county and municipal facilities.

Although the Mexican population in the United States was small in the first decade of the twentieth century, the Mexican prison/jail population was disproportionately high. In fact, Mexicans had the highest ratio of actual to predicted commitment rates of any group measured by Moehling and Piehl. Significantly, Moehling and Piehl controlled for age, especially important with the Mexican population, which was very youthful. Approximately one-third of the Mexicans in the United States (1930) were under age twenty-five.

Because none of the prison censuses reported commitment data broken down by both country of origin and age, the authors created a statistical workaround.

They compared "predicted commitment rates for each immigrant group based on its age distribution in the general population and the age-specific commitment rates of the foreign-born overall." The predicted rate is what one would expect in light of the group's age structure. The higher the ratio of actual to predicted incarceration rates, the "worse" the group's criminality, taking into account its age. As can be seen from table 9.1, the Mexican ratio is far higher than that of any other immigrant group, for instance, more than three times the Italian rate.[16]

TABLE 9.1. Ratio of actual to predicted prisoner commitment rates for major offenses by selected immigrant groups, 1904

| Country of Origin | Actual | Predicted | Ratio of Actual to Predicted |
|---|---|---|---|
| Austria | 72 | 90 | 0.80 |
| Ireland | 60 | 52 | 1.15 |
| Italy | 162 | 97 | 1.67 |
| Mexico | 420 | 79 | 5.32 |
| Poland | 63 | 94 | 0.67 |
| Russia | 89 | 98 | 0.91 |
| Sweden | 28 | 73 | 0.38 |

Source: Moehling and Piehl, "Immigration, Crime, and Incarceration," 758, 759.

The 1930 prisoner count was more useful than the 1904 tally in that it provided age-specific commitment data, although the census used rather broad age categories, for example, 18–24, 25–34, etc. Consequently, Moehling and Piehl were able to calculate commitment rates per 100,000 for various population groups disaggregated by age. Unfortunately, prisoners born in Mexico or of Mexican descent were placed by the census in an "other races" category that also included American Indians, Chinese, Japanese, and all others deemed not white and not black. Mexicans made up the vast majority of these so-called other races—70.3 percent of the prisoners received in 1930—permitting us to attribute to Mexicans most of the "other race" criminality. Table 9.2 presents Moehling and Piehl's figures for incarceration for violent crimes and for homicide in particular.

These data are for males only, which controls for the gender imbalance of the Mexican population.[17]

TABLE 9.2. Commitment rates per 100,000 to state and federal prisons, by race, nativity, age, and offense, males, 1930

VIOLENT CRIMES

| Age | Native Whites | Foreign Whites | Blacks | Other Races |
|---|---|---|---|---|
| 18 to 24 | 68 | 66 | 2 | 84 |
| 25 to 34 | 36 | 24 | 72 | 85 |
| 35 to 44 | 15 | 12 | 4 | 34 |
| 45+ | 7 | 6 | 3 | 22 |

HOMICIDES

| Age | Native Whites | Foreign Whites | Blacks | Other Races |
|---|---|---|---|---|
| 18 to 24 | 7 | 4 | 6 | 18 |
| 25 to 34 | 7 | 5 | 7 | 30 |
| 35 to 44 | 4 | 4 | 3 | 16 |
| 45+ | 2 | 2 | 6 | 10 |

*Source:* Moehling and Piehl, "Immigration and Crime," 42.

As is evident, except for African Americans, "other races" had in each age category the highest commitment rates of all groups for violent crimes and for homicides. Since, as we noted, Mexicans were 70 percent of this other race category, their violent crime and homicide rates must have been significantly higher than that of either native whites or foreign-born whites. In the crucial 25–34 age bracket, for example, other race commitment rates for violent crimes were 236 percent of the native white rate; for homicides, they were over four times the rate for native whites.

The 1930 enumeration of prisoners directly corroborates the high incarceration rates of Mexicans. Table 9.3 presents the homicide and violent crime rates of males from selected racial/ethnic groups. Though age is not accounted for, this table confirms that Mexican rates fell roughly halfway between those of non-Mexican whites and African Americans.

TABLE 9.3. Prison commitment rates per 100,000 of males, nationwide, by racial/ethnic group, 1930

| Group | Homicide | Violent Crime |
|---|---|---|
| African American | 25.04 | 76.95 |
| American Indian | 11.15 | 39.33 |
| Asian | 6.37 | 22.28 |
| Foreign-born white | 2.95 | 13.96 |
| Mexican | 12.92 | 37.57 |
| Native white | 3.11 | 18.62 |

Source: Bureau of the Census, *Prisoners 1929 and 1930*, table 24.

Note: "Asian" refers to prisoners of Chinese, Japanese, Filipino, Hindu, and Korean extraction, plus all other racial or ethnic groups not included in any of the other categories. "Violent Crime" is defined as homicide, rape, robbery, and assault.

As alluded to earlier, the Wickersham Commission presented three studies of Mexican crime, in California, Texas, and Illinois. These reports unwittingly corroborated the findings of Moehling and Piehl. I say "unwittingly" because the authors of these reports did not have the census population data necessary for constructing crime rates, and perhaps as a consequence, downplayed Mexican crime.

California was a major population center for Mexican migrants. Lured by the employment opportunities presented by the railroads and the big farms, Mexicans became by World War I "the most important single ethnic group in the agriculture of the Imperial Valley of California," having replaced American southerners, Chinese, Japanese, and others. By 1930, there were 368,000 Mexicans in California, 6.5 percent of the state's population. Forty-five percent of these Mexicans (167,000) resided in Los Angeles County.[18]

Economist Paul S. Taylor, writing in the Wickersham report, presented data on incarceration in the California state prisons at San Quentin and Folsom. In

1929, there were 6,970 prisoners in these institutions, for an imprisonment rate of 122.8 per 100,000. The tally of Mexican prisoners in that year totaled 758, for a rate of 206 per 100,000, or 168 percent of the general population's rate. The principal offenses of the Mexican prisoners were narcotics and deadly weapons violations plus assaults with those weapons.

Taylor also presented data on arrests in the city of Los Angeles, which show, for crimes against persons, rates of 159.5 per 100,000 for native-born Americans, and 215.2 for those born in Mexico. For rates by race the differential is even greater. For the so-called red race, the "great majority" of which, according to Taylor, was Mexican, the rate for crimes against the person was 312 per 100,000; for all races combined it was 145.9.[19]

We have some valuable confirmatory data for Los Angeles derived from the Los Angeles County homicide database maintained by the late Eric Monkkonen. Taking a three-year average of homicides for 1929 to 1931, and calculating rates by using the census population figures for 1930, I obtained an average of 117 homicides per year for a rate of 5.28 per 100,000. The database disaggregated Mexican victims and victims with Spanish surnames. Combining both columns (as the overwhelming majority of Spanish-surnamed residents undoubtedly were Mexicans) the result was an average 22 homicides per year with a rate of 13.37. In short, the homicide victim rate for Mexicans in Los Angeles was two and one-half times the rate for the general population of the county.

There is more evidence still for Los Angeles. Emory Bogardus, a sociologist at the University of Southern California in the 1930s, produced a slim volume sympathetic to the Mexican immigrant. Bogardus conceded, however, that Mexicans "rank abnormally high in crimes of personal violence against each other. They have," he explained, "brought their customs with them relative to settling their own disputes." Bogardus presented Mexican arrest data for Los Angeles County for the fiscal year ending June 1933. Table 9.4, drawn from Bogardus, lists Mexican arrests for crimes of violence (plus burglary), along with the percent of total arrests that these figures represent and my computation of the arrest rates per 100,000. All calculations were based on the 1930 Census, which indicates that Mexicans were 7.6 percent of the total county population. Note that the proportion of Mexican arrests for each crime far exceeds the proportion of Mexicans in the county population.[20]

Table 9.4. Arrests of Mexicans, selected offenses, Los Angeles County, fiscal year 1933

| Offense | No. of Arrests of Mexicans | Mexican % of Arrests | Arrest Rate of Mexicans |
|---|---|---|---|
| Assault/battery | 168 | 28.2 | 100.6 |
| Murder | 17 | 18.0 | 10.2 |
| Rape/sex offenses | 101 | 15.6 | 60.5 |
| Burglary | 157 | 12.0 | 93.9 |

Source: Bogardus, *Mexican in United States*, 53, 54.

The final Wickersham report of relevance, by Paul Warnshuis, examined Mexican crime in Illinois. The Chicago data were especially revealing. Warnshuis presented figures on arrests of males processed in Chicago's municipal courts over a two-year period, 1928 and 1929. I averaged the data for these years and once again utilized 1930 Census figures for the population at risk. For charges involving crimes against persons the average annual total for all male Chicagoans was 7,459, for a rate of 436 per 100,000. For the same category of offenses charged against Mexican-born males, the average was 104.5 per year, which yields a rate of 1,044 per 100,000. That is 2.4 times the rate for all accused males.[21]

In short, in both California and Illinois, two areas of high concentration of Mexican immigrants, the data point to high violent crime. Our final piece of evidence—national mortality data—does not paint as negative a picture, but doesn't disconfirm the state and local analyses either.

It was not until 1931 that the Census Bureau was satisfied that it had a reasonably accurate count of deaths of Mexicans in the United States. Of those deaths 124 were attributable to homicide. With a 1930 Census population of 1,422,533 Mexicans nationwide, the homicide victimization rate for 1931 was 8.72 for every 100,000 people.[22] Significantly, this is *lower* than the homicide rate for the entire U.S. population, which was 9.3; and lower still than Douglas Lee Eckberg's estimate of 9.7. On the other hand, the Mexican homicide rate exceeded the rate for whites, which was 5.8 in 1931, but was well below the "colored" rate of 36.3.[23]

I conclude that Mexicans did indeed have high violent crime rates, but that given the concentration of the population in the Southwest and Illinois, plus the strong likelihood that the principal victims were other Mexicans, the impact on the vast majority of Americans was minimal.

It is also noteworthy that the Mexicans who arrived in the first half of the twentieth century were different from most other immigrants to the United States. A significant proportion of Mexican immigrants never identified with this country, never sought citizenship in great numbers, and did not remain here once the job market shrank, as it did with a vengeance during the Great Depression of the 1930s. (This sojourner mentality was common among early Italian immigrants as well, but not among succeeding Italian arrivals.) It is estimated that from one-third to one-half of the Mexican population returned to the homeland during the depression, some forcibly repatriated. This reverse immigration also tempered the Mexican crime situation. Concern with Mexican crime would remain muted from the 1930s until the post-1960s era.[24]

# V

# GANGS

# 10

## Prohibition and the 1920s

If the daily press were a safe index to the moral and spiritual life of our nation we might well feel alarm for the future. The forces of law and order seem to be powerless in face of the ever mounting crime rate, and the sensational murders, the sensational court trials, and the organized lawlessness appear to be indicative of a contempt for law and order which, instead of decreasing with growing material progress, seems to be on the increase.
—THORSTEN SELLIN

All I do is to supply a public demand. I do it in the best and least harmful way I can.
—AL CAPONE

America in the 1920s was assuming many of the characteristics that would come to be associated with the United States clear into the next century. The country was young, dynamic, impatient, and aggressive. It offered, as the admiring English historian Paul Johnson declared, "much to shock, enthrall and fascinate." His list included mass motoring, "screaming advertising," endless movies, records sold by millions, twenty-four-hour radio, comic strips in newspapers, the latest in photojournalism, and, thanks in large measure to its vibrant black subculture, a new genre of "pop" music called jazz.[1]

Electricity and the automobile, the two great inventions that came into their own in the 1920s, helped knit a common American culture by breaking down the vast distances that separated the far-flung populace. But they also facilitated crime, the former enabling conspirators, from bookies to bootleggers, instantly to communicate telephonically with one another as well as their clientele. Likewise, the automobile made possible the quick strike and getaway, a blessing for big-city mobsters as well as for small town bank robbers. Police departments quickly adopted the new technologies too: telephones to summon assistance, radios to dispatch personnel, and automobiles to patrol and respond to calls.

Perhaps no event of the 1920s, however, would have a greater impact on crime than the seemingly quixotic crusade against alcohol. Conventional wisdom sees Prohibition as an embarrassingly silly episode in overcriminalization, a lesson that law must never be permitted to so outrun public opinion that enforcement becomes hopeless and the law itself ridiculous. There is something to this view, but it is not entirely accurate.[2]

First of all, as will be discussed, Prohibition had widespread public support, at least in its early years, and even a bit after that outside of the great metropolises. Moreover, a close examination of Prohibition will show that it had some positive benefits, such as shutting down big-city saloons, the hubs of vice, corruption, and much of the criminal violence of the late nineteenth and early twentieth centuries. For another, the noble experiment seems to have dramatically reduced alcohol consumption in this country, a reduction that, reinforced by state and local post-prohibition regulations, lasted for some forty years. Given the well-established link between alcohol and violence we cannot rule out the possibility that Prohibition actually reduced crime. For all that, it seems undeniable that the bootlegger wars—a direct by-product of Prohibition—contributed to the murder toll in some of America's biggest municipalities. As we will see, however, that contribution was not as great as is commonly believed.

## HISTORICAL BACKGROUND

While the federal government was seeking to closely regulate the drinking habits of Americans in the 1920s, it was permissive when it came to business and industry. The great moral crusade was accompanied by a laissez faire, devil-take-the-hindmost attitude toward the economy. "The business of America," Calvin Coolidge aphorized, "is business." For most of the decade, and most of the population, this hands-off approach seemed to work. Growth was the watchword of the era: "Cities were bigger, buildings taller, roads longer, fortunes greater, automobiles faster, colleges larger, night clubs gayer, crimes more numerous, corporations more powerful, speculation more frenzied than ever before in history, and the soaring statistics gave to most Americans a sense of satisfaction if not of security."[3]

The statistics indeed were impressive. From 1920 to 1929, the nation's gross domestic product rose 42 percent. The unemployment rate averaged just 5.5 percent. Disposable personal income went from $71.5 billion to $83.3 billion, a jump of 16.5 percent. There were, to be sure, some economic trouble spots. After 1920, farming went into a twenty-year slump. Midwestern farm bankruptcies quadrupled in 1922 and doubled again the next year. In the overwhelmingly rural South tenant farming (56 percent white) was rapidly replacing family-owned agriculture. By 1930, 42 percent of all American farms were tenant-run. To make matters worse, a boll weevil infestation tore through southern cotton fields, driving many farmers off the land. This would prove an important "push" factor in the first great African American migration to northern cities.[4]

The big cities, though thriving, weren't entirely placid either, especially in the aftermath of World War I. The year 1919 saw an "unprecedented wave" of labor unrest, including a general strike in Seattle, nationwide work stoppages by steelworkers and coal miners, even a police strike in Boston. Between a spate of unsolved bombings and frightening reports of revolution in Russia, some even feared a Bolshevik uprising in the United States. The Red Scare led to the arrest and deportation of nearly one thousand alien radicals, the ousting of a Socialist member of the U.S. House of Representatives from Milwaukee, and the ejection of five elected Socialists from the New York State Assembly. Anxieties over Reds eased only when uprisings announced for May Day 1920 fizzled.[5]

Racial tensions also flared in 1919. As wartime jobs opened in northern cities blacks migrated there in large numbers. As soon as the United States demobilized, however, which was very rapidly, these opportunities began to shrink. Returning veterans, largely working-class whites, now found that they had to compete with blacks for jobs and housing, both of which had grown scarce. Race riots broke out in Chicago, where thirty-eight people died, in Washington, DC, and in a score of smaller cities.[6]

But the worst racial turmoil of the 1920s took place in a southern city, Tulsa, Oklahoma, in 1921. Here the provocation was an inflammatory newspaper account of a black man's sexual assault on a young white woman—the classic southern white alarm bell. Following press reports of preparation for a lynching, whites and blacks mobilized, armed themselves, and violence quickly escalated. Whites, who far outnumbered blacks, began burning black businesses and ultimately launched an attack on the African American community. Nearly the entire black residential and business areas of Tulsa were laid waste. Death estimates, for both blacks and whites, range from 75 to 100.[7]

## WORLD WAR I

The First World War (1914–18) had a substantial impact on the decade that followed. It inured Americans to a greater role for the federal government in their lives, including national efforts to regulate alcoholic beverages. It galvanized the American economy, although the rapid postwar demobilization caused a short-run tailspin. Removing millions of young men from civilian life also seems to have reduced crime, but that too proved temporary.

The functional equivalent of Pearl Harbor or the World Trade Center attack of 2001 was the sinking of the *Lusitania* by the Germans in 1915, killing over 1,100 people, including 128 Americans. The nation, though stunned by the assault, was at first unenthusiastic about going to war. Woodrow Wilson won reelection in 1916 with a "he kept us out of the war" slogan. But when the Germans stepped up the naval attacks, sinking eight American vessals in early 1917, war became inevitable, and Congress declared it in April of that year.

The federal government moved quickly to take command of industry, labor, and agriculture, nationalizing the rail and telegraph lines, shipbuilding and shipping. Control of the Atlantic being vital, a major shipbuilding program, employing thousands, was launched. Twenty-five million men, roughly half the male population, were swiftly registered for the draft, the wartime army reaching an eventual strength of almost 4 million. In spring 1918, the Germans went on an offensive in Europe, and England and France grew desperate for America's help. Convoys took wave after wave of doughboys "over there," as the popular ditty referred to Europe, until 1.75 million had disembarked. The American commitment helped turn the tide and the German offensive collapsed. Fearing invasion of the homeland and wracked by internal turmoil, Germany sued for peace. On November 11, 1918, an armistice ended the conflict.[8]

Though not much remembered nowadays, alcohol prohibition actually began during the war. In an effort to conserve food, Congress in 1917 passed the Lever Act, which prohibited the manufacture of distilled spirits (hard liquor) from any produce that was used for food. To keep the troops from overindulging, the government adopted measures to bar alcohol sales to servicemen.[9] After the

Armistice these wartime restrictions were extended to the immediate postwar demobilization period and expanded to all alcoholic beverages, not just liquor, domestic sales of which were prohibited.[10] Of course, the more permanent effort to regulate alcohol was just around the corner. In 1917, Congress approved the Eighteenth Amendment to the Constitution, the first section of which said: "After one year from the ratification of this article the manufacture, sale, or transportation of intoxicating liquors within, the importation thereof into, or the exportation thereof from the United States and all territory subject to the jurisdiction thereof for beverage purposes is hereby prohibited." The Amendment was swiftly ratified, the thirty-sixth state (out of forty-eight total) approving in January 1919. By the following autumn Congress adopted enabling legislation, the National Prohibition Act, known as the Volstead Act after Rep. Andrew Volstead of Minnesota. The law became effective on January 17, 1920.[11]

Interestingly, then, alcohol consumption in the United States started declining *before* the "real" Prohibition began. Here are some figures for spirits, wine, and beer consumed along with absolute alcohol intake, all in gallons per capita. As can be seen, total alcohol consumed during the war years fell by 23 percent from the five immediately preceding years and consumption of beer, the working man's beverage, declined 28 percent.[12]

TABLE 10.1. Alcohol consumption in the United States, 1911–1919

| | Spirits | | Wine | | Beer | | Total |
| | Bev. | Abs. Alc. | Bev. | Abs. Alc. | Bev. | Abs. Alc. | Abs. Alc. |
|---|---|---|---|---|---|---|---|
| 1911–1915 | 2.09 | 0.94 | 0.79 | 0.14 | 29.53 | 1.48 | 2.56 |
| 1916–1919 | 1.68 | 0.76 | 0.69 | 0.12 | 21.63 | 1.08 | 1.96 |

*Source:* Lender and Martin, *Drinking in America*, 205.

*Note:* "Bev." = alcoholic beverages, consumption in gallons per capita. "Abs. Alc." = amount of alcohol consumed in gallons per capita.

Wartime regulation not only reduced alcohol consumption; it prepared the nation for the more permanent prohibition laws of the 1920s—and it was widely believed that they would be permanent. What was the impact all of this—the war and pre-Prohibition prohibition—on violent crime? Having taken all those young males off Main Street one might expect conscription also to have served as crime control. Reductions in alcohol consumption should have intensified the impact. There was, in fact, a diminution in crime, but the effect, like the mobilization itself, didn't last long.[13] Here are some figures pertaining to the mini crime drop:

- In Chicago, the murder rate, which had been hovering around 10 per 100,000 in 1916 and 1917, fell to 8.6 in 1918, but jumped the next year to 11.3. Felony arrests in Chicago dropped markedly in the same years, from 546 per 100,000 in 1917, to 460 in 1918.[14]
- New York City homicide rates went from 4.4 in 1915 and 1916 to 3.9 in 1917 and 4.2 the next year. Hardly a crime crash but nonetheless a dip. By 1920 homicide rates rose to 5.5. Arrest rates in New York declined significantly in 1918, as table 10.2 shows. Note the 28 percent drop in violent crime arrest rates from 1917 to 1918.[15]

TABLE 10.2. Arrest rates per 100,000 males, age 16 and over, New York City, 1916–1920

|      | Offenses against | | Robbery | Burglary | Larceny |
|------|---------|----------|---------|----------|---------|
|      | Persons | Property | | | |
| 1916 | 698.5 | 817.2 | 61.3 | 124.9 | 161.2 |
| 1917 | 643.4 | 893.1 | 63.4 | 147.5 | 206.7 |
| 1918 | 465.2 | 739.2 | 56.2 | 110.3 | 177.8 |
| 1919 | 447.4 | 820.5 | 83.5 | 150.6 | 200.2 |
| 1920 | 427.0 | 757.8 | 74.5 | 143.6 | 180.6 |

Source: Willbach, "Trend of Crime New York," 69.

- Criminologists Edwin H. Sutherland and C. E. Gehlke reported notable downturns in burglary and homicide arrests in selected cities during the war. The homicide data are especially noteworthy since in five cities (Baltimore, Buffalo, Chicago, Cleveland, and St. Louis) homicide arrests had climbed dramatically from 1911 until 1917, declining sharply in 1918, only to resume their upward ascent after the war.[16]

- National mortality datasets, though inconsistent with one another, all show a decline in homicides in 1918.[17] If we use sociologist Douglas Lee Eckberg's recalculation of the official rates we find the following:

  | | |
  |------|-----|
  | 1917 | 9.1 |
  | 1918 | 7.9 |
  | 1919 | 8.2 |

- The official rates, drawn from vital statistics data compiled by the National Center for Health Statistics, likewise show a homicide falloff in 1918:

  | | |
  |------|-----|
  | 1917 | 6.9 |
  | 1918 | 6.5 |
  | 1919 | 7.2 |

- A survey of forty prisons and reformatories revealed an 18 percent decline in penal populations from 1915 to 1918.[18]

  | | |
  |------|--------|
  | 1915 | 35,203 |
  | 1916 | 33,891 |
  | 1917 | 32,127 |
  | 1918 | 28,991 |

Another complicating factor was the massive influenza pandemic of 1918–19, which coincided with the last year of the war. Although figures are not certain, an often-cited estimate of American deaths from influenza and pneumonia is 675,000 over the ten month period from September 1918 to June 1919.[19] One peculiarity of this pandemic was its impact on the young population, especially the most crime-prone ages. Forty-two percent of all the influenza and pneumonia deaths occurred between the ages of twenty and thirty-nine. This fact probably reflected the enormous outbreak among the U.S. armed forces both here and in Europe. Historian of the pandemic Alfred W. Crosby wrote that it "struck the two armed services earlier and more severely than the civilian population: and, to a considerable extent, the armed forces were the foci from which the civilian population received the disease."[20] Although infants under five were also hard hit (21 percent of total mortalities), the senior population escaped relatively unscathed: ages seventy to seventy-nine were only 4.2 percent of all pandemic fatalities. In addition, males died in greater numbers than females; men comprised, for example, 61 percent of the victims in their thirties.[21]

Given the pandemic's assault on the young, especially males, one might well have expected a decline in crimes of violence. But I don't think this occurred. To test the hypothesis I compared homicides in 1916 and 1918 for the five states that suffered the most pandemic fatalities (ranked from high to low): Pennsylvania, Maryland, New Jersey, Connecticut, and Colorado. (I chose 1916 because of proximity in time to 1918, the pandemic year, without the confounding factor of war conscription, which began in 1917.) Surprisingly, each of these five states had more homicides in 1918 than they had experienced in 1916. Together, their homicide total increased by 9 percent.[22] Official mortality figures for the whole country show a 3.2 percent increase from 1916 to 1918, but Douglas Lee Eckberg's widely accepted estimates indicate an 11.2 percent drop.[23]

For comparison, I examined homicides for the same years, 1916 and 1918, in the five states that were least impacted by the pandemic (ranked from low to high): Michigan, Minnesota, Wisconsin, Indiana, and Washington. Two of these states had fewer homicides in 1918, one had a mere 0.1 percent increase, and two saw significantly higher homicide totals in the pandemic year. Collectively, homicides in these states declined by 3 percent in 1918.

In short, the states experiencing the most pandemic mortalities saw a big rise in homicides while the states that had the fewest infection deaths had a mixed homicide record, with overall declines. Based on these unexpected outcomes I infer that the worst pandemic in U.S. history, despite its toll among young males, did not generate significant falloffs in homicide.

What are we to make of all this? Evidently, World War I, and more precisely, the induction of young men, reduced violent crime. The reduction was relatively small and the postwar upturn similarly modest. The so-called Spanish Flu, which cruelly impacted young people, might have been expected to further curtail crime but apparently did not. The impact of wartime prohibition on violent crime is unclear. It may have helped curb it, but since 1917 and 1918 also were draft years it is difficult to disentangle the effects of alcohol reduction from the impact of conscription. Moreover, when the alcohol restrictions were extended in 1919, the year in which most of the soldiers had returned to civilian life, the crime record was mixed. Most accounts (as shown above) indicate an uptick, suggesting that alcohol regulation alone had little effect.

## THE TWENTIES

The end of the war was followed by a period of disillusionment. "People felt it was about time to relax," wrote historian/eyewitness Frederick Lewis Allen, "to look after themselves, rather than after other people and the world in general; and to have a good time." There would be seven "fat years," as Allen called them, from 1923 to 1929, sandwiched between two economic contractions, the second of which would prove the worst economic disaster in the nation's history. The earlier slowdown, 1920–21, was due to the simultaneous rapid demobilization of the army and the canceling of government contracts, causing unemployment to reach nearly 9 percent in 1921.[24]

Ironically, just as Americans were ready to let their hair down and let go of their puritan inhibitions, the anti-alcohol crusade reached its zenith. There is less of a contradiction here than is often thought. It is true that Prohibition in part was about moralizing and combating sin, reining in dissolute immigrants and the corrupt big-city politicians associated with them. It was a triumph, albeit temporary, in a culture war: "the victory of Protestant over Catholic, rural over urban, tradition over modernity, the middle class over both the lower and upper strata."[25]

But to see Prohibition solely as a moral crusade or as some sort of war against the working class is to miss the crime connection as well as the broader issue of social engineering. The reality is that temperance was a goal, not just of prudes and zealots, but of Progressives. Seen nowadays as a conservative scheme, "prohibition was actually written into the Constitution as a progressive reform." It is the Progressives who believed that the ills of humanity could be dramatically reduced through law and reform of institutions. How telling that muckraker Upton Sinclair and activist Jane Addams joined in the condemnation of alcohol.[26]

Crime was one of Prohibition's biggest targets. An academic writing in 1918 dramatically stated the contemporary understanding of the connection between alcohol and crime. Purple prose aside, the linkage retains acceptability with present-day criminologists.

In its use and traffic alcohol appears as a powerful antisocial force. Especially is it a social menace with respect to crime. The results of the most cautious research show that it is a producer of criminals and of crime on an enormous scale. What else could one expect? Has not the scientific laboratory proved that the habitual use of alcohol, in whatever quantity, disintegrates the moral character? It impairs the judgment, clouds the reason, and enfeebles the will; while at the same time it arouses the appetites, inflames the passions, releases the primitive beast from the artificial restraint of social discipline. All the conditions are favorable to the generation of crime.[27]

At the heart of the alcohol-crime nexus was the big-city saloon, a major source of urban violence and corruption from the late nineteenth century on. Not only did young men gather there, overindulge, and kill one another—recall that one-fifth of late nineteenth-century Chicago homicides were saloon killings—but corrupt politicians, relying on equally corrupt police middlemen, received regular payoffs from the management, as they did from operators of illegal gambling and prostitution establishments. Reformers were endlessly frustrated in seeking to close down these "dens of iniquity." Why not attack the root cause, the alcohol that fueled the operation? Not only would the saloon die out, reducing its attendant corruption and crime, but public health would be improved, public sidewalks and roadways would become safer, American workers would be more efficient, American families better cared for. It is no coincidence that the most influential organization in the campaign for the Eighteenth Amendment was the Anti-Saloon League of America. Prohibition, in short, was the culmination of a three-decade battle waged by reformers against the saloon and its associated crime and corruption.[28]

Paradoxically, Prohibition succeeded in killing the saloon while nevertheless triggering a whole new violent crime spree.

## ENFORCING PROHIBITION

On January 17, 1920, the Volstead Act went into effect. It did not ban drinking per se. It did prohibit the manufacture, sale, transport, import, furnishing, or possession of any intoxicating liquor, defined as any beverage containing 0.5 percent or more of alcohol by volume. Exempt were, among other things, wine for "sacramental purposes," as well as "medicinal preparations."[29]

Contrary to common belief, there was widespread support for the Volstead Act, at least at the outset. Keep in mind that it was passed in the afterglow of successful wartime prohibition, and the Eighteenth Amendment, the foundation for the act, already had received the approval of forty-five states at the time Volstead was adopted. Moreover, every state but one passed "little Volstead Acts," as they shared concurrent responsibility for enforcement. In addition to those who were motivated by religious beliefs, the law had the support of business (hoping for a more sober workforce), the middle class (as a crime control and clean government measure), and women's groups (who sought more responsible husbands and fathers)—a formidable set of backers.[30]

Initially the Volstead Act was effective, and from the world war to the early 1920s alcohol consumption fell sharply. As already noted, total consumption shrank 23 percent during the war years and some think the decline, and a rather steep decline at that, continued in 1921 and 1922. Congress seriously underfunded enforcement, however, and outside of the South and West, state enforcement apparatuses were even more starved for funds.

Support for Volstead began to ebb after 1922, and from 1925 on there was "widespread violation of the law." The disobedience, however, should not be exaggerated. As a general rule, compliance varied with the level of urbanization. The bigger the city, the more the law was flouted. Places like New York City, Chicago, and New Orleans were known for their defiance, about which stories are legion. In New York, for example, Governor Al Smith served liquor at public receptions, Big Apple mayor Jimmy Walker "trampled on" the state prohibition statute, and 52nd Street between Fifth and Sixth Avenues was said to be "an almost unbroken row of speakeasies." But then as now New York was not America, and there were thousands of small towns and rural areas that remained dry as dust throughout the decade.[31]

Teetotaling was not simply a matter of policing as the price of alcohol surged during Prohibition. Historian David Kyvig pointed out that by 1928 beer prices had gone up 600 percent compared with 1916 while the cost of gin rose 520 percent. This alone would have curtailed consumption, though as Kyvig added, one could always make one's own, which many poor urban dwellers did. Indeed, "alky cooking" for bootleggers became an income supplement in the ethnic slums.[32]

Impoverished parts of the South also joined the bootlegging bandwagon. Moonshining had long gone on in Appalachia as far back as the federal excise law of 1791, but Prohibition gave new encouragement to the practice. At first there simply were more individual moonshiners, but improved methods of producing high-quality booze in large amounts made the lone producer obsolete. The illicit still, operated in remote areas (and not just in the South), became the principal source of whiskey for the nation. The federal government and the states seized these plants by the thousands but new ones were quickly established.[33]

Nonetheless, Prohibition apparently drove consumption down and perhaps even more significantly it drove down consumption of *beer*, the favorite beverage of the lower classes. Before the world war, alcohol intake through beer had accounted for 58 percent of total consumption. During the Volstead years it is estimated that only 15 percent of the alcohol consumed was in the form of beer, 75 percent as hard liquor. This suggests that those most likely to drink and engage in violent crime were indulging less. Were they actually less violent? For that matter, since alcohol consumption remained low (relative to the late nineteenth and early twentieth centuries) for several decades *after* Prohibition, can it be said that the Great Crusade had a positive impact on violent crime for a good part of the twentieth century? I'll return to these issues near the end of the chapter.[34]

Congress, fully expecting general compliance and effective local enforcement (the Eighteenth Amendment authorized concurrent federal and local enforcement), initially created a force of only 1,500 federal agents housed in the Treasury Department and paid them less than $3,000 a year. The force size was totally inadequate and soon was doubled. Many of the agents, appointed by politicians as they were not part of the civil service system, proved corrupt; understandable perhaps given the low pay and the money that could be made through bribe taking. From 1920 to 1931, 1,600 agents were fired, 257 prosecuted.

The very act of enforcing Prohibition caused some deaths, although these would be considered justifiable homicides, not crimes. According to a study by the Association Against the Prohibition Amendment, over 1,000 people died during federal enforcement efforts from 1920 to 1929, including 184 citizens and 79 officers. The rest of the victims presumably were suspected law violators. State and local enforcement led to 700 additional deaths. But these fatalities paled by comparison with the "enforcement" practices of the mobs themselves.[35]

Enforcement frustrations led to an organized vigilante movement with links to the resurgent Ku Klux Klan. But raids on homes and gun violence, even deaths, roused strong opposition that curbed private enforcement after 1925.[36]

Prohibition resulted in an expanded federal criminal justice role, a forerunner of the drug enforcement efforts that began in the late 1960s. "Even with its vast corruption, inefficacy, and insufficient funding," wrote Lisa McGirr, "Prohibition marked the birth of a qualitatively new and enduring role of the federal state in crime control."[37] In 1920, 15 percent of all terminated federal prosecutions were Prohibition cases. By 1928, they were an extraordinary two-thirds of all federal criminal cases. The number of federal prison inmates also grew considerably in the 1920s, in great part due to Volstead. In 1920, federal prisons held five thousand inmates. By the end of the decade the total had jumped to twelve thousand, over one-third of which were liquor violations. Overcrowding became a major problem in federal prisons as well as in many of the states. The growing federal activity in law enforcement also produced several important U.S. Supreme Court decisions involving the Fourth Amendment, rulings that gave agents considerable latitude.[38]

## THE ETHNIC CONNECTION

There was an unmistakable link between bootlegging, other organized crime activities, and the European ethnic groups that had recently arrived in the United States. The main reason for this of course was the opportunity for big and quick financial rewards that organized crime provided. The alternatives for ambitious but impatient young males in the big-city ethnic enclaves were limited. Entertainment and sports, such as boxing, were lucrative, but required special talents. (Moreover, in the 1920s, entertainment, sports, and politics were intimately tied to organized crime, so that anyone active in the former was likely to end up mingling with gangsters.) Professions meant years of schooling and required high levels of intelligence. Successful businesses needed startup capital and contacts, couldn't be built overnight, and faced high failure rates. Mom-and-pop stores demanded continuous work for steady but small returns. Toiling in the factories and menial service or clerical jobs in the private sector or the city bureaucracies provided neither big money nor glamour. Organized crime on the other hand promised both. The biggest gangsters wore flashy clothes, drove fine cars, had pretty girls on their arms. They often supported community charities and were generous to the needy. They were local folk heroes, an image enhanced by the movies (which, by the way, had grown immensely popular in the 1920s). That most ended up prematurely dead or in prison did not seem to dull their luster.[39]

Prohibition meant new opportunities, especially in the big metropolises, where the ethnic immigrants were influential and demand for alcohol remained strong. "Prohibition was a lucky break for all gangsters," historian Thomas Reppetto observed, but "the Italians were better able to profit from it."[40] A 1931 study of fifty-eight "top and middle-management syndicate leaders operating in ten cities" found that three-quarters were born in Italy, though most had come over as children and were raised in America.[41] One reason for Italian involvement is that Italian Americans already were running, and quite effectively too, gambling, prostitution, and other illegal operations. During the decade before Prohibition for instance, Italians "reaped great profits from vice operations in Philadelphia, Boston, Milwaukee, Denver, San Francisco, and elsewhere."[42] It often simply was a matter of retrofitting the already existing criminal syndicates to the realities of the new market.

Not only were the Italian-American gangsters well organized, they were culturally at ease with the kinds of violence needed to maintain operations. The Illinois Crime Survey, which closely examined Chicago murder cases over a two-year period, made note of the racial and ethnic background of the murder victims. Overwhelmingly, in the case of gang killings, the victims were of Italian ancestry: 39 of 74 (53 percent) in 1926; 35 of 56 (63 percent) in 1927. This of course reflects the high Italian involvement in organized crime. It should be emphasized that virtually all of this violence was directed at competing syndicates; rarely, except by accident, were ordinary citizens (customers after all) harmed by the mobsters.[43]

Italians weren't the only ethnics to profit from organized crime. Mark Haller reported that a study of Chicago organized crime leaders found that 31 percent were of Italian background, 29 percent were Irish, 20 percent Jewish, and 12 percent black. Not one was native white of native white parents. It is also noteworthy that the more law-abiding and less violent ethnics, like the Germans and Scandinavians, scarcely played any role in organized crime.

There was something of a division of labor among the various immigrant groups active in organized crime, a reflection of cultural proclivities, but also of local situations. The need for "muscle," for instance, provided a role for young Italians with a penchant for violence. "There was, in all probability," observed Haller, "a relationship between the cultural factors that sanctioned violence and private revenge in Europe and the factors that sanctioned the violence with which Italian bootleggers worked their way into a central position in Chicago's organized crime." Another reason bootlegging was attractive to Chicago's Italians is that it provided them "with an opportunity to break into a major field of organized crime that was not already monopolized by the Irish." By the time of Prohibition Chicago's Irish already had established themselves in labor racketeering and gambling.[44]

Jews, in keeping with their cultural inclinations and occupational specialties, were the most likely to provide "professional or expert services" to the syndicates. In Chicago they were a majority of the bail bondsmen, over half the fences who disposed of stolen goods (through Jewish junk dealers and retailers), and were heavily overrepresented among defense attorneys in the criminal courts. By the 1920s, however, Jews too saw opportunities as gangsters. In the late 1920s and early 1930s, Boston's mob was headed by Charles "King" Solomon and after Solomon's murder, Hyman Abrams. In Detroit the Jewish-operated Purple Gang ran liquor-laden boats from Canada (the "Jewish Navy") until it was pushed aside by Italians. In New York City the "number one man in bootlegging—and in almost every other illegal enterprise—was the remarkable Arnold Rothstein," who from his table at Lindy's restaurant "presided over bookmaking operations, Wall Street bucket shops, and international drug rings." Illegal gambling seems to have had a special appeal for Jewish criminals.[45]

Poles also were drawn to organized crime. Philadelphia mobster Mickey Duffy was really Michael Cusick; Chicago gangster Hymie Weiss was born Wajciechowski; and George "Bugs" Moran, famous for losing seven associates in the Saint Valentine's Day Massacre, was Polish, not Irish. Hamtramck, the Polish section of greater Detroit, had a reputation for bootlegging; apparently liquor flowed freely there.[46]

Blacks had their own organized crime specialization in illegal vice operations. More than one-third of Chicago's pimps in the early 1920s were African American. The proximity of the vice district to the South Side black residential community facilitated black employment of various kinds, from prostitutes to maids to entertainers. The numbers racket also supported many African Americans, even through the Great Depression.[47]

## WAS CRIME INCREASING?

We already have seen that Prohibition increased federal criminal prosecutions and imprisonment for violation of federal alcohol restrictions. I now ask whether violent crime escalated in the 1920s, and if so, whether Prohibition was a causal factor.

The general public at the time apparently thought that crime and disrespect for law were on an inexorable upward trajectory. A former Chicago judge, recalling the dry law era, thought that U.S. cities were swept by "a typhoon of crime," undoubtedly "the greatest crime spree in the nation's history." The sheer brazenness of some of the gang murders and the intense media coverage no doubt contributed to these perceptions. To the extent that press coverage is a reflection, not just a determinant, of public concerns, crime seems to have been something of a preoccupation in the 1920s. A 1926 study of twelve daily newspapers in New York City (!), found 4,712 items on crime published in a single month, enough to fill six three-hundred-page books. Even so, press coverage of crime was not comprehensive. H. C. Brearley tallied 650 homicides in his native South Carolina between 1925 and 1928, an estimate he thought conservative. But he found that South Carolina's biggest newspaper, *The State*, covered only 321 of the cases, less than half. Brearley concluded that "newspapers spend much space upon a few sensational crimes" while covering "only a small proportion of the total number of slayings." It is, of course, doubtful that media treatment of crime is much different today.[48]

As for the alleged crime wave, experts of the day were more cautious than the media or the public. But, as discussed earlier, they were stymied by incomplete and questionable data. Analysts understood that mortality statistics on homicide provide one of the most reliable indicators of crime, avoiding the vagaries of erratic police and court activity. However, the failure of the United States to collect mortality figures for the entire country throughout the first three decades of the century made reliance on these statistics problematic. The "registration area," that is, the states and cities reporting their homicides to the federal government, began in the Northeast and only gradually expanded to the southern and southwestern states. (See table with note 17 on p. 335.)

Nationwide homicide data show a significant increase over this time period, but since the South and Southwest had higher homicide rates than the rest of the country, the increase probably was an artifact of the gradual addition of those high-homicide states and cities. Moreover, as the Census Bureau conceded, there was a second problem with the data aside from missing states: mortality statistics prior to 1905 were untrustworthy.

Frederick L. Hoffman, one of the earliest proponents of mortality statistics as an indicator of crime, deftly managed the problem of the expanding registration area. He examined rates for twenty-eight cities that had been reporting homicides from the turn of the century up into the 1920s. These rates, unaffected by additions to the registration area, had doubled between 1900 and 1924, from 5.1 per 100,000 to 10.3. Hoffman concluded that murder was "unquestionably on the increase," and what's more, the criminal justice system, judging by the gap between the number of homicides and the number of murder convictions, was badly serving the American public. Note, however, that Hoffman relied on data from 1900 on, even though figures for the earliest years were less than reliable.[49]

Edwin H. Sutherland, generally considered the father of American criminology, also wrote during the twenties, and he was doubtful that murder was on the rise. He pointed out that homicide is not identical with murder (since a killing, should it result in arrest and prosecution, may be excusable or justifiable) and produced homicide data showing inconsistent results. For 61 cities in the death registration area from 1912 to 1922, Sutherland found that 29 had lower rates at the end of the study period; 29 had higher; and 3 had the same rates. Likewise, for 23 states during the same years, he found 11 with higher rates, 11 with lower, one unchanged. He inferred that homicide rates were little changed from the beginning to the end of the decade. Of course, this analysis, which ends with 1922, tells us little about the rest of the 1920s.[50]

H. C. Brearley, who in the early 1930s wrote a comprehensive tract on homicide in the United States, offered a compromise. He concluded that homicide may have increased over the first decades of the century, but the increase probably was "much smaller" than the data indicate. Present-day analysis has borne out Brearley's surmise. Douglas Lee Eckberg, utilizing multiple regression techniques, developed estimated nationwide rates for 1900 to 1932 that proved to be significantly higher than the official figures while following a similar pattern of oscillations. If we use Eckberg's reworking of the mortality figures, the differences between the beginning of the twentieth century and the 1920s are narrowed considerably. According to Eckberg's data, the average homicide rate for 1900–1909 was 7.6 per 100,000, whereas the average for 1920 to 1929 was 8.95. This represents a clear rise, but it is not (as Hoffman thought) a doubling. Nevertheless, homicide rates had climbed 17.8 percent between the turn of the century and the 1920s—a substantial increase.[51]

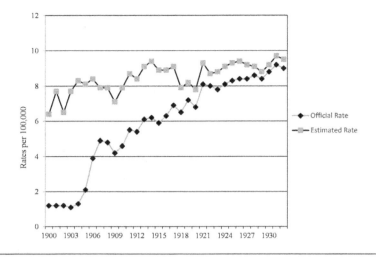

FIGURE 10.1. Homicide mortality rates per 100,000 for the United States, official and estimated, 1900–1929. *Sources:* Federal Security Agency, *Vital Statistics Rates,* mortality tables, table 12 (official); Eckberg, "Estimates," table 4 (estimated).

## GANG WARS

The violent conflict between bootlegger gangs ferociously competing for "market share" was the classic Hobbesian war of all against all. Given the absence of any mutually-agreed-to rules of conduct and the lack of a superior force to mediate disputes, the mob wars seem to us almost inevitable. That they took everyone by surprise is due to the complete failure to foresee the scope of noncompliance with the alcohol laws.

The audaciousness of the violence and the inability of the authorities to cope with it gave big-city residents the sense that the country was sliding toward anarchy. But whether the bootlegger wars really raised homicide rates and whether they posed an actual threat to the general public are questions requiring more thorough consideration.

The mob violence was, of course, an urban phenomenon. Most of America learned about it through newspapers, the radio, or with even less accuracy, the movies. The number of killings varied with the city and in turn depended on whether one gang bested its rivals, made peace and divided up the market, or continued to wage war. In Chicago, for instance, the legendary bootlegger rivalry hit its peak between 1923 and 1926, during which time an estimated 215 gang members were murdered by competitors, 160 more by police. Thereafter, Chicago calmed a bit, though the death toll was said to be 765 by the time the Eighteenth Amendment was repealed in 1933. New York City was purported to be the scene of over 1,000 gangland hits throughout the Prohibition years, largely because Arnold Rothstein and his associate Waxey Gordon (Irving Wexler) were unable to establish complete control over the biggest market of all. Rothstein himself was assassinated in 1928 by a gambler collecting on a debt.[52]

Al Capone, the most famous of the gangsters, was in many ways typical of the "successful" mob leaders. Born in Brooklyn, a second-generation Italian American, Capone came to control through violence and organizational skill Chicago's leading bootlegging operation. But, as Mafia historian Thomas Reppetto pointed out, his power lasted just three years, "during which he was almost constantly at war with rivals or the law." Capone had been brought to Chicago by John Torrio, who had quietly and relatively nonviolently served as the city's leading organized crime figure until 1925, when he retired to Italy. "In his absence," said Reppetto, "Capone ran things and shooting became the order of the day."

Killing had been made easier in the 1920s by a World War I invention, the Thompson submachine gun, which could fire off a thousand .45-caliber rounds per minute. Developed for the Army by General John Thompson, the "tommy gun" was introduced into Chicago's Beer Wars in 1925. Not to be outgunned by the mobsters, the Chicago police formed an antigangster squad equipped with tommy guns and instructions to shoot to kill.[53]

It was unusual for the general public to be assaulted by mobsters except as bystander casualties. The Illinois Crime Survey, a meticulous investigation of homicide in Chicago and environs over a two-year period, found only two bystanders killed, neither by gangsters. Most of the public probably viewed mob killings with a mix of amazement and anxiety. "The murder and maiming of rival gang members in the scramble to create monopolies and gain larger profits," observed Humbert Nelli, "seemed, to many Americans, to be a modern version of the old Wild West shootout; such events stirred remarkably little anger or dismay." On the other hand, organized crime sometimes contributed to the violence and fear of violence that pervaded many of the metropolitan ethnic neighborhoods.[54]

As for Capone, his flamboyance and brutality proved his undoing. He loved media attention, moving about Chicago in an armored limousine with a phalanx of bodyguards. As he became bolder the federal government stepped up its efforts to get him. In the Illinois primary and elections of 1928, Capone had a ward leader shot, bombed the homes of candidates he opposed, and beat and threatened campaign workers. Naturally, this triggered national news coverage. Several months later, on February 14, 1929, in apparent retaliation for attacks on members of his gang by the rival Bugs Moran organization, alleged Capone hit men disguised as Chicago police machine-gunned seven of Moran's associates in a Chicago garage. Capone himself had an alibi as he was wintering in Florida, but most people thought that he was the instigator, a view only recently challenged. Meanwhile, "the Valentine's Day Massacre set off a public outcry that posed a problem for all mob bosses."[55]

By the end of the decade, Reppetto observed, "the reputation of the whole country, not just Chicago, was at stake; Capone and his gunmen had become worldwide symbols of American lawlessness." President Hoover personally ordered federal agents to put Capone out of business. While Justice Department agents (who were not brought in to enforce Prohibition until 1930) raided illegal breweries and speakeasies, they found it nearly impossible to successfully prosecute the real operators, who were shielded by front men. Treasury agents, meanwhile, had much greater success, as they were able to build tax evasion cases against wealthy mobsters like Capone, reputed to be taking in $50 million dollars a year.[56]

Capone's violent career came crashing down in 1931 when he was convicted of federal tax evasion and sentenced to eleven years in prison. Transferred to Alcatraz in 1934, he was released five years later, at age forty, with dementia due to syphilis. His mind and body deteriorating, Capone was unable to resume his mob activities. He died in 1947, only forty-eight years old, and was quietly buried in Chicago. Capone had done himself in with his penchant for in-your-face aggression. He remains nonetheless a symbol of the era: brash, violent, hedonistic and lawless.[57]

When Prohibition ended in 1933, though the nation was well into the Great Depression, the gangsters were awash in money. They quickly moved into or expanded other illicit activities: gambling was the most profitable, but loan-sharking, prostitution and narcotics also proved lucrative. Legitimate businesses were infiltrated as labor and business racketeering provided another revenue stream. While syndicate rivalries spawned occasional "rubouts," however, open warfare in the streets of American cities would not be seen again until the black gang fights over cocaine in the 1980s.[58]

## HOMICIDE RATES: CHICAGO

The average nationwide homicide rate for 1920 through 1929 was 8.95 per 100,000. To give a sense of the significance of this figure, consider that the average rate for the 1980s, a particularly violent recent decade, was 9.2. To properly compare them, of course, one must take into account the *type* of homicides prevalent in each era, not simply the number of incidents. (Also, the incidence of robbery and other crimes of violence against strangers are a crucial difference between the early and late decades of the twentieth century.)

How much of the violence of the 1920s was attributable to the bootlegger wars? If there had been no gang wars would homicide rates have been as high as they were? One can only hazard some educated guesses because we do not know exactly how many gang victims there were. In New York City, as mentioned earlier, it is estimated that mob killings took around a thousand lives over the entire fourteen-year Prohibition era (1920–33). Eric Monkkonen's homicide tally for that period comes to 5,468, which means that mob hits accounted for, roughly speaking, 18 percent of all the killings during the Prohibition years. This is, to say the least, a significant proportion (though far lower than the drug-related killings in the late 1980s). As for rates, assuming an even distribution of homicides over the period (unlikely as that is), we would have had 71 gang slayings per year. Looking at 1930, where we have the accuracy of the census to determine the population, New York had 6,930,446 people and 478 homicides, for a rate of 6.9 per 100,000. With 71 fewer homicides, the rate would have fallen to 5.9, a decline of 14.5 percent.[59]

For Chicago we have the benefit of the 1929 Illinois Crime Survey, championed by a reform-oriented collaboration of law enforcement and civic elites. Academics at the University of Chicago Department of Sociology, including the well-regarded John Landesco and Ernest W. Burgess, were heavily involved in the design and implementation of the studies. The most valuable work, for our purposes, was the homicide survey conducted by Arthur V. Lashly. Poring over the records of the county coroner, the police, the state's attorney (prosecutor), and the courts, the survey examined and classified each and every homicide in Cook County for 1926 and 1927.

The survey counted 739 homicides in 1926 and 699 the next year, but adjusting these figures to exclude automobile deaths and abortions brings the totals to 584 and 546, respectively. Using 1930 estimates of the population for Cook County (3,982,123), I determined that the adjusted homicide rates were 14.7 per 100,000 in 1926, and 13.7 the next year. Even going back a half century, Chicago (which contained 85 percent of the population of Cook County) had never seen such high rates. According to Chicago crime scholar Jeffrey Adler, the average adjusted homicide rate from 1875 to 1919 was 6.2 per 100,000 and double digit rates were unheard of before 1916.[60]

The Crime Survey, examining coroner's verdicts, determined that in each of the two years studied there had been 380 murders (as distinguished from manslaughters and other legal designations). These murders were then classified according to motive, "gang killings" being one of the categories. Gang killings were defined as killings in which the evidence "clearly pointed to the murder as having been committed by some member of a band of organized criminals and in accordance with gang methods of disposing of their enemies." In 1926, 74 murders were considered gang killings, which comes to 12.7 percent of the adjusted homicide total (584). The next year produced 56 gang killings, 10.3 percent of the 546 homicides. If none of these gang killings had taken place, Cook County's homicide rates would have fallen from 14.7 to 12.8 per 100,000 (1926) and from 13.7 to 12.3 (1927). In other words, the rates would not have declined dramatically and they still would have been at historical highs. These figures vindicate the surmise of some of the experts of the day that the gang murders, largely because they were so sensational, were making a greater impression than was warranted by their numbers.[61]

A major reason for the distress over gang killings is that they were committed with impunity. Not one of the mob hits during the two years covered by the Crime Survey was successfully prosecuted. This failure of the system was attributed to the "gang code of silence even to the grave," the "swift capital punishment inflicted by gangland itself upon informers," plus public indifference to the gangster victim's death or the likely retaliatory murder of his killer.

The biggest murder category was altercation-and-brawl killings, which accounted for 90 of the 1926 murders, compared to 74 gang killings that year. In 1927 there were 111 altercation-and-brawl murders, nearly double the 56 gang cases. Lashly noted that "intoxication was the moving cause in practically every one of these cases," and that the incidence of altercation and brawl killings increased in 1927 because it was easier to obtain alcohol in that year. He added, without giving figures, that this type of homicide was "largely confined to Negroes"; whereas only two of the gang victims were "colored."[62]

TABLE 10.3. Classification of murders in Chicago, 1926 and 1927

| Type of Murder | 1926 | 1927 |
|---|---|---|
| Holdups | 37 (9.7%) | 34 (8.9%) |
| Altercations/brawls | 90 (23.7%) | 111 (29.2%) |
| Domestic | 32 (8.4%) | 23 (6.1%) |
| Jealousy | 31 (8.2%) | 23 (6.1%) |
| Revenge | 14 (3.7%) | 23 (6.1%) |
| Abortion | 16 (4.2%) | 12 (3.2%) |
| Infanticide | 29 (7.6%) | 18 (4.7%) |
| Automobile | 22 (5.8%) | 27 (7.1%) |
| Law enforcer killed | 11 (2.9%) | 9 (2.4%) |
| Unknown motive | 13 (3.4%) | 30 (7.9%) |
| Miscellaneous | 11 (2.9%) | 14 (3.7%) |
| Gang killings | 74 (19.5%) | 56 (14.7%) |
| Total | 380 | 380 |

*Source:* Lashly, "Homicide (in Cook County)," 610.

Automobile homicides increased considerably in the 1920s when Henry Ford brought cars to the mass market, charging only $310 for a new Ford. For 1926 and 1927, there were, on average, a staggering 938 automobile homicides per year in Cook County, and that only includes deaths that were brought to coroner's juries. The automobile death rate per 100,000 was 23.6, two-thirds higher than the county homicide rate shorn of automobile and abortion deaths. Forty-nine of the cases were hit-and-runs by unknown drivers and coroner's juries, apparently outraged, issued murder verdicts; but no murder prosecution ever was successful in an automobile case. In fact, although 250 of the cases before coroner's juries resulted in manslaughter verdicts only a tiny fraction ultimately were convicted.

Despite assumed reductions in drinking and the much lower speeds of automobiles the roads were a lot more dangerous in the 1920s than today. In 2005–9, Cook County had an average of 325 traffic fatalities per year, for a rate of 6.2 per 100,000. The 1920s rate was nearly four times as high, probably because drivers back then had less experience with motorized vehicles.[63]

## HOMICIDE RATES: DETROIT

I turn now to Detroit, where criminologist James Boudouris provided considerable detail on homicides in the late 1920s. Although Boudouris's study captures only the second half of the Prohibition era, it affords some interesting insights into gang war killings.

Located just across the river from Windsor, Ontario, Detroit was the ideal port for smuggling in Canadian liquor. Smuggling operations were led by Jewish gangsters dubbed the "Purple Gang," a pugnacious group "constantly at war with other gangs and each other." After compiling, as Reppetto put it, "an impressive body count," the Purples were by decade's end "virtually eliminated by rivals and the law." As of the early 1930s, the gang came under new management, Italians having pushed aside the Jewish hoodlums.[64]

Boudouris created a typology of Detroit homicides and determined the annual number of killings in each category. The crucial category for our purposes was called "criminal transactions," which Boudouris defined as a homicide that is a "product of the violation of the law." Gang killings were included in this category (although one might question the fit). From 1926 to 1929, the categories with the most homicides, in descending order, were noncriminal or justifiable, friends and acquaintances, domestic relations, and criminal transactions, the latter comprising 12.9 percent of all homicides in this time period.[65]

Most striking for the 1920s, as compared with subsequent years, is the high number of homicides both in absolute numbers and in rates. "In terms of total numbers of homicides," Boudouris wrote, "the 1920s were the most violent and retained this eminence until 1967 and 1968." From 1926 to 1929, Detroit averaged 251 homicides per annum; for all of the 1930s, the average was 118. The magnitude of the rates in the 1920s can best be comprehended by comparing Detroit to other jurisdictions. As is evident from table 10.4, Detroit's rates are comparable to Chicago's and far exceed both New York and nationwide figures. Were gang killings responsible for the outsized homicide count?[66]

TABLE 10.4. Homicide rates per 100,000, selected jurisdictions, 1926–1929

|  | U.S. | NYC | Chicago | Detroit |
|---|---|---|---|---|
| 1926 | 9.4 | 5.14 | 17.5 | 24.3 |
| 1927 | 9.2 | 5.2 | 16.2 | 16.6 |
| 1928 | 9.1 | 5.79 | 20.3 | 14.4 |
| 1929 | 8.8 | 6.03 | 17.3 | 15.8 |

*Sources:* Detroit rates calculated by author from Boudouris, "Classification," 531, 532–33. Population from linear interpolation of census data in U.S. Census Bureau, *Historical Census Statistics* (Working Paper No. 76). Chicago rates from "Homicide in Chicago," http://homicide.northwestern.edu/download/. New York City rates from Monkkonen, "Homicides in New York City." United States rates from Eckberg, "Estimates," 13.

Boudouris examined and classified all of the killings designated "criminal transaction" homicides, which included gang killings. He tallied 130 such homicides in 1926–29, and most significantly found that 40 of them (31 percent) were attributable to gang wars, extortion, "riot snipers," or related incidents. In other words, nearly one-third of the criminal transaction homicides were gang killings or something similar. Needless to say, this is a very high proportion. Also interesting is the decline of this type of homicide over the years. In 1930 to 1934, they were 31 of 106 criminal transaction homicides, 29.3 percent. After Prohibition, which ended in 1933, these killings drastically diminished. In 1935 to 1939, gang-war homicides dropped to 5 of 49 (10 percent) and never again exceeded 5 per year until the late 1960s. The obvious inference is that Prohibition caused a spike in gang killings. However, as a percentage of *all* homicides, not just criminal transactions, gang killings were a mere 4 percent (40/1005). For the second half of the Prohibition era at least, gang murders did not drastically raise the death toll in Detroit.

## ALCOHOL AND HOMICIDE

During the 1920s the nationwide homicide rate averaged 8.95 per 100,000, exceeding 9 in six of the ten years. These were historically high rates. Indeed, until the 1970s they were the highest decadal rates in the twentieth century. Why this happened is not entirely clear. Certainly the bootlegger killings contributed, but as we saw, they explain only a small proportion of the total.

Turning to other possible causes one finds little of explanatory value in economic factors. The economy of the 1920s was sound overall, and 1923 to 1929 (at least until October 1929) were golden years. As noted earlier, GDP and disposable income rose sharply in the 1920s, and the unemployment rate averaged just 5.5 percent. As economist Paul Ryscavage put it, "The prosperity of the 1920s was real. Private gross domestic product (in real terms) rose by 45 percent, from $68.7 billion in 1919 (in 1929 dollars) to $99.3 billion by 1929. The increase dwarfed the 30 percent real growth experienced in the 1909–1919 period. . . . Real private GNP per person rose strongly throughout most of the decade and the real incomes of families and the real wages of workers rose."[67] If anything, there was an inverse relationship between economic well-being and violent crime.

The high rate of violent crime also seems inconsistent with the considerable decline in alcohol consumption. Given the association of drinking with violence, one would expect, even after accounting for gang murders, that crime would have fallen in the Prohibition years. Though it is impossible to know with certainty the quantity of alcohol consumed during Prohibition since alcohol production and distribution were illegal, we are confident that immediately after repeal, and for three decades thereafter, consumption remained at historic lows. As for beer in particular—the poor man's brew, and therefore the drink of those most at risk for violence—consumption did not again reach turn-of-the-century levels until the 1970s.[68]

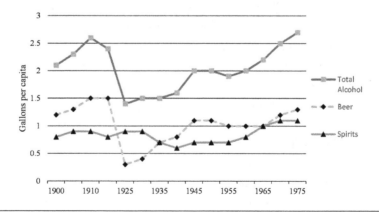

FIGURE 10.2. Alcohol consumption in the United States, 1900–1975. *Source:* Levine and Reinarman, "Prohibition to Regulation," 468. Data based on absolute alcohol consumed per capita, age 15+.

What's more, Prohibition was successful in destroying the saloon, the male gathering place that, from the nineteenth century on, had been the source—indeed, the epicenter—of urban criminal violence. After Prohibition, American drinking habits changed, becoming more of a private, domestic activity. This was made possible by three simultaneous developments. First was improved home refrigeration and bottled (later canned) beer. Second, the states established stringent regulation of alcohol sales, including, for example, no Sunday sales, no dancing or gambling on premises that sold alcoholic beverages, no drinks without the purchase of food, etc. A third factor was the expansion due to the automobile of suburban residential communities in which hitherto communal pleasures were privatized. Historian Jack S. Blocker explained.

> By the end of the 20th century, two thirds of the alcohol consumed by Americans was drunk in the home or at private parties. In other words, the model of drinking within a framework of domestic sociability, which had been shaped by women, had largely superseded the style of public drinking men had created in their saloons and clubs. Prohibition helped to bring about this major change in American drinking patterns by killing the saloon, but it also had an indirect influence in the same direction, by way of the state. . . . Some states retained their prohibition laws—the last repeal occurring only in 1966—but most created pervasive systems of liquor control that affected drinking in every aspect. With the invention of the aluminum beer can and the spread of home refrigeration after the 1930s, the way was cleared for the home to become the prime drinking site.[69]

Did this change in drinking habits affect violent crime? One might have expected it to. We have compelling evidence that arrests for public drunkenness and related offenses sank to a historical low in 1920, and despite occasional upticks, the decline continued right through the 1970s. In fact, whereas drunk and disorderly arrests accounted for more than half of all urban arrests before 1920, they were but one-fourth of apprehensions in the 1970s.[70]

For violent crime, however, there is no comparable evidence. During Prohibition, the apparent drop in alcohol ingestion was not accompanied by a commensurate drop in violent crime, which held steady at rates not seen since the nineteenth century. A recent quantitative study of Chicago confirmed that whereas total homicides and killings unrelated to alcohol consumption rose during Prohibition, alcohol-related homicides were unchanged.[71]

After the 1920s, however, the argument that reduced alcohol consumption tamped down violent crime gains plausibility. Both crime and alcohol ingestion were relatively low in the three decades following Prohibition, and when violent crime rose again in the 1970s, so did alcohol consumption. But it also is plausible to think that other factors in the seventies—such as an expanded youth population that repudiated conventional values—drove up both alcohol consumption and crime rates.

Proof that Prohibition alone raised nationwide murder rates is wanting (notwithstanding the effect of bootlegger gangs on Chicago and a few other big cities). The most elaborate quantitative study to date found no evidence for the proposition, attributing the increased rates in the 1920s to urbanization and the "changing demographic composition of the population," presumably, increasing numbers of African Americans and immigrants in U.S. cities.[72]

This explanation has potency for the big cities of the North and rightly calls attention to crime by blacks. African Americans had, during this period, homicide rates that far exceeded white rates, often by a factor of seven or more. But the preceding conclusions overlook the fact that much of the violent crime of the era, including that of African Americans, took place below the Mason-Dixon line. The southern states, during the 1920s, had higher homicide rates by a considerable margin than the northeastern states, higher indeed than all other regions of the United States.[73] What's more, the entry into the United States of impoverished Mexicans also occurred in the 1920s, and as shown in the last chapter, this too contributed to the escalation in violent crime.

## CONCLUSION

In summation, I suggest that four factors led to the crime surge of the 1920s. They are presented here without regard to their relative significance:

1. First was immigration to the United States of groups that had been violent in their home countries and continued their violent ways here. I speak primarily of southern Italians and Sicilians, who arrived mainly before World War I, and Mexicans, who entered the country largely in the 1920s.

2. Second was Prohibition, a policy that unwittingly produced violent clashes between urban gangs competing with each other for control of the lucrative big-city markets for the proscribed but ever-popular beverages.

3. Third, we had exceptionally high regional crime in the South, especially among African Americans, but also among whites, both of whom shared a culture of violence insulated from the moderating forces (such as reliance on the justice system to resolve disputes) that predominated in the rest of the nation.

4. Fourth and finally, the Great Black Migration effectively transported high African American violence to the big cities of the North, creating slum communities that would produce outsized amounts of such crime for decades.

All four of these developments together brought the average nationwide homicide rate for 1920–29 to 8.95 per 100,000, with rates in excess of 9.0 in six of the ten years.[74] (Excluding 1920, which was something of an outlier, the average jumps to 9.1.) By comparison, the average rate for the 1980s, a very violent recent decade, was 9.2.

# VI

# CRIME AND THE ECONOMY

# 11

# The Great Depression

The whole country is with him. Just so he does something. If he burned down the Capitol, we would cheer and say, "Well, at least we got a fire started anyhow."
—WILL ROGERS ON FDR

The common argument that crime is caused by poverty is a kind of slander on the poor.
—H. L. MENCKEN

## INTRODUCTION

It was an economic maelstrom akin to one of those tsunamis that overwhelms everything in its path. It was totally unexpected and utterly calamitous. But it lasted a lot longer than any tidal wave: literally an entire decade less a few years of recovery in the middle. Those who survived it never would forget. They would live with a permanent sense of foreboding, a gnawing feeling that prosperity was a fragile thing that could evaporate in a flash.

Oddly, given conventional understandings, the great collapse did not trigger a huge upsurge in violent crime. Violence had been elevated throughout the previous decade and the Great Depression seems to have exacerbated the problem, but only modestly. Moreover, once the recovery began, after 1933, crime steadily declined, and it continued to do so even when the economy relapsed in 1937–38. One must, therefore, question the relationship between economic downturns and violence. The position taken here—developed at the end of this chapter—is that the Great Depression, unique in its severity, increased violent crime and the postdepression recovery helped reduce it, but that attempts to discern a general causal link between the economy and violent crime have been and continue to be unpersuasive. What's more, as will be shown, other factors not directly related to economics contributed greatly to the downturn.

First, I will analyze the Great Depression itself, to see how it came about and the terrible damage it caused. Then, as was the pattern of previous chapters, the crime situation will be examined in detail.

## THE GREAT DEPRESSION

The Great Depression was unexpected because the 1920s were so very prosperous. Fueled by advertising and mass consumer goods—new Fords sold for less than $300—the American economy of the twenties soared. In the last half of the decade the average annual unemployment rate was 3.1 percent of the workforce, bottoming at a remarkable 1.8 percent in 1926. Wall Street was positively giddy. Shares bought and sold went from $250 million in 1921 to $1.1 billion in 1929. The Dow Jones average leapt from $63.90 (1921) to $381.17 (1929). Low interest rates (around 3 to 5 percent) encouraged borrowing, including—and this proved disastrous—a credit system to buy stocks. Buying "on margin" it was called. The investor would borrow from the broker most of the cost of the stock purchase; the brokers in turn borrowed from the banks. As long as stocks continued to climb everyone made money. In autumn 1929 they stopped climbing.

Even before the Panic of '29 many had been left behind. As was discussed in previous chapters, well in advance of the depression, the South, black and white, was buffeted by a series of disasters that were driving people off the farms. In the North, those with limited skills and little education—new African American migrants and recent foreign immigrants especially—had difficulty making ends meet. Roughly 40 percent of the American population was impoverished *before* the depression, and the Brookings Institution estimated that 60 percent of Americans earned below the $2,000 needed for basic necessities. In many respects though, when the thunderclap struck, the left-behinds suffered less than the middle class. Their expectations were low; the middle class, on the other hand, really believed there would be, as Herbert Hoover's 1928 campaign promised, a chicken for every pot and a car in every garage.[1]

Although October 29, 1929, Black Tuesday, is often cited as the day that Wall Street crashed, there had been, in fact, a series of down days followed by comebacks throughout that fall. It was all a matter of confidence. Once that confidence evaporated, once the investors began to really believe that the bull market was over, that truly ended it. Shareholders then sold in mass, hoping to unload stocks before their value tumbled. Brokers made margin calls, seeking payment for the loans they had made to investors. As share values fell, investors simply let the brokers keep the stocks that had secured the loans. Brokers, saddled with deflating investments, were unable to repay the banks. And so the panic on Wall Street spiraled out to the banking system, and then to the home mortgage system, and outward to the economy generally. One could almost hear the confidence hissing out of the economy like air in a punctured balloon. As prospective buyers of goods and services, in anticipation of difficult times ahead, began to defer their purchases, merchants stopped hiring. With business sluggish layoffs soon followed. Those laid off cut back on *their* purchases and soon found it hard to pay bills. Their creditors couldn't collect and soon they too were in trouble. And on it went, casting the entire nation into a mood of black despair.[2]

Perhaps the fatal coffin nail was the failure of the banking system. Roughly a year after the Wall Street collapse, 1,352 banks failed; the next year, 1931, 2,294 more went under. In all, between 1930 and 1933, roughly 30 percent of all U.S. banks shut down. Depositors panicked, sometimes managing to recover part of their savings, sometimes losing everything. (Federal deposit insurance, a New Deal innovation, didn't yet exist.) State governments declared bank holidays to prevent runs on the banks and give them time to raise capital. "The banking system," said historian David Kyvig, "was completely immobilized." Not only did individuals lose their savings, but institutional depositors as well—churches, charities, businesses, and local governments—either lost or could not access their money. As a result, they were unable to pay wages, make purchases, extend charity, or meet debts. In 1933, 1,300 local governments—cities, towns, counties, and school districts—plus three states, defaulted on obligatory payments.

Once the banks failed, credit dried up and the home mortgage went with it. Worse still, layoffs and reduced wages prevented homeowners from making payments on existing mortgages. At the start of 1933, over 40 percent of home mortgages were in default. Some who had lost their homes built makeshift shacks on vacant land; "Hoovervilles" people called them in mordant tribute to the president. Mortgaged farmland also went into default and banks foreclosed on thousands of farms. The banks took the land, but without buyers, were unable to sell it.

Perhaps the truest measure of public misery—and the one most closely associated with crime—was the unemployment rate. It was, in a word, staggering.

"By 1932," Kyvig wrote, "an estimated 28 percent of the nation's households, containing 34 million people, did not have a single employed wage earner." Young workers and seniors were hit hardest, perhaps reflecting hiring preferences given to men with families. Black females also were thrown out of work in record numbers; most had been employed in domestic service, a luxury middle-class people no longer could afford. Even when jobs were available, hours and wages were sharply reduced. Steel foundries, for example, went to a four-day, then a three-day workweek. National income in 1933 fell to only 54 percent of 1929 levels.

As the depression broadened and deepened, private and community philanthropic organizations were quickly overwhelmed. Soup kitchens drew impossibly long lines. People began rummaging for food in big-city garbage dumps. New York City officials reported 29 deaths due to malnutrition in 1933, 110 in 1934. In Appalachia, some families subsisted on dandelions and wild blackberries; others ate every other day. Apple growers, in an effort to sell produce while aiding the needy, sold crates of fruit to the jobless, who then resold apples on the streets at 5 cents each. The streetcorner apple seller, along with the soup kitchen queue and the pop song "Brother, Can You Spare A Dime," became the grim symbols of the era.[3]

Herbert Hoover's administration, no doubt unfairly, took much of the blame for the catastrophe. The president's reputation was badly tarnished when he called the Army in to break up a Washington, DC, encampment of nearly twenty thousand World War I veterans pressing for an early retirement bonus. (The money, for patriotic service, was not due to be paid until 1945, but the vets, like everyone else, were desperate.) The routing of the "Bonus Army" by troops and tanks etched in the public mind an image of "heartless Hoover." This was especially ironic since Hoover's career had been made by his extraordinary work on food relief for Europeans during the First World War, an effort that kept millions from starving.

It also is not true to say that his administration did nothing about the depression. Most notably, in 1932, Hoover got Congress to approve the Reconstruction Finance Corporation, which made $2 billion in loans to banks and financial institutions in order to reinvigorate the economy. He also created the Emergency Relief Act, which made loans to states for work relief and was extended by his successor in 1933.[4]

Nonetheless, whatever Hoover did or did not do, the depression was getting worse, not better. The upcoming presidential election of 1932 offered a desperate country an opportunity for new leadership. Franklin Roosevelt's campaign struck just the right chord. He promised to "build from the bottom up and not from the top down," to "put their faith once more in the forgotten man at the bottom of the economic pyramid." In his nomination speech during the summer of 1932, he pledged "a new deal for the American people." Roosevelt won in a landslide, taking 42 of the 48 states. At his inaugural in March 1933, with one-quarter of the workforce unemployed, FDR rallied support for "our greatest primary task": putting people to work. In perhaps his most inspiring words, he told the American public that "the only thing we have to fear is fear itself—nameless, unreasoning, unjustified terror which paralyzes needed efforts to convert retreat into advance."[5]

## THE NEW DEAL

Roosevelt tackled the depression with tremendous gusto. The day after his inauguration on March 4, 1933, he issued a presidential proclamation declaring a bank holiday (although thirty-eight states already had closed banks temporarily). He then called Congress into special session, the famous 100-day Congress, which passed a succession of enactments to provide farm and unemployment relief and reform the banking system. (The New Deal agricultural legislation, discussed in chapter 3, will be passed over here.) One of those early measures, the Emergency Banking Act, created a mechanism to certify banks for soundness and allow them to reopen. Later that June, the FDIC (Federal Deposit Insurance Corporation) was created, restoring public confidence by insuring bank deposits. This was accompanied by the Homeowners Refinancing Act, which helped refinance 20 percent of the mortgages in the United States.[6]

But the part of Roosevelt's New Deal that most directly affected the public, especially that segment of the population that might be expected to turn to crime, was the work relief programs and the policies aimed at youth. The work programs, which employed millions, were at first met with great enthusiasm; later they came to be seen by many as make-work boondoggles. The debates over these policies provided a foretaste of postwar disputes about the role, size, and effectiveness of the federal government—debates that continue to this day.

The 1933 Congress first extended Hoover's program to lend money to the states for relief, recast under FDR as the Federal Emergency Relief Administration (FERA). States and cities were supposed to match each dollar of federal money with three dollars of local. FERA was said to have employed as many as 2.5 million people at various points during the depression.

Because the matching and planning mechanism of FERA was slow to get underway, Congress also passed the Civil Works Administration (CWA) to spend federal monies on work relief without a state or local match. The CWA employed workers on public projects such as street paving and the construction of roads, schools, and airports. Although the CWA lasted only a few months, it served as the model for the Works Progress Administration (WPA), established in 1935. The WPA's $5 billion budget was the biggest single appropriation in U.S. history to that time. At its maximum effectiveness, it put 3.3 million people to work on the construction of thousands of hospitals, schools, airports, streets, highways, sidewalks, utility plants, parks, and recreation facilities. The WPA even employed forty thousand artists and intellectuals on cultural projects. Perhaps one-third of all the unemployed in the United States received WPA checks, averaging $50 a month, some in payment for work, the rest in direct cash payments (the "dole").[7]

For African Americans, one of the groups hit hardest by the depression, these relief programs were a lifeline. In 1933, more than 2 million blacks received FERA relief (jobs or cash), which was, as a percentage of each race, nearly double the white rate (17.8 to 9.5 percent of whites). Within two years the number of blacks on relief jumped to 3.5 million. When added to the 200,000 blacks working on WPA projects in 1935, this brought the proportion of African Americans receiving New Deal benefits to almost 40 percent of the nation's black population.[8]

Perhaps the most popular New Deal program of all was the Civilian Conservation Corps (CCC), which was aimed at young men from poor families. Initially, membership was limited to males, ages eighteen to twenty-five, whose fathers were on relief, but Congress later expanded the age boundaries and dropped the relief requirement altogether. The young men in the CCC were sent to quasi-military camps run by the Army to do conservation work on public lands. They were paid $30 a month, $25 of which was sent to the enrollee's family. At its peak in 1935, over half a million males were serving in 2,600 camps in every state in the country.[9]

It is natural to ask whether the CCC was in some measure responsible for the crime decline of the 1930s. Although there is little to suggest that the Corps was aimed at crime control, the young male target group certainly was appropriate. There even were camps for blacks, segregated of course, and located in the South where the bulk of the African American population still lived. These might have taken a bite out of African American crime, which, as will be discussed, accounted for nearly half of the homicides in the United States. On the other hand, the program's impact on big-city youth and northern blacks apparently was minimal. And we have no data on crime within the camps, which, given the nature of the population and the availability of tools as weapons, might have been significant. So while it is reasonable to think that the CCC may have reduced violent crime during the depression, there is no solid proof of this.[10]

A second youth program, the National Youth Administration (NYA), established in 1935 as part of the WPA, funded part-time jobs for high school and college students. It also provided cash relief with on-the-job training for unemployed youth who were not in school. The NYA employed approximately one half million youth per year, males and females, between the ages of sixteen and twenty-four. Participants received their benefits while living at home (or on their college campuses); unlike the CCC there were no camps out in the countryside. It is estimated that the NYA served at most 37 percent of the jobless and out-of-school youth population.[11] As with the CCC, the impact of the NYA on crime remains a matter of conjecture.

The various New Deal work relief programs raise an interesting question about measuring unemployment during the depression. If, on the one hand, one is trying to determine how many people were unable to obtain (or had stopped seeking) jobs in the private sector or regular public sector positions, then it is sensible to discount those on work relief. If, on the other hand, crime is caused by impoverishment or by anger, frustration, and mental depression due to being out of work, then recipients of work relief should be considered employed. The difference, as figure 11.1 shows, could be substantial.[12]

For those who were working—and most Americans managed to hold onto their jobs—paychecks were getting thinner. The 1930s was an era of strong labor union activity as workers pressed for higher pay. The Roosevelt administration gave unions a big boost by backing the National Labor Relations Act of 1935 (also known as the Wagner Act, in honor of its primary sponsor, New York senator Robert Wagner). This law compelled employers to bargain with unions adopted by workers through elections overseen by an impartial government agency, the National Labor Relations Board (NLRB). It also barred the dismissal of workers for union activity. The Wagner Act gave unions a major base in the big manufacturing industries—automobile, steel, and rubber. Membership in the United Automobile Workers, for example, reached about 350,000 in 1937, ten times the membership of the previous year. Between the time the National Labor Relations Act was upheld by the Supreme Court and the end of 1940, the NLRB supervised

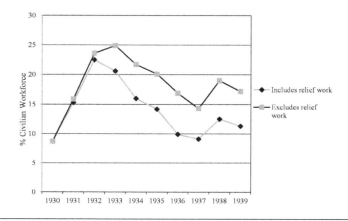

FIGURE 11.1. Estimated U.S. unemployment rates, 1930–39. *Source:* Smiley, "Recent Unemployment," 488.

over three thousand elections. But even if workers won the right to bargain collectively management didn't have to accept their terms. Strikes and picket lines became more frequent, and workers sometimes went a step further and called illegal sit-down strikes, sitting in the plant but refusing to work. When employers sent in security forces to break the picket lines or clear the plants violence ensued.

Over one-third of the U.S. workforce had become unionized by the 1930s, and the effect probably was to raise wages generally, although the biggest increases would come in the 1940s, during the war mobilization. President Roosevelt sought to give federal protection to all workers unionized or not by, in his words, "putting a floor" under wages. This was accomplished by the Fair Labor Standards Act (1938), which set minimum wages (initially 40 cents an hour) and maximum hours of work. Perhaps the most significant impact was the two-day weekend, which became the new standard for the American workforce.[13]

The New Deal, for all practical purposes, ended with the minimum wage law. Before 1937, recovery seemed assured as unemployment drifted downward and the latest congressional elections, along with the public opinion polls, indicated strong opposition to new spending measures. "The New Deal declined after 1937," wrote Richard Polenberg, "because most Americans did not want to extend it much further." But then, whether because government spending diminished, or because the government intervened excessively in the first place, the economy took a nosedive. "In the fall of 1937, the economy suddenly went into a tailspin.

The rate of decline over the next ten months was sharper even than in 1929: industrial production fell by 33 percent, industrial stock prices by 50 percent, and national income by 12 percent. Nearly four million people lost their jobs, boosting total unemployment to 11.5 million."[14]

This depression-within-the-depression is significant to our analysis of crime in the 1930s. As will be seen, from 1934 on violent crime trended down seemingly in tandem with the recovery. But as also will be seen, the downward trend continued even when, in 1937–38, the recovery stalled. If economic gains drove the crime fall, then why didn't the economic reversal send crime rates northward again? Before addressing the impact of the economy on crime I will examine in detail violent crime in the 1930s.

## CRIME IN THE DEPRESSION YEARS

Judging by the newspaper headlines, the country was in the grip of a crime wave from 1932 to 1934. The press coverage reflected (as media reporting usually does) the number of high-profile crimes which seemed to proliferate in those years. But the statistical measures for once bear out the media's message: in 1933 the nationwide homicide mortality rate hit a high for the century (which was of course only three decades old) of 9.7 per 100,000. In fact, the homicide rate exceeded 9.0 in every year from 1930 to 1934. Only in the Great Crime Surge of the 1970s would we again begin seeing rates that alarming.[15]

The big name criminals of the early 1930s have become fodder for generations of movie makers: "Pretty Boy" Floyd, "Baby Face" Nelson, "Ma" Barker, John Dillinger, Bonnie and Clyde Barrow. All (except perhaps for Ma Barker) were violent robbers and murderers during the late 1920s and early depression years. All (including Barker) were captured or killed by local law enforcement agents or by the then new Federal Bureau of Investigation, which was just making a name for itself. The year 1934 alone saw the deaths of Dillinger, Bonnie and Clyde, Pretty Boy Floyd, and Baby Face Nelson. Rivaling the bank robber murderers for public attention were the kidnappers. In 1932, following the sensational kidnapping and killing of Charles Lindbergh's infant son, there was a rash of copycat crimes, including twenty-seven major kidnapping cases in 1933 alone.[16]

The crime spike of the early 1930s coincided with the Great Depression, but the uptick only continued and exacerbated the persistently elevated violence of the 1920s. In numerical terms the worst years of the depression were associated with a 3 percent increase in homicides. The average rate for 1925–29 was 9.2 homicides per 100,000; for 1930–34, it was 9.5.[17] But to suggest that the depression *caused* the crime wave of the early 1930s is to raise an intriguing question about the relationship between violent crime and the general economy. How is it that both the prosperity of the 1920s and the collapse of the 1930s were associated with high crime rates?

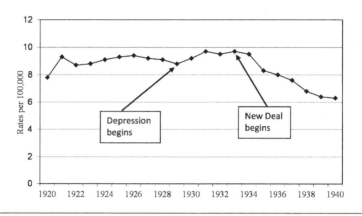

FIGURE 11.2. Homicide mortality rates per 100,000, 1920–40. *Sources:* Eckberg, "Estimates," table 4 (1920–32); Federal Security Agency, *Vital Statistics Rates,* mortality tables, table 12 (1933–40).

For over a century theorists have wrestled with the relationship between economic recessions and crime, but the results of their explorations have been mixed at best. Some have found a positive relationship between unemployment or recessions and criminality, some a negative relationship, and some no connection whatsoever. To further complicate the picture it also has been suggested that the effect on property crimes differs from the impact on crimes of violence.[18] This seems plausible in that joblessness might encourage one to steal what one cannot lawfully obtain, whereas murder, assault, and rape do not, at least at first blush, appear to be rationally related to employment. This last statement, however, may not apply to robbery which is a hybrid of theft and violence. Moreover, murder and assault often accompany robbery, and the former may increase as a consequence of an upsurge in the latter. Finally, since the rise in crime in the early years of the Great Depression was modest, while the decline in the later years was rather dramatic we must consider the possibility that economic recovery, especially from a severe downturn, may have more of an impact on violent crime (in a positive sense) than does a major depression. I will consider each of the preceding points momentarily.

First, however, I need to complete the discussion of the magnitude and trend of violent crime in the 1930s, for there are additional data on national, state, and city rates. They are, by and large, corroborative of one another, confirming that violent crime rose in the early years of the depression, fell off sharply as the recovery advanced, and continued to decline even when the recovery slowed.

Crime data took some significant leaps forward in the 1930s, so that from roughly 1933 on one can be very confident about its accuracy. First, the death registration area was complete by 1933, that is, all states (forty-eight at the time) henceforth provided to the federal government mortality data in accordance with national and international standards. These data, as I have noted several times, are the most reliable we have in that they are untainted by some of the problems plaguing police department records, such as the reliance on public cooperation in reporting crime. Nevertheless, since they are mortality data they are limited to homicidal offenses.

Second, the FBI's *Uniform Crime Reports (UCR)*, which rely on data collected from local police departments, became increasingly accurate from 1933 on as more departments throughout the United States cooperated. The *UCR*, unlike mortality data, provides invaluable information on a range of offenses, including the most significant violent crimes: murder and manslaughter, robbery, rape, and aggravated assault. A big caveat with the *UCR* is that the only crimes counted were those "known to the police," that is, reported by private citizens or observed by the police themselves. For homicide, this is not much of a limitation as police awareness of wrongful deaths is not as dependent on citizen reporting as it is for other violent crimes.[19]

I begin with homicide mortality data. As figure 11.2 shows, nationwide homicide rates, which had been hovering around 9 per 100,000 throughout the most of the 1920s, rose to 9.2 in 1930, the year after the Wall Street crash. Rates then spiked to a high of 9.7 in 1931, and oscillated between 9.7 and 9.5 for the next three years, some of the worst years of the crash.[20] As the recovery proceeded from 1934 to 1937, homicide likewise declined, dropping 20 percent during this time period. Then, even though the economy stalled in 1937–38, homicide rates continued to fall, bottoming at 6.4 per 100,000 as the decade passed into history.

The FBI's *Uniform Crime Reports* tell a similar tale, with the composite rate for four violent crimes—murder and nonnegligent manslaughter, robbery, rape, and aggravated assault—subsiding 31 percent between 1933 (the first year for reliable nationwide data) and 1936.[21]

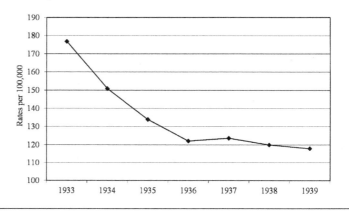

FIGURE 11.3. Violent crimes reported to the police, rates per 100,000, 1933–39. *Source:* Office of Management & Budget, *Social Indicators*, 64. Based on *UCR* and unpublished FBI data.

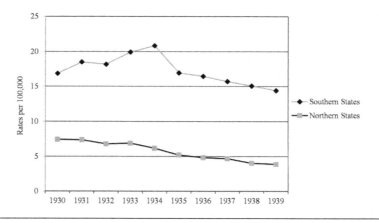

FIGURE 11.4. Homicide mortality rates per 100,000 in five northern industrial states and twelve southern states, 1930–39. *Sources:* Bureau of the Census, *Mortality Statistics* (annual reports, 1930–36); Bureau of the Census, *Vital Statistics, pt. 1* (annual reports, 1937–39).

State-level homicide rates declined in the second half of the decade. Figure 11.4 covers five northern industrial states, which were especially hard hit by the economic collapse, and twelve southern states. Note the downhill trajectory after 1933 in the North and one year later in the South, despite the massive economic slump.[22]

State and federal imprisonment rates also eased, but the decline was modest. From 1930 to 1934, the average rate was 55.9 per 100,000. For 1935–39, it was 51.3, an 8 percent reduction.[23]

## AFRICAN AMERICAN CRIME

The depression hit the black communities of the North early. As Drake and Cayton put it, African Americans were "a barometer" of the impending disaster. In 1930, when white unemployment in the North was around 8 percent, black unemployment already exceeded 10 percent, and in the East North Central states (Illinois, Indiana, Michigan, Ohio, and Wisconsin) it approached 15 percent. Layoffs of African Americans began in 1929, the year of the stock market panic. When factories cut production, unskilled black labor "was usually the first to go." When white homeowners balanced budgets, black servants were dismissed. Illegal gambling ("policy") soon became the black community's biggest employer. By mid-1930, "every bank in Black Metropolis was closed." It wasn't until 1933 that equivalent pain spread to the rest of America.[24]

It should be kept in mind that the overwhelming majority of African Americans—79 percent—were still down South, where the unemployment situation, while scarcely good, was at least less bad. The effect of the contraction in the North was to slow down the Great Migration, which in the 1930s was half of what it had been in the previous decade. Still, with the cotton market continuing to collapse and federal relief benefits (part of the New Deal) more attractive in the North, thousands more migrants left the South. (Federal relief payments being more generous in the North, blacks concluded that outside of Dixie emergency employment policies were less likely to be discriminatory.) Black Chicago, for example, grew by 19 percent, nearly 44,000 people, during the depression years (though in the 1920s, the growth rate had been 114 percent).[25]

Turning to the black crime situation in the 1930s, one finds that the racial gap remained as wide as it had been before the great decline. Consolidated police reports for the entire nation (the *Uniform Crime Reports*) became available in the 1930s, revealing enormous disparities between white and black arrests for crimes of violence.

TABLE 11.1. Four-year average arrest rates per 100,000 of males in U.S. for violent crimes, by race, 1935–1938

| Offense | White | Black | Black/White Ratio |
|---|---|---|---|
| Criminal homicide | 6.9 | 34.7 | 5.0 |
| Robbery | 16.6 | 58.1 | 3.5 |
| Assault | 27.5 | 166.9 | 6.1 |
| Rape | 7.4 | 18.9 | 2.6 |

Source: von Hentig, "Criminality of Negro," 666.

Nationwide prisoner counts (also collected by the federal government) produced comparable outcomes.

TABLE 11.2. Five-year average incarceration rates per 100,000 of males in U.S. for violent crimes, by race, 1932–1936

| Offense | White | Black | Black/White Ratio |
|---|---|---|---|
| Homicide | 3.6 | 25.3 | 7.0 |
| Robbery | 9.7 | 25.1 | 2.6 |
| Aggravated assault | 1.9 | 17.0 | 8.9 |
| Rape | 2.0 | 4.5 | 2.3 |

Source: von Hentig, "Criminality of Negro," 664.

And homicide mortality data, more reliable than the criminal justice figures, confirmed the disturbingly outsized black violence. In North Carolina, undoubtedly typical of the South in this respect, 71 percent of all homicides in the decade were black-on-black killings.[26] Nationwide, over the entire decade, black homicide mortality victims were 48 percent of the total, even though blacks were less than 10 percent of the general population.[27] The African American rates were nearly eight times higher than white: an average 38.7 per 100,000 for African

Americans to 4.9 for whites. But the trends were different for the races. White homicides rose more and fell further during the 1930s. If one compares the second half of the preceding decade, 1925 to 1929, with the first half of the 1930s, 1930 to 1934, white homicides rose an average 12.8 percent, while black killings barely edged up .08 percent. In the second half of the decade, 1935 to 1939, white rates dropped nearly 30 percent, black just under 8 percent. If the Great Depression was the principal causal factor in these homicide trends—and that is a very big "if"—one would conclude that the crash, and even more the recovery, had a much bigger impact on whites than on blacks. Notwithstanding differences in the magnitude of the respective responses, however, the *direction* of the responses was the same: both races suffered more homicides in the worst years of the disaster and fewer in the recovery years. The coefficient of correlation for black and white homicides in the 1930s was +.769 (significant at the .01 level).[28]

Table 11.3 shows the change in homicide rates per 100,000 for whites and blacks from 1925 to 1939, using five-year averages.

TABLE 11.3. Homicide mortality rates in U.S., by race, five-year averages and percentage change, 1925–1939

|  | Blacks | Whites |
|---|---|---|
| 1925–1929 | 39.98 | 5.14 |
| 1930–1934 | 40.3 (+.08%) | 5.8 (+12.8%) |
| 1935–1939 | 37.1 (−7.9%) | 4.1 (−29.3%) |

Source: Federal Security Agency, *Vital Statistics Rates,* table 16.

Note: Percentage change, in parentheses, is from immediately preceding quinquennium.

## CRIME AND THE ECONOMY

This brings us to the question of the economy and crimes against the person. As previously observed, the quantitative studies of the relationship between general economic conditions and crime are all over the lot. Some find a positive relationship, some a negative, some no relationship whatsoever. Few have zeroed in on the depression years, although this is surprising since data are available and the strength of the relationship is underscored by the magnitude of the crisis. Two sophisticated attempts to relate crime to the economy in the 1930s produced somewhat contradictory outcomes.

A study by Andrew Henry and James Short on both homicide and suicide and the relation of each to "the business cycle," which they measured by an index of manufacturing, found that "crimes of violence against persons rise in prosperity and fall during depression."[29] This conclusion runs counter to contemporary assumptions that economic downturns, not upswings, beget higher violent crime.

A second study on the economy and crime during the depression years, this by M. H. Brenner in the 1970s, demonstrated that homicide varied positively with employment and inversely with the nation's Gross National Product (GNP).[30] In other words, as economic output increases, homicide falls; and (contrary to expectations) as employment rises so does homicide. However, with nonhomicidal offenses, such as robbery and larceny, the rates are inversely related both to employment and GNP. Consequently, one would expect the nonhomicidal crimes to increase during depression years, but one also would expect contradictory economic impacts on murder.

The homicide results are surprising. Why should joblessness, especially the massive joblessness of the Great Depression, have *reduced* killing? Brenner's explanation is that the income loss of some portions of the population (due to unemployment, work-week and salary reductions, etc.) provides relative advantage to other sectors, namely those lower in the socioeconomic pecking order. As the homicide rate of this latter group declines it pulls down overall homicide rates.[31]

If one examines unemployment and homicide during the 1930s, without adjusting for other factors, the results contradict Brenner's findings. As a general proposition, when unemployment peaked during the start of the decade homicide also was high, and as unemployment diminished the killing declined. The coefficient of correlation between unemployment and homicide during the 1930s was +0.59.[32]

As for GNP and homicide, Brenner's findings are confirmed by the unadjusted correlation of homicide mortality data and GDP (Gross Domestic Product: a measure comparable to GNP). As figure 11.6 indicates, there was during the 1930s a remarkable degree of correspondence between the nation's economic output and homicide. Indeed, the coefficient of correlation was −.90. In plain words, as economic output declined homicide rose or remained high; as output increased homicides diminished.[33]

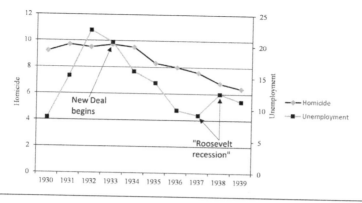

FIGURE 11.5. Homicide rates per 100,000 and unemployment rates during the Great Depression. *Sources:* Smiley, "Recent Unemployment," 488 (treating emergency government workers as employed); Eckberg, "Estimates," 13 (homicide 1930–32); Federal Security Agency, *Vital Statistics Rates*, mortality tables, table 12 (homicide 1933–39).

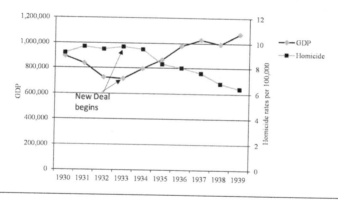

FIGURE 11.6. Homicide rates per 100,000 and GDP, 1930–39. *Sources:* MeasuringWorth, http://measuringworth.com/ (real GDP in 2005 dollars); Eckberg, "Estimates," 13 (homicide 1930–32); Federal Security Agency, *Vital Statistics Rates*, mortality tables, table 12 (homicide 1933–39).

There have been numerous critiques of Brenner's methods as well as of his hypotheses,[34] but it would be more fruitful at this point to present my own explanation for violent crime during the 1930s. To restate the basic facts, violent crime was elevated throughout the 1920s; it peaked in the worst years of the depression (the early 1930s) and declined thereafter. The correlation with unemployment and economic production was marked and significant. It would seem therefore that the economy impacted violent crime, and the ways in which it did will be explored directly below. But immediately following that discussion I will show that noneconomic factors, namely the end of Prohibition and the curtailment of immigration and domestic migration, also played significant roles.

It is reasonable to believe that an economic catastrophe of the magnitude of the Great Depression may well have increased violence. With massive unemployment lasting years, it would have been understandable that tempers were frayed and conflicts of an interpersonal nature, such as between acquaintances or spouses, would become more common. A study of marital relations in the 1930s found that "mounting economic pressures in the Great Depression damaged marital relationships through husbands who became worrisome, unstable, and explosive." The strains on families for many became nearly intolerable. In New York City, for example, arraignments for abandonment nearly tripled between 1928 and 1931. Female homicide victimizations, probably due to domestic murders, rose nationwide during the early years of the depression.[35] It also is credible to think that as robbery increased (which it did) robbery-murders proliferated. It is even possible that the lower class that invariably is responsible for the overwhelming bulk of violence was enlarged by the depression; that masses of people lost what tenuous holds they had on a working-class existence and were propelled onto the lowest rungs of the socioeconomic ladder. Could such people have engaged in violent crime? It seems perfectly plausible to think so.

But attempts to generalize from this extraordinary situation and conclude that economic downturns always or even usually cause violent crime go too far. In the first place we know that prosperity, such as in the 1920s, had a stronger association with violence than the depression. Second, even during the 1930s, the response to the economy was uneven. While it is true that homicide rates rose during the worst years of the big bust, they declined just after the initiation of the New Deal, a slide that continued even in the face of the so-called Roosevelt Recession of 1937–38. Finally, I would observe that numerous attempts to quantify a general relationship between crime and the economy have come to grief. An examination of sixty-three studies that sought to establish a statistical association between unemployment and crime discerned a "consensus of doubt" among analysts. Of 138 measures of a purported link between unemployment and crimes of violence, only 24 percent were statistically significant.[36]

The Great Depression was *sui generis* and extraordinary times may have produced an extraordinary crime response. The sheer magnitude of the collapse—with soaring levels of unemployment persisting for so many years—marks it as a unique period in American history, one without parallel in the twentieth century. Before 1933, moreover, it was a period without the elaborate governmental social safety net that the New Deal first put into motion.

By employing millions and giving millions of others cash payments, the New Deal may have reduced crime. It is reasonable to think that robbery and theft to provide necessities, such as food and clothing, might have been averted in some cases. And by alleviating the frustration and despair of the long-term unemployed and giving people a glimmer of hope for the future, the New Deal also may have cut down on crimes of violence. A quantitative study correlating depression relief spending with crime found that each dollar per capita of spending produced measurable reductions in most violent crimes.[37]

It is even possible that some of the more unusual and creative New Deal programs, though not designed for such a purpose, decreased crime. For instance, as was mentioned earlier, it has been claimed that the Civilian Conservation Corps, which effectively isolated between one-quarter and one-third of the nation's poor young men—a highly criminogenic group—served as a crime control program. Even President Roosevelt thought in retrospect that "crime prevention has been an important by-product" of the CCC.[38]

While the New Deal apparently played a role in the crime slide that occurred between 1933 and 1940, other events also contributed. Simultaneous with the reduction in crime came the elimination of national Prohibition and a sharp decline both in foreign immigration and domestic migration. I turn attention to these two developments.

## PROHIBITION, IMMIGRATION, AND MIGRATION

The repeal of the Eighteenth Amendment in 1933 marked the end of Prohibition. While this did not mean an end to the gangs, which moved into other activities, it did write finis to their open warfare on the streets. The impact on crime may be inferred from developments in Detroit, where we have the benefit of a systematic study of homicide. It was found that murders attributable in part to gangs, which had contributed nearly one-third of all homicides involving "criminal transactions," fell off sharply after 1933. From 1926 to 1929, gang murders constituted 40 out of 130 criminal transaction homicides (31 percent). From 1930 to 1934, for most of which Prohibition was still in force, they were at 29 percent (31 of 106). By 1935–39, however, gang killings dropped by 84 percent to 5 out of 49 criminal transaction homicides.[39]

Crime historian Eric Monkkonen once astutely observed that the end of gangland killings was unlikely to affect *female* homicide rates. Consequently, if female rates went down during the 1930s, it must not be because of the end of Prohibition. In fact, female homicide rates did not decline significantly until 1938, seemingly ignoring both the economy and the laws on alcohol.[40]

Furthermore, despite the end of Prohibition, alcohol ingestion remained low in the United States and this too may have reduced violent crime. State and local drinking regulations continued in effect after national Prohibition was repealed, and these laws along with the straitened circumstances of the depression kept alcohol consumption down throughout the 1930s. Total consumption, which had hit highs of two and one-half gallons per capita before Prohibition (and would attain such levels again in the 1970s), sank to a gallon and a half per capita during the depression, a 40 percent decline. Combined with the end of the gang wars, it is highly likely that continued low levels of alcohol consumption contributed to the crime fall that began after 1933.[41]

A second factor in the late 1930s crime decline was the slowing, and in some cases the reversal, of domestic migration and foreign immigration to northern cities. As we saw in chapter 10, the enormous movement of people, especially young men, into the big industrial cities of the North contributed to the crime rise of the 1920s. That flow was cut off by the Great Depression as job opportunities in manufacturing rapidly dried up. In the case of African Americans, the Great Migration stalled as the outflow from the South in the 1930s dropped 50 percent compared with the previous decade. In addition, some blacks returned to the South, where the economy, though hardly robust, probably was better than in the industrial states. From 1935 to 1940, nearly 26,000 African Americans embarked on a reverse migration.[42]

Foreign immigration tailed off even more precipitously. Despite the restrictive immigration quota laws of the 1920s, an average of over 412,000 immigrants had arrived in the United States each year from 1920 to 1930. Between 1931 and 1940, by contrast, the annual average was under 53,000, a decline of 87 percent.

It seems very likely that the falloff in migration and immigration contributed to reduced crime in the big cities of the North, the destination for the vast bulk of the influx. This would have occurred for two reasons. First, in the case of southern Italians and Sicilians, as well as African Americans (and perhaps white southerners as well)—groups with high rates of violent crime at their place of origin—the slowdown simply kept more potential offenders out of the Northeast. Second, urban tensions created by the massive inflows of population to the slums and ghettos of the big cities (such as derive from competition for scarce jobs and housing)—a major problem in the 1920s—were eased by the reduced inmigration.[43]

As was the case with the end of Prohibition, the impact on crime of the diminished migration and immigration remains speculative. Nevertheless, it is plausible to think that since these factors contributed to elevated crime rates in the 1920s, their attenuation in the 1930s played a part in the decline of crime in the second half of that troubled decade.

One final consideration before I conclude. One must determine whether or not demographic factors, such as age and gender, were significant in the 1930s, since an excess or dearth of young men would have had a profound effect on crime rates. The thirties was a baby-bust decade—marriage and birth rates plunged—no doubt due to the economic strains on families. The U.S. population, which had grown 16 percent in the 1920s and 15 percent in the 1940s, rose only 7 percent in the 1930s, making the thirties generation the smallest in the century. This baby-bust cohort reached high crime age in the 1950s, when crime was indeed low. But there is no reason to think that the baby bust had any bearing on crime in the 1930s.[44]

The young male population which had been responsible for the violence of the 1920s would have moved into its late thirties during the depression years, perhaps "aging out" of violent crime. However, the demographic data indicate that they were replaced in the 1930s by comparable numbers of young males. The male population of the United States between the ages of twenty and twenty-nine shrank a bit in 1930, but returned to near 1920 levels by the end of the decade. In 1920, this cohort was 8.6 percent of the total national population; it dipped to 8.3 percent in 1930, but rose to 8.5 percent in 1940. Thus, age was not the main reason for the crime fall.[45]

As for gender, the results were mixed. For the youngest group, 15–24 year olds, the male-to-female ratio rose from 96.8 (1920) to 97.9 (1930) and then to 98.5

(1940). For the next oldest age cohort, however, the 25 to 44 group, there was a significant decline in male prevalence; the male-to-female ratio dropped from 105.1 to 101.8 to 98.5.[46] All in all, considering both age and gender, it is difficult to see much of an impact on crime from such demographic characteristics.

## CONCLUSION

Before the decade ended an influential article published in the *American Socio-logical Review* offered a theory of crime that emphasized—appropriately enough to the era—monetary success. Crime, Robert K. Merton explained, was the product of the strain between American society's unrelenting demand for pecuniary success and its failure to provide most of its citizens with the opportunities to achieve such success by legitimate means.

> On the one hand, they are asked to orient their conduct toward the prospect of accumulating wealth and on the other, they are largely denied effective opportunities to do so institutionally. The consequences of such structural inconsistency are psychopathological personality, and/or antisocial conduct, and/or revolutionary activities. It is only when a system of cultural values extols, virtually above all else, certain common symbols of success for the population at large while its social structure rigorously restricts or completely eliminates access to approved modes of acquiring these symbols for a considerable part of the same population, that antisocial behavior ensues on a considerable scale.[47]

Merton's "structural-strain" theory became the one of the most influential of what we might call the "adversity theories" of crime. Thinkers on the political left quickly adopted the position that reducing the "strain" by uplifting the poor, that is, redistributing wealth, was the ultimate solution to the crime problem.

It is perhaps understandable that in the dark days of the greatest depression in the twentieth century, only a few years after violent crime rose to new heights, one might conclude that the maldistribution of wealth provided the key to the country's social maladies. The irony is that the next several decades would witness a meteoric increase in national wealth and an enormous expansion of the middle class—followed by the greatest escalation in violent crime in over a century.

If there were any validity at all to the notion that violent crime is solely or even mainly a product of economic turbulence, the 1920s and the 1960s would be remembered as eras of peace and harmony while the 1930s would be known for its rampant lawlessness. That it was exactly the opposite—that the prosperous twenties produced runaway crime while the calamitous thirties saw steady declines in violence—tells us one of two things. Either economic decline for some strange reason makes people *less* prone to violence, or it has very little to do with violent crime.

The former view is hardly intuitive. Economic catastrophe could, one may suppose, create a kinship of the suffering, a sort of we're-all-in-this-together type of attitude that makes people empathize with one another. This in turn could make it less likely that they will physically hurt their fellow-sufferers. It has been said that the Great Depression "softened" class, ethnic, and regional conflicts and that the near-universal hard times fostered a "heightened sense of unity, understanding, and compassion among the nation's citizens."[48] But even if this were true about the depression years it hardly follows that *economic* disaster in particular produces such eras of good feeling. It is just as likely—even more plausible—that a popular war or a period of great prosperity would generate such a positive social outlook.

The second proposition—that the economy has very little to do with violent crime one way or the other—is better aligned with the historical record. Americans suffered terribly in the 1930s. It was a bleak era that ended only when the nation mobilized for the Second World War. And yet every reliable measure of crime available essentially tells the same story: violent crime remained elevated through the twenties, rose modestly until 1933, then went steadily down. This downturn occurred *despite* the depression. We know this because of the so-called Roosevelt Recession of 1937 to 1938. Although this late decade crash was in some respects as bad as the 1929 collapse, crime continued to decline, and indeed, fell to new lows. If ever the economic downturn theory of crime applied, the 1937–38 crash, coming at the tail end of the grimmest decade of the twentieth century, should have left blood in the streets.

For that matter, in the late twentieth and early twenty-first centuries, there seemed to be an inverse relationship between crimes of violence and economic hardship. From 1993 to 2011, violent crime rates tumbled 72 percent while unemployment rates rose 29 percent.[49]

The conclusion seems patent. Murder, robbery, and violent crime in general do not necessarily increase when people are unemployed, or when they are destitute, or even when they are, as so many were in the 1930s, hungry and desperate. Downturns may increase robberies; and they may not. They may strain marriages and cause wife-abuse and killing; and they may not. Depressions may increase compassion for one's fellow-man or they may heighten social divisions. There simply is no consistent relationship between economic trends and violent crime rates.

# Conclusion

## THE TWO CRIME BOOMS

The United States went through two major crime booms in the twentieth century, each followed by sharp downturns. As I write we are still enjoying the crime trough that followed boom number two, what I call the crime tsunami. As to what comes next, I will venture some rather optimistic views at the end of this chapter.

Prior to the twentieth century violent crime in the United States had declined significantly between the Civil War and the early 1890s. If we average the homicide victimization rates of New York City and Chicago for 1875 to 1899—national homicide mortality figures didn't exist in the nineteenth century—the result is an impressively low 4.3 per 100,000. Even our present-day crime trough can't match this rate.[1]

Violent crime climbed steadily in the early twentieth century, starting in the 1910s, ratcheting upward (except for the World War I years) right through the mid-1930s. The first twentieth-century crime boom was, in fact, one of the biggest in U.S. history, eclipsed only by the crime tsunami of the post-1960s era.

But there was a big difference between violent crime in the pre-1940 era and afterward. That difference was robbery, or the "mugging" of strangers. Robbery was much more prevalent in the post-1960s boom.

It was attacks by strangers that made the late twentieth-century crime wave so devastating. High as the murder rates were in the early decades of the century, victimization was by and large avoidable. If one didn't associate with violent young men, especially young men who drank, one faced an infinitely greater likelihood of injury or death from an errant automobile or a dangerous work site than from a criminal assault. The chances of being robbed, or worse still, robbed

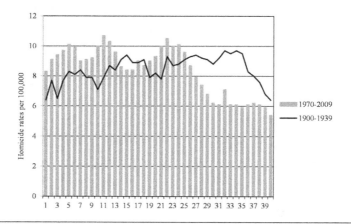

FIGURE 12.1. Two twentieth-century crime booms: 1900–1939 and 1970–2009. *Sources:* Eckberg, "Estimates," 13 (homicide 1930–32); Federal Security Agency, *Vital Statistics Rates,* mortality tables, table 12 (homicide 1933–39); National Center for Health Statistics, *Health, United States, 2017,* table 29, https://www.cdc.gov/nchs/hus/contents2017.htm#Table_029.

and physically assaulted (or even killed), were, by conservative estimate, at least two to four times as great in the post-1960s crime wave.

Furthermore, the apprehension of crime, which soared starting in the late 1960s, was almost as harmful to American society as the actuality. By 1972, four out of ten Americans were afraid to walk alone in their communities at night, and for African Americans, the poor, the elderly, and big-city dwellers, the figure was one out of two.[2]

Fear of crime led people to alter their behaviors in numerous ways, wreaking havoc with American lifestyles. Metro area residents became cautious about travel to big-city downtowns, especially on public transportation and at nighttime. Tourism declined as well. This hurt restaurants, shops, and downtown entertainment venues, damaging urban economies. People became wary of crime when they selected a place to live or enrolled their children at school. "Hardening" targets, such as residential and commercial properties, along with automobiles, became a must. Locks, bolts, and security lights proliferated. Security businesses mushroomed and security guards became ubiquitous. Violent crime in the pre-1940 era, bad as it was, had never been like this.

Robbery had been of little concern in the late 1800s, but increased markedly as the new century began. As crime historian Roger Lane observed, despite the prevalence of handguns in the waning decades of the nineteenth century, "armed robbery was for unclear reasons virtually unknown then in the urban east."[3] This soon began to change. Jeffrey Adler's incisive work on Chicago ably documents the developments in the Windy City up to 1920. He showed that between 1890 and 1920, the population rose 146 percent and homicides increased 376 percent—but robbery-homicides jumped 1,950 percent.[4]

As disturbing as early twentieth-century robbery growth was, it paled beside the end-of-century rates. Chicago provides proof of this, as its police department kept accurate records throughout the century, enabling us to track changes in a single jurisdiction with the same police force. From 1920 to 1970, robbery rates in Chicago rose 325 percent, and by 1980, they had climbed 392 percent. Judging by Chicago's experience, robbery was much more of a threat in the post-1960s era than in the first crime wave.[5]

Boston is another city with credible police records affording us crime data over a long time span. Robbery arrest rates per 100,000 soared in Boston, more than tripling between 1937–51 and 1970–71, and increasing sevenfold by the early 1980s.[6]

A final piece of evidence is the proportion of prisoners convicted of robbery at various points over the course of the twentieth century. In 1904, a mere 1 percent of all state and federal commitments were for robbery. In 1910, the proportion was 5 percent. By 1933, when violent crime peaked for the prewar period, the percentage rose to 12, trailing off to about 9 during the great crime dip of the 1940s and 1950s. By 1970, however, 14 percent of all those sentenced to one year or more in prison were robbers, and in 1981, the figure had escalated to 18 percent.[7]

Thus, the best evidence suggests that stranger violence—robbery is perpetrated by strangers in roughly eight out of every ten cases—was a much bigger problem near the end than at the start of the twentieth century.

## EUROPE AND AMERICA

It is instructive to compare developments here with those in Europe and the United Kingdom. As table 12.1 depicts, overseas homicides were low in the last quarter of the nineteenth century by American standards, Italy alone suffering more per capita murders than the United States. But as the twentieth century progressed European homicide rates tumbled dramatically, while our rates grew out of all proportion, leading analysts to talk about "American exceptionalism."

From 1900 to 1924, for example, American rates were averaging 8.3 per 100,000, four and one-half times the Euro/UK average of 1.8. This gap, despite occasional expansions and contractions, became typical of the relationship. (Recently, however, we've begun to see a reversal of the usual pattern: American violent crime rates have been on the way down since the mid-1990s, while European rates have been climbing.)[8]

TABLE 12.1. Homicide victimization rates per 100,000, Europe and United States, 1875–1949

|  | England | Holland/ Belgium | Scandi- navia | Germany/ Switz. | Italy | U.S. |
|---|---|---|---|---|---|---|
| 1875–1899 | 1.3 | 1.5 | 0.9 | 2.2 | 5.5 | 4.3 |
| 1900–1924 | 0.8 | 1.7 | 0.8 | 2.0 | 3.9 | 8.3 |
| 1925–1949 | 0.8 | 1.3 | 0.6 | 1.4 | 2.6 | 7.5 |

Sources: Eisner, "Modernization," 629 (Europe); Monkkonen, "Homicides in New York City"; Jeffrey S. Adler, private communication (Chicago); Eckberg, "Estimates" (U.S. 1900–1932).

Note: Data for United States, 1875–99, are averages for New York City and Chicago.

The difference between the social compositions of Europe and America explains the enormous gulf between our violent crime and theirs. The violent subcultures of various American social groups—white southerners, certain immigrant groups (southern Italians, for example), and African Americans—combined with a culture of gun violence that makes killing easy have been responsible for our sky-high violent crime rates. Europe and the United Kingdom never had such a tinderbox social makeup (although the recent influx of Muslims from the Middle East may change this), and even widespread gun ownership (as in Switzerland) has never produced murders on anything like the scale seen here.

There also were secondary factors instrumental in our early twentieth-century crime boom. The rise of big metropolitan areas at the close of the nineteenth century provided more people, greater wealth, more attractive goods, and improved mobility—all conducive to robbery. Bear in mind, however, that while Europe also grew big cities it had nowhere near our crime. While New York City reveled in turn-of-the-century homicide rates of 3.5 per 100,000, London's rates were 0.8.

Some might think that our unique experience with Prohibition helps explain the crime wave during the 1920s. However, while booze gangs added to homicide totals in some of our big cities and frightened the public with their brazen violence, Prohibition on balance wasn't responsible for the crime escalation. It even helped reduce crime over the long term. Not only did Prohibition kill the saloon—crime central for big cities—it also spawned state and local regulations that, along with canned and bottled beer, domesticated imbibing, thereby minimizing the stranger quarrels that escalate into drunken brawls or shootouts. (See chapter 10.)

And when it comes to saloon violence we should recall the role of demographics, yet another significant secondary factor. The bulk of violent crime is committed by young males, and many of the violent immigrant groups had relatively few females, at least initially, making these groups even more violent per capita than they might otherwise have been. (Demographics also became significant in the second twentieth-century crime escalation with the rise of the Baby Boomers.)

Nor did poverty or sharp economic downturns cause the first crime wave. The 1920s boom came amidst an economic expansion so great that one might conclude that prosperity, not economic slump, is a correlate of crime. Moreover, in several periods of calamitous economic adversity—the Panic of 1893, the second half of the Great Depression of the 1930s, and the Great Recession of the post-2008 era—violent crime was not a major worry.

One also must consider the role of weakness in the criminal justice system, which caused crime spikes in the nineteenth-century West and South. When law enforcement is feeble, as it was in the rural South and the wide open spaces of the West, it creates incentives to crime as well as to vigilantism. It wasn't happenstance that lynching was mainly associated with these areas. The strengthening of police, courts, prisons, and the other components of the criminal justice system ultimately reduced both crime and private enforcement in the United States.

## THE PRESENT AND BEYOND

Crime historian Eric Monkkonen once hypothesized that violent crime runs in cycles. "Violence provokes a multitude of control efforts," he contended, "many of which have long lags before their side effects show up in the murder rates, [whereupon] . . . the cumulative effect ultimately drives the rates down. When the murder rate ebbs, control efforts get relaxed, thus creating the multiple conditions causing the next upswing."[9]

If Monkkonen was right, then contemporary efforts to weaken the criminal justice system, the current trend, are risky. By relaxing the social controls on violence we are, as he put it, "creating the multiple conditions causing the next upswing."

But he may have been mistaken. Monkonnen's hypothesis emphasizes the strength of the criminal justice system. The thesis of this book is that groups with subcultures of violence have been responsible for a great deal of our violent crime and that the potency of the criminal justice system is a significant but secondary factor.

It could be—here's my optimistic scenario—that as groups with high violence subcultures move into the middle class, crime, despite the weakened social controls, will remain low and get even lower. Bourgeois values, however much derided by some, vaccinate against violence. For the middle class, the risks of personal injury, loss of status, and criminal justice sanctions are a great deterrence to violence. Besides, middle-class people can afford to go to law to resolve disputes.[10]

In the period covered by this book the immigrant Irish had already begun moving up the social ladder. By the 1950s they were joined by Italian and Chinese immigrants. The violent crime rates of each of these groups diminished accordingly. The same undoubtedly will happen—it is already happening—to Latinos and African Americans in our day. The opportunity for social advance by people of color is one of the great benefits of the civil rights movement of the 1960s.[11]

So if we look back at the key factors in crime booms over the last century-and-a-half the picture in the first decades of the twenty-first century looks promising. The population is aging, groups with high violence subcultures are advancing socioeconomically, the opioids problem is not increasing violent crime rates (partly because youth gangs don't control distribution), and the United States is becoming more and more of a middle-class nation. Although the immigration issue has become a political lightning rod of late, it is not unreasonable to believe that entry into the United States of Latino groups with high crime rates will eventually be addressed. And relatively nonviolent Asian immigration is expected to outstrip Hispanic immigration in the first half of this century.[12] In short, the great crime booms of the early and late twentieth century may turn out to be of historical interest only in the twenty-first.

# NOTES

## PREFACE

1. Federal Bureau of Investigation, *Crime in the United States, Uniform Crime Reporting Statistics*, https://www.ucrdatatool.gov/Search/Crime/Crime.cfm. According to the FBI, violent crime encompasses four different offenses: criminal homicide (murder and non-negligent manslaughter), robbery, rape and sexual assault, and assault (usually aggravated assault). The violent crime rates in 1960 were 160.9 per 100,000; in 1990, they were 729.6 per 100,000. These rates are based on records of police departments across the United States that report to the FBI crimes known to them (whether or not solved by police).

2. Barry Latzer, *The Rise and Fall of Violent Crime in America* (New York: Encounter Books, 2016).

3. Roger Lane, *Murder in America: A History* (Columbus: Ohio State University Press, 1997), 189.

4. Mark Cooney, "The Decline of Elite Homicide," *Criminology* 35, no. 3 (1997): 381.

5. H. V. Redfield, *Homicide, North and South* (Philadelphia: J. B. Lippincott, 1880).

6. A quantitative analysis demonstrated the vitality of the southern white honor culture in the 1990s: Richard E. Nisbett and Dov Cohen, *Culture of Honor: The Psychology of Violence in the South* (Boulder, CO: Westview, 1996). I found persistently high homicide mortality rates for southern whites in the twenty-first century after adjusting for Hispanic ethnicity and age: Latzer, *Rise and Fall*, 214, fig. 4.18.

7. For most of American history, until the Great Migration of the twentieth century, the overwhelming majority of blacks resided in the South. In 1910, 89 percent of the black population lived there. This dipped to 85 percent in 1920 and 79 percent in 1930, as blacks migrated north. U.S. Census Bureau, *Historical Census Statistics on Population Totals by Race, 1790 to 1990, and by Hispanic Origin, 1970 to 1990, for the United States, Regions, Divisions, and States*, by Campbell Gibson and Kay Jung, Working Paper No. 56 (Washington, DC: GPO, 2002), tables 1, 4. By the turn of the twenty-first century, after the Great Migration had ended, 55 percent of blacks lived in the South. U.S. Census Bureau, *The Black Population: 2000* (2001), 3, fig. 2, https://www.census.gov/prod/2001pubs/c2kbr01–5.pdf.

8. Elijah Anderson, *Code of the Street: Decency, Violence, and the Moral Life of the Inner City* (New York: W. W. Norton, 1999), 76.

9. Anderson, *Code of the Street*, 75.

10. Latzer, *Rise and Fall*, 216.

## CHAPTER ONE

1. David Hackett Fischer, *Albion's Seed: Four British Folkways in America* (New York: Oxford University Press, 1989); Grady McWhiney, *Cracker Culture: Celtic Ways in the Old South* (Tuscaloosa: University of Alabama Press, 1988).

2. John Hope Franklin, *The Militant South, 1800–1861* (Cambridge, MA: Harvard University Press, 2002, 1956), 2.

3. Redfield, *Homicide.*

4. Redfield, *Homicide,* 87, 88.

5. Redfield, *Homicide,* 15.

6. Redfield, *Homicide,* 55.

7. Redfield, *Homicide,* 188–89.

8. H. C. Brearley, who analyzed southern homicide in the first half of the twentieth century, said that "during the five years from 1920 to 1924 the rate of homicide per 100,000 population for the southern states was a little more than two and a half times greater than for the remainder of the United States." H. C. Brearley, "The Pattern of Violence," in *Culture in the South,* ed. W. T. Couch (Chapel Hill: University of North Carolina Press, 1934), 681. As for southern black homicides, rates in the South for 1920 and 1925 ranged from 2.2 (South Carolina) to 6.1 (Tennessee) times the rates of southern whites: H. C. Brearley, *Homicide in the United States* (Chapel Hill: University of North Carolina Press, 1932), 99.

9. W. J. Cash, *The Mind of the South* (Garden City, NY: Doubleday, 1941, 1954), "Preview to Understanding," 1–2.

10. Cash, *Mind of the South,* 412.

11. Dickson D. Bruce, Jr., *Violence and Culture in the Antebellum South* (Austin: University of Texas Press, 1979).

12. Charles Reagan Wilson and William Ferris, eds., *Encyclopedia of Southern Culture* (New York: Anchor Books, 1989), 4:343–417.

13. For a compendium of the many thousands of ethnic groups worldwide, only some of which are "regional" in that they have a major presence in a particular geographical region, see David H. Levinson, *Ethnic Groups Worldwide: A Ready Reference Book* (Phoenix, AZ: Oryx, 1998).

14. Thomas Sowell, *Race and Culture: A World View* (New York: Basic Books, 1994), 63. "The integration of the South into the economy and mass culture of the nation," said Ayers, "accelerated in the late 1890s and early 1900s." But "the South tentatively rejoined national life only to discover, and often reaffirm, the distance that separated its people from other Americans." Edward L. Ayers, *The Promise of the New South: Life after Reconstruction* (New York: Oxford University Press, 1992), 310.

15. "For the South is differentiated from the rest of the country, not only in having a large negro population, but also, as is often overlooked, in not having any appreciable foreign population. And, because of this latter fact, the white South is undoubtedly closer to the colonial times in social type and mental outlook than any other region." U.S. Department of Commerce, Bureau of the Census, *Immigrants and Their Children 1920,* by Niles Carpenter (Washington, DC: GPO, 1927), 35.

16. Fischer, *Albion's Seed;* McWhiney, *Cracker Culture.* Historian McWhiney called these British immigrants "Celts," while admitting that the descent of the Irish, Scottish and Welsh from ancient Celts is questionable (*Cracker Culture,* xxiii).

17. Fischer, *Albion's Seed,* 6.

18. Fischer, *Albion's Seed,* 6.

19. Fischer, *Albion's Seed,* 633–34.

20. Fischer, *Albion's Seed*, 626, 629.

21. Fischer, *Albion's Seed*, 766.

22. Richard Maxwell Brown, *Strain of Violence* (New York: Oxford University Press, 1975), 99–100, 102; Richard Maxwell Brown, *The South Carolina Regulators* (Cambridge, MA: Harvard University Press, 1963); Randolph Roth, *American Homicide* (Cambridge, MA: Harvard University Press, 2009), 205–6.

23. William Lynwood Montell, *Killings: Folk Justice in the Upper South* (Lexington: University Press of Kentucky, 1986), xiv, xv, 24, 39, 144, 164.

24. Fischer, *Albion's Seed*, 767.

25. Otis K. Rice, "Hatfields and McCoys," in *Encyclopedia of Southern Culture,* ed. Wilson and Ferris, 4:402–3.

26. Elliott J. Gorn, "'Gouge and Bite, Pull Hair and Scratch': The Social Significance of Fighting in the Southern Backcountry," *American Historical Review* 90, no. 1 (1985): 20.

27. Gorn, "'Gouge and Bite,'" 33.

28. Gorn, "'Gouge and Bite,'" 19, 22.

29. Bertram Wyatt-Brown, *Southern Honor: Ethics and Behavior in the Old South* (New York: Oxford University Press, 1982), 354.

30. Personal communication from Matthew Byron, professor of history at Young Harris College, Georgia.

31. Edward L. Ayers, *Vengeance and Justice: Crime and Punishment in the 19th-Century American South* (New York: Oxford University Press, 1984), 15; Edward L. Ayers, "Honor," in *Encyclopedia of Southern Culture,* ed. Wilson and Ferris, 4:363.

32. Michael Stephen Hindus, *Prison and Plantation: Crime, Justice, and Authority in Massachusetts and South Carolina, 1767–1878* (Chapel Hill: University of North Carolina Press, 1980), 44.

33. Bruce, *Violence and Culture*, 43; Roth, *American Homicide*, 214.

34. Roth, *American Homicide*, 218, 219.

35. Ayers, *Vengeance and Justice*, 29–31, 75.

36. Ayers, *Vengeance and Justice*, 74n5, 75n10. The overwhelming majority of the defendants in antebellum southern courts were white, as blacks, being slaves, were in most cases punished by their masters. While free blacks were subject to trial in the regular courts and could have been sentenced to the Georgia penitentiary, that prison's inmate population was, throughout the 1850s, entirely white: Ayers, *Vengeance and Justice*, 61n57.

37. Hindus, *Prison and Plantation*. The Massachusetts study covered 1833–38, 1849–52, and 1854–59. The South Carolina study covered different years for different counties, all within the period 1800 to 1860.

38. Hindus, *Prison and Plantation*, 78, 125–26. "Presentments" in nineteenth-century South Carolina were public comments prepared by grand juries on their own initiative at the start of each court term, i.e., twice a year in each judicial district. Another North-South comparison study supports the conclusion that the North took violent crime more seriously than the South. David J. Bodenhamer found that "for the antebellum decades, the mean sentence for violent offenders in Indiana was 8.2 years compared to 3.6 years in Georgia": David J. Bodenhamer, "Criminal Sentencing in Antebellum

America: A North-South Comparison," *Historical Social Research* 15, no. 4 (1990): 84. One may question whether Indiana is representative of northern states.

39. Redfield, *Homicide*, 193.

40. Ayers, *Vengeance and Justice*, 100n64. Ayers also informs us that a greater proportion of rural than urban defendants were middle-class; 12 percent of Savannah's accused owned some property, compared with two-thirds of the defendants in rural Greene and Whitfield counties (116).

41. Charles Dickens, *American Notes for General Circulation* (Leipzig: Bernhard Tauchnitz, 1842), 296.

42. Roth, *American Homicide*, 202–5; Hindus, *Prison and Plantation*, 103–4, 157. An execution database created by M. Watt Espy lists only 111 executions in South Carolina between 1800 and 1855, including whites and blacks, slave and free: M. Watt Espy, "Executions in the United States, 1608–2002: The ESPY File," Inter-University Consortium for Political and Social Research, Study No. 8451 (2016), https://doi.org/10.3886/ICPSR08451.v5. Espy's is the most comprehensive tally of executions in the United States extant, but researchers consider it inexact.

43. Ayers, *Vengeance and Justice*, 11. The "brutalizing effect" remark was by Fox Butterfield, who traced the family of black criminal Willie Bosket back to antebellum Edgefield County, South Carolina, a district notorious for its violence: Fox Butterfield, *All God's Children: The Bosket Family and the American Tradition of Violence* (New York: Knopf, 1995), 21.

44. McWhiney, *Cracker Culture*, 51.

45. Ayers, *Vengeance and Justice*, 116n28. Slave population figures were derived from the 1860 Census: Department of the Interior, Bureau of the Census, *Population of the United States in 1860* (Washington, DC: GPO, 1864). Ayers estimated that "nearly 60 percent of the slaves in Savannah lived away from the immediate control of their masters": *Vengeance and Justice*, 103.

46. Montell said there were only two black families in the entire area. Montell, *Killings*, 35.

47. Whether the South has been historically more militaristic than the rest of America is unclear. Historian Dickson Bruce thought antebellum southerners ambivalent toward military conflict. "Southern attitudes toward war were quite similar to their attitudes toward other forms of violence in society," that is, war was "a dangerous necessity." Bruce, *Violence and Culture*, 175–6. For a view that southerners exalted military ideals and virtues, see Rod Andrew, *Long Gray Lines: The Southern Military School Tradition, 1839–1915* (Chapel Hill, NC: University of North Carolina Press, 2001).

48. For example, rural Louisiana, 1865–84, was 40 percent white, but whites committed three-quarters of the murders: Gilles Vandal, "Black Violence in Post-Civil War Louisiana," *Journal of Interdisciplinary History* 25, no. 1 (1994): 52, 53.

49. Roth, *American Homicide*, 332, 335, 337, 338, 347–48, 352.

50. Roth, *American Homicide*, 162, 348. The three Georgia counties were Franklin, Jasper, and Wilkes.

51. Gilles Vandal, *Rethinking Southern Violence: Homicides in Post-Civil War Louisiana, 1866–1884* (Columbus: Ohio State University Press, 2000), 49, 54, 64.

52. Roth, *American Homicide*, 418.

53. Roth, *American Homicide*, 420, 421n74.

54. Ayers's data were drawn from a database developed by Monkkonen. Eric Monkkonen, "Police Departments, Arrests and Crime in the United States, 1860–1920," Inter-University Consortium for Political and Social Research, Study No. 7708, 2006, https://doi.org/10.3886/ICPSR07708.v2.

55. Ayers, *Vengeance and Justice*, 180.

56. Roth, *American Homicide*, 421.

57. "The South has been cynically and not inaccurately described as 'that part of the United States lying below the Smith and Wesson line,' a reference to the prevailing custom of carrying revolvers—and using them." Brearley, "Pattern of Violence," 678.

## CHAPTER TWO

1. W. E. B. DuBois, *The Philadelphia Negro: A Social Study* (New York: Schocken Books, 1899, 1967), 241.

2. Du Bois found that 57 percent of the black prisoners in Eastern Penitentiary had been born in the South (*Philadelphia Negro*, 253). His findings were partially confirmed by contemporary historian Roger Lane, who observed that a large proportion of Philadelphia's blacks, criminals and non-, had been from the South, mostly from Washington, DC, and Baltimore and environs: Lane, *Roots of Violence in Black Philadelphia, 1860–1900* (Cambridge, MA: Harvard University Press, 1986), 164.

3. Lane, *Roots of Violence*, 143.

4. Only Virginia's and Maryland's penitentiaries had significant numbers of free blacks, 29.5 percent and 43.8 percent, respectively. Ayers, *Vengeance and Justice*, 61n57.

5. Monroe N. Work, "Negro Criminality in the South," *Annals of the American Academy of Political and Social Science* 49 (1913): 74.

6. Hindus, *Prison and Plantation*, 139. Slaves could get the death penalty for such offenses as wounding a white man, a third conviction for striking a white man, poisoning or attempted poisoning, burning crops, insurrection, and assault with intent to rape a white woman (Hindus, *Prison and Plantation*, 131).

7. Hindus, *Prison and Plantation*, 141–42. Hindus found 1,044 black prosecutions for identified offenses in Anderson and Spartanburg Counties, South Carolina, 1818–60. Of the 1,044 cases, 408 (39 percent) were for theft crimes (including various larcenies and burglary), whereas 181 (17.3 percent) were for violent crimes (including assault, murder, poisoning, rape, attempted rape, riot and fighting). Slave theft commonly was a group crime, which is why it was prosecuted in court, not just punished on the plantation (Hindus, *Prison and Plantation*, 140).

8. Hindus, *Prison and Plantation*, 63.

9. Arthur F. Howington, "The Treatment of Slaves and Free Blacks in the State and Local Courts of Tennessee" (PhD diss., Vanderbilt University, 1982), 324, table 25; see Arthur F. Howington, *What Sayeth the Law: The Treatment of Slaves and Free Blacks in the State and Local Courts of Tennessee* (New York: Garland Publishing, 1986).

10. Jeff Forret, *Slave Against Slave: Plantation Violence in the Old South* (Baton Rouge: Louisiana State University Press, 2015), 292, 295.

11. Forret, *Slave Against Slave*, 45; Roth, *American Homicide*, 226. See also Philip J. Schwarz, *Twice Condemned: Slaves and the Criminal Laws of Virginia, 1705–1865* (Baton Rouge: Louisiana State University Press, 1988). Schwarz's study shows that from 1855 to 1864 Virginia slaves were convicted of murder 7.5 times per year on average (233). Given the Virginia slave population of 490,865, the

murder conviction rate of slaves is a very low 1.53 per 100,000. Of course, convictions are always less numerous than actual crimes.

12. Forret, *Slave Against Slave*, 71–72.

13. Forret, *Slave Against Slave*, 67. Roth reports that blacks in the plantation counties of Georgia and South Carolina used guns in only 7 percent of prewar homicides: Roth, *American Homicide*, 352.

14. George R. Bentley, *A History of the Freedmen's Bureau* (Philadelphia: University of Pennsylvania Press, 1955), 76, 176.

15. Ayers, *Vengeance and Justice*, 152.

16. Ayers, *Vengeance and Justice*, 172.

17. Leon F. Litwack, *Been in the Storm So Long: The Aftermath of Slavery* (New York: Alfred A. Knopf, 1979), 313.

18. U.S. Department of Commerce, Bureau of the Census, *The Social and Economic Status of the Black Population in the United States: An Historical View, 1790–1978,* Current Population Reports, Special Studies, Series P-23, No. 80 (Washington, DC: GPO, 1979), tables 11, 17. Black population percentages in 1870 were: Alabama, 48 percent; Florida, 49 percent; Georgia, 46 percent; Louisiana, 50 percent; Mississippi, 54 percent; North Carolina, 37 percent; South Carolina, 59 percent; Texas, 31 percent; and Virginia, 42 percent.

19. Joel Williamson, *The Crucible of Race: Black-White Relations in the American South since Emancipation* (New York: Oxford University Press, 1984), 57, 58.

20. Meier and Rudwick, *From Plantation to Ghetto,* 154; Christopher R. Adamson, "Punishment after Slavery: Southern State Penal Systems, 1865–1890," *Social Problems* 30, no. 5 (1983): 555–69, 559. In addition to criminal provisions, the Black Codes established rigid employment contract rules for blacks, limits on firearm ownership, and in a minority of states, segregated public transportation policies. However, these laws also established black rights to own property and to initiate civil suits.

21. Ayers, *Vengeance and Justice*, 165.

22. Allen W. Trelease, *White Terror: The Ku Klux Klan Conspiracy and Southern Reconstruction* (Baton Rouge: Louisiana State University Press, 1995), 311.

23. Trelease, *White Terror,* 415. The Klan prosecutions were based on the Enforcement Act of 1870, passed by the Republican Congress. Trelease reports 7,372 prosecutions between 1870 and 1897, 5,172 in the South. He says, however, that fewer than one in five cases resulted in conviction; two-thirds of the prosecutions were dropped or dismissed (417n86). The Klan enjoyed a nominal resurgence in the 1920s, but the twentieth-century Klan was not a continuation of the nineteenth-century terror organization.

24. Meier and Rudwick, *From Plantation to Ghetto,* 172.

25. *Plessy v. Ferguson,* 163 U.S. 537 (1896).

26. C. Vann Woodward, *Reunion & Reaction: The Compromise of 1877 and the End of Reconstruction* (Boston: Little, Brown, 1951), 4.

27. John W. Blassingame, "Before the Ghetto: The Making of the Black Community in Savannah, Georgia, 1865–1880," *Journal of Social History* 6, no. 4 (1973): 463–88.

28. Blassingame, "Before the Ghetto," 481.

29. James O. Breeden, "Science and Medicine," in *Encyclopedia of Southern Culture*, ed. Wilson and Ferris, 4:126.

30. Howard N. Rabinowitz, *Race, Ethnicity, and Urbanization* (Columbia: University of Missouri Press, 1994), 179.

31. H. H. Proctor and M. N. Work, "Atlanta and Savannah," in *Some Notes on Negro Crime particularly in Georgia*, ed. W. E. B. Du Bois (Atlanta: Atlanta University Press, 1904), 50.

32. Roger Lane, "Urban Police and Crime in Nineteenth-Century America," *Crime & Justice* 15 (1992): 12. Atlanta, for example, did not set up its police signal system utilizing call boxes until 1901. Thomas H. Martin, *Atlanta and Its Builders: A Comprehensive History of the Gate City of the South* (Atlanta: Century Memorial, 1902), 512–13.

33. Rabinowitz, *Race, Ethnicity*, 170–72.

34. Ayers, *Vengeance and Justice*, 229.

35. Quoted in Rabinowitz, *Race, Ethnicity*, 178.

36. *Atlanta Constitution*, August 26, 1883, quoted in Rabinowitz, *Race, Ethnicity*, 177.

37. Rabinowitz, *Race, Ethnicity*, 173, 174.

38. Ayers, *Vengeance and Justice*, 223.

39. Both the above newspapers are so quoted in Ayers, *Vengeance and Justice*, 229–30.

40. Quoted in Eugene J. Watts, "The Police in Atlanta, 1890–1905," *Journal of Southern History* 39, no. 2 (1973): 172.

41. Proctor and Work, "Atlanta and Savannah," 50. The Census of 1900 counted 89,872 Atlantans, 35,727 black (39.8 percent). U.S. Census Bureau, *Historical Census Statistics on Population Totals by Race, 1790 to 1990, and by Hispanic Origin, 1970 to 1990, For Large Cities and Other Urban Places in the United States*, by Campbell Gibson and Kay Jung, Population Division, Working Paper No. 76 (Washington, DC: GPO, 2005), table 11.

42. Louisville and Charleston figures from Frederick L. Hoffman, "The Race Traits and Tendencies of the American Negro," *Publications of the American Economic Association* 11, nos. 1/3 (1896): 226–27.

43. Proctor and Work, "Atlanta and Savannah," 49. In Savannah, 1895–97, public order offenses, mainly drunkenness and disorderly conduct, comprised 69.9 percent of all arrests of blacks (51).

44. Vance McLaughlin and Richard R. E. Kania, "Savannah Homicides in a Century of Change: 1896 to 1903 and 1986 to 1993," *Sociation Today* 6, no. 1 (2008), http://www.ncsociology.org/sociationtoday/v61/savannah.htm. These writers found ninety-seven homicides in which the race of both the offender and victim were known. Of these, African Americans were arrested for seventy-two, or 74.2 percent.

45. Ayers, *Vengeance and Justice*, 231n16.

46. Work, "Negro Criminality in the South," 79. Work was quoting William H. Samford (erroneously identified as "Sanford"), a nineteenth-century Alabama prosecutor and defense attorney.

47. Du Bois, *Some Notes*, 15. In Savannah in 1903, less than 29 percent of the black population, ages six to eighteen, was enrolled in school: Proctor and Work, "Atlanta and Savannah," 52.

48. In *Strauder v. West Virginia*, 100 U.S. 303 (1879), the Supreme Court struck down a statute restricting jury service to whites. Exclusions nevertheless continued, but without written laws.

49. *The Booker T. Washington Papers*, ed. Louis R. Harlan (Urbana: University of Illinois Press, 1974), 3:29.

50. Ayers, *Vengeance and Justice*, 212. Ayers may have been including work for public entities, such as county chain gangs. In 1886, 15 percent of the 64,349 prisoners in the United States (n = 9,699) worked under the lease system in thirteen states, ten of which had been slave states: Alex Lichtenstein, *Twice the Work of Free Labor: The Political Economy of Convict Labor in the New South* (London: Verso Books, 1996), 19.

51. Ayers, *Vengeance and Justice*, 221–22.

52. Ayers, *Vengeance and Justice*, 196.

53. [State of Georgia], *Biennial Report of the Principal Keeper of the Georgia Penitentiary From the 20th of October, 1880, to the 20th of October, 1882* (James P. Harrison, State Printer, n.d.), 3, 11, https://babel.hathitrust.org/cgi/pt?id=uiug.30112000799442&view=1up&seq=1.

54. Ayers, *Vengeance and Justice*, 186.

55. Ayers, *Vengeance and Justice*, 199–201.

56. Williamson, *Crucible of Race*, 58.

57. Ayers, *Vengeance and Justice*, 225.

58. Ayers, *Vengeance and Justice*, 180.

59. W. E. B. Du Bois, *The Souls of Black Folk: Essays and Sketches* (New York: Bantam Classic, 1904, 1953), 125.

60. W. E. B. Du Bois, *Some Notes*, 6.

61. See, e.g., Charles H. Otken, *The Ills of the South* (New York: G. P. Putnam's Sons, 1894), 219.

62. Tables 2.4 and 2.5 were drawn from Ayers, *Vengeance and Justice*, 250n56, who in turn relied on a dataset attributed to Eric Monkkonen, presumably the one presented in Eric H. Monkkonen, *Police in Urban America 1860–1920* (Cambridge: Cambridge University Press, 1981), app. B, 169. If so, then the southern cities are: New Orleans, Louisville, and Richmond, and probably the border cities Baltimore, St. Louis, and Washington, DC.

63. Ayers, *Vengeance and Justice*, 225n3.

64. Ayers, *Vengeance and Justice*, 176. Philip Alexander Bruce wrote in 1889: "The most confirmed criminal habit of the plantation negro is petit larceny; this infirmity is so common that there are comparatively few individuals of his race and condition who will not yield to the temptation to take what does not belong to them": Philip Alexander Bruce, *The Plantation Negro as a Freeman: Observations on His Character, Condition, and Prospects in Virginia* (New York: G. P. Putnam's Sons, 1889), 87. The Mississippi Supreme Court once declared that the former slaves were "given rather to furtive offenses than to the robust crimes of the whites": *Ratliff v. Beale*, 74 Miss. 247, 266, 20 So. 865, 868 (1896).

65. Du Bois, *Philadelphia Negro*, 249.

66. Redfield, *Homicide*, 103. Redfield counted homicides in Kentucky and Texas for 1878, and South Carolina for 1877. Of the 657 cases in which the race was known, 532 involved white killers, 125 black.

67. Roth, *American Homicide*, 351.

68. Vandal, "Black Violence in Post-Civil War Louisiana," 59–60.

69. Randolph Roth, *American Homicide Supplemental Volume*, AH tables 22, 23, 2010, https://cjrc.osu.edu/research/interdisciplinary/hvd/ahsv.

70. Roth, *American Homicide Supplemental Volume*, AH table 24.

71. Roth, *American Homicide Supplemental Volume*, AH table 31.

72. Roth, *American Homicide Supplemental Volume*, W fig. 53.

73. Foner, *Reconstruction*, 150.

74. Foner, *Reconstruction*, 81. "In fact," Foner points out, "a majority of freedmen did not abandon their home plantations in 1865" (81).

75. The black population of the South's ten biggest cities doubled between 1865 and 1870, while white residents increased 10 percent: Foner, *Reconstruction*, 81–82.

76. Barry A. Crouch, "A Spirit of Lawlessness: White Violence; Texas Blacks, 1865–1868," *Journal of Social History* 18 (Winter 1984): 220. This study relied on data compiled by the Texas Freedmen's Bureau.

77. Nick Lyons, *1897 Sears Roebuck & Co. Catalogue* (New York: Skyhorse Publishing, 2007), 534.

78. Philip Coehlo and James Shepherd, "The Impact of Region Difference in Prices and Wages on Economic Growth: The United States in 1890," *Journal of Economic History* 34 (1979): 77.

79. Lee Kennett and James LaVerne Anderson, *The Gun in America: The Origins of a National Dilemma* (Westport, CT: Greenwood Press, 1975), 155, 156.

80. John Hammond Moore, *Carnival of Blood: Dueling, Lynching, and Murder in South Carolina, 1880–1920* (Columbia: University of South Carolina Press, 2006), 127.

81. Hoffman, "Race Traits," 220.

82. Department of the Interior, Census Office, *Eleventh Census: 1890*, vol. 4, *Report on Vital and Social Statistics in the United States* (Washington, DC, 1896), sec. 1, 1. The eight states are Massachusetts, Connecticut, New Hampshire, Vermont, Rhode Island, New York, New Jersey, and Delaware. Compliance was spotty until the 1920s, and it took until 1933 for all states to enroll in the so-called death registration: U.S. Department of Commerce, Bureau of the Census, *Mortality Statistics 1932* (Washington, DC: GPO, 1935), 2–5.

83. Census Office, *Eleventh Census: 1890, Vital and Social Statistics*, part 3, table 17.

84. Bureau of the Census, *Social and Economic Status*, table 6.

85. Census Office, *Eleventh Census: 1890*, vol. 4, part 2, tables 7, 8. The nine cities are Baltimore, Boston, Brooklyn, Chicago, Cincinnati, New York, Philadelphia, St. Louis, and Washington, DC.

86. McLaughlin and Kania, "Savannah Homicides in a Century of Change," http://www.ncsociology.org/sociationtoday/v61/savannah.htm. Black males were apprehended for sixty murders, of which fifty-four of the victims were of the same race. This study relied on Savannah newspapers, annual health officers' reports, and public health department certificates and registrations.

87. Ayers, *Vengeance and Justice*, 231n16. Ayers stated that there were sixty-nine incidents, but his detailed account lists seventy.

88. Clare V. McKanna, Jr., *Homicide, Race, and Justice in the American West, 1880–1920* (Tucson: University of Arizona Press, 1997), 149.

89. Stewart E. Tolnay and Amy Kate Bailey, "Creating a New Database for the Study of Southern Lynchings: Public Use Microdata, The Historical United States County Boundary Files 1790–1999

and Forensic Demography," 2006, http://racialviolenceus.org/Articles/TolnayBailey_Database
_Lynchings.pdf, table 1, 7.

90. Ayers, *Promise of New South,* 157.

91. Ayers, *Promise of New South,* 156–57.

92. Tolnay and Bailey counted 805 black and 123 white victims for the decade 1890–99. Tolnay
and Bailey, "Creating a New Database," table 1, 7, http://racialviolenceus.org/Articles/TolnayBailey
_Database_Lynchings.pdf. Tolnay and Beck estimate that 6 percent of the blacks lynched between
1882 and 1930 in ten southern states were attacked by other blacks or integrated lynch mobs: Stewart
Emory Tolnay and E. M. Beck, *A Festival of Violence: An Analysis of Southern Lynchings, 1882–1930*
(Champaign: University of Illinois Press, 1995), ix.

93. Tolnay and Beck, *Festival of Violence,* 92.

94. Tolnay and Beck, *Festival of Violence,* 96. The exact figure was 25.4 percent, not including
incidents in which the motivation was unknown.

95. Ayers, *Vengeance and Justice,* 243.

96. See E. M. Beck and Stewart E. Tolnay, "The Killing Fields of the Deep South: The Market
for Cotton and the Lynching of Blacks, 1882–1930," *American Sociological Review* 55, no. 4 (1990):
526–39; Susan Olzak, "The Political Context of Competition: Lynching and Urban Racial Violence,
1882–1914," *Social Forces* 69, no. 2 (1990): 395–421.

97. Moore, *Carnival of Blood,* 128, 129.

98. Work, "Negro Criminality in the South," 75.

99. Williamson, *Crucible of Race,* 58–59.

100. Roth, *American Homicide,* 430–31, 433.

101. Lawrence W. Levine, *Black Culture and Black Consciousness* (New York: Oxford University
Press, 1977), 407–8.

102. Williamson, *Crucible of Race,* 59.

103. Sowell, *Black Rednecks and White Liberals* (San Francisco: Encounter Books, 2005), 27.

104. Roth, *American Homicide,* 434.

## CHAPTER THREE

1. "By the 1820s, the homicide rate in the slaveholding South was at least twice what it had been
at its low point in the mid-eighteenth century, and much higher than in the rest of the United States":
Roth, *American Homicide,* 200.

2. http://www.census.gov/geo/www/us_regdiv.pdf. The Census Bureau has used different definitions over the course of the twentieth century.

3. Jacqueline Jones, *The Dispossessed: America's Underclasses from the Civil War to the Present* (New
York: Basic Books, 1992), 82, 89, 101; Cash, *Mind of the South,* 418; Dewey W. Grantham, *The South
in Modern America: A Region at Odds* (New York: HarperCollins, 1994), 51.

4. Grantham, *South in Modern America,* xv–xvi, 92, 157; James N. Gregory, *The Southern Diaspora:
How the Great Migrations of Black and White Southerners Transformed America* (Chapel Hill: University
of North Carolina Press, 2005), 22.

5. Jones, *The Dispossessed*, 129, 130, 133, 135, 148, 149, 159. During the 1920s, nearly 1.5million whites left the South, compared with a black migration of under 811,000. Gregory, *Southern Diaspora*, 330.

6. Grantham, *South in Modern America*, 28, 91.

7. Grantham, *South in Modern America*, 53–54; Bureau of the Census, *Social and Economic Status*, tables 63, 88, tables 68, 91.

8. Cash, *Mind of the South*, 425.

9. Howard W. Odum, *Southern Regions of the United States* (Chapel Hill: University of North Carolina Press, 1936), 141, 142.

10. Grantham, *South in Modern America*, 102.

11. Grantham, *South in Modern America*, 102.

12. Grantham, *South in Modern America*, 102, 104; David E. Kyvig, *Daily Life in the United States, 1920–1940: How Americans Lived Through the "Roaring Twenties" and the Great Depression* (Chicago: Ivan R. Dee, 2002, 2004), 8.

13. Grantham, *South in Modern America*, 135. Lynching figures are from the Archives at Tuskegee Institute, http://192.203.127.197/archive/handle/123456789/507. *Powell v. Alabama*, 287 U.S. 45 (1932), established a constitutional right to counsel at state expense but only in limited circumstances, viz., where the defendants faced capital charges and were indigent as well as incapable of self-defense.

14. Gregory, *Southern Diaspora*, 330.

15. Gregory, *Southern Diaspora*, 16, 163.

16. Gregory, *Southern Diaspora*, 83, 94, 160, 162–63; J. Trent Alexander, "Great Migrations: Race and Community in the Southern Exodus, 1917–1970" (PhD diss., Carnegie Mellon University, 2001), 44, 51–52.

17. The Census Bureau collected mortality data beginning in 1880 from a steadily expanding list of states and cities, the so-called death registration area. The southern states were especially slow in cooperating, and it was not until 1933 that the entire country was enrolled. Bureau of the Census, *Mortality Statistics 1932*, 2–5.

Inclusion of southern states in the death registration area, by year

| State | Year | State | Year | State | Year |
|---|---|---|---|---|---|
| Kentucky | 1911 | Louisiana | 1918 | Arkansas | 1927 |
| Virginia | 1913 | Florida | 1919 | Georgia | 1928 |
| North Carolina | 1916 | Mississippi | 1919 | Oklahoma | 1928 |
| South Carolina | 1916 | Alabama | 1925 | Texas | 1933 |
| Tennessee | 1917 | West Virginia | 1925 | | |

18. Frederick L. Hoffman, "The Homicide Record of American Cities, 1882–1911," *Spectator*, October 3, 1912, 154.

19. The South Atlantic Division included Delaware, Maryland, District of Columbia, Virginia, West Virginia, North Carolina, South Carolina, Georgia, and Florida. The North Atlantic Division con-

sisted of Kentucky, Tennessee, Alabama, Mississippi, Louisiana, Texas, Indian Territory, Oklahoma, and Arkansas.

20. Gregory, *Southern Diaspora*, 18; U.S. Census Bureau, *Historical Census Statistics* (Working Paper No. 56), tables 2, 3, 4.

21. Patrol officers per 100,000 for ten northern and ten southern cities, selected unsystematically, reveals that northern rates were 21 percent higher. Department of Commerce, Bureau of the Census, *General Statistics of Cities: 1915* (Washington, DC: GPO, 1916), 9–10; table 2, 60. Patrol count was for 1915; city populations were 1914 estimates.

Patrol officers per 100,000 of the general population for ten northern and ten southern cities

| Northern Cities | Patrol Rate | Southern Cities | Patrol Rate |
|---|---|---|---|
| New York | 150.1 | Washington, DC | 146.1 |
| Chicago | 88.0 | Louisville | 126.2 |
| Philadelphia | 171.0 | Atlanta | 101.5 |
| Detroit | 151.8 | Birmingham | 84.7 |
| Cleveland | 78.8 | Richmond | 104.4 |
| St. Louis | 167.2 | San Antonio | 111.2 |
| Boston | 178.0 | Memphis | 97.7 |
| Pittsburgh | 105.2 | Dallas | 111.9 |
| Buffalo | 113.2 | Nashville | 87.9 |
| Milwaukee | 104.2 | Average | 103.1 |
| Average | 130.8 | | |

22. Brearley, *Homicide*, 23.

23. The West was defined as California, Colorado, Idaho, Montana, Nevada, Oregon, Utah, Washington, and Wyoming. Missing states—Georgia, Nevada, New Mexico, Oklahoma, South Dakota, and Texas—had not provided data to the Census Bureau.

24. Jeffrey S. Adler, "Murder, North and South: Violence in Early-Twentieth-Century Chicago and New Orleans," *Journal of Southern History* 74, no. 2 (2008): 297–324.

25. Adler, "Murder, North and South," 312, 312n51.

26. Adler, "Murder, North and South," 315–16.

27. Adler, "Murder, North and South," 305.

28. Andrew A. Bruce and Thomas S. Fitzgerald, "A Study of Crime in the City of Memphis, Tennessee," *Journal of the American Institute of Criminal Law & Criminology* 19, no. 2 (August 1928 suppl.): 3–127. Hoffman's statement appeared in the *Spectator*, June 14, 1923, 3, a publication of Hoffman's employer, the Prudential Insurance Company.

29. Chicago's rate was calculated by Professor Jeffrey S. Adler, who at my request kindly provided the figures. They are derived from his research for Jeffrey S. Adler, *First in Violence, Deepest in Dirt: Homicide in Chicago, 1875–1920* (Cambridge, MA: Harvard University Press, 2006). The 9.7 rate was adjusted by Adler to exclude homicides due to automobile accidents, abortions, infanticides, and types of killings not prosecuted throughout the time period of his study. The unadjusted rate for Chicago was 12.51, more than three times the rate for Memphis. The New York City rate

was calculated from Monkkonen's New York City homicide database: Eric H. Monkkonen, "Homicides in New York City, 1797–1999 [And Various Historical Comparison Sites]" (Ann Arbor, MI: Inter-University Consortium for Political and Social Research, Study No. 3226, 2001), https://doi .org/10.3886/ICPSR03226.v1.

30. Bruce and Fitzgerald, "A Study of Crime," 94.

31. The figure for Chicago, provided by Adler, is for adjusted white homicide victimizations in 1920.

32. Grantham, *South in Modern America*, 90, 116.

33. Cash, *Mind of the South*, 366, 369, 370.

34. Arthur M. Schlesinger, Jr., *The Age of Roosevelt: The Coming of the New Deal* (New York: Houghton Mifflin, 1958), 375; Grantham, *South in Modern America*, 117.

35. Grantham, *South in Modern America*, 118, 119; Cash, *Mind of the South*, 373.

36. Cash, *Mind of the South*, 376, 418–19.

37. The Index Crimes initially included murder, non-negligent manslaughter, aggravated assault, robbery, burglary, larceny, auto theft, and rape. Part II offenses included such things as prostitution, drunkenness, forgery, driving while intoxicated, etc.

38. Stuart Lottier, "Distribution of Criminal Offenses in Sectional Regions," *Journal of Criminal Law and Criminology* 29, no. 3 (1938): 330, 339, 344.

39. Austin L. Porterfield, "A Decade of Serious Crimes in the United States: Some Trends and Hypotheses," *American Sociological Review* 13, no. 1 (1948): 49. Since Index Crimes included burglary, larceny, and auto theft, which were nonviolent offenses, this is an imperfect measure of purely violent crime.

40. In the last years of the 1930s, however, white southern homicide rates declined, as did homicide rates throughout the United States. For 17 southern states, white homicide victimization rates fell from an average of 7.35 per 100,000 in 1935 to 5.39 in 1940, a drop of almost 27 percent. Federal Security Agency, U.S. Public Health Service, National Office of Vital Statistics, *Vital Statistics Rates in the United States 1900–1940*, by Forrest E. Linder and Robert D. Grove (Washington, DC: GPO, 1947), mortality tables, table 20.

41. U.S. National Emergency Council, *Report on Economic Conditions of the South* (Washington, DC: GPO, 1938), 46.

## CHAPTER FOUR

1. Isabel Wilkerson, *In the Warmth of Other Suns* (New York: Random House, 2010), 9.

2. Social psychologist John Dollard, writing in the 1930s, defined caste as that which "defines a superior and inferior group and regulates the behavior of the members of each group": John Dollard, *Caste and Class in a Southern Town*, 3d ed. (Garden City, NY: Doubleday, 1949), 62.

3. Department of Commerce, Bureau of the Census, *Negroes in the United States*, Bulletin 129 (Washington, DC: GPO, 1915), 32, table 1, 36. The situation hadn't changed much by 1920 when, of 920,000 black farmers living in the South, 24 percent owned land. The size of the average black farm, however, had increased markedly to 77 acres, with an average value of $1,588. White farms remained more valuable, worth on average $3,911: R. Douglas Hurt, ed., *African-American Life in the Rural South, 1900–1950* (Columbia: University of Missouri Press, 2003), 2. The cotton market

turmoil of the 1920s ruined black farmers, reducing the total to only 40,000 by 1930: Jones, *The Dispossessed,* 96.

4. Robert A. Margo, "Accumulation of Property by Southern Blacks Before World War I: Comment and Further Evidence," *American Economic Review* 74, no. 4 (1984): 770. The ratio of white-to-black assessed wealth for 1910 was 6.3 in Arkansas, 24.6 in Louisiana, 9.2 in North Carolina, and 9.6 in Virginia (1910–14 dollars): Margo, "Accumulation of Property".

5. Hortense Powdermaker, *After Freedom: A Cultural Study in the Deep South* (New York: Viking, 1939), 130–31; Lemann, *Promised Land,* 17. Of course, southern winters were not as bitter, or as long, as northern.

6. Bureau of the Census, *Social and Economic Status,* tables 63, 68; Lemann, *Promised Land,* 17; Grantham, *South in Modern America,* 54.

7. George Edmund Haynes, "Conditions Among Negroes in the Cities," *Annals of the American Academy of Political and Social Science* 49 (1913): 105–19. Haynes listed the following southern cities as having black populations exceeding 40,000 in 1910: Atlanta, GA / 51,902; Baltimore, MD / 84,749; Birmingham, AL / 52,305; Louisville, KY / 40,522; Memphis, TN / 52,441; New Orleans, LA / 89,262; Richmond, VA / 46,733; Washington, DC / 94,446.

8. "Most of the shootings and serious fights in the community take place on Saturday night or in the early hours of Sunday morning": Powdermaker, *After Freedom,* 169.

9. Butterfield, *All God's Children,* 62; Charles S. Johnson, *Growing Up in the Black Belt: Negro Youth in the Rural South* (Washington, DC: American Council on Education, 1941), 153.

10. Dollard, *Caste and Class,* 279.

11. "[Black] women referred both to violence and to fear of violence, and this motif recurs constantly throughout the middle and lower classes": Powdermaker, *After Freedom,* 170.

12. Butterfield, *All God's Children,* 63.

13. Brearley, *Homicide,* 110.

14. Thorsten Sellin, "The Negro Criminal. A Statistical Note," *Annals of the American Academy of Political and Social Science* 140 (1928): 58–59.

15. Guy B. Johnson, "The Negro and Crime," *Annals of the American Academy of Political and Social Science* 217 (1941): 99.

16. Dollard, *Caste and Class,* 279.

17. In his study of the treatment of murder defendants in the 1930s, sociologist Guy Johnson found that the overwhelming majority of indicted murder defendants in Richmond, Virginia; five counties in North Carolina; and Fulton County, Georgia, were black. The percentages of blacks indicted (my calculations) were 90.5 percent, 80.1 percent, and 92.6 percent, respectively. Eighty-two percent of the indictments involved blacks accused of murdering other African Americans. Johnson, "Negro and Crime," table 1. However, we cannot tell from Johnson's work how many homicides of blacks were seriously pursued by the authorities and how many cases were dropped before the indictment stage. Some analysts think that most black victim cases were not taken seriously. See, for example, Adler's study of New Orleans in the 1920s: Jeffrey S. Adler, *Murder in New Orleans: The Creation of Jim Crow Policing* (Chicago: University of Chicago Press, 2019).

18. Dollard, *Caste and Class,* 281.

19. U.S. Department of Commerce and Labor, Bureau of the Census, *Special Reports. Prisoners and Juvenile Delinquents in Institutions 1904* (Washington, DC: GPO, 1907), tables 6, 9. The early twentieth-century censuses defined "colored" as persons of Negro descent, Chinese, Japanese, and American Indians. The South Atlantic states, which consisted of Delaware, Maryland, Washington, DC, Virginia, West Virginia, North Carolina, South Carolina, Georgia, and Florida, had negligible numbers of Chinese and Japanese and relatively few Native Americans. Their "colored" population therefore was overwhelmingly African American. The West, on the other hand, would have had enough Chinese, Japanese, and American Indians to make their prisoner and general population tallies poor substitutes for a count of African Americans.

20. Matthew J. Mancini, "Race, Economics, and the Abandonment of Convict Leasing," *Journal of Negro History* 63, no. 4 (October 1978): 343, 349.

21. The high southern white rate for murder is partly responsible for the regional difference in black-to-white commitment ratios. The southern white commitment rate for grave homicide was 0.8 per 100,000, which is 2.6 times the northern white rate of 0.3.

22. U.S. Department of Commerce, Bureau of the Census, *Prisoners 1923* (Washington, DC: GPO, 1926), table 36, 68. U.S. Bureau of the Census, *Social and Economic Status,* 9.

23. Howard W. Odum, "Social and Mental Traits of the Negro: Research into the Conditions of the Negro Race in Southern Towns" (PhD diss., Columbia University, 1910), 202–4.

24. Federal Security Agency, *Vital Statistics Rates,* mortality tables, table 16.

25. Department of Commerce, Bureau of the Census, *Mortality Statistics 1920* (Washington, DC: GPO, 1922), 64–65; Department of Commerce, Bureau of the Census, *Mortality Statistics 1929* (Washington, DC: GPO, 1932), table BH, 43.

26. Brearley, *Homicide,* 101.

27. Dollard, *Caste and Class,* 267–68.

28. Latzer, *Rise and Fall,* 128–41.

29. Sowell, *Black Rednecks.*

30. Gregory, *Southern Diaspora,* 100, 330; U.S. Census Bureau, *Demographic Trends,* 83.

31. Gregory, *Southern Diaspora,* 100, 118, 119, 120. Not all of New York's black migrants could be counted as southerners as roughly 17 percent (in 1930) came from the Caribbean (Jamaica, Trinidad, Barbados), a source of cultural conflict within black neighborhoods (119).

32. U.S. Department of Commerce, Bureau of the Census, *Historical Statistics of the United States, Colonial Times to 1970, Bicentennial Edition, Part 1* (Washington, DC: GPO, 1975), 105. On the economic impact of World War I, see Hugh Rockoff, "Until It's Over, Over There: The U.S. Economy in World War I," NBER Working Paper 10580, 2004, http://www.nber.org/papers/w10580.

33. Meier and Rudwick, *From Plantation to Ghetto,* 216; Stewart E. Tolnay, "The African American 'Great Migration' and Beyond," *Annual Review of Sociology* 29 (2003): 214–16; Robert Higgs, "The Boll Weevil, the Cotton Economy, and Black Migration 1910–1930," *Agricultural History* 50, no. 2 (1976): 335–50; Hurt, *African-American Life,* 1–3.

34. Tolnay, "Great Migration," 215.

35. Lemann, *Promised Land,* 40.

36. Tolnay, "Great Migration," 217.

37. Tolnay, "Great Migration," 217; Louis M. Kyriakoudes, "'Lookin' for Better All the Time': Rural Migration and Urbanization in the South, 1900–1950," in *African-American Life*, 14, 16. As of 1930, black migrants to New York City came from the following states: Virginia, 44,471; South Carolina, 33,765; North Carolina, 26,120; Georgia, 19,546; Florida, 8,249; all other states, 6,656 or less each: Gilbert Osofsky, *Harlem: The Making of a Ghetto: Negro New York, 1890–1930* (New York: Harper & Row, 1963, 1966), 129.

38. Tolnay, "Great Migration," 218; Drake and Cayton, *Black Metropolis: A Study of Negro Life in a Northern City* (Chicago: University of Chicago Press, 1945, 1962), 57, 73. *Black Metropolis* is the classic study of black Chicago in the first half of the twentieth century.

39. Drake and Cayton, *Black Metropolis*, 58, 61, 62; Adler, *First in Violence*, 123; Gregory, *Southern Diaspora*, 118, 119, 121, 123; Roger Lane, *William Dorsey's Philadelphia and Ours: On the Past and Future of the Black City in America* (New York: Oxford University Press, 1991), 74.

40. Drake and Cayton, *Black Metropolis*, 60, 81; Gregory, *Southern Diaspora*, 131–35; Osofsky, *Harlem*, 135.

41. Adler, *First in Violence*, 142, 243, 248, 265–67; Allan H. Spear, *Black Chicago: The Making of a Negro Ghetto, 1890–1920* (Chicago: University of Chicago Press, 1967), 216. The newspaper headline was recounted in Walter F. White, "Chicago and Its Eight Reasons," *The Crisis* 18 (1919): 295. *The Crisis* was the NAACP monthly.

42. Meier and Rudwick, *Plantation to Ghetto*, 217.

43. Arthur V. Lashly, "Homicide (in Cook County)," in *The Illinois Crime Survey*, pt. 2, chap. 13 (Chicago: Illinois Association for Criminal Justice, 1929), 601. U.S. Census Bureau, Population Division, *Population of Counties by Decennial Census: 1900 to 1990*, by Richard Forstall, 1995, http://www.nber.org/data/census-decennial-population.html. The homicide total included justifiable homicides (mainly fights), as well as killings by police, which Lashly noted, never were prosecuted. The 1930 Cook County population figure, 3,982,123, was used here to determine the overall homicide rate, which was the average for the two-year period (Lashly, "Homicide (in Cook County)". County population figures by race were not available, therefore the black victimization rate was calculated with the black population figure for the city of Chicago for 1930, which was 233,903. U.S. Census Bureau, *Historical Census Statistics* (Working Paper No. 76), table 14.

44. Lashly, "Homicide (in Cook County)," 616–17, 618, 624.

45. Kenneth L. Kusmer, *A Ghetto Takes Shape: Black Cleveland, 1870–1930* (Urbana: University of Illinois Press, 1976), 220.

46. Brearley, *Homicide*, 99. In 1930, African Americans were 97 percent of the "colored" population in the Northeast, 89 percent in the Midwest. Odum, *Southern Regions*, 468.

47. Brearley, *Homicide*, 218–19.

48. Cairo, at the southernmost tip of the state, may have hosted the bootlegger gang wars that broke out in southern Illinois in the mid-1920s, thereby elevating white rates: Gary DeNeal, *A Knight of Another Sort: Prohibition Days and Charlie Birger* (Carbondale: Southern Illinois University Press, 1998).

49. James Boudouris, "Trends in Homicide, Detroit: 1926–1968" (PhD diss., Wayne State University, 1970), table 22, 175.

50. Bruce and Fitzgerald, "A Study of Crime," 20.

51. Drake and Cayton, *Black Metropolis*, 78, 80. The 1920 Census did not record employment status so there is uncertainty about unemployment prior to the 1930 Census. For a more negative view on black conditions in the 1920s, a view supported by very limited data, see Theodore Kornweibel, Jr., "An Economic Profile of Black Life in the Twenties," *Journal of Black Studies* 6, no. 4 (1976): 307–20. As for migrant returns, black migrants returned at one-third the white migrant rates. From 1935 to 1940 only 1.8 percent of black migrants went back to the South: Gregory, *Southern Diaspora*, 16, 331.

### CHAPTER FIVE

1. W. Eugene Hollon, *Frontier Violence: Another Look* (New York: Oxford University Press, 1974), 203.

2. Richard White, *"It's Your Misfortune and None of My Own": A New History of the American West* (Norman: University of Oklahoma Press, 1991), 336.

3. Richard Maxwell Brown, "Violence," in *The Oxford History of the American West*, ed. Clyde A. Milner, II, Carol A. O'Connor, and Martha A. Sandweiss (New York: Oxford University Press, 1994), 415.

4. Brown, "Violence," 410.

5. White, *"It's Your Misfortune,"* 329.

6. White, *"It's Your Misfortune,"* 339.

7. American Indian and white concepts of land ownership were very different. To whites, if land was owned, it was set aside for private use in accordance with the owner's wishes. To Native Americans, land ownership meant common possession by the tribe for common benefit, that is, for hunting and gathering. Native land wasn't fenced and tribal ownership wasn't recorded, unless it was the subject of an agreement with whites.

8. Brown, "Violence," 395.

9. Richard Maxwell Brown, "Western Violence: Structure, Values, Myth," *Western Historical Quarterly* 24, no. 1 (1993): 10.

10. Brown, "Violence," 394, 395.

11. The rule became a source of controversy in early 2012, when a Sanford, Florida, Neighborhood Watch organizer, George Zimmerman, was accused of second-degree murder in the shooting death of Trayvon Martin, a seventeen-year-old who, Zimmerman claimed, attacked him. Zimmerman was Hispanic, Martin black, so there was a racial undercurrent in the case. On July 13, 2013, Zimmerman was acquitted of all charges: Arian Campo-Flores and Lynn Waddell, "Jury Acquits Zimmerman of All Charges," *Wall Street Journal*, July 14, 2013. Florida is one of eighteen states which, since 2005, have passed so-called Stand Your Ground laws, which waive any duty to retreat by someone faced with an imminent deadly threat: Chandler McClellan and Erdal Tekin, "Stand Your Ground Laws and Homicides," Institute for the Study of Labor, Discussion Paper 6705 (2012), ftp://ftp.iza.org/RePEc/Discussionpaper/dp6705.pdf, accessed 8/28/12.

12. *Brown v. United States*, 256 U.S. 335, 343 (1921).

13. Adolphe Quetelet, *A Treatise on Man and the Development of His Faculties* (New York: Burt Franklin, 1842, 1968). The propensity to crime, wrote Quetelet, "attains its maximum about the age of 25 years." "The difference of sexes has also a great influence on the propensity to crime" (95).

14. Robert R. Dykstra, *The Cattle Towns: A Social History of the Kansas Cattle Trading Centers* (New York: Knopf, 1968), 100–107.

15. Gun control in the nineteenth-century West didn't usually work. Laws against carrying concealed weapons were commonplace—and commonly ignored: McKanna, *Homicide, Race, and Justice,* 24.

16. White, *"It's Your Misfortune,"* 330.

17. Mabel A. Elliott, "Crime and the Frontier Mores," *American Sociological Review* 9, no. 2 (1944): 189.

18. Roth, *American Homicide,* 380–81.

19. Robert R. Dykstra, "Overdosing on Dodge City," *Western Historical Quarterly* 27, no. 4 (1996): 508, 509; Randolph Roth, Michael D. Maltz, and Douglas L. Eckberg, "Homicide Rates in the Old West," *Western Historical Quarterly* 42 (2011): 175, 176.

20. Roger D. McGrath, "Violence and Lawlessness on the Western Frontier," in *Violence in America, Volume 1: The History of Crime,* ed. Ted Robert Gurr (Newbury Park, CA: Sage Publications, 1989), 122–45.

21. McGrath, "Violence and Lawlessness," 1:123.

22. McGrath, "Violence and Lawlessness," 1:133.

23. McGrath, "Violence and Lawlessness," 1:137.

24. McGrath, "Violence and Lawlessness," 1:124.

25. McGrath, "Violence and Lawlessness," 1:125, 131.

26. McGrath, "Violence and Lawlessness," 1:127.

27. McGrath, "Violence and Lawlessness," 1:123.

28. McGrath, "Violence and Lawlessness," 1:139.

29. McGrath, "Violence and Lawlessness," 1:137–39.

30. Hubert Howe Bancroft, *The Works of Hubert Howe Bancroft: Popular Tribunals,* vol. 1 (San Francisco: History Co., 1887). "Petty and poor offenders only were punished. Able counsel was secured by money, false witnesses were suborned, and judges and jailers made lenient. I do not mean to say that all officials, nor the half of them, were open to bribery. There were some as pure judges on the bench then as now. Yet money, if not directly, then indirectly, would buy acquittal or pardon" (1:317).

31. Paul T. Hietter, "A Surprising Amount of Justice: The Experience of Mexican and Racial Minority Defendants Charged with Serious Crimes in Arizona, 1865–1920," *Pacific Historical Review* 70, no. 2 (2001): 213. This study covered four Arizona counties. For white defendants, the conviction ratio was 51 percent; for Hispanics, 74.4 percent.

32. McKanna, *Homicide, Race, and Justice,* 96.

33. McKanna, *Homicide, Race, and Justice,* 93. Study of seven counties, 1850–1900. For Hispanics, the conviction rate was much higher, at 54 percent (71).

34. U.S. Department of Justice, Bureau of Justice Statistics, *Felony Defendants in Large Urban Counties, 2009—Statistical Tables* (Washington, DC: GPO, 2013), 22. However, nearly all of the adjudications were the result of guilty pleas, not trials.

35. Brown, *Strain of Violence,* 97.

36. Michael J. Pfeifer, *Rough Justice: Lynching and American Society, 1874–1947* (Urbana: University of Illinois Press, 2004), 39, 42. Pfeifer states that 61 percent of the lynchings in Washington were by private mobs (42).

37. White, *"It's Your Misfortune,"* 333.

38. Stephen J. Leonard, *Lynching in Colorado, 1859–1919* (Boulder: University Press of Colorado, 2002).

39. Wyoming lynched three between 1910 and 1947, California seven. From 1900 to 1947, Washington vigilantes took two lives: Pfeifer, *Rough Justice*, 159–60, 180–82.

40. Clare V. McKanna, Jr., "Enclaves of Violence in Nineteenth-Century California," *Pacific Historical Review* 73, no. 3 (2004): 391–423.

41. David Peterson del Mar, *Beaten Down: A History of Interpersonal Violence in the West* (Seattle: University of Washington Press, 2002), 75. Oregon's 1895 homicide rate was 6.3 per 100,000.

42. Kevin J. Mullen, *Dangerous Strangers: Minority Newcomers and Criminal Violence in the Urban West, 1850–2000* (New York: Palgrave Macmillan, 2005), 47. Rates went from 39.9 to 7.88 per 100,000.

43. Hietter, "Surprising Amount of Justice," 213, 215.

44. Pfeifer, *Rough Justice*, 2–3, 122.

45. White, *"It's Your Misfortune,"* 346–49.

46. White, *"It's Your Misfortune,"* 347. *Pettibone v. United States*, 148 U.S. 197 (1893).

47. Brown, "Violence," 411.

48. McKanna, *Homicide, Race, and Justice*, 81–114.

49. McKanna, *Homicide, Race, and Justice*, 81–82.

50. McKanna, *Homicide, Race, and Justice*, 85–88.

51. White estimates that 70–80 percent of all Italian migrants were young men without families: White, *"It's Your Misfortune,"* 449.

52. McKanna, *Homicide, Race, and Justice*, 83, 95, 96.

53. McKanna, *Homicide, Race, and Justice*, 101.

54. Mullen, *Dangerous Strangers*, 89.

55. Mullen, *Dangerous Strangers*, 86, 91. From 1890 to 1920, Mullen tallied 74 homicides by Italians in San Francisco. During that same period Chicago had 400 murders by the Black Hand alone (92).

56. This certainly was true in Chicago: Adler, *First in Violence*, 173.

57. Rudolph J. Vecoli, *"Contadini* in Chicago: A Critique of *The Uprooted*," *Journal of American History* 51, no. 3 (1964): 40.

58. Mullen, *Dangerous Strangers*, 56, 78.

59. Richard White, *Railroaded: The Transcontinentals and the Making of Modern America* (New York: W. W. Norton, 2011), 293–305; Lane, *Murder in America*, 172.

60. White, *"It's Your Misfortune,"* 341; Mullen, *Dangerous Strangers*, 53.

61. The Chinese Exclusion Act of May 6, 1882, Pub. L. No. 47–126, 22 Stat. 58 (1882). The act was renewed for ten years in 1892 and made permanent in 1902. It was not repealed until World War II, when China was an ally. The Magnuson Act of December 17, 1943, Pub. L. No. 78–199, 57 Stat. 600 (1943), permitted Chinese nationals already residing in the United States to become naturalized citizens.

62. White, *"It's Your Misfortune,"* 341. Census figures show a drop in the Chinese population of California from 72,472 in 1890 to 45,753 in 1900, a decline of 36.9 percent: U.S. Department of the

Interior, Census Office, *Twelfth Census of the United States, Taken in the Year 1900, vol. 1, pt. 1* (Washington, DC: GPO, 1901), general tables, table 13.

63. Crude opium was first brought into North America by European explorers and settlers. Colonists considered it a pain reliever. Opium in alcohol extract—laudanum—was used by Benjamin Franklin to relieve the pain of kidney stones: David F. Musto, "Opium, Cocaine and Marijuana in American History," *Scientific American* 265 (1991): 40–47; John Helmer, *Drugs and Minority Oppression* (New York: Seabury Press, 1975), 18–19.

64. Helmer, *Drugs and Minority Oppression,* 27.

65. Helmer, *Drugs and Minority Oppression,* 30, 33.

66. The Narcotics Act of December 14, 1914, Pub. L. No. 63–223, 38 Stat. 785 (1914), also known as the Harrison Act, did not prohibit outright narcotics use or distribution, but rather, imposed registration and record-keeping requirements on the production and sale of opiates and cocaine. By 1914, forty-seven states had adopted some form of legislation regulating opium or cocaine distribution: Gerald T. McLaughlin, "Cocaine: The History and Regulation of a Dangerous Drug," *Cornell Law Review* 58 (1973): 566.

67. Brian Paciotti, "Homicide in Seattle's Chinatown, 1900–1940: Evaluating the Influence of Social Organizations," *Homicide Studies* 9, no. 232 (2005).

68. McKanna, *Race and Homicide,* 37.

69. Paciotti, "Homicide," 231–32.

70. McKanna, *Race and Homicide,* 33, 41; Mullen, *Dangerous Strangers,* 65, 74.

71. Mullen, *Dangerous Strangers,* 68, 70.

72. Page Act of March 3, 1875, Pub. L. No. 43–141, 18 Stat. 477 (1875). Between 1876 and 1882, when the Exclusion Act curtailed Chinese migration generally, the number of Chinese women entering the United States declined 68 percent as compared with the previous seven-year period: George Anthony Peffer, "Forbidden Families: Emigration Experiences of Chinese Women under the Page Law, 1875–1882," *Journal of American Ethnic History* 6, no. 1 (1986): 29.

73. A 2009 sample of felony defendants in large urban counties yielded a 66 percent conviction rate within one year of having been charged: Bureau of Justice Statistics, "Felony Defendants," 22.

74. McKanna, *Race and Homicide,* 39, 49, 93.

75. Mullen, *Dangerous Strangers,* 72–74.

76. McKanna found that of a sample of California prisoners convicted of murder or manslaughter, 46 percent of the Chinese got life sentences, but only 27 percent of the American Indians, 19 percent of the Hispanics and 26 percent of the whites. He found this anomalous since, with the help of the Six Companies, Chinese defendants had lawyers more often than other impoverished accused: McKanna, *Race and Homicide,* 97, 98.

77. McKanna, *Race and Homicide,* 74.

78. An 1863 California law said: "No Indian peoples or person having one half or more Indian peoples blood, or Mongolian or Chinese, shall be permitted to give evidence in favor of, or against, any white man." The California Supreme Court held, astonishingly, that this law did not violate the equal protection of the laws clause of the Fourteenth Amendment. *People v. Brady,* 40 Cal. 198 (1870).

79. Robert M. Utley, *The Indian Frontier of the American West 1846–1890* (Albuquerque: University of New Mexico Press, 1984), 4.

80. Utley, *The Indian Frontier*, 4.

81. Utley, *The Indian Frontier*, 11.

82. Utley, *The Indian Frontier*, 169–70.

83. Utley, *The Indian Frontier*, 229.

84. Utley, *The Indian Frontier*, 164.

85. Utley, *The Indian Frontier*, 184, 193, 201.

86. Utley, *The Indian Frontier*, 251.

87. For numerous fascinating examples of this Messiah phenomenon throughout history, see Norman Cohn, *The Pursuit of the Millennium* (New York: Oxford University Press, 1970).

88. Utley, *The Indian Frontier*, 254–57.

89. Utley, *The Indian Frontier*, 210.

90. Utley, *The Indian Frontier*, 213–15; Johnson, *History of the American People*, 522.

91. Farming "demeaned Sioux manhood": Utley, *The Indian Frontier*, 239.

92. White, *"It's Your Misfortune,"* 115.

93. *Elk v. Wilkins*, 112 U.S. 94 (1884), held that, the Fourteenth Amendment notwithstanding, American Indians were not citizens unless made so by Congress.

94. U.S. Constitution, art. 1, sec. 8, gives Congress power "[t]o regulate Commerce with foreign Nations, and among the several States, and with the Indian Tribes."

95. *Cherokee Nation v. State of Georgia*, 30 U.S. 1, 13 (1831).

96. *Worcester v. State of Georgia*, 31 U.S. 515 (1832).

97. Indian Citizenship Act of June 2, 1924, Pub. L. No. 68–125, 43 Stat. 253 (1924).

98. Utley, *The Indian Frontier*, 219–20.

99. *Ex Parte Crow Dog*, 109 U.S. 556 (1883).

100. Indian Major Crimes Act, 23 Stat. 385 (1885).

101. Kevin K. Washburn, "American Indians, Crime, and the Law," *Michigan Law Review* 104 (2006): 709–77.

102. Utley, *The Indian Frontier*, 59.

103. Utley, *The Indian Frontier*, 263.

104. Glenn Shirley, *West of Hell's Fringe: Crime, Criminals, and the Federal Peace Officer in Oklahoma Territory, 1889–1907* (Norman: University of Oklahoma Press, 1978), 4, 7, 9, 29.

105. The Curtis Act, 55 Pub. L. No. 517, 30 Stat. 495 (1898), abolished all tribal courts in Indian Territory and transferred all civil and criminal cases to the federal courts operating in the Oklahoma Territory. Utley, *Indian Frontier*, 265–66.

106. Shirley, *West of Hell's Fringe*, 420.

107. Shirley, *West of Hell's Fringe*, v.

108. Shirley, *West of Hell's Fringe*, 33.

109. Shirley, *West of Hell's Fringe*, 132.

110. Shirley, *West of Hell's Fringe*, 132, 242.

111. Shirley, *West of Hell's Fringe*, v.

112. Jerrold E. Levy and Stephen J. Kunitz, "Indian Reservations, Anomie, and Social Pathologies," *Southwestern Journal of Anthropology* 27, no. 2 (1971): 101.

113. McKanna, *Homicide, Race, and Justice*, 41. Homicide indictment rates also tumbled. In the 1880s, the white rate was 44 per 100,000, and the Apache rate was 51. In the next decade, the Apache rate remained high (49), while the white rate dropped to 29. By the twentieth century, Apache rates plummeted by 55 percent, essentially on a par with white rates (152). Contemporary black homicide rates are from Bureau of Justice Statistics, *Homicide Trends*.

114. Levy and Kunitz, "Indian Reservations," 101.

115. David Lester, *Crime and the Native American* (Springfield, IL: Charles C. Thomas, 1999), 26. Presumably the author meant 2,151 arrests per 100,000, the equivalent of 21.51 per 1,000. See also Jeffrey Ian Ross, ed., *American Indians at Risk* (Santa Barbara: Greenwood Press, 2014), 1:65–66.

116. McKanna, *Race and Homicide*, 14.

117. Bureau of Justice Statistics, "Homicide Trends."

118. McKanna, *Race and Homicide*, 74. Roth reports much higher homicide victimization rates for American Indians than for whites, e.g., 70 versus 11 per 100,000, respectively, 1881–1900. But 63 percent of the Native victims were killed by nonindigenous or unknown perpetrators, whereas only 20 percent of the whites were slain by nonwhites or unknowns. Thus, the Native victimization rate may not be a good indicator of Native offending. Roth, *American Homicide, Supplemental Volume*, AH tables 33, 34, 2010, https://cjrc.osu.edu/research/interdisciplinary/hvd/ahsv. Roth contended that in California in the 1880s and 1890s, "Native Americans continued to suffer catastrophic rates of intraracial and interracial violence": Roth, *American Homicide*, 408.

119. McKanna, *Race and Homicide*, 29, 30, 31, 74. There are conflicting data on American Indian conviction rates. In San Bernardino County, California, for 1870–1900, Vanessa Gunther found only a 50 percent conviction rate for violent felony accusations against indigenous peoples. However, when the victims were white, conviction was "almost guaranteed": Vanessa Gunther, "Indians and the Criminal Justice System in San Bernardino and San Diego Counties, 1850–1900," *Journal of the West* 39, no. 4 (2000): 32.

120. McKanna, *Race and Homicide*, 19–22.

121. Utley, *The Indian Frontier*, 17; see Peter C. Mancall, *Deadly Medicine: Indians and Alcohol in Early America* (Ithaca, NY: Cornell University Press, 1995).

122. McKanna, *Race and Homicide*, 21.

123. Gunther, "Indians and the Criminal Justice System," 32.

124. Levy and Kunitz, "Indian Reservations," 109.

125. Lester, *Crime and the Native American*, 28.

126. Manuel G. Gonzales, *Mexicanos: A History of Mexicans in the United States* (Bloomington: Indiana University Press, 1999), 32–33, 38–40, 47.

127. McKanna, *Race and Homicide*, 53.

128. Mullen, *Dangerous Strangers*, 35, 37.

129. White, *"It's Your Misfortune,"* 335. The murders occurred between August 1850 and October 1851.

130. Mullen, *Dangerous Strangers*, 39.

131. T. R. Fehrenbach, *Lone Star: A History of Texas and the Texans* (Cambridge, MA: Da Capo Press, 1968, 2000), 508, 510, 511.

132. Fehrenbach, *Lone Star,* 511–21.

133. Gonzales, *Mexicanos,* 109; Brown, "Violence," 418; White, *"It's Your Misfortune,"* 335; John Boessenecker, "California Bandidos: Social Bandits or Sociopaths?" *Southern California Quarterly* 80, no. 4 (1998): 419–34.

134. McKanna, *Race and Homicide,* 72.

135. Gonzales, *Mexicanos,* 108.

136. Richard Nostrand, "The Hispano Homeland in 1900," *Annals of the Association of American Geographers* 70, no. 3 (1980): 392–93. "Hispanics" encompasses all people of Spanish descent, including those who came from Mexico or other countries in Central or South America. "Hispanos" refers to the residents of the American Southwest who descended from settlers at the time of the Mexican occupation, or even earlier.

137. Nostrand, "Hispano Homeland," 382–83.

138. Robert W. Larson, "The White Caps of New Mexico: A Study of Ethnic Militancy in the Southwest," *Pacific Historical Review* 44, no. 2 (1975): 171–85.

139. Donna Crail-Rugotzke, "A Matter of Guilt: The Treatment of Hispanic Inmates by New Mexico Courts and the New Mexico Territorial Prison, 1890–1912," *New Mexico Historical Review* 74 (1999): 300–301.

140. Crail-Rugotzke said that from 1900 to 1910, Mexican immigrants made up 5.4–6.4 percent of the New Mexico population (300, 303).

141. Laura E. Gómez, "Race, Colonialism, and Criminal Law: Mexicans and the American Criminal Justice System in Territorial New Mexico," *Law & Society Review* 34, no. 4 (2000): 1138.

142. Crail-Rugotzke, "Matter of Guilt," 307.

143. The Edmunds-Tucker Act of March 3, 1887, Pub. L. No. 49-397, 24 Stat. 635 (1887), strengthened the Edmunds Anti-Polygamy Act of March 22, 1882, Pub. L. No. 47-47, 22 Stat. 30b (1882).

144. Crail-Rugotzke, "Matter of Guilt," 302.

145. Gómez, "Race, Colonialism," 1130, 1131n2. As of 1890, New Mexico had nineteen counties. Hispanos were sheriffs in eight of those counties, and half-hispanos married to hispana women were sheriffs in two other counties. Nostrand, "Hispano Homeland," 393n20.

146. Gómez, "Race, Colonialism," 1136, 1137, 1149, 1171.

147. Gómez, "Race, Colonialism," 1138, 1150.

148. Hietter, "Surprising Amount of Justice," 194, 200, 202, 204, 211, 214.

149. Samuel P. Huntington, *Political Order in Changing Societies* (New Haven, CT: Yale University Press, 1968), 5.

150. Huntington defined a political organization as "an arrangement for maintaining order, resolving disputes [and] selecting authoritative leaders": Huntington, *Political Order,* 8. See also Roth, *American Homicide,* 378.

151. Brown, "Western Violence," 5–20.

152. Frederick Jackson Turner, *The Frontier in American History* (New York: Henry Holt, 1920), 2–3, 37.

153. Richard Slotkin, *Gunfighter Nation: The Myth of the Frontier in Twentieth-Century America* (New York: Atheneum, 1992), 13.

### CHAPTER SIX

1. Bureau of the Census, *Historical Statistics*, Series A 57–72, Series A 119–134.

2. U.S. Census Bureau, *Historical Census Statistics* (Working Paper No. 76), table 33.

3. Jacob Riis, who had exposed the deplorable conditions in the tenements of New York City, reported in 1890 that more than nine thousand homeless young men lodged nightly in the Bowery district and that the police put up 147,634 per year in crude police station barracks: Jacob A. Riis, *How the Other Half Lives: Studies among the Tenements of New York* (New York: Charles Scribner's Sons, 1890), 89. In 1896, Theodore Roosevelt, then Commissioner of Police in New York, abolished the practice of lodging the homeless. Lane, *Murder in America,* 212.

4. Luc Sante, *Low Life: Lures and Snares of Old New York* (New York: Farrar, Straus, & Giroux, 1991), 178. Youth gangs were "the basic unit of social life among young males in New York in the nineteenth century" (197).

5. According to Eric A. Johnson, "the Germans who have contributed most significantly to the long-standing myth that cities promote crime and disorder are among the founding fathers of modern sociology: Georg Simmel, Ferdinand Toennies, and Max Weber. Their works stand alongside those of their French contemporary Emile Durkheim as classical bulwarks protecting the anti-urban mythos": Eric A. Johnson, "Cities Don't Cause Crime: Urban-Rural Differences in Late Nineteenth- and Early Twentieth-Century German Criminality," *Social Science History* 16, no. 1 (1992): 139–40.

6. Edwin G. Burrows and Mike Wallace, *Gotham: A History of New York City to 1898* (New York: Oxford University Press, 1999), 1111.

7. Census Office, *Eleventh Census: 1890, Part I* (Washington, DC: GPO, 1895), clxii. "Foreign extraction" here refers to persons, including those born abroad, with one or both foreign-born parents. The percentage of the population with foreign parents was nearly as high for other big cities, e.g., Chicago, 78 percent; San Francisco, 78; Cleveland, 75; and Brooklyn, 71: Census Office, Eleventh Census., Part I.

8. New Yorkers born in Germany numbered 210,723, 13.9 percent of the city's population. There were 425,876 New Yorkers with one or both parents born in Germany: Census Office, Eleventh Census, Part I, table 34, clxix; Sante, *Low Life*, 15.

9. Stephan Thernstrom, ed., *Harvard Encyclopedia of American Ethnic Groups* (Cambridge, MA: Harvard University Press, 1980), 413; Donald L. Miller, *City of the Century: The Epic of Chicago and the Making of America* (New York: Simon & Schuster, 1996), 469.

10. Frederick M. Binder and David M. Reimers, *All the Nations under Heaven* (New York: Columbia University Press, 1995), 97.

11. Richard O'Connor, *Hell's Kitchen: The Roaring Days of New York's Wild West Side* (New York: J. B. Lippincott, 1958), 135.

12. Eric H. Monkkonen, *Murder in New York City* (Berkeley: University of California Press, 2001), 138.

13. Census Office, *Eleventh Census: 1890, Part I* (Washington, DC: GPO, 1895), clxix.

14. Nathan Glazer and Daniel Patrick Moynihan, *Beyond the Melting Pot; The Negroes, Puerto Ricans, Jews, Italians, and Irish of New York City* (Cambridge, MA: MIT Press, 1963), 219.

15. Paul A. Gilje, *The Road to Mobocracy: Popular Disorder in New York City, 1763–1834* (Chapel Hill: University of North Carolina Press, 1987), 128.

16. Glazer and Moynihan, *Beyond the Melting Pot*, 219. This immigration wave was augmented by a wavelet in the late 1870s, also due to agricultural depression in Ireland: Burrows and Wallace, *Gotham*, 1112.

17. Lane, *Murder in America*, 183.

18. Monkkonen, *Murder in New York City*, 21. The average homicide rate for New York City, 1826–35, was 3.1; for 1850–59 it was 7.5. In 1863, the rate was 16.69; in 1864, 15.34. Monkkonen's dataset is available at Monkkonen, "Homicides in New York City," https://doi.org/10.3886/ICPSR03226.v1.

19. Eric H. Monkkonen, "Diverging Homicide Rates: England and the United States, 1850–1875," in *Violence in America, Volume 1*, 90–91. There were 290 homicide victims for whom identity was known; of these, 242 were foreign-born, 28 were native-born whites. Of 242 killers, identity known, 196 were foreign, 24 native white. Monkkonen's lower bounds estimates were that 39 percent of the victims and 31 percent of the killers were foreign-born.

20. Monkkonen, *Murder in New York City*, 76, 138.

21. Schecter considers 105, the official toll, too low, deeming the "sober contemporary estimate" of five hundred a suitable upper limit: Barnet Schecter, *The Devil's Own Work: The Civil War Draft Riots and the Fight to Reconstruct America* (New York: Walker, 2005), 252.

22. Herbert Asbury, *The Gangs of New York: An Informal History of the Underworld* (New York: Thunder's Mouth Press, 1927, 2001), 112.

23. Michael A. Gordon, *The Orange Riots: Irish Political Violence in New York City, 1870 and 1871* (Ithaca, NY: Cornell University Press, 1993), 2.

24. Lane, *Roots of Violence*, 141. By 1888–1901, the citywide rate was 2.1 per 100,000; for the Irish it was 1.8.

25. Sante, *Low Life*, 18, 197.

26. Sante, *Low Life*, 214.

27. Sante, *Low Life*, 222.

28. O'Connor, *Hell's Kitchen*, 55.

29. O'Connor, *Hell's Kitchen*, 171, 182.

30. O'Connor, *Hell's Kitchen*, 194.

31. Sante, *Low Life*, 26, 33, 39; H. W. Brands, *The Reckless Decade: America in the 1890s* (New York: St. Martin's Press, 1995), 98–99; Burrows and Wallace, *Gotham*, 1117.

32. Brands, *Reckless Decade*, 99; Robert H. Bremner, *From the Depths: The Discovery of Poverty in the United States* (New Brunswick, NJ: Transaction Publishers, 1956, 1992), 82.

33. Riis, *How the Other Half Lives*, 26, 33–34.

34. Riis, *How the Other Half Lives*, 88–89. Others put the number lodged at only 45,000 per year. See Moses King, *King's Handbook of New York City* (Boston: Moses King, 1892), 486.

35. Monkkonen, *Police in Urban America*, 108–9, 127.

36. Riis, *How the Other Half Lives*, 185.

37. Robert Hunter, *Poverty* (New York: Macmillan, 1907), 27, 44.

38. Robert Coit Chapin, *The Standard of Living Among Workingmen's Families in New York City* (Philadelphia, Wm. F. Fell, 1909), 241, 245. The investigators, who made no attempt to randomize in the contemporary social science sense, interviewed 391 families with an average of three children and residing in Manhattan, Brooklyn, and the Bronx.

39. The Census Bureau established $19,749 as the poverty threshold for a family of four in 2017, and found that 12.3 percent of all U.S. families fell below this threshold. The 2017 threshold for individuals (under age 65) was $12,752; 11.2 percent of individuals ages 18 to 64 were below this threshold in 2017: U.S. Census Bureau, *Income and Poverty in the United States: 2017,* by Kayla Fontenot, Jessica Semega, and Melissa Kollar, Current Population Reports, P60–263 (Washington, DC: GPO, 2018), 47, tables B-1, B-2.

40. Hunter, *Poverty,* 19, 24, 27.

41. Paul Boyer, *Urban Masses and Moral Order in America, 1820–1920* (Cambridge, MA: Harvard University Press, 1978), 126; Burrows and Wallace, *Gotham,* 1186. If the city's population was 1,515,301, as the 1890 Census indicated, the percentage of unemployed would come to 4.6: U.S. Census Bureau, *Historical Census Statistics* (Working Paper No. 76), table 33. This seems suspiciously low during a year when the national rate was 12.33 percent. See Christina Romer, "Spurious Volatility in Historical Unemployment Data," *Journal of Political Economy* 94, no. 1 (1986): 31.

42. Hunter, *Poverty,* 28–29.

43. Romer, "Spurious Volatility," 31. From December 2007 to June 2009, the United States underwent a recession with unemployment rates comparable to the 1890s. For 2008–12, the average unemployment rate was 8.3 percent: U.S. Department of Labor, Bureau of Labor Statistics, "Labor Force Statistics from the Current Population Survey," http://data.bls.gov/timeseries/LNU04000000?years_option=all_years&periods_option=specific_periods&periods=Annual+Data.

44. Hunter, *Poverty,* 344. The contemporary death rate from all unintentional injuries is 40.6 per 100,000: U.S. Department of Health and Human Services, Centers for Disease Control and Prevention, National Vital Statistics Reports, "Deaths: Final Data for 2006," vol. 57, no. 14, April 17, 2009, tables 18, 89, http://www.cdc.gov/nchs/data/nvsr/nvsr57/nvsr57_14.pdf.

45. Binder and Reimers, *All the Nations Under Heaven,* 94, 99, 140; Burrows and Wallace, *Gotham,* 1116, 1122. While police and firefighters were nearly all Irish, Italian immigrants did manage to get city jobs with the Sanitation Department.

46. David R. Johnson, *American Law Enforcement: A History* (St. Louis: Forum Press, 1981), 63.

47. James Lardner and Thomas Reppetto, *NYPD: A City and Its Police* (New York: Henry Holt, 2000), 67.

48. Sante, *Low Life,* 236.

49. O'Connor, *Hell's Kitchen,* 97.

50. Kenneth T. Jackson, ed., *The Encyclopedia of New York City* (New Haven, CT: Yale University Press, 1991) 1149–50, 1237; Johnson, *American Law Enforcement,* 59, 67.

51. William L. Riordon, *Plunkitt of Tammany Hall* (Digireads.com Publishing, 2010), 9–10.

52. Edward Robb Ellis, *The Epic of New York City* (New York: Kodansha International, 1997), 433 (quoting from the Lexow Committee Report).

53. King, *King's Handbook,* 484; Sante, *Low Life,* 241, 249.

54. Johnson, *American Law Enforcement*, 60.

55. King, *King's Handbook*, 235, 453–54, 456, 460; Sante, *Low Life*, 245–46.

56. Sante, *Low Life*, 242, 247–48; Johnson, *American Law Enforcement*, 60.

57. Ellis, *Epic of New York City*, 430–31; Parkhurst's remark is from Boyer, *Urban Masses*, 165.

58. Ellis, *Epic of New York City*, 434.

59. Ellis, *Epic of New York City*, 436–39.

60. Sante, *Low Life*, 287–88; Johnson, *American Law Enforcement*, 66.

61. Boyer, *Urban Masses*, 146, 150, 155, 165.

62. Sante, *Low Life*, 121; Boyer, *Urban Masses*, 193.

63. Monkkonen, *Murder in New York City*, 21.

64. *Annual Report of the Board of City Magistrates of the City of New York (First Division), For the Year Ending December 31, 1901* (New York: J. W. Pratt, 1902), 25, 27. The magistrates' report presents data on arraignments, which, as they are the initial court appearance for an arrested person, may be taken as a proxy for arrest. Rates were calculated by using federal census data for 1900 for the Manhattan and Bronx population and Monkkonen's intercensal population estimate for 1892.

65. *Annual Report of the Board of City Magistrates*, 3, 20, 36.

66. Monkkonen, "Homicides in New York City," https://doi.org/10.3886/ICPSR03226.v1.

67. Adler, *First in Violence*, 279.

68. The homicide rate is based on Adler's data for 1890–99. Adler took his book title from Lincoln Steffens, "Chicago: Half Free and Fighting On," *McClure's Magazine* 21, no. 6 (1903): 563.

69. U.S. Census Bureau, *Historical Census Statistics* (Working Paper No. 76), table 14. The exact figure for 1900 is 1,698,575.

70. Census Office, *Eleventh Census: 1890, Part I* (Washington, DC: GPO, 1895), clxii. That is, 856,754 Chicagoans had one or both parents born abroad. In 1900, 587,112 Chicagoans were born in a foreign country, 34.56 percent of the city's population: U.S. Census Office, *Twelfth Census, 1900, Population*, pt. 1, table 35, 796.

71. Census Office, *Eleventh Census: 1890, Report on Population 1890*, clxix.

72. Drake and Cayton, *Black Metropolis*, 47. In 1890, blacks numbered around 15,000, 1.3 percent of the population. This figure doubled by 1900, but blacks were still only 1.9 percent of Chicago (Drake and Cayton, *Black Metropolis*, 8, 9). Russians numbered 11,294; Italians, 8,219: Census Office, *Eleventh Census: 1890, Report on Population 1890*, clxix.

73. Clifford R. Shaw and Henry D. McKay, *Juvenile Delinquency and Urban Areas* (Chicago: University of Chicago Press, 1942, 1969), 156. This described the 1898 population with foreign-born fathers in eight inner-city areas as designated by Shaw and McKay.

74. Adler, *First in Violence*, 170.

75. Adler, *First in Violence*, 127, 133.

76. Adler, *First in Violence*, 168. The Scandinavian rates were for 1910 only, but there is nothing to indicate that Scandinavian rates were different in other years in this time period.

77. Adler, *First in Violence*, 60n41.

78. Miller, *City of the Century*, 275.

79. Miller, *City of the Century*, 197, 199.

80. Miller, *City of the Century,* 218, 219, 424, 427, 457.

81. Data on Chicago's homicide rates were kindly provided by Jeffrey S. Adler in email communication on file with the author. Professor Adler provided two sets of data, "crude homicide rates" and "adjusted rates," a distinction designed to differentiate criminal from noncriminal homicides. Adjusted rates exclude automobile accidents, abortion-related deaths, infanticides, and forms of homicide not treated as crimes throughout the time period of Adler's study. The adjusted rates are used in this chapter as they better reflect murders. The average adjusted homicide rate for Chicago, 1875–1879, was 3.11; for 1890–1899, it was 5.55.

82. Adler, *First in Violence,* 7.

83. Adler, *First in Violence,* 20; Shaw and McKay, *Juvenile Delinquency,* 156.

84. Adler, *First in Violence,* 15, 16, 17, 39. My enumeration of the different types of killings was based on an email communication from Professor Adler on file with the author.

85. Adler, *First in Violence,* 23; Census Office, *Eleventh Census: 1890,* general tables, table 19, and *Report on Vital and Social Statistics in the United States, Part II—Vital Statistics. Cities of 100,000 Population and Upward,* 14.

86. Adler, *First in Violence,* 7, 17, 23, 24.

87. Adler, *First in Violence,* 241.

88. Adler, *First in Violence,* 242; "Weltering in Blood," *Chicago Tribune,* March 8, 1875, 1.

89. Eric H. Monkkonen, "Homicide in Los Angeles, 1827–2002," *Journal of Interdisciplinary History* 36, no. 2 (2005): 172; Robert M. Fogelson, *The Fragmented Metropolis: Los Angeles, 1850–1930* (Cambridge, MA: Harvard University Press, 1967), 21; John Boessenecker, *Gold Dust and Gunsmoke: Tales of Gold Rush Outlaws, Gunfighters, Lawmen, and Vigilantes* (New York: John Wiley & Sons, 1999), 323. Boessenecker reported ninety homicides in Los Angeles County from 1855 to 1859.

90. Oscar Osburn Winther, "The Rise of Metropolitan Los Angeles, 1870–1900," *Huntington Library Quarterly* 10, no. 4 (1947): 399.

91. Fogelson, *Fragmented Metropolis,* 67, 72; Census Office, *Eleventh Census: 1890, pt. 1,* clxii; U.S. Census Office, *Twelfth Census, 1900, Population, pt. 1,* tables 34, 35, 57.

92. U.S. Census Office, *Twelfth Census,* tables 19, 20.

93. Eric Monkkonen, "Homicide in Los Angeles, 1830–2003," Historical Violence Database, Criminal Justice Research Center, Ohio State University, 2003, http://cjrc.osu.edu/researchprojects /hvd/usa/la/; Monkkonen, "Homicides in New York City," https://doi.org/10.3886/ICPSR03226.v1; Chicago data provided by Jeffrey S. Adler, email communication on file with the author; Roth, *American Homicide,* 355, 403.

94. David T. Courtwright, *Violent Land: Single Men and Social Disorder from the Frontier to the Inner City* (Cambridge, MA: Harvard University Press, 1996), 150.

95. Fogelson, *Fragmented Metropolis,* 64, 82.

96. Monkkonen, "Homicide in Los Angeles, 1830–2003"; Adler, *First in Violence,* 33. The 58 percent figure is for murders that did not occur during brawls; for brawl-murders, guns were used only 42 percent of the time, brawlers grabbing whatever was at hand to do the job (Adler, *First in Violence,* 33).

97. McKanna, *Race and Homicide.* McKanna found 1,317 homicides over the half-century in the seven counties that he studied; he was able to identify the race/ethnicity of the perpetrator in 1,175 of

the incidents. The number killed by each group was: American Indians, 106; Chinese, 103 (indicted for murder); Hispanics, 175; and whites, 791. The inordinately high number of white killings may reflect a high murder rate or the predominance of whites in the population or both (McKanna, *Race and Homicide*, 7, 14, 49, 53, 74).

98. Mullen, *Dangerous Strangers*, 30, 78; Fogelson, *Fragmented Metropolis*, 82.

99. Mullen, *Dangerous Strangers*, 14; William Issel and Robert W. Cherny, *San Francisco, 1865–1932: Politics, Power, and Urban Development* (Berkeley: University of California Press, 1986), 12, 13; U.S. Census Bureau, *Historical Census Statistics* (Working Paper No. 76), table 5.

100. Mullen, *Dangerous Strangers*, 51, 52, 55, 56.

101. Lane, *Murder in America*, 183; Monkkonen, *Murder in New York City*, 138.

102. O'Donnell found high rates of homicide in Ireland during the famine years, 1845–50, as compared to other periods in Ireland's history. Homicide rates for 1841–50 were 3.87 per 100,000: Ian O'Donnell, "Lethal Violence in Ireland, 1841 to 2003," *British Journal of Criminology* 45 (2005): 676, 677. This is consistent with scholarship that points to an Irish affinity for brawling: Carolyn A. Conley, *Melancholy Accidents: The Meaning of Violence in Post-Famine Ireland* (Lanham, MD: Lexington Books, 1999), 36, 215. But other scholars argue that Ireland was not especially violent in this period, pointing to the unusually high number of baby killings—44 percent of all homicides in the 1840s—which, they contend, should be seen as different from ordinary male-perpetrated violence: Richard McMahon, "'A violent society'? Homicide Rates in Ireland, 1831–1850," *Irish Economic and Social History* 36, no. 1 (2009): 13. The availability of guns may be significant in explaining the increased Irish violence in the United States. Firearms seldom were used to kill in Ireland, but account for 55 percent of the Irish homicides in San Francisco over the second half of the nineteenth century: Mullen, *Dangerous Strangers*, 59.

103. Between 1851 and 1880, the ratio of male-to-female Irish immigrants was 1.14 to 1; from 1880 to 1910 the ratio was .98 to 1: Roger Daniels, *Coming to America: A History of Immigration and Ethnicity in American Life* (New York: HarperCollins, 2002), 141. For the city as a whole, the male/female ratio dropped from 1.31:1 in 1890, to 1.17:1 in 1900: Fogelson, *Fragmented Metropolis*, 82.

104. Mullen, *Dangerous Strangers*, 66, 72, 76, 78. In the 1890s, the Chinese male homicide rate was 30.8, 2.41 times the white male rate of 12.8: Mullen, *Dangerous Strangers*, 66; Issel and Cherny, *San Francisco*, 71. Roth said that Chinese intraracial murder rates in 1880s/1890s San Francisco were 25 per 100,000, while killings of Chinese by non-Chinese and unknowns "fell to low levels": Roth, *American Homicide*, 408.

105. Federal Bureau of Investigation, *Crime in the United States, 1990*, table 6, https://ucr.fbi.gov/crime-in-the-u.s.; Mullen, *Dangerous Strangers*, 47.

106. Philip L. Fradkin, *The Great Earthquake and Firestorms of 1906: How San Francisco Nearly Destroyed Itself* (Berkeley: University of California Press, 2005), 68, 80, 189–90; Mullen, *Dangerous Strangers*, 87.

## CHAPTER SEVEN

1. Emile Durkheim, *Suicide: A Study in Sociology* (Glencoe, IL: Free Press, 1897, 1951), 353.

2. Ted Robert Gurr, "Historical Trends," in *Violence in America, Volume 1*, 35, 37.

3. Boston's homicide rates may have risen from the 1880s to the 1890s, but it is difficult to tell without a full decadal average for the 1880s.

4. Gurr, "Historical Trends," in *Violence in America, Volume 1,* 31, 42; Eric A. Johnson, *Urbanization and Crime: Germany, 1871–1914* (Cambridge: Cambridge University Press, 1995), 129. A meta-analysis of violent crime in Europe between 1875 and 1899 found the following national rates per 100,000: England, 1.3; Netherlands and Belgium, 1.5; Scandinavia, 0.9; Germany and Switzerland, 2.2; and Italy, 5.5: Manuel Eisner, "Long-Term Historical Trends in Violent Crime," *Crime & Justice* 30 (2003): 99.

5. Gurr, "Historical Trends," in *Violence in America, Volume 1,* 34.

6. Pieter Spierenburg, "Democracy Came Too Early: A Tentative Explanation for the Problem of American Homicide," *American Historical Review* 111 (2006): 108 (italics removed); see also, Pieter Spierenburg, *A History of Murder: Personal Violence in Europe from the Middle Ages to the Present* (Cambridge: Polity Books, 2008).

7. Spierenburg, "Democracy Came Too Early," 113.

8. Spierenburg, "Democracy Came Too Early," 112. By the mid-1880s, Lane observed, "police in Philadelphia and elsewhere had in effect established a practical monopoly on the use of collective force": Lane, *Violent Death,* 12.

9. A recent Supreme Court case, *District of Columbia v. Heller,* 554 U.S. 570 (2008), held, 5–4, that the Second Amendment created an "individual right to bear arms."

10. Roth offered four correlations with homicide rates: "1. The belief that government is stable and that its legal and judicial institutions are unbiased and will redress wrongs and protect lives and property. 2. A feeling of trust in government and the officials who run it, and a belief in their legitimacy. 3. Patriotism, empathy, and fellow feeling arising from racial, religious, or political solidarity. 4. The belief that the social hierarchy is legitimate, that one's position in society is or can be satisfactory and that one can command the respect of others without resorting to violence." Roth, *American Homicide,* 18.

11. Gary LaFree, *Losing Legitimacy: Street Crime and the Decline of Social Institutions in America* (Boulder, CO: Westview Press, 1998), 111–12.

12. Sidney Verba, Kay Lehman Schlozman, and Henry E. Brady, *Voice and Equality: Civic Voluntarism in American Politics* (Cambridge, MA: Harvard University Press, 1995), 349.

13. Monkkonen, *Murder in New York City,* 115–16. Monkkonen worried that "the true figure could have been huge, masked by the unreported relationships" (115); Roger Lane, *Violent Death in the City: Suicide, Accident, and Murder in Nineteenth-Century Philadelphia* (Cambridge, MA: Harvard University Press, 1979, 83. Contemporary statistics are from Bureau of Justice Statistics, "Homicide Trends." This latter work indicates that in 35 percent of the incidents the relationship was unknown. Counting the unknown cases, stranger killings were reduced to 14 percent of the total; family killings, 15 percent; murders by acquaintances, 32 percent.

14. Lane, *Roots of Violence,* 14, 103.

15. Lane, *Roots of Violence,* 139.

16. Adler, *First in Violence,* 241, 243, 247–48.

17. Bureau of Justice Statistics, "Homicide Trends," http://bjs.ojp.usdoj.gov/content/homicide /tables/totalstab.cfm. Franklin E. Zimring and Gordon Hawkins, *Crime Is Not the Problem: Lethal Violence in America* (New York: Oxford University Press, 1997), 69. Zimring and Hawkins say that "the vast majority" of murders during felony involved robbery, and that "four times as many Americans are killed in robberies each year as are killed in burglary, arson, and rape combined" (68).

18. Adler, *First in Violence*, 243, 247, 248, 265.

19. Adler, *First in Violence*, 266, 268.

20. Adler, *First in Violence*, 269.

21. Adler, *First in Violence*, 244–45.

22. Sam Bass Warner, *Streetcar Suburbs: The Process of Growth in Boston, 1870–1900* (Cambridge, MA: Harvard University Press, 1962, 1978) 15–16; David Ward, *Cities and Immigrants: A Geography of Change in Nineteenth-Century America* (New York: Oxford University Press, 1971) 5, 106, 125.

23. Ward, *Cities and Immigrants*, 5, 94, 105; Warner, *Streetcar Suburbs*, 34, 58, 60.

24. Ward, *Cities and Immigrants*, 5, 134; Alan Trachtenberg, *The Incorporation of America: Culture and Society in the Guilded Age* (New York: Hill & Wang, 1982, 2007), 130. "Between 1870 and 1900," Trachtenberg reported, "the volume of advertising multiplied more than tenfold, from 50 to 542 millions of dollars per year" (136).

25. Marcus Felson and Lawrence E. Cohen, "Human Ecology and Crime: A Routine Activity Approach," *Human Ecology* 8, no. 4 (1980): 394.

## CHAPTER EIGHT

1. Bureau of the Census, *Immigrants and Their Children*, 64.

2. Robert F. Foerster, *The Italian Emigration of Our Times* (Cambridge, MA: Harvard University Press, 1919), 327. From 1910 to 1914, 1,104,833 Italians migrated to the United States and 405,723 (37 percent) departed: U.S. Department of Commerce, Bureau of Foreign and Domestic Commerce, *Statistical Abstract of the United States 1930* (Washington, DC: GPO, 1930), table 106.

3. Lloyd P. Gartner, "Jewish Migrants En Route from Europe to North America: Traditions and Realities," *Jewish History* 1, no. 2 (1986): 52, 55.

4. Foerster, *Italian Emigration*, 328; Luciano J. Iorizzo and Salvatore Mondello, *The Italian-Americans* (Youngstown, NY: Cambria Press, 2006), 76–77, 106. Many Italians migrated to Brazil and Argentina during this same time period, over 1 million to Argentina between 1896 and 1914. But the North American exodus was three times greater (Iorizzo and Mondello, *The Italian-Americans*, 62–63). Seventy-eight percent of Italian immigrants lived in cities in 1910: U.S. Department of Commerce, Bureau of the Census, *Prisoners and Juvenile Delinquents in the United States 1910* (Washington, DC: GPO, 1918), 128.

5. Glazer and Moynihan, *Beyond the Melting Pot*, 183; Foerster, *Italian Emigration*, 58, 59, 60, 64, 89, 95; Iorizzo and Mondello, *Italian-Americans*, 19, 20, 21, 56, 57, 58, 60, 62, 63. Regarding malaria, Foerster stated that it killed 21,000 Italians in 1887, declining to 3,100 in 1912: Foerster, *Italian Emigration*, 60.

6. The quoted statement, from artist and statesman Massimo d'Azeglio, actually said: "pur troppo, s'è fatta l'Italia, ma non si fanno gl'Italiani": "we have made Italy, but unfortunately we are not mak-

ing Italians": Mark I. Choate, *Emigrant Nation: The Making of Italy Abroad* (Cambridge, MA: Harvard University Press, 2008), 18, 101n1. Iorizzo and Mondello, *Italian-Americans*, 102, 105, 106, 111.

7. Luigi Barzini, *The Italians* (New York: Atheneum, 1964), 193, 194; Iorizzo and Mondello, *Italian-Americans*, 207.

8. Barzini, *The Italians*, 253–54.

9. Humbert S. Nelli, *The Business of Crime: Italians and Syndicate Crime in the United States* (New York: Oxford University Press, 1976), xii. My analysis was drawn from Nelli's discussion, but Nelli used the term "mafia" in somewhat different senses.

10. Barzini, *The Italians*, 59–260; Iorizzo and Mondello, *Italian-Americans*, 23.

11. Barzini, *The Italians*, 260–63.

12. Iorizzo and Mondello, *Italian-Americans*, 23.

13. Nelli, *Business of Crime*, 11.

14. Jean-Claude Chesnais, *Histoire de la violence en occident de 1800 à nos jours* (Paris: Editions Robert Laffont, 1981), 65: "D'acte d'honneur, de devoir sacré à l'égard de la famille ou du clan dans la civilisation agraire, la vengeance devient meurtre, crime contre la société, dans la civilisation industrielle."

15. Chesnais, *Histoire de la violence*, 64. As these are conviction rates, it is expected that they significantly undercount actual homicides.

16. Eisner, "Long-Term Historical Trends," 99. Eisner presented the following rates, based on "national statistics," for 1875–99: England, 1.3; Netherlands and Belgium, 1.5; Scandinavia, 0.9; Germany and Switzerland, 2.2; Italy, 5.5 (99).

17. Chesnais, *Histoire de la Violence*, 66. The rates are for homicide cases referred to the public prosecutor between 1884 and 1886.

18. Barzini, *The Italians*, 272–73.

19. Iorizzo and Mondello, *Italian-Americans*, 164, 166; Glazer and Moynihan, *Beyond the Melting Pot*, 185, 190.

20. Glazer and Moynihan, *Beyond the Melting Pot*, 190, 199, 206; John H. Mariano, *The Second Generation of Italians in New York City* (Boston: Christopher Publishing House, 1921), 32.

21. Bureau of the Census, *Prisoners and Juvenile Delinquents 1904*, table 23. Major offenses were defined as "all crimes that are universally held to be of a grave nature." These were said to include the most aggravated crime against chastity, federal offenses, including perjury and counterfeiting, all crimes against the person, and arson, burglary, forgery, and embezzlement (table 23, page 28).

22. Bureau of the Census, *Prisoners and Juvenile Delinquents 1904*, table 24.

23. Carolyn Moehling and Anne Morrison Piehl, "Immigration, Crime, and Incarceration in Early Twentieth-Century America," *Demography* 46, no. 4 (2009): 757, 758. The "actual" rate was not provided by the 1904 Census data. It was constructed by Moehling and Piehl using data from the 1904 prison census on commitments plus population estimates constructed from the 1910 IPUMS data set. (IPUMS, the Integrated Public Use Microdata Series, provides information about individual persons and households in nearly all the detail originally recorded by the census enumerations; see http://usa.ipums.org/usa/data.shtml.) The "predicted" commitment rates were calculated using the age distributions by country of birth constructed from the 1910 IPUMS database and applying the commitment rates by age for the foreign-born population as a whole.

24. Moehling and Piehl, "Immigration, Crime, and Incarceration," 759. Moehling and Piehl thought the Mexican data problematic because of seasonal migration and the failure to differentiate U.S.-born Mexicans and Mexican-born immigrants (758).

25. Bureau of the Census, *Prisoners and Juvenile Delinquents 1910*, table 148. It should be kept in mind that the majority of both the Austrians and the Russians undoubtedly were Jews, and that the Mexican rates may well have conflated those actually born in Mexico and persons of Mexican descent born here. The distinction between "Grave" and "Lesser" homicide was made by the Census Department, but not defined.

26. Monkkonen, "Police Departments," https://doi.org/10.3886/ICPSR07708.v2. On the other hand, Eckberg's estimated national homicide rates showed no spike. His figures for the last half of the first decade are as follows: 1905, 8.1; 1906, 8.4; 1907, 7.9; 1908, 7.9; 1909, 7.1: Eckberg, "Estimates," 13.

27. From 1970 to 1994, after which rates began to decline, the average homicide rate for New York City was 23.1, more than four times the average for the 1920s: Monkkonen, "Homicides in New York City, https://doi.org/10.3886/ICPSR03226.v1.

28. U.S. Immigration Commission, *Immigration and Crime* (Washington, DC: GPO, 1911).

29. U.S. Immigration Commission, *Immigration and Crime*, 1, 2.

30. The commission also gathered data from outside New York. For a complete description of its crime data sources, see U.S. Immigration Commission, *Immigration and Crime*, 10.

31. U.S. Immigration Commission, *Immigration and Crime*, 11. In defining public policy and chastity offenses the commission referred to the "customary classification" of the Census. Consequently, the definitions for those categories, following, were taken from Bureau of the Census, *Prisoners and Juvenile Delinquents 1904*, 20: "Gainful": blackmail, extortion, burglery, forgery, fraud, larceny, receiving stolen property, robbery; "Personal violence": abduction, kidnapping, assault, homicide, rape; "Public policy": perjury, counterfeiting, federal law violations, drunkenness, disorderly conduct, liquor law violations, vagrancy, incorrigibility, truancy; "Against chastity": adultery, bigamy, polygamy, seduction, crime against nature, incest, fornication, prostitution; "Unclassified": abandonment, abortion, arson, attempted suicide, cruelty to children, malicious mischief.

32. There were 1,769 total convictions, 34 percent of which (n = 88) were of immigrant Italians, and 5 percent of which were second-generation Italians (n = 14). Of the 26 total homicide convictions, immigrant Italians committed 11 (42 percent), second-generation Italians 1 (4 percent): U.S. Immigration Commission, *Immigration and Crime*, 68.

33. U.S. Immigration Commission, *Immigration and Crime*, 14. Regarding the "second generation issue" we note that the crime pattern from immigrants to offspring has not been consistent over the course of the twentieth century.

34. U.S. Immigration Commission, *Immigration and Crime*, 123.

35. U.S. Immigration Commission, *Immigration and Crime*, 88, 90.

36. Kate Holladay Claghorn, "Crime and Immigration (Report of Committee of the Institute)," *Journal of the American Institute of Criminal Law and Criminology* 8, no. 5 (1918): 675–93. This was a psychiatric study. The investigators classified crimes as "having their impulse in the instinct of pugnacity," "in the instinct of sex," "in an abnormal sex instinct," and "in the acquisitive instinct."

Italians committed 31 "pugnacity" offenses, but I included among their crimes of violence one child rape, two kidnappings, one arson, and one dynamiting, for a total of 36 (53 percent).

37. Iorizzo and Mondello, *Italian-Americans*, 286–87. In 1910, New York State had 472,201 Italian immigrants; Pennsylvania, 196,122; New Jersey, 115,446. After Massachusetts came Illinois with 72,163; California, 63,615; and Connecticut, 56,954 (286–87).

38. United States Immigration Commission, *Immigration and Crime*, 161, 169.

39. Roger Lane, "On the Social Meaning of Homicide Trends in America," in *Violence in America, Volume 1: The History of Crime,* ed. Ted Robert Gurr (Newbury Park, CA: Sage Publications, 1989), 71.

40. Adler, *First in Violence,* 168–70.

41. Mullen, *Dangerous Strangers,* 88, 89.

42. McKanna, *Homicide, Race, and Justice,* 83, 95, 98, 101.

43. Eliot Lord, John J. D. Trenor, and Samuel J. Barrows, *The Italian in America* (New York: B. F. Buck, 1905), 215.

44. Adler, *First in Violence,* 171, 175; "Prior to the 1920s, Italian-American crime was essentially intracommunity crime involving family feuds, extortion, petty thefts" (Iorizzo and Mondello, *Italian-Americans,* 190).

45. Francis A. J. Ianni, "The Mafia and the Web of Kinship," *Public Interest* 22 (1971): 88. See Thomas M. Pitkin and Francesco Cordasco, *The Black Hand: A Chapter in Ethnic Crime* (Totowa, NJ: Littlefield, Adams, 1977): "That the Black Hand sprang from Mafia and Camorra roots cannot be doubted" (224).

46. Humbert S. Nelli, "The Hennessy Murder and the Mafia in New Orleans," *Italian Quarterly* 19 (1975): 77–95. American media, including the *New York Times,* defended the lynching, suggesting that the accused Italians were clearly guilty and that the jury that had acquitted them had been corrupted: "The New Orleans Affair," *New York Times,* March 16, 1891, 4.

47. Thomas Reppetto, *American Mafia: A History of Its Rise to Power* (New York: Henry Holt, 2004), 28, 29, 32, 33, 46, 48; Pitkin and Cordasco, *Black Hand,* 119.

48. U.S. Department of Commerce, Bureau of the Census, *Thirteenth Census of the United States Taken in the Year 1910, vol. 1, Population 1910* (Washington, DC: GPO, 1913), table 20.

49. Glazer and Moynihan, *Beyond the Melting Pot,* 185n7. In 1910, males born in Italy, ages 20–29, were 31 percent of the Italian immigrant population. By 1930, they were 16 percent: U.S. Department of Commerce, Bureau of the Census, *Fifteenth Census of the United States: 1930, Population vol. 2* (Washington, DC: GPO, 1933), table 9. U.S. Department of Commerce, Bureau of the Census, *Age of the Foreign-Born White Population By Country of Birth* (Washington, DC: GPO, 1933), table 26.

50. Jenna Weissman Joselit, *Our Gang: Jewish Crime and the New York Jewish Community, 1900–1940* (Bloomington,: Indiana University Press, 1983), 28, 32:

51. Hans Rogger, *Russia in the Age of Modernisation and Revolution 1881–1917* (London: Longman, 1983), 200–206; Gartner, "Jewish Migrants," 58, 62.

52. Gartner noted that "Galicia was relatively free of pogroms, yet its Jews emigrated in greater proportion than those in Russia": Gartner, "Jewish Migrants," 51.

53. Rudolf Wassermann, *Beruf, Konfession und Verbrechen: Eine Studie über die Kriminalität der Juden in Vergangenheit und Gegenwart* [Occupation, Religion and Crime: A Study of the Criminality of Jews

Past and Present] (München: Ernst Reinhardt, 1907), 66. Fewer than one-quarter of the Jews emigrating to America self-identified as laborers. Nearly two-thirds told the immigration authorities that they had been involved in manufacturing in Europe and half of these said they had worked in clothing production. But these latter self-reports may have been tailored (no pun intended) to the perceived preferences of the immigration authorities. Arcadius Kahan, "Economic Opportunities and Some Pilgrims' Progress: Jewish Immigrants from Eastern Europe in the U.S., 1890–1914," *Journal of Economic History* 38, no. 1 (1978): 237. "The vast majority of Poland's Jews," another source reports, "were traders and middlemen, keepers of shops and inns, artisans and landlords' agents": Rogger, *Russia in the Age,* 199.

54. Jenna Weissman Joselit, "Dark Shadows: New York Jews and Crime, 1900–1940" (PhD diss., Columbia University, 1980), 10n1, and *Our Gang,* 43.

55. Wassermann, *Beruf, Konfession,* 73, 78.

56. Joselit, *Our Gang,* 25, 42, 43, 45, 135.

57. Albert Fried, *The Rise and Fall of the Jewish Gangster in America,* rev. ed. (New York: Columbia University Press, 1993), 26.

58. Joselit, "Dark Shadows," 124, 132.

59. Vecoli, "*Contadini* in Chicago," 409.

60. Leonard Dinnerstein, Roger L. Nichols, and David M. Reimers, *Natives and Strangers* (New York: Oxford University Press, 1979), 239–40.

61. Immigration Act of 1924, Pub. L. No. 68–139, 43 Stat. 153 (1924). Helen F. Eckerson, "Immigration and National Origins," *Annals of the American Academy of Political and Social Science 367* (1966): 8–9. The partiality toward northern and western Europe was reflected in President Hoover's 1929 proclamation establishing immigration allocations in accordance with the 1924 law: Proclamation No. 1872, 46 Stat. 2984 (1929). The following are examples of quota allotments established by the proclamation: Germany: 25,957; Great Britain and Northern Ireland: 65,721; Greece: 307; Italy: 5,802; Poland: 6,524; Rumania: 295; Russia: 2,784.

## CHAPTER NINE

1. L. H. Gann and Peter J. Duignan, *The Hispanics in the United States: A History* (Boulder, CO: Westview, 1986), 36; Bureau of the Census, *Fifteenth Census: 1930, Population, vol. 2* (Washington, DC: GPO, 1933), 27. The Census Bureau had definition problems with Mexicans. Before 1930, the Census considered Mexicans "white." For the 1930 census Mexicans were differentiated from whites, but no distinction was drawn between Mexicans born in the United States and those born in Mexico. The 1930 definition was: "all persons born in Mexico, or having parents born in Mexico, who are not definitely white, Negro, Indian, Chinese, or Japanese": *Fifteenth Census: 1930.* The 1940 and subsequent censuses placed Mexicans back into the white category.

2. Gann and Duignan, *Hispanics,* 33, 37.

3. James A. Sandos and Harry E. Cross, "National Development and International Labour Migration: Mexico 1940–1965," *Journal of Contemporary History* 18, no. 1 (1983): 45–46.

4. Francisco Arturo Rosales, "The Regional Origins of Mexicano Immigrants to Chicago During the 1920s," *Aztlán: A Journal of Chicano Studies* 7, no. 2 (1976): 193; Enrique Krauze, *Mexico: Biography of Power: A History of Modern Mexico, 1810–1996* (New York: HarperCollins, 1997), 422–23.

5. Gann and Duignan, *Hispanics*, 37; Mark Reisler, "The Mexican Immigrant in the Chicago Area during the 1920's," *Journal of the Illinois State Historical Society* 66, no. 2 (1973): 146.

6. Donald R. Taft, "Nationality and Crime," *American Sociological Review* 1, no. 5 (1936): 729; National Commission on Law Observance and Enforcement, *Report on Crime and the Foreign Born,* pt. 3, "The Mexican Immigrant and the Problem of Crime and Criminal Justice" (Washington, DC: GPO, 1931), 272, 275, 276; Gann and Duignan, *Hispanics*, 37, 42, 43; Bureau of the Census, *Fifteenth Census: 1930, Population, vol. 3*, table 1.

7. Gann and Duignan, *Hispanics*, 41, 42, 46, 47. Scholars report ten lynchings of Mexicans in the United States between 1921 and 1930. In the previous decade, 1911–20, 124 lynchings were reported, but this includes killings of bandits and revolutionaries who crossed into Texas during the Mexican Revolution: William D. Carrigan and Clive Webb, "The Lynching of Persons of Mexican Origin or Descent in the United States, 1848 to 1928," *Journal of Social History* 37, no. 2 (2003): 423.

8. All figures are for 1930: Dinnerstein, Nichols, and Reimers, *Natives and Strangers*, 214–16; Bureau of the Census, *Fifteenth Census: 1930, Population, vol. 3*, pt. 1, table 17, pt. 2, table 17. The Newlands Reclamation Act of 1902, Pub. L. No. 57–161, 32 Stat. 388 (1902), funded irrigation projects throughout the West and Southwest. The newly irrigated fields provided jobs to thousands of unskilled workers.

9. Gann and Duignan, *Hispanics*, 52, 55–59; Abraham Hoffman, "Stimulus to Repatriation: The 1931 Federal Deportation Drive and the Los Angeles Mexican Community," in *Historical Themes and Identity: Mestizaje and Labels*, ed. Antoinette Sedillo López (New York: Garland Publishing, 1995), 309–24; Gonzales, *Mexicanos*, 149.

10. Pablo Piccato, *City of Suspects: Crime in Mexico City, 1900–1931* (Durham, NC: Duke University Press, 2001), 81, 82, 83, 88, 89, 91, 98.

11. Piccato, *City of Suspects*, 79, 99, 100. The Federal District, administered by Mexico's federal government through an appointed governor, encompassed 571 square miles, and contained, in addition to the capital, twenty-two autonomous municipalities. As a point of comparison, the five boroughs of New York City cover 301 square miles.

12. National Commission, *Report on Crime*, pt. 3, 240, 412. As my discussion of crime in Mexico showed, Mexicans frequently used knives to assault one another—not a good reason to excuse Mexicans from complying with U.S. laws.

13. F. Arturo Rosales, *¡Pobre Raza!: Violence, Justice, and Mobilization among México Lindo Immigrants, 1900–1936* (Austin: University of Texas Press, 1999), 82, 87. Rosales did not spell out the time frame for the thousands of killings by Rangers; presumably, several decades.

14. Rosales, *¡Pobre Raza!*, 91.

15. Rosales, *¡Pobre Raza!*, 55, 65.

16. Moehling and Piehl, "Immigration, Crime, and Incarceration," 757, 758, 759. As the authors point out, there were special problems with the data on Mexicans. First, because of the seasonal nature of Mexican employment the general census may have miscounted the population "at risk" for incarceration. Second, because prison and jail administrators commonly failed to distinguish Mexican-born inmates from American natives of Mexican descent the institutional head-count

may have overstated the Mexican-born population. These problems may have led to distortions in the Mexican commitment rate, but it is not clear that they account for the outsized Mexican rates. We cannot be certain that the general population survey undercounted Mexicans because we don't know whether the survey took place during harvest times or at some other point; nor do we know whether the seasonal workers returned to Mexico in the off-season. As for prison counts distorting the number of Mexican-born inmates, it is unlikely that the population of Americans of Mexican heritage was significant when compared to the number of recent arrivals from Mexico (Moehling and Piehl, "Immigration, Crime, and Incarceration," 758).

17. Carolyn Moehling and Anne Morrison Piehl, "Immigration and Crime in Early 20th Century America" (2007), 42, ftp://snde.rutgers.edu/Rutgers/wp/2007–04.pdf. This essay was an earlier draft of the Moehling and Piehl article published in *Demography*. The earlier draft provided data for "other races" that was not presented in the *Demography* version. In a private communication with Professor Moehling, she confirmed the validity of these data. U.S. Department of Commerce, Bureau of the Census, *Prisoners in State and Federal Prisons and Reformatories 1929 and 1930* (Washington, DC: GPO, 1932), table 21.

18. Gann and Duignan, *Hispanics*, 37–38; Bureau of the Census, *Fifteenth Census: 1930, Population*, vol. 3, pt. 1, table 17.

19. National Commission, *Report on Crime*, pt. 3, 202, 213, 214. Crimes against the person include various assault charges, battery, blackmail, failure to render aid, kidnaping, manslaughter, murder, and robbery (214).

20. Emory S. Bogardus, *The Mexican in the United States* (San Francisco: R and E Research Associates, 1934, 1970), 53, 54. Bogardus did not present data on arrests for robbery.

21. National Commission, *Report on Crime*, pt. 3, 279. The 1930 male Mexico-born population of Chicago numbered 10,009: Bureau of the Census, *Fifteenth Census: 1930, vol. 2*, chap. 5, table 9. Chicago's total male population in 1930 was 1,710,663: U.S. Department of Commerce, Bureau of the Census, *Fifteenth Census of the United States: 1930, Metropolitan Districts, Population and Area* (Washington, DC: GPO, 1932), table A.

22. Prior censuses grouped Mexicans with "whites." Starting in 1931, the total number of deaths reported for Mexicans increased, "which is doubtless attributable," the Census asserted, "mainly to improvement in the completeness of the returns." U.S. Department of Commerce, Bureau of the Census, *Mortality Statistics 1931* (Washington, DC: GPO, 1935), 9, tables 7, BG. It is interesting that 67.74 percent of the Mexican homicides were caused by firearms, a result nearly identical to the proportion of firearm deaths for all homicides (67.5 percent): U.S. Department of Commerce, Bureau of the Census, *Mortality Statistics 1931*, table 7, 47.

23. U.S. Department of Commerce, Bureau of the Census, *Mortality Statistics 1931*, 47. For Eckberg's rate estimates, see Eckberg, "Estimates."

24. Because the 1940 census folded the Mexican population into the white we do not have accurate figures on the number of Mexicans in the United States in 1940. Recent scholarship has it that approximately one-third of the Mexican population returned during the Great Depression, while acknowledging that the figure may be closer to one-half. Gonzales, *Mexicanos*, 149.

**CHAPTER TEN**

1. Paul Johnson, *A History of the American People* (New York: HarperCollins, 1998), 698.

2. The Eighteenth Amendment, Oliver and Hilgenberg asserted, "did prove impossible to enforce, and its sad 13 years as the law of the land further illustrates an important point: Any policy or law that does not enjoy widespread public confidence, that does not have substantial public support, is destined to fail": William M. Oliver and James F. Hilgenberg, *A History of Crime and Criminal Justice in America* (Durham, NC: Carolina Academic Press, 2010), 236. This overlooks the fact that Prohibition did have substantial public support initially and for several years in the early 1920s.

3. Allan Nevins, Henry Steele Commager, and Jeffrey Morris, *A Pocket History of the United States* (New York: Pocket Books, 1992), 411.

4. GDP figures are from http://www.measuringworth.com. Unemployment rates are from Romer, "Spurious Volatility." Disposable income figures are from Bureau of the Census, *Historical Statistics,* 224. The farming discussion was derived from Kyvig, *Daily Life,* 14, 182; and Nevins, Commager, and Morris, *Pocket History,* 407. As for the boll weevil, Tolnay and Beck wrote: "One important precipitating cause of black migration was the relentless march of the boll weevil on a northeasterly course through the South": Stewart E. Tolnay and E. M. Beck, "Black Flight: Lethal Violence and the Great Migration, 1900–1930," *Social Science History* 14, no. 3 (1990): 353.

5. Kyvig, *Daily Life,* 7.

6. Kyvig, *Daily Life,* 8. It is estimated that from 1910 to 1920, 454,000 African Americans left the South. Of these, 244,000 migrated to North Central states, 182,000 to northeastern states. Bureau of the Census, *Social and Economic Status,* table 8.

7. Kyvig, *Daily Life,* 171. Kyvig reported the death toll as "at least 75 residents, perhaps as many as 250" (171). Historians John Hope Franklin and Scott Ellsworth, writing for a state commission created to examine the incident, put the count at 75–100, adding that one credible source from the period reported around 300 deaths: 1921 Tulsa Race Riot Commission, *Tulsa Race Riot: A Report by the Oklahoma Commission to Study the Tulsa Race Riot of 1921,* (2001), 23, http://www.okhistory.org/trrc/freport.htm.

8. Nevins, Commager, and Morris, *Pocket History,* 393–99; Edward M. Coffman, *The War to End All Wars: The American Military Experience in World War I* (Lexington: University Press of Kentucky, 1986). Coffman estimated the peak strength of the Army at 4 million (55). The male population in 1918 was 52 million: Bureau of the Census, *Historical Statistics,* 9. If Nevins, Commager, and Morris are right about 25 million men registering for the draft, then 48 percent of the total male population did so.

9. Lisa McGirr, *The War on Alcohol: Prohibition and the Rise of the Amercian State* (New York, W. W. Norton, 2016), 32.

10. Food and Fuel Control Act, Pub. L. No. 65–41, 40 Stat. 276 (1917). Just after the Armistice of November 1918, Congress passed the War-Time Prohibition Act, Pub. L. No. 65–243, 40 Stat. 1045 (1918), which, effective June 30, 1919, banned the sale of beer, wine, or liquor until the president declared that demobilization was terminated. These laws were repealed simultaneously with the approval of the Volstead Act enforcing Prohibition.

11. Mark Edward Lender and James Kirby Martin, *Drinking in America: A History* (New York: Free Press, 1987), 129–30.

12. Lender and Martin, *Drinking in America,* 205. Even before World War I there were subnational efforts to regulate alcohol: J. C. Burnham, "New Perspectives on the Prohibition 'Experiment' of the 1920's," *Journal of Social History* 2, no. 1 (1968): 55. "Beginning in 1907 a large number of state and local governments enacted laws or adopted constitutional provisions that dried up—as far as alcoholic beverages were concerned—a substantial part of the United States"(Burnham, "New Perspectives").

13. The army discharged over 800,000 men within two months of the November 1918 Armistice, and by July 1919, 2.7 million: Coffman, *War to End,* 357.

14. Homicide data were provided by Professor Jeffrey S. Adler. Arrest data are from Edith Abbott, "Recent Statistics Relating to Crime in Chicago," *Journal of the American Institute of Criminal Law & Criminology* 13 (1922): 334. Abbott thought World War I probably was responsible for the decline in arrests (334–35). Her data came from annual reports of the Chicago Police Department.

15. Homicide rates: Monkkonen, "Homicides in New York City, https://doi.org/10.3886/ICPSR03226.v1. Arrest rates: Harry Willbach, "The Trend of Crime in New York City," *American Institute of Criminal Law & Criminology* 29 (1938–39): 69.

16. Edwin H. Sutherland and C. E. Gehlke, "Crime and Punishment," in *Recent Social Trends in the United States, Report of the President's Research Committee on Social Trends* (New York: McGraw-Hill, 1933), 1127. Sutherland and Gehlke found a steady march upward in homicide arrests in the five selected cities from 1911 on, broken only by the wartime dip.

17. H. C. Brearley, a criminologist writing in 1932, also reported a wartime decline in homicide. He reported the following rates: 1917–7.7, 1918–6.8, 1919–7.5: Brearley, *Homicide,* 16. For a report utilizing National Center for Health Statistics data, see A. Joan Klebba, "Homicide Trends in the United States, 1900–74," *Public Health Reports* 90, no. 3 (1975): 195–204. Eckberg's recalculation is described in Eckberg, "Estimates." Homicide statistics produced by the Metropolitan Life Insurance Company also showed a drop in 1918. The company's figures were: 1917–7.4, 1918–6.2, 1919–6.9. Reported in Betty B. Rosenbaum, "The Relationship between War and Crime in the United States," *Journal of Criminal Law and Criminology* 30, no. 5 (1940): 732.

18. Rosenbaum, "The Relationship between War and Crime," 730.

19. Alfred W. Crosby, *America's Forgotten Pandemic: The Influenza of 1918* (Cambridge: Cambridge University Press, 2003), 206. The Census Bureau, comparing deaths from influenza and pneumonia in 1915 to corresponding incidents in 1918 and 1919, produced the somewhat lower figure of 548,452 for the registration states of 1915. U.S. Department of Commerce, Bureau of the Census, *Mortality Statistics 1919* (Washington, DC: GPO, 1921), 30.

20. Crosby, *America's Forgotten Pandemic,* 56.

21. Bureau of the Census, *Mortality Statistics 1919,* 30.

22. U.S. Department of Commerce, Bureau of the Census, *Mortality Statistics, 1916* (Washington, DC: GPO, 1918), table 5. U.S. Department of Commerce, Bureau of the Census, *Mortality Statistics, 1918* (Washington, DC: GPO, 1920), table 5.

23. Compare Federal Security Agency, *Vital Statistics Rates,* mortality tables, table 12, with Eckberg, "Estimates," 13.

24. Frederick Lewis Allen, *The Big Change: America Transforms Itself 1900–1950* (New York: Bantam Books, 1952, 1961), 116, 123; Kyvig, *Daily Life,* 6, 9.

25. Joseph R. Gusfield, *Symbolic Crusade: Status Politics and the American Temperance Movement* (Urbana: University of Illinois Press, 1986), 7.

26. James H. Timberlake, *Prohibition and the Progressive Movement, 1900–1920* (Cambridge, MA: Harvard University Press, 1963), 2; Kyvig, *Daily Life*, 8–9; McGirr, *War on Alcohol*, 25. Of course, contemporary progressivism and the progressive movement of the early twentieth century are not identical, despite some similarities, e.g., policies to constrain capitalism.

27. George Elliott Howard, "Alcohol and Crime: A Study in Social Causation," *American Journal of Sociology* 24, no. 1 (1918): 61–62. Contemporary data indicate that 37 percent of all state inmates imprisoned for violent crimes had been, at the time of the offense, under the influence of alcohol or both alcohol and drugs: U.S. Department of Justice, Bureau of Justice Statistics, *Survey of State Prison Inmates, 1991*, by Allen Beck et al. (Washington, DC: GPO, 1993), 26. For a discussion of alcohol and violence, see Robert Nash Parker, *Alcohol and Homicide: A Deadly Combination of Two American Traditions* (Albany: State University of New York Press, 1995).

28. Kyvig, *Daily Life*, 20. On saloon homicide, see Adler, *First in Violence*, 15–18. Saloons were on the decline by the twentieth century, in part because of license fees and regulations. Adler pointed out that in 1895 there had been one saloon for every 232 Chicago residents, but by 1910, the ratio already had fallen to one in 307 (39).

29. National Prohibition Act, Pub. L. No. 66–66, 41 Stat. 305 (1919); see Title II.

30. Kyvig, *Daily Life*, 44.

31. Burnham, "New Perspectives," 57–59; Kyvig, *Daily Life*, 21, 22; Reppetto, *American Mafia*, 107, 109.

32. Kyvig, *Daily Life*, 22; David E. Kyvig, *Repealing National Prohibition* (Chicago: University of Chicago Press, 1979), 25; Mark H. Haller, "Organized Crime in Urban Society: Chicago in the Twentieth Century," *Journal of Social History* 5, no. 2 (1971–72): 224.

33. National Commission on Law Observance and Enforcement, *Report on the Enforcement of the Prohibition Laws of the United States* (Washington, DC: GPO, 1931), 28–29. The Wickersham Report stated that more than 2,300 stills were seized in 1913, before national Prohibition, and that in 1929, "well over twelve times as many" were seized; this figure was for the entire country, not just the South (29).

34. Lender and Martin, *Drinking in America*, 146. After Prohibition, absolute alcohol consumption remained low until the late 1960s. From 1891 to 1915, consumption averaged 2.37 gallons. In 1934, after Prohibition, consumption had fallen to only .97 gallons and did not reach pre-Prohibition levels until 1966–70 (2.45 gallons): Lender and Martin, *Drinking in America*, 205–6.

35. Kyvig, *Repealing*, 20, 23, 31, 108; Brearley, *Homicide*, 46–47. Reppetto claimed that a Prohibition agent could make $50,000 a year "on the side" in New York City: Reppetto, *American Mafia*, 93.

36. McGirr, *War on Alcohol*, 122–53.

37. McGirr, *War on Alcohol*, xxi.

38. Kyvig, *Repealing*, 30, 108; McGirr, *War on Alcohol*, 202. Supreme Court cases on the Fourth Amendment, which constrains the power of the police to search for and seize evidence, were rare before the 1920s. *Olmstead v. United States*, 277 U.S. 438 (1928), upheld the authority of federal agents to tap the telephone lines of Roy Olmstead, one of Seattle's top bootleggers, without obtaining a search

warrant. *Carroll v. United States,* 267 U.S. 132 (1925), approved a warrantless search of a moving automobile in which bottles of contraband whiskey were hidden.

39. Haller, "Organized Crime," 211.

40. Reppetto, *American Mafia,* xii.

41. Nelli, *Business of Crime,* 201–2.

42. Nelli, *Business of Crime,* 121.

43. Lashly, "Homicide (in Cook County)," 610. It was not clear whether the "Italians" referred to in the survey were born in Italy or born in the United States to Italian immigrant parents.

44. Haller, "Organized Crime," 211, 217, 219, 222.

45. Haller, "Organized Crime," 220; Nelli, *Business of Crime,* 168–69; Reppetto, *American Mafia,* 103. A "bucket shop" was an illegal gambling operation in which the customers bet on the rise and fall of stock prices, which were posted.

46. Nelli, *Business of Crime,* 169–70.

47. Haller, "Organized Crime," 220–24.

48. Brearley, *Homicide,* 25–26; Joseph L. Holmes, "Crime and the Press," *Journal of the American Institute of Criminal Law & Criminology* 20, no. 1 (1929): 6–59. The "typhoon of crime" remark was by John H. Lyle, a Chicago trial judge in the 1920s: John H. Lyle, *The Dry and Lawless Years* (Englewood Cliffs, NJ: Prentice-Hall, 1960), 121. Public-opinion polls were unscientific in the 1920s, so it is difficult to know exactly what the public thought. See Maurice C. Bryson, "The Literary Digest Poll: Making of a Statistical Myth," *American Statistician* 30, no. 4 (1976): 184–85. One commentator, writing in 1926, declared: "The world at large is definitely under the impression that there is an enormous increase in crime in the United States and that this is of recent origin": Ellen C. Potter, "Aspects of Crime in Relation to the Crime Wave," *Annals of the American Academy of Political and Social Science* 125 (1926): 1. In a survey from 1922, conducted by *Leslie's Weekly,* 73 percent of the respondents thought that "the present situation dangerously threaten[ed] our institutions by breeding disrespect for laws." This was one of several surveys on Prohibition of the period, reported in George MacAdam, "Counting Noses, Wet and Dry," *New York Times,* August 20, 1922.

49. Frederick L. Hoffman, *The Homicide Problem* (Newark, NJ: Prudential Press, 1925), 96. The quote is from Frederick L. Hoffman, "The Increase in Murder" *Annals of the American Academy of Political and Social Science* 125 (1926): 28.

50. Edwin H. Sutherland, "Murder and the Death Penalty," *Journal of the American Institute of Criminal Law & Criminology* 15, no. 4 (1925): 524. Oddly, Sutherland does not identify the states or cities.

51. Brearley, *Homicide,* 18; Eckberg, "Estimates," 1–16.

52. Kyvig, *Repealing,* 27; Reppetto, *American Mafia,* 97, 103, 110. In the 1920s, killings by police generally were treated as justifiable homicides and not prosecuted, but they were counted as homicides by the federal Division of Vital Statistics, so they contributed to the homicide rate tabulation: Brearley, *Homicide,* 203.

53. Reppetto, *American Mafia,* 94, 99, 114, 115.

54. Lashly, "Homicide (in Cook County)," 594; Haller, "Organized Crime," 228; Nelli, *Business of Crime,* 149.

55. Reppetto, *American Mafia,* 113–14, 116, 117, 119, 120, 121. Jonathan Eig claimed that the massacre was an act of revenge for the killing of a policeman's son by members of the Moran gang, and that Capone had nothing to do with it: Jonathan Eig, *Get Capone. The Secret Plot That Captured America's Most Wanted Gangster* (New York: Simon & Schuster, 2010), 251–53.

56. Reppetto, *American Mafia,* 114, 122; Kyvig, *Repealing,* 31.

57. Reppetto, *American Mafia,* 127, 131; Eig, *Get Capone,* 394–96.

58. Nelli, *Business of Crime,* 219.

59. Monkkonen, "Homicides in New York City, https://doi.org/10.3886/ICPSR03226.v1. Andrew Karmen found that in 1986, 33 percent of New York City murders were drug-related, 31 percent in 1991. Karmen, *New York Murder,* 39.

60. Lashly, "Homicide (in Cook County)," 599, 601; U.S. Census Bureau, "Population of Counties," http://www.nber.org/data/census-decennial-population.html. Chicago homicide rates for 1875–1919 were provided by Jeffrey S. Adler and are on file with the author. These rates were adjusted by Adler to exclude automobile accidents, abortion-related deaths, infanticides, and forms of homicide not enforced throughout the time period.

61. Lashly, "Homicide (in Cook County)," 594.

62. Lashly, "Homicide in Cook County," 610, 612, 636.

63. Of 203 automobile homicide cases taken into the criminal justice system, 111 were no billed by a grand jury, 17 were tried and acquitted, and only two were convicted. The rest received various other treatments. Lashly, "Homicide (in Cook County)," 602, 634; U.S. Dept of Transportation, National Highway Traffic Safety Administration, "Traffic Safety Facts, Cook County, Illinois 2005–2009," http://www-nrd.nhtsa.dot.gov/departments/nrd-30/ncsa/STSI/17_IL/2009/Counties /Illinois_Cook%20County_2009.PDF. The price of a Ford was for 1921: Kyvig, *Daily Life,* 31.

64. James Boudouris, "A Classification of Homicides," *Criminology* 11 (1973–74): 525–40; Reppetto, *American Mafia,* 102, 149. Boudouris's study covered homicides in Detroit from 1926 to 1968.

65. Boudouris, "Classification," 529, 532. It is not clear why Boudouris considered gang killings a "product of the violation of the law."

66. Boudouris, "Classification," 531, 532–33. Detroit's homicide rates were calculated by using Boudouris's homicide data and a linear interpolation of census data for Detroit. Detroit's population for 1920 was 993,678; for 1930 it was 1,568,662: U.S. Census Bureau, *Historical Census Statistics* (Working Paper No. 76), table 23. Chicago homicide rates are from the Chicago homicide database, "Homicide in Chicago 1870–1930," http://homicide.northwestern.edu/download/. New York City rates are from Monkkonen, "Homicides in New York City," https://doi.org/10.3886/ICPSR03226.v1. National rates are from Eckberg, "Estimates," 13.

67. Paul Ryscavage, *Income Inequality in America: An Analysis of Trends* (Armonk, NY: M.E. Sharpe, 1999), 138.

68. Harry G. Levine and Craig Reinarman, "From Prohibition to Regulation: Lessons from Alcohol Policy for Drug Policy," *Milbank Quarterly* 69, no. 3 (1991): 468. Data are based on absolute alcohol consumed per capita, age fifteen or over.

69. Kyvig, *Repealing*, 188–89; Jack S. Blocker, "Did Prohibition Really Work? Alcohol Prohibition as a Public Health Innovation," *American Journal of Public Health* 96, no. 2 (2006): 241.

70. Eric H. Monkkonen, "A Disorderly People? Urban Order in the Nineteenth and Twentieth Centuries," *Journal of American History* 68, no. 3 (1981): 542, 543. Monkkonen said that arrests for public disorder offenses had been declining well before the 1920s, and he concluded that Prohibition had accelerated the decline (547). The link between alcohol and violent crime, some contend, is stronger even than that for other illicit substances. Robert Nash Parker and Kathleen Auerhahn, "Alcohol, Drugs, and Violence," *Annual Review of Sociology* 24 (1998): 291–311: "When violent behavior is associated with a substance that substance is, overwhelmingly, alcohol. Study after study indicates that, even in samples containing relatively high baseline rates of illicit drug use, violent events are overwhelmingly more likely to be associated with the consumption of alcohol than with any other substance" (306–7).

71. Mark Asbridge and Swarna Weerasinghe, "Homicide in Chicago from 1890 to 1930: Prohibition and Its Impact on Alcohol- and Non-Alcohol-Related Homicides," *Addiction* 104, no. 3 (2009): 360.

72. Emily Greene Owens, "Are Underground Markets Really More Violent? Evidence from Early 20th Century America," *American Law and Economics Review* 13, no. 1 (2011): 41. Owens's controls included state urbanization levels and state non-native, Catholic, and black populations (24). A contrary conclusion was drawn by Jensen from a more limited quantitative analysis. "Despite the fact that alcohol consumption is a positive correlate of homicide (as expected)," wrote Jensen, "Prohibition and its enforcement increased the homicide rate": Gary F. Jensen, "Prohibition, Alcohol, and Murder: Untangling Countervailing Mechanisms," *Homicide Studies* 2000, no. 4: 31.

73. Brearley, *Homicide*, 18–23, 97. African American drinking patterns did not track those of whites. The first black migration, despite Prohibition, stimulated black alcohol use, and ingestion increased even more during the second migration just after World War II: Denise Herd, "Migration, Cultural Transformation and the Rise of Black Liver Cirrhosis Mortality," *British Journal of Addiction* 80 (1985): 397–410. We cannot rule out the possibility that Prohibition contributed to changes in alcohol consumption only among whites, changes that eventually reduced white violence, while factors such as northward migration, in part contemporaneous with Prohibition, were having the opposite effect on African Americans.

74. As national mortality rates are considered unreliable prior to 1933, figures presented here are based on generally accepted estimates. Eckberg, "Estimates."

## CHAPTER ELEVEN

1. Kyvig, *Daily Life*, 211, 212, 214. For unemployment data, see Gene R. Smiley, "Recent Unemployment Rate Estimates for the 1920s and 1930s," *Journal of Economic History* 43, no. 2 (1983): 488.

2. Robert S. McElvaine, *The Great Depression: America, 1929–1941* (New York: Random House, 1993), 46–48; Kyvig, *Daily Life*, 216–17.

3. Kyvig, *Daily Life*, 209, 217–21, 223–25. More than nine thousand banks failed in the four-year period 1930–33, "the highest concentration of bank suspensions in the nation's history": Elmus Wicker, *The Banking Panics of the Great Depression* (Cambridge: Cambridge University Press, 1996),

xv. By contrast, in the recent recession that began in 2008, 414 banks closed between 2008 and the end of 2011: Federal Deposit Insurance Corporation, "Failed Bank List," http://www.fdic.gov/bank /individual/failed/banklist.html.

4. Kyvig, *Daily Life,* 228–29; see also Richard Norton Smith, *An Uncommon Man: The Triumph of Herbert Hoover* (New York: Simon & Schuster, 1984).

5. William E. Leuchtenburg, *Franklin D. Roosevelt and the New Deal, 1932–1940* (New York: Harper & Row, 1963), 4–5, 8, 41, 195.

6. Kyvig, *Daily Life,* 232–33.

7. Kyvig, *Daily Life,* 245–46.

8. Raymond Wolters, "The New Deal and the Negro," in *The New Deal,* vol. 1, ed. John Braeman, Robert H. Bremner, and David Brody (Columbus: Ohio State University Press, 1975), 188. At this time about 79 percent of blacks still lived in the South: U.S. Census Bureau, *Historical Census Statistics* (Working Paper No. 56), tables 1, 4.

9. John A. Salmond, *The Civilian Conservation Corps, 1933–1942: A New Deal Case Study* (Durham, NC: Duke University Press, 1967). The average ages of CCC enrollees were eighteen to nineteen. Exceptions to the age limits were established for veterans and American Indians, who had a special CCC program and their own camps. In 1937, Congress changed the age limits to seventeen to twenty-eight, and it eliminated the requirement that the father must be on relief (Salmond, *Civilian Conservation Corps*).

10. For a claim that the CCC served a crime-control function, see John A. Pandiani, "The Crime Control Corps: An Invisible New Deal Program," *British Journal of Sociology* 33, no. 3 (1982): 348–58.

11. Richard A. Reiman, *The New Deal & American Youth: Ideas & Ideals in a Depression Decade* (Athens: University of Georgia Press, 2010), 2.

12. Smiley, "Recent Unemployment," 488.

13. Kyvig, *Daily Life,* 300, 330. The National Labor Relations Act, Pub. L. No. 74–198, 49 Stat. 449 (1935), was upheld by the Supreme Court on April 12, 1937. *NLRB v. Jones & Laughlin Steel Corp.* 301 U.S. 1 (1937).

14. Richard Polenberg, "The Decline of the New Deal," in *The New Deal,* vol. 1, ed. John Braeman, Robert H. Bremner, and David Brody (Columbus: Ohio State University Press, 1975), 255. Polenberg, probably in accord with most writers, attributed the slump to sudden sharp cuts in government spending intended to balance the budget. For a contrary view—that the New Deal itself hurt the economy—see Amity Shlaes, *The Forgotten Man: A New History of the Great Depression* (New York: HarperCollins, 2007), 8–10; see also Robert Higgs, *Depression, War and Cold War: Studies in Political Economy* (New York: Oxford University Press, 2006). "It is time," argued Higgs, "for economists and historians to take seriously the hypothesis that the New Deal prolonged the Great Depression by creating an extraordinarily high degree of regime uncertainty in the minds of investors" (24).

15. Douglas Eckberg's estimated rates (which ran to 1932, at which point the rates compiled by the National Center for Health Statistics (NCHS) were considered highly accurate) indicate a 9.7 rate for 1931: Eckberg, "Estimates." The NCHS rates underestimated homicides by approximately 0.5 per 100,000. Official: Federal Security Agency, *Vital Statistics Rates,* table 12. Estimated: Eckberg, "Estimates," 13.

Homicide mortality rates, 1930–1934

| Year | Official | Estimated |
|------|----------|-----------|
| 1930 | 8.8 | 9.2 |
| 1931 | 9.2 | 9.7 |
| 1932 | 9.0 | 9.5 |
| 1933 | 9.7 | |
| 1934 | 9.5 | |

16. Bryan Burrough, *Public Enemies: America's Greatest Crime Wave and the Birth of the FBI, 1933–34* (New York: Penguin Books, 2004), 6–7, 13–14.

17. Rates for 1920–32 are based on Eckberg, "Estimates," 13. Rates for 1933–40 are from Federal Security Agency, *Vital Statistics Rates,* mortality tables, table 12.

18. As two criminologists observed, "the unemployment-crime relationship (hereafter denoted the U-C relationship) has been the object of much research attention in sociology and related social sciences. Yet this research has failed to produce consensus about the direction of the relationship: some studies find a positive U-C effect, others conclude that the effect is negative, and still others infer that the relationship is essentially null": David Cantor and Kenneth C. Land, "Unemployment and Crime Rates in the Post–World War II United States: A Theoretical and Empirical Analysis," *American Sociological Review* 50, no. 3 (1985): 317. A striking illustration of the different impact of national economy on crime was offered by Sir Leon Radzinowicz, who found that in Poland, 1927–34, crimes against the person decreased during depressions and increased during prosperous times, whereas property crimes increased during depressions: Leon Radzinowicz, "The Influence of Economic Conditions on Crime," *Sociological Review* 33, no. 2 (1941): 151.

19. For comparisons of the *UCR* and the National Center for Health Statistics (NCHS) homicide mortality data, see David Cantor and Lawrence E. Cohen, "Comparing Measures of Homicide Trends: Methodological and Substantive Differences in the Vital Statistics and Uniform Crime Report Time Series (1933–1975)," *Social Science Research* 9 (1980): 121–45. For national homicide trends Cantor and Cohen urge caution in using 1933–1935 *UCR* data, but find that the correlation between the *UCR* and NCHS data for 1936 to 1973 is an impressively high .97 (123). The FBI data have undergone revisions from time to time. Cantor and Cohen recommended a version of the data for 1933 through 1972 prepared by the federal Office of Management and Budget: U.S. Office of Management and Budget, *Social Indicators 1973* (Washington, DC: GPO, 1973), table 2/1. That dataset is used in this book for the period starting with 1933.

20. Big-city homicides generally spiked from 1929 to 1933, but not in every city. For instance, Chicago went from 404 to 516 killings (+28 percent), while New York tallied 458 homicide deaths in 1929, 552 in 1933 (+21 percent). But Philadelphia's homicides declined, 175 to 137 (−22 percent), as did killings in New Orleans (118 to 98, −17 percent): Bureau of the Census, *Mortality Statistics 1929,* table 9; U.S. Department of Commerce, Bureau of the Census, *Mortality Statistics 1933* (Washington, DC: GPO, 1936), table 9.

21. Office of Management and Budget, "Social Indicators," table 2/1.

22. In calculating the homicide rates for 1930–34, 1930 census population data were used; for 1935–40, 1940 population data were used.

23. U.S. Department of Justice, Bureau of Justice Statistics, "Historical Corrections Statistics in the United States, 1850–1984," by Margaret Werner Cahalan (Washington, DC: GPO, 1986), tables 3–8.

24. Drake and Cayton, *Black Metropolis,* 83–84; Gregory, *Southern Diaspora,* 99; Richard K. Vedder and Lowell Gallaway, "Racial Differences in Unemployment in the United States, 1890–1990," *Journal of Economic History* 52 (1992), 699. 699.

25. Gregory estimated that black migration totaled 391,641 in the 1930s, 810,614 in the 1920s: Gregory, *Southern Diaspora,* 330; Drake and Cayton, *Black Metropolis,* 88; U.S. Census Bureau, *Historical Census Statistics;* Bureau of the Census, "Population of 100 Largest Cities," Working Paper No. 27, table 14.

26. Harold Garfinkel, "Research Note on Inter- and Intra-Racial Homicides," *Social Forces* 27, no. 4 (1949): 370. Garfinkel collected mortality data for ten North Carolina counties for the entire decade, 1930 to end of 1939. Of 821 cases, 70.7 percent were black-on-black, only 2.9 percent were white-on-black, which was half the percentage of black-on-white killings (6.2 percent) (370).

27. From 1930 to 1939, there were 104,629 homicide victimizations in the United States, of which nonwhites were 49,903, or 47.7 percent of the total. Data for 1930–36 from annual publication *Mortality Statistics,* by U.S. Department of Commerce, Bureau of the Census, table 5. Data for 1937–39, annual publication of *Vital Statistics of the United States,* table 14, by U.S. Department of Commerce, Bureau of the Census. For 1937 and 1938, victims are designated "white" and "Negro." In all other years the designations are "white" and "all other races." This has little bearing on the homicide data because in this time period blacks were the overwhelming majority of all nonwhites.

28. Federal Security Agency, *Vital Statistics Rates,* mortality tables, table 16.

29. Andrew F. Henry and James F. Short, *Suicide & Homicide: Some Economic, Sociological and Psychological Aspects of Aggression* (New York: Free Press, 1954), 46–47.

30. M. Harvey Brenner, "Economic Crises and Crime," in *Crime In Society,* ed. Leonard D. Savitz and Norman Johnston (New York: John Wiley & Sons, 1978), 555–72.

31. Brenner, "Economic Crises and Crime," 569–70.

32. The coefficient of correlation was significant at the .10 level. Unemployment rates, from Smiley, "Recent Unemployment," 488, treated emergency government workers as employed. Homicide rates for 1930–32 are based on Eckberg, "Estimates," 13. Homicide rates for 1933–39 are from Federal Security Agency, *Vital Statistics Rates,* mortality tables, table 12.

33. The coefficient of correlation was significant at the .01 level. The distinction between Gross Domestic Product (GDP) and Gross National Product (GNP), which concerns whether the goods are located in the United States or abroad, is not significant here. See http://www.bea.gov/glossary/glossary.cfm.

34. For example, James Q. Wilson and Philip J. Cook, "Unemployment and Crime—What Is the Connection?" *Public Interest* 79 (1985): 3–8. Wilson and Cook point out that Brenner did not take sentencing or age into account in constructing his multiple regression analysis, but their critique, as with that of other commentators, is centered on Brenner's post–World War II work.

35. Jeffrey K. Liker and Glen H. Elder, Jr., "Economic Hardship and Marital Relations in the 1930s," *American Sociological Review* 48, no. 3 (1983): 356; Pandiani, "Crime Control Corps," 348.

Female homicide victimization rates from 1921 to 1929 averaged 3.3 per 100,000. During the worst depression years, 1930–33, they jumped to an average of 3.6, a 9 percent increase: Federal Security Agency, *Vital Statistics Rates*, mortality tables, table 15.

36. Theodore G. Chiricos, "Rates of Crime and Unemployment: An Analysis of Aggregate Research Evidence," *Social Problems* 34 no. 2 (1987): 193. It appears that few of these studies covered the pre–World War II period.

37. Ryan S. Johnson, Shawn Kantor, and Price V. Fishback, "Striking at the Roots of Crime: The Impact of Social Welfare Spending on Crime During the Great Depression," NBER Working Paper No. 12825, rev. March 2010, http://www.nber.org/tmp/70986-w12825.pdf. "An added dollar of per capita relief spending was associated with a reduction per 100,000 people of 0.06 murders[, 0.49 robberies] and 1.76 aggravated assaults, but an increase of 0.05 rapes" (12).

38. Roosevelt's remark, part of an address to the National Parole Conference in 1939, was quoted in Pandiani, "Crime Control Corps," 352.

39. Boudouris, "Classification of Homicides," 536. Boudouris defined criminal transaction homicides as "a product of the violation of the law, as when a holdup man kills a store owner or police officer" (529). A list of all criminal transaction homicides by incident type has a category labeled "Gang war, extortion, riot snipers, misc." (536). I assume that the vast majority of the homicides falling into this category were gang killings.

40. Monkkonen, *Murder in New York City*, 17. Monkkonen probably was discussing female homicides in New York City. The national averages reveal the following. Female rates in the 1920s (1921–29) averaged 3.3 per 100,000. In the heart of the depression (1930–33), they averaged 3.6. For the remainder of the decade (1934–39), the mean was 3.2, a decline especially noticeable in 1938 (2.9) and 1939 (2.7): Federal Security Agency, *Vital Statistics Rates*, mortality tables, table 16. These figures suggest that economic decline raised female homicides in the early 1930s, but had no effect in the latter part of the decade. As for Prohibition, since there is no noticeable decline until 1938, five years after repeal, there is no conclusion to be drawn from female homicides.

41. Total alcohol consumption in the United States, which had hit a high of 2.6 gallons per capita in 1910, fell to 1.4 gallons per capita in 1925, rose only to 1.5 gallons in 1930, and remained unchanged in 1935. Consumption then increased slightly to 1.6 gallons per capita in 1940: Levine and Reinarman, "Prohibition to Regulation," 468. The nexus between alcohol and violent crime is generally accepted by contemporary analysts. See, e.g., Parker, *Alcohol and Homicide*.

42. Gregory, *Southern Diaspora*, 330, 331.

43. Southern whites, as I have shown, had high violent crime rates. Unfortunately, we do not know whether their violence continued at high rates when they migrated out of the South. Also, many of the white Dust Bowl migrants went to agricultural settings in California, as opposed to northern industrial states.

44. Kyvig, *Daily Life*, 228.

45. U.S. Census Bureau, *Demographic Trends*, table 5, A-7. The 15–24 age cohort rose between 1920 and 1940. This group was 17.1 percent of the total male population in 1920, 17.9 percent in 1930, and 18.0 percent in 1940 (U.S. Census Bureau, *Demographic Trends*, table 5, A-10).

46. U.S. Census Bureau, *Demographic Trends*, , table 5, A-11.

47. Robert K. Merton, "Social Structure and Anomie," *American Sociological Review* 3, no. 5 (1938): 679, 680.

48. Grantham, *South in Modern America,* 131. Randolph Roth contended that the steady decline in homicide rates in the 1930s "coincided once again with the stabilization of the federal government, the reestablishment of its legitimacy, and the gradual restoration of Americans' faith in the country, their leadership, and one another": Roth, *American Homicide,* 441. Talk of an era of good feeling seems strained for the late 1930s. While Franklin Roosevelt retained the approbation of the American public, his popularity had eroded considerably by the last years of the decade. Faith and confidence in the federal government were in decline. "In August 1939 Roosevelt's approval rating fell below 50 percent for the first time since George Gallup began routinely monitoring it several years earlier": Matthew A. Baum and Samuel Kernell, "Economic Class and Popular Support for Franklin Roosevelt in War and Peace," *Public Opinion Quarterly* 65, no. 2 (2001): 200.

49. U.S. Department of Justice, Bureau of Justice Statistics, *Criminal Victimization, 2011,* by Jennifer L. Truman and Michael Planty (Washington, DC: GPO, 2012), 1. The unemployment rate in 1993 was 6.9 percent; in 2011 it was 8.9 percent: U.S. Department of Labor, Bureau of Labor Statistics, https://www.bls.gov/.

## CONCLUSION

1. The national murder/manslaughter rate for 2017 was 5.4 per 100,000: Federal Bureau of Investigation, *Crime in the United States 2017,* table 16, https://ucr.fbi.gov/crime-in-the-u.s. New York City's 2017 homicide rate was a strikingly low 3.9 per 100,000 (FBI, *Crime in the United States,* table 6). But 1882 and 1883 beat even that figure with rates below 3: Monkkonen, "Homicides in New York City, https://doi.org/10.3886/ICPSR03226.v1.

2. Gallup surveys included the following question: "Is there any area around here—that is, within a mile—where you would be afraid to walk alone at night?" In 1965, 34 percent of the respondents said yes, and in 1972, the figure rose to 41 percent. By group, responses in the affirmative in 1972 were as follows: blacks, 49 percent; residents of cities over 1 million, 53 percent; ages 50 and over, 49 percent; income under $3,000 per year, 58 percent: Hazel Erskine, "The Polls: Fear of Violence and Crime," *Public Opinion Quarterly* 38, no. 1 (1974): 137, 138, 140, 141.

3. Lane, *Roots of Violence,* 103.

4. Adler, *First in Violence,* 269.

5. Harry Willbach, "The Trend of Crime in Chicago," *American Institute of Criminal Law & Criminology* 31 (1940–41): 722; Chicago Police Department, *Statistical Summary 1980,* 12, https://home.chicagopolice.org/inside-the-cpd/statistical-reports/annual-reports/.

6. Rates from 1937 to 1951 are annual averages derived from graphic representations in Ferdinand, "Criminal Patterns," 93. Rates for 1970–71 and 1981–82 are based on Boston Police reports of the number of arrests for year-long periods running from July 1 to June 30: City of Boston, *Annual Report of the Police Commissioner for the City of Boston,* http://archive.org/stream/annualreportof po1970bost#page/n6/mode/1up (1970–71); http://archive.org/stream/annualreportofpo8182bost #page/n0/mode/1up (1981–82).

7. Bureau of the Census, *Prisoners and Juvenile Delinquents 1904,* table xiv; Bureau of Justice Statistics, *Historical Corrections Statistics,* table 3–17. Robbers are difficult to apprehend, in large measure because they are strangers to the victim. It is possible that over the course of the twentieth century, police improved their capacity to arrest robbers, but robbery clearances declined after the 1960s. It is also possible that over the century, courts convicted a bigger percentage of accused robbers or judges sentenced more of them to prison terms. I am not aware of any evidence for these propositions.

8. Paolo Buonanno et al., "Crime in Europe and the United States: Dissecting the 'Reversal of Misfortunes,'" *Economic Policy* 26, no. 67 (2011): 348–85. By the late 1990s the plotlines for violent crime rates in the United States and Europe crossed; thereafter, as U.S. rates continued to fall, European rates rose (352). This trend is contrary to all of modern history.

9. Monkkonen, *Murder in New York City,* 22–23.

10. Cooney, "Decline of Elite Homicide," 381.

11. "The [non-Hispanic] white share of the middle class fell to 55 percent in 2017, and will drop below half to 49 percent within the next quarter-century." Ethnic and racial minorities are projected to be a majority of the middle-class by 2042: Richard V. Reeves and Camille Busette, "The middle class is becoming race-plural, just like the rest of America," February 27, 2018, https://www.brookings.edu/blog/social-mobility-memos/2018/02/27/the-middle-class-is-becoming-race-plural-just-like-the-rest-of-america/.

12. "Asian immigrants are projected to make up a larger share of all immigrants, becoming the largest immigrant group by 2055 and making up 38% of the foreign-born population by 2065": Pew Research Center, "Modern Immigration Wave Brings 59 Million to U.S., Driving Population Growth and Change Through 2065," September 28, 2015, https://www.pewresearch.org/hispanic/2015/09/28/modern-immigration-wave-brings-59-million-to-u-s-driving-population-growth-and-change-through-2065/.

# SELECTED BIBLIOGRAPHY

A complete bibliography may be found on the book's webpage on the Louisiana State University Press website, https://lsupress.org/.

Adler, Jeffrey S. *First in Violence, Deepest in Dirt: Homicide in Chicago, 1875–1920.* Cambridge, MA: Harvard University Press, 2006.

———. *Murder in New Orleans: The Creation of Jim Crow Policing.* Chicago: University of Chicago Press, 2019.

———. "Murder, North and South: Violence in Early-Twentieth-Century Chicago and New Orleans." *Journal of Southern History* 74 (2008): 297–324.

Ayers, Edward L. *Vengeance and Justice: Crime and Punishment in the 19th-Century American South.* New York: Oxford University Press.

Barzini, Luigi. *The Italians.* New York: Atheneum, 1964.

Beck, E. M., and Stewart E. Tolnay. "The Killing Fields of the Deep South: The Market for Cotton and the Lynching of Blacks, 1882–1930." *American Sociological Review* 55 (1990): 526–39.

———. "When Race Didn't Matter: Black and White Mob Violence against Their Own Color." In *Under Sentence of Death: Lynching in the South,* edited by W. Fitzhugh Brundage, 132–51. Chapel Hill: University of North Carolina Press, 1997.

Bienen, Leigh B., and Brandon Rottinghaus. "Learning From the Past, Living in the Present: Understanding Homicide in Chicago, 1870–1930." *Journal of Criminal Law and Criminology* 92 (2002): 437–54.

Blassingame, John W. "Before the Ghetto: The Making of the Black Community in Savannah, Georgia, 1865–1880." *Journal of Social History* 6 (1973): 463–88.

Bodenhamer, David J. "Criminal Sentencing in Antebellum America: A North-South Comparison." *Historical Social Research* 154 (1990): 77–94.

Boessenecker, John. "California Bandidos: Social Bandits or Sociopaths?" *Southern California Quarterly* 80 (1998): 419–34.

———. *Gold Dust and Gunsmoke: Tales of Gold Rush Outlaws, Gunfighters, Lawmen, and Vigilantes.* New York: John Wiley, 1999.

Bogardus, Emory S. *The Mexican in the United States.* 1934. Reprint, San Francisco: R and E Research Associates, 1970.

Boudouris, James. "A Classification of Homicides." *Criminology* 11 (1973–74): 525–40.

———. "Trends in Homicide, Detroit: 1926–1968." PhD diss., Wayne State University, 1970.

Brearley, H. C. *Homicide in the United States.* Montclair, NJ: Patterson Smith, 1969, 1932.

———. "The Pattern of Violence." In *Culture in the South,* edited by W. T. Couch, 678–92. Chapel Hill: University of North Carolina Press, 1934.

Brenner, M. Harvey. "Economic Crises and Crime." In *Crime In Society,* edited by Leonard D. Savitz and Norman Johnston, 555–72. New York: John Wiley & Sons, 1978.

Brown, Richard Maxwell. *Strain of Violence.* New York: Oxford University Press, 1975.

———. "Violence." In *The Oxford History of the American West,* edited by Clyde A. Milner, Carol A. O'Connor, and Martha A. Sandweiss, 393–425. New York: Oxford University Press, 1994.

Bruce, Andrew A., and Thomas S. Fitzgerald. "A Study of Crime in the City of Memphis, Tennessee." Journal of the American Institute of Criminal Law & Criminology 19 (August 1928 Supplement): 3–127.

Bruce, Dickson D., Jr. *Violence and Culture in the Antebellum South.* Austin: University of Texas Press, 1979.

Burrough, Bryan. *Public Enemies: America's Greatest Crime Wave and the Birth of the FBI, 1933–34.* New York: Penguin Books, 2004.

Butterfield, Fox. *All God's Children: The Bosket Family and the American Tradition of Violence.* New York: Alfred A. Knopf, 1995.

Cantor, David, and Lawrence E. Cohen. "Comparing Measures of Homicide Trends: Methodological and Substantive Differences in the Vital Statistics and Uniform Crime Report Time Series (1933–1975)." *Social Science Research* 9 (1980): 121–45.

Cantor, David, and Kenneth C. Land. "Unemployment and Crime Rates in the Post-World War II United States: A Theoretical and Empirical Analysis." *American Sociological Review* 50 (1985): 317–32.

Capeci, Dominic. *The Harlem Riot of 1943.* Philadelphia: Temple University Press, 1977.

Capeci, Dominic J., Jr., and Martha Wilkerson. "The Detroit Rioters of 1943: A Reinterpretation." *Michigan Historical Review* 16 (1990): 49–72.

Cash, W. J. *The Mind of the South.* 1941. Reprint, Garden City, NY: Doubleday, 1954.

Chesnais, Jean-Claude. *Histoire de la violence en occident de 1800 à nos jours.* Paris: Editions Robert Laffont, 1981.

Chicago Historical Homicide Project. "Homicide in Chicago 1870–1930." http://homicide.northwestern.edu/.

Chicago Police Department. *Chicago Police Annual Report 1970.* 1971? https://portal.chicago
police.org/portal/page/portal/ClearPath/News/Statistical%20Reports/Annual%20
Reports/1970_AR.pdf, 18.

Chin, Ko-lin. *Chinese Subculture and Criminality.* Westport, CT: Greenwood Press, 1990.

Chiricos, Theodore G. "Rates of Crime and Unemployment: An Analysis of Aggregate
Research Evidence." *Social Problems* 34 (1987): 187–212.

City of New York, Board of City Magistrates. *Annual Report of the Board of City Magistrates
of the City of New York (First Division), For the Year Ending December 31, 1901.* New York:
J. W. Pratt, 1902.

Claghorn, Kate Holladay. "Crime and Immigration (Report of Committee of the Institute)." *Journal of the American Institute of Criminal Law and Criminology* 8 (1918):
675–93.

Clarke, James W. "Black-on-Black Violence." *Society* 33 (1996): 46–50.

———. *The Lineaments of Wrath: Race, Violent Crime, and American Culture.* New Brunswick, NJ: Transaction Publishers, 2001.

Conley, Carolyn A. "The Agreeable Recreation of Fighting." *Journal of Social History* 33
(1999): 57–72.

———. *Melancholy Accidents: The Meaning of Violence in Post-Famine Ireland.* Lanham,
MD: Lexington Books, 1999.

Cook, Waldo L. "Murders in Massachusetts." *Publications of the American Statistical Association* 3 (1893): 357–78.

Cooney, Mark. "The Decline of Elite Homicide." *Criminology* 35 (1997): 381–407.

Courtwright, David T. *Violent Land: Single Men and Social Disorder from the Frontier to the
Inner City.* Cambridge, MA: Harvard University Press, 1996.

Crail-Rugotzke, Donna. "A Matter of Guilt: The Treatment of Hispanic Inmates by New
Mexico Courts and the New Mexico Territorial Prison, 1890–1912." *New Mexico Historical Review* 74 (1999): 295–314.

Crouch, Barry A. "A Spirit of Lawlessness: White Violence; Texas Blacks, 1865–1868,"
*Journal of Social History* 18 (1984): 217–32.

Del Mar, David Peterson. *Beaten Down: A History of Interpersonal Violence in the West.*
Seattle: University of Washington Press, 2002.

Department of Health, City of Memphis. *A Study of Violent Deaths Registered in Atlanta,
Birmingham, Memphis and New Orleans for the Years 1921 and 1922,* by J. J. Durrett and
W. G. Stromquist. Memphis, TN: Davis Printing, [1924?].

Dollard, John. *Caste and Class in a Southern Town,* 3d ed. Garden City, NY: Doubleday, 1949.

Drake, St. Clair, and Horace R. Cayton. *Black Metropolis: A Study of Negro Life in a Northern
City.* 1945. Reprint, Chicago: University of Chicago Press, 1962, 1970.

Du Bois, W. E. B. "Crime in Georgia." In *Some Notes on Negro Crime particularly in Georgia*, edited by W. E. B. Du Bois, 2–9. Atlanta: Atlanta University Press, 1904.

———. *The Philadelphia Negro: A Social Study.* 1899. Reprint, New York: Schocken Books, 1967.

Durkheim, Emile. *Suicide: A Study in Sociology.* Translated by John A. Spaulding and George Simpson. 1897. Reprint, Glencoe, IL: Free Press, 1951.

Duwe, Grant. "The Patterns and Prevalence of Mass Murder in Twentieth-Century America." *Justice Quarterly* 21 (2004): 729–61.

Dykstra, Robert R. *The Cattle Towns: A Social History of the Kansas Cattle Trading Centers.* New York: Alfred A. Knopf, 1968.

———. "Overdosing on Dodge City." *Western Historical Quarterly* 27 (1996): 505–514.

Eckberg, Douglas Lee. "Estimates of Early Twentieth-Century U.S. Homicide Rates: An Econometric Forecasting Approach." *Demography* 32 (1995): 1–16.

Eig, Jonathan. *Get Capone: The Secret Plot That Captured America's Most Wanted Gangster.* New York: Simon & Schuster, 2010.

Eisner, Manuel. "Long-Term Historical Trends in Violent Crime." *Crime & Justice* 30 (2003): 83–142.

Elias, Norbert. *The Civilizing Process: Sociogenetic and Psychogenetic Investigations.* 1994. Revised edition, Oxford: Blackwell Publishing, 2000.

Elliott, Mabel A. "Crime and the Frontier Mores." *American Sociological Review* 9 (1944): 185–92.

Elofson, Warren M. "Law and Disorder on the Ranching Frontiers of Montana and Alberta/Assiniboia, 1870–1914." *Journal of the West* 42 (2003): 40–51.

Espy, M. Watt, and John Ortiz Smykla. "Executions in the United States, 1608–2002: The Espy File." Ann Arbor, MI: Inter-University Consortium for Political and Social Research, Study No. 8451. 2016. https://doi.org/10.3886/ICPSR08451.v5. Available at http://www.deathpenaltyinfo.org/executions-us-1608–2002-espy-file.

Fairlie, Robert W., and William A. Sundstrom. "The Racial Unemployment Gap in Long-Run Perspective." *American Economic Review* 87 (1997): 306–10.

Falkner, Roland P. "Crime and the Census." *Annals of the American Academy of Political and Social Science* 9 (1897): 42–69.

Federal Bureau of Investigation. *Crime in the United States; Uniform Crime Reports* (multiple years).

Felson, Marcus, and Lawrence E. Cohen. "Human Ecology and Crime: A Routine Activity Approach." *Human Ecology* 8 (1980): 389–406.

Ferdinand, Theodore N. "The Criminal Patterns of Boston since 1849." *American Journal of Sociology* 73 (1967): 84–99.

Fischer, David Hackett. *Albion's Seed: Four British Folkways in America.* New York: Oxford University Press, 1989.

Foerster, Robert F. *The Italian Emigration of Our Times.* Cambridge, MA: Harvard University Press, 1919.

Fogelson, Robert M. *The Fragmented Metropolis: Los Angeles, 1850–1930.* Cambridge, MA: Harvard University Press, 1967.

Forret, Jeff. "Conflict and the "Slave Community": Violence among Slaves in Upcountry South Carolina." *Journal of Southern History* 74 (2008): 551–88.

———. *Slave Against Slave: Plantation Violence in the Old South.* Baton Rouge: Louisiana State University Press, 2015.

Fosdick, Raymond B. *American Police Systems.* New York: Century, 1920.

Fried, Albert. *The Rise and Fall of the Jewish Gangster in America,* rev. ed. New York: Columbia University Press, 1993.

Gann, L. H., and Peter J. Duignan. *The Hispanics in the United States: A History.* Boulder, CO: Westview Press, 1986.

Garfinkel, Harold. "Research Note on Inter- and Intra-Racial Homicides." *Social Forces* 27 (1949): 369–81.

Gastil, Raymond. "Homicide and a Regional Culture of Violence." *American Sociological Review* 36 (1971): 412–27.

[Georgia.] *Biennial Report of the Principal Keeper of the Georgia Penitentiary From the 20th of October, 1880, to the 20th of October, 1882.* [Georgia.]: James P. Harrison, State Printer, n.d.). https://babel.hathitrust.org/cgi/pt?id=uiug.30112000799442&view=1up&seq=1.

Glazer, Nathan, and Daniel Patrick Moynihan. *Beyond the Melting Pot; The Negroes, Puerto Ricans, Jews, Italians, and Irish of New York City.* Cambridge, MA: M.I.T. Press, 1963.

Gómez, Laura E. "Race, Colonialism, and Criminal Law: Mexicans and the American Criminal Justice System in Territorial New Mexico." *Law & Society Review* 34 (2000): 1129–1202.

Gonzales, Manuel G. *Mexicanos: A History of Mexicans in the United States.* Bloomington: Indiana University Press, 1999.

Gorn, Elliott J. "'Good-Bye Boys, I Die a True American': Homicide, Nativism, and Working-Class Culture in Antebellum New York City." *Journal of American History* 74 (1987): 388–410.

———. "'Gouge and Bite, Pull Hair and Scratch': The Social Significance of Fighting in the Southern Backcountry." *American Historical Review* 90 (1985): 18–43.

Grantham, Dewey W. *The South in Modern America: A Region at Odds.* New York: Harper-Collins, 1994.

Green, Edward. "Race, Social Status, and Criminal Arrest." *American Sociological Review* 35 (1970): 476–90.

Gregory, James N. *The Southern Diaspora: How the Great Migrations of Black and White Southerners Transformed America.* Chapel Hill: University of North Carolina Press, 2005.

Gunther, Vanessa. "Indians and the Criminal Justice System in San Bernardino and San Diego Counties, 1850–1900." *Journal of the West* 39 (2000): 26–34.

Gurr, Ted Robert. "Historical Trends in Violent Crime: A Critical Review of the Evidence" *Crime and Justice* 3 (1981): 295–353.

———. "Historical Trends in Violent Crime: Europe and the United States." In *Violence in America, Volume 1: The History of Crime,* edited by Ted Robert Gurr, 21–54. Newbury Park, CA: Sage Publications, 1989.

Gutman, Herbert B. *The Black Family in Slavery and Freedom, 1750–1925.* New York: Pantheon Books, 1976.

Hackney, Sheldon. "Southern Violence." *American Historical Review* 74 (1969): 906–25.

Haller, Mark H. "Organized Crime in Urban Society: Chicago in the Twentieth Century." *Journal of Social History* 5 (1971–72): 210–34.

Hayner, Norman S. "Social Factors in Oriental Crime." *American Journal of Sociology* 43 (1938): 908–19.

Haynes, George Edmund. "Conditions Among Negroes in the Cities." *Annals of the American Academy of Political and Social Science* 49 (1913): 105–19.

Helmer, John. *Drugs and Minority Oppression.* New York: Seabury Press, 1975.

Henry, Andrew F., and James F. Short. *Suicide & Homicide: Some Economic, Sociological and Psychological Aspects of Aggression.* Glencoe, IL: Free Press, 1954.

Hietter, Paul T. "A Surprising Amount of Justice: The Experience of Mexican and Racial Minority Defendants Charged with Serious Crimes in Arizona, 1865–1920." *Pacific Historical Review* 70 (2001): 183–219.

Hindus, Michael Stephen. *Prison and Plantation: Crime, Justice, and Authority in Massachusetts and South Carolina, 1767–1878.* Chapel Hill: University of North Carolina Press, 1980.

Hines, Elizabeth, and Eliza Steelwater. Project HAL: Historical American Lynching. http://people.uncw.edu/hinese/HAL/HAL%20Web%20Page.htm#HAL%20History.

Hoffman, Frederick L. *The Homicide Problem.* Newark, NJ: Prudential Press, 1925.

———. "The Increase in Murder." *Annals of the American Academy of Political and Social Science* 125 (1926): 20–29.

———. "The Race Traits and Tendencies of the American Negro." *Publications of the American Economic Association* 11 (1896): 1–329.

Hollon, W. Eugene. *Frontier Violence: Another Look.* New York: Oxford University Press, 1974.

Holmes, Joseph L. "Crime and the Press." *Journal of the American Institute of Criminal Law & Criminology* 20 (1929): 6–59.

Howard, George Elliott. "Alcohol and Crime: A Study in Social Causation." *American Journal of Sociology* 24 (1918): 61–80.

Howington, Arthur F. "The Treatment of Slaves and Free Blacks in the State and Local Courts of Tennessee." PhD diss., Vanderbilt University, 1982.

———. *What Sayeth the Law: The Treatment of Slaves and Free Blacks in the State and Local Courts of Tennessee*. New York: Garland Publishing, 1986.

Hunter, Robert. *Poverty*. New York: Macmillan, 1907.

Huntington, Samuel P. *Political Order in Changing Societies*. New Haven, CT: Yale University Press, 1968.

Hurt, R. Douglas, ed. *African-American Life in the Rural South, 1900–1950*. Columbia: University of Missouri Press, 2003.

Ianni, Francis A. J. "The Mafia and the Web of Kinship." *Public Interest* 22 (1971): 78–100.

Iorizzo, Luciano J., and Salvatore Mondello. *The Italian-Americans*. Youngstown, NY: Cambria Press, 2006.

Issel, William, and Robert W. Cherny. *San Francisco, 1865–1932: Politics, Power, and Urban Development*. Berkeley: University of California Press, 1986.

Jackson, Kenneth T., ed. *The Encyclopedia of New York City*. New Haven, CT: Yale University Press, 1991.

Jensen, Gary F. "Prohibition, Alcohol, and Murder: Untangling Countervailing Mechanisms." *Homicide Studies* 4 (2000): 18–36.

Johnson, Charles S. *Growing Up in the Black Belt: Negro Youth in the Rural South*. Washington, DC: American Council on Education, 1941.

———. *The Negro in American Civilization: A Study of Negro Life and Race Relations in the Light of Social Research*. New York: Henry Holt, 1930.

Johnson, David R. *American Law Enforcement: A History*. St. Louis: Forum Press, 1981.

Johnson, Eric A. "Cities Don't Cause Crime: Urban-Rural Differences in Late Nineteenth- and Early Twentieth-Century German Criminality." *Social Science History* 16 (1992): 129–76.

Johnson, Guy B. "The Negro and Crime." *Annals of the American Academy of Political and Social Science* 217 (1941): 93–104.

Johnson, Ryan S., Shawn Kantor, and Price V. Fishback. "Striking at the Roots of Crime: The Impact of Social Welfare Spending on Crime During the Great Depression." NBER Working Paper No. 12825, rev. March 2010. http://www.nber.org/tmp/70986-w12825.pdf.

Jones, Jacqueline. *The Dispossessed: America's Underclasses from the Civil War to the Present*. New York: Basic Books, 1992.

Joselit, Jenna Weissman. "Dark Shadows: New York Jews and Crime, 1900–1940." PhD diss., Columbia University, 1980.

———. *Our Gang: Jewish Crime and the New York Jewish Community, 1900–1940*. Bloomington: Indiana University Press, 1983.

Kaplan, Michael. "New York City Tavern Violence and the Creation of a Working-Class Male Identity." *Journal of the Early Republic* 15 (1995): 591–617.

Kennett, Lee, and James LaVerne Anderson. *The Gun in America: The Origins of a National Dilemma*. Westport, CT: Greenwood Press, 1975.

Klebba, A. Joan. "Homicide Trends in the United States, 1900–74." *Public Health Reports* 90 (1975): 195–204.

Kornweibel, Theodore, Jr. "An Economic Profile of Black Life in the Twenties." *Journal of Black Studies* 6 (1976): 307–20.

Kusmer, Kenneth L. *A Ghetto Takes Shape: Black Cleveland, 1870–1930*. Urbana: University of Illinois Press, 1976.

Kyvig, David E. *Daily Life in the United States, 1920–1940: How Americans Lived Through the "Roaring Twenties" and the Great Depression*. Chicago: Ivan R. Dee, 2004.

———. *Repealing National Prohibition*. Chicago: University of Chicago Press, 1979.

LaFree, Gary. *Losing Legitimacy: Street Crime and the Decline of Social Institutions in America*. Boulder, CO: Westview Press, 1998.

Lane, Roger. "Crime and Criminal Statistics in Nineteenth-Century Massachusetts." *Journal of Social History* 2 (1968): 156–63.

———. *Murder in America: A History*. Columbus: Ohio State University Press, 1997.

———. "On the Social Meaning of Homicide Trends in America." In *Violence in America, Volume 1: The History of Crime*, edited by Ted Robert Gurr, 55–79. Newbury Park, CA: Sage Publications, 1989.

———. *Roots of Violence in Black Philadelphia, 1860–1900*. Cambridge, MA: Harvard University Press, 1986.

———. "Urban Police and Crime in Nineteenth-Century America." *Crime & Justice* 15 (1992): 1–50.

———. *Violent Death in the City: Suicide, Accident, and Murder in Nineteenth-Century Philadelphia*. Cambridge, MA: Harvard University Press, 1979.

———. *William Dorsey's Philadelphia and Ours: On the Past and Future of the Black City in America*. New York: Oxford University Press, 1991.

Lardner, James, and Thomas Reppetto. *NYPD: A City and Its Police*. New York: Henry Holt, 2000.

Lashly, Arthur V. "Homicide (in Cook County)," Part II, Chap. XIII of *The Illinois Crime Survey*. Illinois Association for Criminal Justice. Chicago: Blakely Printing, 1929.

Latzer, Barry. *The Rise and Fall of Violent Crime in America*. New York: Encounter Books, 2016.

———. "Subcultures of Violence and African American Crime Rates." *Journal of Criminal Justice* 54 (2018): 41–49.

Lee, Matthew R., William B. Bankston, Timothy C. Hayes, and Shaun A. Thomas. "Revisiting the Southern Culture of Violence." *Sociological Quarterly* 48 (2007): 253–75.

Lee, Matthew R., Shaun A. Thomas, and Graham C. Ousey. "Southern Culture and Homicide: Examining the Cracker Culture/Black Rednecks Thesis." *Deviant Behavior* 31 (2009): 60–96.

Lemann, Nicholas. *The Promised Land: The Great Black Migration and How It Changed America*. New York: Alfred A. Knopf, 1991.

Lender, Mark Edward, and James Kirby Martin. *Drinking in America: A History*. New York: Free Press, 1987.

Leonard, Stephen J. *Lynching in Colorado, 1859–1919*. Boulder: University Press of Colorado, 2002.

Lester, David. *Crime and the Native American*. Springfield, IL: Charles C. Thomas, 1999.

Levine, Harry G., and Craig Reinarman. "From Prohibition to Regulation: Lessons from Alcohol Policy for Drug Policy." *Milbank Quarterly* 69 (1991): 461–94.

Levy, Jerrold E., and Stephen J. Kunitz. "Indian Reservations, Anomie, and Social Pathologies." *Southwestern Journal of Anthropology* 27 (1971): 97–128.

Lord, Eliot, John J. D. Trenor, and Samuel J. Barrows. *The Italian in America*. New York: B. F. Buck, 1905.

Lottier, Stuart. "Distribution of Criminal Offenses in Sectional Regions." *Journal of Criminal Law and Criminology* 29 (1938): 329–44.

Lyle, John H. *The Dry and Lawless Years*. Englewood Cliffs, NJ: Prentice-Hall, 1960.

Mancall, Peter C. *Deadly Medicine: Indians and Alcohol in Early America*. Ithaca, NY: Cornell University Press, 1995.

Mancini, Matthew J. "Race, Economics, and the Abandonment of Convict Leasing." *Journal of Negro History* 63 (1978): 339–52.

McGirr, Lisa. *The War on Alcohol: Prohibition and the Rise of the Amercian State*. New York, W. W. Norton, 2016.

McGrath, Roger D. "Violence and Lawlessness on the Western Frontier." In *Violence in America, Volume 1: The History of Crime*, edited by Ted Robert Gurr, 122–45. Newbury Park, CA: Sage Publications, 1989.

McKanna, Clare V., Jr. "Enclaves of Violence in Nineteenth-Century California." *Pacific Historical Review* 73 (2004): 391–423.

———. *Homicide, Race, and Justice in the American West, 1880–1920*. Tucson: University of Arizona Press, 1997.

———. *Race and Homicide in Nineteenth-Century California*. Reno: University of Nevada Press, 2002.

McLaughlin, Gerald T. "Cocaine: The History and Regulation of a Dangerous Drug." *Cornell Law Review* 58 (1972–73): 537–73.

McLaughlin, Vance, and Richard R. E. Kania. "Savannah Homicides in a Century of Change: 1896 to 1903 and 1986 to 1993." *Sociation Today* 6 (2008), http://www.ncsociology.org/sociationtoday/v61/savannah.htm.

McMahon, Richard. "'A Violent Society'? Homicide Rates in Ireland, 1831–1850." *Irish Economic and Social History* 36 (2009): 1–20.

McNair, Glenn. *Criminal Injustice: Slaves and Free Blacks in Georgia's Criminal Justice System.* Charlottesville: University of Virginia Press, 2009.

McWhiney, Grady. *Cracker Culture: Celtic Ways in the Old South.* Tuscaloosa: University of Alabama Press, 1988.

Meier, August, and Elliott Rudwick. *From Plantation to Ghetto.* 1966. Revised edition, New York: Hill & Wang, 1970.

Merton, Robert K. "Social Structure and Anomie." *American Sociological Review* 3 (1938): 672–82.

Miller, Donald L. *City of the Century: The Epic of Chicago and the Making of America.* New York: Simon & Schuster, 1996.

Moehling, Carolyn, and Anne Morrison Piehl. "Immigration, Crime, and Incarceration in Early Twentieth-Century America." *Demography* 46 (2009): 739–63.

Monkkonen, Eric H. "A Disorderly People? Urban Order in the Nineteenth and Twentieth Centuries." *Journal of American History* 68 (1981): 539–59.

———. "Diverging Homicide Rates: England and the United States, 1850–1875." In *Violence in America, Volume 1: The History of Crime,* edited by Ted Robert Gurr, 84–93. Newbury Park, CA: Sage Publications, 1989.

———. "Homicide in Los Angeles, 1827–2002." *Journal of Interdisciplinary History* 36 (2005): 167–83.

———. "Homicide in Los Angeles, 1830–2003." Columbus: Historical Violence Database, Criminal Justice Research Center, Ohio State University. http://cjrc.osu.edu/research projects/hvd/usa/la/.2005.

———. "Homicides in New York City, 1797–1999 [And Various Historical Comparison Sites]." Ann Arbor, MI: Inter-University Consortium for Political and Social Research, Study No. 3226. 2001. https://doi.org/10.3886/ICPSR03226.v1.

———. *Murder in New York City.* Berkeley: University of California Press, 2001.

———. "Police Departments, Arrests and Crime in the United States, 1860–1920." Ann Arbor, MI: Inter-University Consortium for Political and Social Research, Study No. 7708. 2005.

———. *Police in Urban America 1860–1920.* Cambridge: Cambridge University Press, 1981.

Montell, William Lynwood. *Killings: Folk Justice in the Upper South.* Lexington: University Press of Kentucky, 1986.

Moore, John Hammond. *Carnival of Blood: Dueling, Lynching, and Murder in South Carolina, 1880–1920.* Columbia: University of South Carolina Press, 2006.

Mullen, Kevin J. *Dangerous Strangers: Minority Newcomers and Criminal Violence in the Urban West, 1850–2000.* New York: Palgrave Macmillan, 2005.

Musto, David F. "Opium, Cocaine and Marijuana in American History." *Scientific American* 265 (1991): 40–47.

National Commission on Law Observance and Enforcement. *Report on Crime and the Foreign Born*, Part III, "The Mexican Immigrant and the Problem of Crime and Criminal Justice." Washington, DC: Government Printing Office, 1931.

———. *Report on the Enforcement of the Prohibition Laws of the United States*. Washington, DC: Government Printing Office, 1931.

Nelli, Humbert S. *The Business of Crime: Italians and Syndicate Crime in the United States*. New York: Oxford University Press, 1976.

———. "Italians and Crime in Chicago: The Formative Years, 1890–1920." *American Journal of Sociology* 74 (1969): 373–91.

———. "The Hennessy Murder and the Mafia in New Orleans." *Italian Quarterly* 19 (1975): 77–95.

New York City Department of Health, Coroner and Office of Chief Medical Examiner, 1823–1946. http://www.nyc.gov/html/records/html/collections/collections_coroner .shtml.

New York City Police Department. *Annual Report 1917*. New York: Police Department Bureau of Printing, 1917.

Nisbett, Richard E., and Dov Cohen. *Culture of Honor: The Psychology of Violence in the South*. Boulder, CO: Westview Press, 1996.

Nostrand, Richard. "The Hispano Homeland in 1900." *Annals of the Association of American Geographers* 70 (1980): 382–96.

O'Connor, Richard. *Hell's Kitchen The Roaring Days of New York's Wild West Side*. New York: J. B. Lippincott, 1958.

O'Donnell, Ian. "Lethal Violence in Ireland, 1841 to 2003." *British Journal of Criminology* 45 (2005): 671–95.

Odum, Howard W. "Social and Mental Traits of the Negro: Research into the Conditions of the Negro Race in Southern Towns." PhD diss., Columbia University, 1910.

———. *Southern Regions of the United States*. Chapel Hill: University of North Carolina Press, 1936.

Oliver, William M., and James F. Hilgenberg. *A History of Crime and Criminal Justice in America*, 2d ed. Durham, NC: Carolina Academic Press, 2010.

Olzak, Susan. "The Political Context of Competition: Lynching and Urban Racial Violence, 1882–1914." *Social Forces* 69 (1990): 395–421.

Osofsky, Gilbert. *Harlem: The Making of a Ghetto: Negro New York, 1890–1930*. New York: Harper & Row, 1966.

Owens, Emily Greene. "Are Underground Markets Really More Violent? Evidence from Early 20th Century America." *American Law and Economics Review* 13 (2011): 1–44.

Paciotti, Brian. "Homicide in Seattle's Chinatown, 1900–1940: Evaluating the Influence of Social Organizations." *Homicide Studies* 9 (2005): 229–55.

Pandiani, John A. "The Crime Control Corps: An Invisible New Deal Program." *British Journal of Sociology* 33 (1982): 348–58.

Parker, Robert Nash. *Alcohol and Homicide: A Deadly Combination of Two American Traditions.* Albany: State University of New York Press, 1995.

Parker, Robert Nash, and Kathleen Auerhahn. "Alcohol, Drugs, and Violence." *Annual Review of Sociology* 24 (1998): 291–311.

Pfeifer, Michael J. *The Roots of Rough Justice: Origins of American Lynching.* Urbana: University of Illinois Press, 2011.

———. *Rough Justice: Lynching and American Society, 1874–1947.* Urbana: University of Illinois Press, 2004.

Piccato, Pablo. *City of Suspects; Crime in Mexico City, 1900–1931.* Durham, NC: Duke University Press, 2001.

Pitkin, Thomas M., and Francesco Cordasco. *The Black Hand: A Chapter in Ethnic Crime.* Totowa, NJ: Littlefield, Adams, 1977.

Polenberg, Richard. "The Decline of the New Deal." In *The New Deal: The National Level,* edited by John Braeman, Robert H. Bremner, and David Brody, 246–66. Columbus: Ohio State University Press, 1975.

Porterfield, Austin L. "A Decade of Serious Crimes in the United States: Some Trends and Hypotheses." *American Sociological Review* 13 (1948): 44–54.

Potter, Ellen C. "Aspects of Crime in Relation to the Crime Wave." *Annals of the American Academy of Political and Social Science* 125 (1926): 1–19.

Powell, Elwin H. "Crime as a Function of Anomie." *Journal of Criminal Law, Criminology, and Police Science* 57 (1966): 161–71.

Proctor, H. H., and M. N. Work. "Atlanta and Savannah." In *Some Notes on Negro Crime particularly in Georgia,* edited by W. E. B. Du Bois, 49–52. Atlanta: Atlanta University Press, 1904.

Rabinowitz, Howard N. *Race, Ethnicity, and Urbanization.* Columbia: University of Missouri Press, 1994.

Radzinowicz, Leon. "The Influence of Economic Conditions on Crime." *Sociological Review* 33 (1941): 139–53.

Redfield, H. V. *Homicide, North and South.* Philadelphia: J. B. Lippincott, 1880.

Reisler, Mark. "The Mexican Immigrant in the Chicago Area during the 1920's." *Journal of the Illinois State Historical Society* 66 (1973): 144–58.

Reppetto, Thomas. *American Mafia: A History of Its Rise to Power.* New York: Henry Holt, 2004.

Ridings, Jim. *Images of America: Chicago to Springfield: Crime and Politics in the 1920s.* Charleston, SC: Arcadia Publishing, 2010.

Riis, Jacob A. *How the Other Half Lives: Studies Among the Tenements of New York.* New York: Charles Scribner's Sons, 1890.

Rosales, F. Arturo. *¡Pobre Raza!: Violence, Justice, and Mobilization among México Lindo Immigrants, 1900–1936.* Austin: University of Texas Press, 1999.

———. "The Regional Origins of Mexicano Immigrants to Chicago During the 1920s." *Aztlán: A Journal of Chicano Studies* 7 (1976): 187–201.

Rosenbaum, Betty B. "The Relationship between War and Crime in the United States." *Journal of Criminal Law and Criminology* 30 (1940): 722–40.

Ross, Christine, Sheldon Danziger, and Eugene Smolensky. "The Level and Trend of Poverty in the United States, 1939–1979." *Demography* 24 (1987): 587–600.

Roth, Randolph. *American Homicide.* Cambridge, MA: Harvard University Press, 2009.

———. *American Homicide Supplemental Volume (AHSV), American Homicides (AH),* 2010. http://cjrc.osu.edu/researchprojects/hvd/AHSV/tables/AHSV%20American%20Homicides%205-2010.pdf.

Roth, Randolph, Michael D. Maltz, and Douglas L. Eckberg. "Homicide Rates in the Old West." *Western Historical Quarterly* 42 (2011): 173–95.

Rousey, Dennis C. *Policing the Southern City: New Orleans, 1805–1889.* Baton Rouge: Louisiana State University Press, 1996.

Ryscavage, Paul. *Income Inequality in America: An Analysis of Trends.* Armonk, NY: M. E. Sharpe, 1999.

Salmond, John A. *The Civilian Conservation Corps, 1933–1942: A New Deal Case Study.* Durham, NC: Duke University Press, 1967.

Sante, Luc. *Low Life: Lures and Snares of Old New York.* New York: Farrar, Strauss, & Giroux, 1991.

Schwarz, Philip J. *Twice Condemned: Slaves and the Criminal Laws of Virginia, 1705–1865.* Baton Rouge: Louisiana State University Press, 1988.

Sellin, Thorsten. "Crime and Delinquency in the United States: An Over-All View." *Annals of the American Academy of Political and Social Science* 339 (1962): 11–23.

———. "Is Murder Increasing in Europe?" *Annals of the American Academy of Political and Social Science* 125 (1926): 29–34.

———. "The Negro Criminal: A Statistical Note." *Annals of the American Academy of Political and Social Science* 140 (1928): 52–64.

Shaw, Clifford R., and Henry D. McKay. *Juvenile Delinquency and Urban Areas.* Rev. ed. 1942. Reprint, Chicago: University of Chicago Press, 1969.

Shirley, Glenn. *West of Hell's Fringe: Crime, Criminals, and the Federal Peace Officer in Oklahoma Territory, 1889–1907.* Norman: University of Oklahoma Press, 1978.

Smiley, Gene R. "Recent Unemployment Rate Estimates for the 1920s and 1930s." *Journal of Economic History* 43 (1983): 487–93.

Smolensky, Eugene, and Robert Plotnick. "Inequality and Poverty in the United States: 1900 to 1990." Institute for Research on Poverty Discussion Paper No. 998–93. 1992. http://www.irp.wisc.edu/publications/dps/pdfs/dp99893.pdf.

Sowell, Thomas. *Black Rednecks and White Liberals.* San Francisco: Encounter Books, 2005.

———. *Race and Culture: A World View.* New York: Basic Books, 1994.

Spear, Allan H. *Black Chicago: The Making of a Negro Ghetto, 1890–1920.* Chicago: University of Chicago Press, 1967.

Spierenburg, Pieter. "Democracy Came Too Early: A Tentative Explanation for the Problem of American Homicide." *American Historical Review* 111 (2006): 104–14.

———. *A History of Murder: Personal Violence in Europe from the Middle Ages to the Present.* Cambridge, UK: Polity Press, 2008.

Sundstrom, William A. "Last Hired, First Fired? Unemployment and Urban Black Workers during the Great Depression." *Journal of Economic History* 52 (1992): 415–29.

Sutherland, Edwin H. "Crime." In *American Society in Wartime,* edited by William Fielding Ogburn. 1943. Reprint, New York: Da Capo Press, 1972.

———. "Murder and the Death Penalty." *Journal of the American Institute of Criminal Law & Criminology* 15 (1925): 522–29.

———. *Principles of Criminology,* 3d ed. Chicago: J. B. Lippincott, 1939.

Sutherland, Edwin H., and Donald R. Cressey. *Criminology,* 8th ed. Philadelphia: J. B. Lippincott, 1970.

Sutherland, Edwin H., and C. E. Gehlke. "Crime and Punishment." In *Recent Social Trends in the United States,* 2:1114–67. Report of the President's Research Committee on Social Trends. New York: McGraw-Hill, 1933.

Taft, Donald R. "Nationality and Crime." *American Sociological Review* 1 (1936): 724–36.

Thernstrom, Stephan, ed., *Harvard Encyclopedia of American Ethnic Groups.* 1980. Reprint, Cambridge, MA: Belknap Press of Harvard University, 1994.

Timberlake, James H. *Prohibition and the Progressive Movement, 1900–1920.* Cambridge, MA: Harvard University Press, 1963.

Tolnay, Stewart E. "The African American 'Great Migration' and Beyond." *Annual Review of Sociology* 29 (2003): 209–32.

———. "The Living Arrangements of African American and Immigrant Children, 1880–2000." *Journal of Family History* 29 (2004): 421–45.

Tolnay, Stewart E., and Amy Kate Bailey. "Creating a New Database for the Study of Southern Lynchings: Public Use Microdata, *The Historical United States County Boundary Files 179–1999* and Forensic Demography." 2006. http://paa2006.princeton.edu/download .aspx?submissionId=60387.

Tolnay, Stewart Emory, and E. M. Beck. "Black Flight: Lethal Violence and the Great Migration, 1900–1930." *Social Science History* 14 (1990): 347–70.

———. *A Festival of Violence: An Analysis of Southern Lynchings, 1882–1930.* Champaign: University of Illinois Press, 1995.

Trelease, Allen W. *White Terror: The Ku Klux Klan Conspiracy and Southern Reconstruction.* Baton Rouge: Louisiana State University Press, 1971.

U.S. Bureau of the Census. *The Social and Economic Status Black Population in the United States: An Historical View, 1790–1978,* Current Population Reports, P-23, No. 80. Washington, DC: Government Printing Office, 1979.

U.S. Congress, Congressional Research Service, *American War and Military Operations Casualties: Lists and Statistics,* by Nese F. DeBruyne, RL32492, 2018, https://fas.org/sgp/crs/natsec/RL32492.pdf.

U.S. Department of Commerce, Bureau of the Census. *Immigrants and Their Children 1920,* by Niles Carpenter. Washington, DC: Government Printing Office, 1927.

———. *Mortality Statistics* (various years).

———. *Prisoners 1923.* Washington, DC: Government Printing Office, 1926.

———. *Prisoners and Juvenile Delinquents in the United States 1910.* Washington, DC: Government Printing Office, 1918.

———. *Prisoners in State and Federal Prisons and Reformatories 1929 and 1930.* Washington, DC: Government Printing Office, 1932.

———. *The Social and Economic Status of the Black Population in the United States: An Historical View, 1790–1978,* Current Population Reports, Special Studies, Series P-23, No. 80. Washington, DC: Government Printing Office, 1979.

———. *Vital Statistics of the United States* (various years).

U.S. Department of Commerce and Labor, Bureau of the Census. *Special Reports, Prisoners and Juvenile Delinquents in Institutions 1904.* Washington, DC: Government Printing Office, 1907.

U.S. Department of the Interior, Census Office. *Report on Crime, Pauperism, and Benevolence in the United States at the Eleventh Census: 1890.* Washington, DC: Government Printing Office, 1896.

———. *Report on the Defective, Dependent, and Delinquent Classes of the Population of the United States.* Washington, DC: Government Printing Office, 1888.

U.S. Immigration Commission. *Immigration and Crime.* Washington, DC: Government Printing Office, 1911.

U.S. National Emergency Council. *Report on Economic Conditions of the South.* Washington, DC: Government Printing Office, 1938.

U.S. Office of Management and Budget. *Social Indicators 1973.* Washington, DC: Government Printing Office, 1973.

U.S. Public Health Service, National Office of Vital Statistics. *Vital Statistics Rates in the United States 1900–1940,* by Forrest E. Linder and Robert D. Grove. Washington, DC: Government Printing Office, 1947.

Utley, Robert M. *The Indian Frontier of the American West 1846–1890*. Albuquerque: University of New Mexico Press, 1984.

Vandal, Gilles. "Black Violence in Post–Civil War Louisiana." *Journal of Interdisciplinary History* 251 (1994): 45–64.

———. *Rethinking Southern Violence: Homicides in Post–Civil War Louisiana, 1866–1884*. Columbus: Ohio State University Press, 2000.

Vedder, Richard K., and Lowell Gallaway. "Racial Differences in Unemployment in the United States, 1890–1990." *Journal of Economic History* 52 (1992): 696–702.

Von Hentig, Hans. *Crime: Causes and Conditions*. New York: McGraw-Hill, 1947.

———. "The Criminality of the Negro." *Journal of Criminal Law and Criminology* 30 (1940): 662–80.

Warner, Sam Bass. *Crime and Criminal Statistics in Boston*. Cambridge, MA: Harvard University Press, 1934.

———. *Streetcar Suburbs: The Process of Growth in Boston, 1870–1900*. 1962. Reprint, Cambridge, MA: Harvard University Press, 1978.

Washburn, Kevin K. "American Indians, Crime, and the Law." *Michigan Law Review* 104 (2006): 709–77.

Wassermann, Rudolf. *Beruf, Konfession und Verbrechen: Eine Studie über die Kriminalität der Juden in Vergangenheit und Gegenwart*. München: Ernst Reinhardt, 1907.

Watts, Eugene J. "The Police in Atlanta, 1890–1905." *Journal of Southern History* 39 (1973): 165–82.

Weiner, Neil Alan, and Margaret A. Zahn. "Violence Arrests in the City: The Philadelphia Story, 1857–1980." In *Violence in America, Volume 1: The History of Crime*, edited by Ted Robert Gurr, 107–21. Newbury Park, CA: Sage Publications, 1989.

White, Richard. *"It's Your Misfortune and None of My Own": A New History of the American West*. Norman: University of Oklahoma Press, 1991.

Willbach, Harry. "The Trend of Crime in Chicago." *American Institute of Criminal Law & Criminology* 31 (1940–41): 720–27.

———. "The Trend of Crime in New York City." *American Institute of Criminal Law & Criminology* 29 (1938–39): 62–75.

Williamson, Joel. *The Crucible of Race: Black-White Relations in the American South since Emancipation*. New York: Oxford University Press, 1984.

Wilson, Charles Reagan, and William Ferris, eds. *Encyclopedia of Southern Culture*. New York: Anchor Books, 1989.

Wolfgang, Marvin, and Franco Ferracuti. *The Subculture of Violence: Towards an Integrated Theory in Criminology*. London: Tavistock Publications, 1967.

Woodward, C. Vann. *Reunion & Reaction: The Compromise of 1877 and the End of Reconstruction*. Boston: Little, Brown, 1951.

———. *The Strange Career of Jim Crow*, 2d rev. ed. New York: Oxford University Press, 1966.

Work, Monroe N. "Crime in Cities." In *Some Notes on Negro Crime particularly in Georgia*, edited by W. E. B. Du Bois, 18–32. Atlanta: Atlanta University Press, 1904.

———. "Negro Criminality in the South." *Annals of the American Academy of Political and Social Science* 49 (1913): 74–80.

Wyatt-Brown, Bertram. *Southern Honor: Ethics and Behavior in the Old South.* New York: Oxford University Press, 1982.

Zehr, Howard. *Crime and the Development of Modern Society: Patterns of Criminality in Nineteenth Century Germany and France.* Totowa, NJ: Rowman & Littlefield, 1976.

Zimring, Franklin E., and Gordon Hawkins. *Crime Is Not the Problem: Lethal Violence in America.* New York: Oxford University Press, 1997.

# INDEX

Abbott, Edith, 252, 363n14

Addams, Jane, 182, 271

Adler, Jeffrey S., 71, 110, 185, 189, 190, 191, 206, 207, 235, 284, 336n29, 337n31, 338n17, 351n76, 351n81, 352n84, 352n96, 364n28, 366n60

adversities, crime and, xi, xii, 89, 91, 118, 316, 323

African Americans: age of, and crime, xiv, 44, 255; arrests of, 21, 30, 31, 32, 33, 34, 35, 40, 43, 48, 96, 102, 308, 331n43; biased sentencing of, 28, 32, 38, 44, 92, 94, 96, 327n36; courts and, 27, 28, 32, 35–37, 41, 42, 45, 92, 114, 117, 327n36; education of, 26, 36, 51, 53, 58, 89, 107, 296; employment of, 27, 37, 47, 53, 86, 87, 89, 106, 107, 108, 110, 265, 277, 298, 300, 307, 330n20, 340n51; execution of, 17, 25, 48, 328n42, 329n6; homicide mortality of, 3, 44, 48, 96, 99, 102, 103, 114, 118, 119, 308, 346n113; housing of, 34, 61, 89, 106, 109, 119, 209, 265, 315; incarceration rates of, 67; migration of, 27, 28, 29, 30, 50, 52, 55, 57, 61, 62, 69, 84–85, 105–10, 111, 114, 119, 149, 168, 215, 233, 265, 291, 307, 312, 313, 314, 315, 325n7, 334n5, 339n37, 362n4, 367n73, 369n25; police and, 30, 31, 32–35, 41, 48, 67, 72, 90, 101, 111, 113, 114, 117, 307–8, 340n43; (black) police officers, 30, 31, 33; rural residency of, 27, 45, 53, 84, 85, 89, 90, 100, 101, 328n48; subculture of violence and, xii, xiii, xiv, 26, 42, 43, 50–52; unemployment rates of, 87, 88, 89, 99, 118, 307; urban residency of, 27, 45, 61, 84, 85, 90, 100, 101, 339n37; violent crime of, xiii, 24–28, 32, 33, 34, 35, 39–46, 50–53, 85, 89, 90–105, 112, 113, 118–21, 308–9; women, 29, 51, 86–87, 91, 338n11

Allen, Frederick Lewis, 271

American Indians. *See* Native Americans

Anderson, Elijah, xiii

assault rate, 67

Atlanta, Ga., 30, 31, 33, 46, 50, 57, 75, 76, 89, 331n32, 338n7

Auerhahn, Kathleen, 366n70

Ayers, Edward L., 13, 14, 15, 16, 17, 19, 32, 36, 37, 38, 46, 47, 326n14, 327n36, 328n40, 328n45, 329n4, 332n50, 332n62, 333n87

Baltimore, Md., 89, 268, 329n2, 332n62, 333n85

Bancroft, Hubert Howe, 134, 342n30

Barzini, Luigi, 218, 219, 222

Birmingham, Ala., 57, 75, 77, 89, 98, 99

Black Codes, 28, 330n20

Black Hand. *See* Italians

blacks. *See* African Americans

Blocker, Jack S., 289

blood feuds, 11, 59, 83, 141

Bodenhamer, David J., 327n38

Bogardus, Emory, 257, 361n20

boll weevil, 77, 107, 265, 362n4

Boston, Mass., 168, 193, 199, 201, 265, 276, 321, 333n85, 372n6

Boudouris, James, 118, 286, 287, 366nn64–66, 371n39

Brearley, H. C., 22, 54, 68, 69, 74, 92, 100, 103, 114, 115, 278, 279, 326n8, 329n57, 363n17, 365n52

Philadelphia, Penn., xi, 24, 106, 108, 109, 111, 168, 172, 193, 199, 201, 205, 206, 233, 234, 244, 276, 277, 329n2, 333n85, 354n8

Piccato, Pablo, 250, 251

Piehl, Anne Morrison, 224, 225, 226, 253, 254, 256, 356nn23–24, 360n16, 361n17

pleas, guilty, 126, 136, 154, 159, 160, 342n34

*Plessy v. Ferguson,* 29

Poland. *See* Poles

Polenberg, Richard, 302, 368n14

Poles, 187, 192, 199, 201, 223, 225, 232, 234, 239, 277, 359n61, 369n18

police: constitutional limitations on, 364n38; crime data and, 305, 321, 325n1, 365n52, 372n6; Mexicans and, 252, 253; in nineteenth century, 177–81, 354n8; number of, per capita, 67; technology and, 264, 331n32. *See also* Chicago, Ill.: police in; New York City, N.Y.: police in

Porterfield, Austin, 80, 337n39

poverty, crime and, ix, x, xi, 4, 23, 24, 55, 83, 139, 168, 182, 189, 198, 199, 323

prisoner (imprisonment) data, 39, 64, 65, 96, 98, 223, 234, 257, 307

Proctor, H. H., 331n43, 331n47

Prohibition: African Americans and, 277, 290, 367n73; alcohol consumption and, 264, 267, 268, 273, 274, 288, 290, 314, 364n34, 366n70, 366n72, 367n73, 371n41; bootlegger gangs and, 117, 119, 246, 263, 273, 276, 280–82, 283, 287; Chicago crime and, 276, 277, 280, 281, 282, 283–86, 289, 290, 364n28, 366n60, 366n66, 369n20; Detroit crime and, 277, 286–87, 313–14, 366n64, 366n66; federal enforcement agents and, 274, 275, 282, 303, 364n38; federal prosecutions and, 275, 277; Italians and, 276, 277, 286, 356n9, 365n43; Jews and, 277; Poles and, 277; the South and, 60, 273, 274, 278, 364n33; state enforcement of, 273, 274, 303; violent crime and, 268, 270, 272, 274, 277–91; Volstead

Act (National Prohibition Act), 267, 272, 273, 274, 275, 362n10

Puritans, 9, 10

Quetelet, Adolphe, 129, 341n13

race riots, 3, 28, 34, 111, 117, 121, 127, 265, 349n21, 362n7

Radzinowicz, Leon, 369n18

Reconstruction, 11, 18, 19, 20, 22, 26, 28, 29, 41, 50, 52, 53, 130, 333nn74–76

Redfield, H. V., xii, 5, 6, 16, 41, 332n66

registration area (reported homicides), 64, 68, 78, 99, 278, 279, 305, 335n17

Regulators, 10, 11, 133

Reinarman, Craig, 366n68, 371n41

Reppetto, Thomas, 276, 281, 282, 286, 364n35

retreat rule (self-defense), 128, 341n11

Richmond, Va., 27, 33, 94, 95, 209, 332n62, 338n7, 338n17

Riis, Jacob, 174, 175, 348n3, 349n34

Rockefeller, John D., 137

Roosevelt, Franklin D., 77, 299, 301, 302, 312, 313, 317, 371n48

Roosevelt, Theodore, 150, 175, 181, 236, 348n3

Rosales, Francisco (F. Arturo), 253, 360n13

Roth, Randolph, 11, 14, 19, 20, 22, 42, 51, 52, 130, 160, 203, 204, 328n50, 330n13, 334n1, 346n118, 353n104, 354n10, 371n48

rough-and-tumble, 12, 13

routine activities theory, 209, 210

rurality, crime and, 4, 5, 15, 19, 20, 28, 42, 45, 46, 48, 55, 58, 83, 85, 90, 100, 101, 111, 136, 198, 199, 218, 250, 251, 323, 328n40, 328n48, 339n37, 348n5

Ryscavage, Paul, 288

Salmond, John A., 368n9

saloons, crime and, xi, 30, 110, 111, 132, 137, 138, 156, 162, 178, 179, 189, 190, 191, 206, 207, 208, 264, 272, 289, 323, 364n28

CPSIA information can be obtained
at www.ICGtesting.com
Printed in the USA
LVHW091312080321
680873LV00002B/13

9 780807 174296